THE
DIPLOMATIC
RECORD
1991-1992

Published in cooperation with the

INSTITUTE FOR THE STUDY OF DIPLOMACY

School of Foreign Service, Georgetown University

THE DIPLOMATIC RECORD 1991-1992

edited by
Hans Binnendijk
and Mary Locke
INSTITUTE FOR THE STUDY OF DIPLOMACY

WESTVIEW PRESS
Boulder • San Francisco • Oxford

The Diplomatic Record

Production of *The Diplomatic Record* is made possible by a grant from the Harriman Foundation.

Published in 1993 in the United States of America by Westview Press, Inc., 5500 Central Avenue, Boulder, Colorado 80301-2877, and in the United Kingdom by Westview Press, 36 Lonsdale Road, Summertown, Oxford OX2 7EW

Library of Congress ISSN: 1052-0309
ISBN: 0-8133-1687-1
ISBN: 0-8133-1688-X (pbk.)

Printed and bound in the United States of America

∞ The paper in this publication meets the requirements of the American National Standard for Permanence of Paper for Printed Library Materials Z39.48-1984.

10   9   8   7   6   5   4   3   2   1

Contents

DEPARTMENTS

Editors' Note

In diplomacy, as in good driving, periodic glances in the rearview mirror are recommended. Seeing where you have been gives you a better sense of where you are. It is also useful to have early warning of the occasional fast-moving vehicle rapidly approaching from behind.

No matter what our readers' occupation—practitioner, scholar, journalist, or student of international affairs—this third volume of *The Diplomatic Record* is the recommended look in the rearview mirror. It gives a panoramic glimpse of territory just covered. Theories describing what the post-Cold War world will look like are useful, but it will take several years to prove their validity. This volume reveals to readers the impact of recent events on diplomacy a year or so into the post-Cold War world.

As in past volumes, this collection of essays concentrates on diplomatic negotiations, the process that, with skill and luck, can prevent wars or settle them quickly after fighting begins. Negotiations can involve economic, scientific, and other nonsecurity issues as well as efforts to regulate international behavior and avoid escalation of disagreements into security problems. But this volume differs from its predecessors in that the impact of the end of the Cold War has profoundly affected the nature and course of every negotiation considered by our authors.

The essays are divided into five broad topics—disintegration in the East, integration in the West, new relations with old allies, changes in the Third World, and multilateral diplomacy. Chapters 1 through 3 assess diplomatic initiatives designed to deal with fragmentation in Eastern Europe and the former Soviet Union. Chapters 4 through 6 analyze diplomatic activities associated with economic integration in North America and European union as well as with German unification. Chapters 7 and 8 examine emerging new relationships between the United States and its two closest allies in Asia—Japan and the Philippines. Chapters 9, 10, and 11 review three new opportunities for peace in the Third World that flow from the end of the Cold War. And Chapter 12 and the section entitled "Looking Ahead" offer, among other things, a look at the United Nations and other international mechanisms for dealing with problems in an increasingly multilateral world.

In the first essay, William Green Miller goes to the source of change: the disintegration of the Soviet Union. He describes a "cautious, uncertain, and reactive" US policy working on two tracks, struggling to maintain good relations with both Mikhail Gorbachev and Boris Yeltsin as they battled for power. Miller tells in vivid detail how the United States leaned first toward Gorbachev and stuck with him officially during most of 1991, but about mid-year began to pay more attention to Yeltsin as his boldness, courage, and parliamentary skills became increasingly evident.*

Next, Ivo H. Daalder describes a dramatic shift of means and goals in American nuclear diplomacy. In July 1991, the United States and the USSR signed the Strategic Arms Reduction Talks (START) agreement, culminating a decade of laborious negotiation. After the August coup attempt in the USSR, priorities changed to enhancing secure command and control over Soviet nuclear forces, preventing instant nuclear proliferation, eliminating ground-based tactical nuclear weapons, and seeking deeper reductions in strategic nuclear warheads. Because negotiators needed to keep pace with the radical political changes described by Miller, they shed formality and effective verification in favor of reciprocal unilateral pronouncements. From the signing of a START protocol that will concentrate all nuclear weapons in Russia by 2000 to the massive strategic nuclear reductions announced at the Yeltsin-Bush summit in June 1992, US diplomacy successfully took advantage of opportunities created by Soviet disintegration.

---

*On December 25, 1991, several of the former Soviet republics made the following changes in their names:

      Byelorussia – Belarus
      Kirghizia – Kyrgyzstan
      Moldavia – Moldova
      Tadzhikistan – Tajikistan
      Turkmenia – Turkmenistan

We will be using the new names in this volume of *The Diplomatic Record* except in the chronology, where the old names appear in entries occurring prior to the change.

European Community (EC) efforts to mediate the Yugoslav conflict is a case of diplomatic failure, even more serious because the fragmentation of Yugoslavia may be a model for post-Cold War crises. In Chapter 3, John Zametica argues that the EC representatives started too late, dealt initially with the wrong leaders, were unable to narrow their differing views on local sovereignty until late in the negotiations, and used ineffective economic sanctions as their primary tool. The best efforts of Lord Carrington and his colleagues may have been doomed from the outset because most of the parties in Yugoslavia stood to benefit from conflict and the EC was unable to raise the stakes by threatening massive peace-enforcement operations.

As nations east of the former Iron Curtain disintegrate, the most pronounced phenomenon west of that line is union. In Chapter 4, Alan K. Henrikson describes trilateral negotiations to create a North American Free Trade Agreement (NAFTA). The United States has supported the concept of an economic zone from "the Yukon to the Yucatan" to strengthen its political and economic posture in the world. After dealing with labor, environmental, and human rights interest groups that oppose the effort, the US Congress gave President Bush "fast track" authority for the negotiations. The negotiations concluded in August and the congressional review will be completed in 1993.

Whereas a NAFTA would create a loose economic association, the European Community embarked on a much more ambitious plan for economic, monetary, and political union. In Chapter 5, Jenonne Walker provides keen insights into the give-and-take that culminated in the December 1991 Maastricht summit agreement. She describes bold US tactics to influence the results and concludes that although the United States and Britain may have gained some concessions on security issues, the final text closely tracks French and German positions.

In Chapter 6, Flora Lewis takes a look at the politics and improvised diplomacy of German unification. Although these events took place in 1989 and 1990, we have included her essay because it provides a unique behind-the-scenes assessment based on interviews with the principal actors. Lewis tells the tale of division in the East German Politburo, of Hungary's decision to open the Iron Curtain, of German Chancellor Helmut Kohl's willingness to seize the opportunity, and of the diplomatic "triple play" from Bonn to Washington to Moscow. US diplomacy was guided by the two Roberts, Robert Zoellick at the State Department and Robert Blackwill at the National Security Council, who together worked in secret to pull off the diplomatic coup of the decade. The successful unification of Germany has changed the political map of Europe and stimulated the process of regional integration.

As the once-dominant security issues recede in Asia, US relations with its close Asian allies have been strained by trade and aid disputes. In Chapter 7, Alan William Wolff and Thomas A. Kalil take a snapshot look at the never-ending trade negotiations between the United States and Japan. With the end of the Cold War, they argue, it is no longer the case that trade constitutes "low politics" as opposed to the "high politics" of national security. They cite predictions that US competitiveness may improve as defense spending declines, possibly helping to balance US-Japan trade. But they also point out that the common interest in containing Soviet power was the glue that held the US-Japan alliance together and that trade issues could now dominate the relationship. And, on the trade front, they see plenty of reasons to be pessimistic.

The Philippine base negotiations took place in a climate in which the Cold War "seemed very much over," writes Richard L. Armitage in Chapter 8. As the chief negotiator, he is able to describe in unusual detail the ups and downs of addressing demands for increased financial assistance in return for an asset that had diminished in value because of the end of the Cold War and, later, because of the eruption of Mt. Pinatubo.

The end of the Cold War has brought greater prospects for peace to many areas of the Third World. This volume examines the Korean peninsula, Cambodia, and El Salvador. In addition, Operation Desert Storm created new opportunities for peace in the Middle East. At historic meetings in Madrid and Washington, Israeli and Arab leaders began a process that could settle disputes in that troubled region. Next year we will review progress in the Middle East.

Robert A. Scalapino in his piece on North-South Korean negotiations notes in Chapter 9 that the Soviet Union's recognition of South Korea and Moscow's later demand for hard-currency transactions and global market prices for oil, among other goods, shook North Korea to its core and contributed to its making major policy adjustments during negotiations with the South. The domestic circumstances of the two Koreas combined with policy shifts on the part of the major powers to create a climate for advances that few could have envisaged in relations between the two mortal enemies.

After the first Sino-Soviet summit in thirty years in May 1989, both the Soviets and Chinese sought a solution to problems in Indochina. In Chapter 10, Robert G. Sutter shows that the Cambodian breakthrough came at a time when the Soviet Union was facing major problems at home and the Chinese, possibly to appear less isolated after the Tiananmen Square massacre, were showing new flexibility in dealing with former adversaries.

In Chapter 11, Thomas Dodd argues that the end of the Cold War has released Central America from its anguished role as a focal point of superpower rivalry. This gradual but far-reaching development was symbolized in December 1991 when the United States and the Soviet Union jointly persuaded government and rebel forces in El Salvador to agree on an internationally supervised cease-fire. Professor Dodd tells the story of how regional and local efforts successfully combined to end insurgencies and begin the difficult process of bringing democracy to the region.

Former US ambassador to the United Nations Donald F. McHenry describes in Chapter 12 the selection of a new secretary-general for the UN that for the first time was free of the shadow of the Cold War. During the past four decades, the successful candidate was the one least likely to rock the boat so delicately balanced between East and West. But, as Ambassador McHenry reports, the UN could not completely escape its past. Though the selection process did not split along East-West lines, it was still mired in political maneuvering and the pursuit of national ambitions.

*   *   *

We would urge readers looking for pieces to complete the analytical puzzle of the new world to peruse the chronology. Covering the period from July 1991 through June 1992, it offers an intriguing view of events occurring simultaneously around the world. For example, during the month of December 1991:

- UN special envoy Cyrus Vance warned that the latest breakdown of the Yugoslav truce threatened UN peacekeeping efforts.
- EC nations furthered their union in Maastricht.
- The second round of Middle East peace talks began in Washington, DC.
- South Korea stated that all nuclear weapons had been removed from its soil.
- The Soviet Union ceased to exist and President Gorbachev resigned on Christmas Day.
- The Philippines declared that the United States must withdraw from Subic Naval Base by the end of 1992.

■ UN Secretary-General Javier Pérez de Cuéllar brokered a cease-fire agreement between the El Salvadoran government and opposition guerrilla forces.

It was a year of momentous events that had impact directly and indirectly on diplomatic negotiations around the world. We hope you agree that this volume of *The Diplomatic Record* captures the essence of the changed world in which we are living. We have again included an essay entitled "Looking Ahead" (by Steven Philip Kramer), which previews next year's edition, as well as a bibliography of recently published volumes for further reading. We owe a large debt to Pamela Harriman, without whose generous support this volume would never have been written.

Hans Binnendijk
Mary Locke

About the Editors and Authors

Richard L. Armitage served as the special negotiator for the Philippine base negotiations and is currently serving as deputy to the coordinator for US assistance to the new independent states of the former Soviet Union.

Hans Binnendijk is the director of the Institute for the Study of Diplomacy and the Marshall B. Coyne Research Professor of Diplomacy at Georgetown University, Washington, DC.

Ivo H. Daalder is the director of research at the Center for International Security Studies and is a visiting assistant professor at the School of Public Affairs, University of Maryland. He is the author, most recently, of *The Nature and Practice of Flexible Response* (New York: Columbia University Press, 1991); *Strategic Defenses in the 1990s: Criteria for Deployment* (New York: St. Martin's Press, 1991); and *Cooperative Arms Control: A New Agenda for the Post-Cold War Era* (College Park, MD: Center for International Security Studies at Maryland, 1992).

Thomas Dodd is an associate professor of history at the School of Foreign Service, Georgetown University, Washington, DC.

Alan K. Henrikson is the director of the Fletcher Roundtable on a New World Order at the Fletcher School of Law and Diplomacy, Tufts University, Medford, MA, where he teaches American diplomatic history and international negotiation. He also is the counselor on Canadian affairs at the Center for International Affairs, Harvard University, Cambridge, MA.

Thomas A. Kalil is an international trade specialist with the law firm of Dewey Ballantine in Washington, DC.

Steven Philip Kramer was a research associate of the Institute for the Study of Diplomacy from 1991 to 1992.

Flora Lewis is a senior columnist for the *New York Times*.

Mary Locke is an author and editor. She was previously the managing editor of the *European Community* magazine and has also served on the staff of the Senate Foreign Relations Committee.

Donald F. McHenry, who served as US permanent representative to the United Nations from 1979 to 1981, is currently a university research professor of diplomacy and international affairs at the School of Foreign Service, Georgetown University, Washington, DC.

William Green Miller is the president of the American Committee on Relations with Russia and the Independent States (formerly the American Committee on US-Soviet Relations).

Robert A. Scalapino is the Robson Research Professor of Government Emeritus at the University of California, Berkeley.

Robert G. Sutter is a senior specialist at the Congressional Research Service.

Jenonne Walker is a senior associate at the Carnegie Endowment for International Peace.

Alan William Wolff is the managing partner of Dewey Ballantine's Washington law office and leads the firm's international trade practice. He served as US deputy special representative for trade negotiations from 1977 to 1979.

John Zametica is a research fellow in European security at the University of Westminster, London. He is the author of *The Yugoslav Conflict*, Adelphi Paper No. 270 (London: International Institute for Strategic Studies, 1992).

ESSAYS

ESSAYS

1

American Diplomacy and Soviet Disintegration

William Green Miller

O N CHRISTMAS DAY, 1991, Mikhail S. Gorbachev resigned his post as president of the Union of Soviet Socialist Republics. The red flag with the hammer-and-sickle emblem of the Soviet Union was lowered for the last time, and only the white, blue, and red flag of Russia flew over the Kremlin and the vast territories of Russia. Gorbachev's resignation was a dramatic, somewhat poignant formality marking the end of the Soviet system. The Soviet Union had formally ceased to exist on December 21, when the Commonwealth of Independent States (CIS) was created by agreement of eleven of the fifteen republics of the Soviet Union.

The Soviet empire had collapsed, the Berlin Wall had crumbled, and East European nations had declared independence. The East and the West were finally beginning to heal the wounds caused by revolution, cataclysmic world war, and an ideological confrontation that had divided the world into hostile camps. The end of the Cold War marked the first stage of a revolutionary change in the internal structure of the Soviet Union.

Diplomacy among the United States, the disintegrating Soviet Union, and the newly independent Russian republic, particularly in 1991, is a record of extraordinary complexity and radical change. Relations were determined by the revolutionary internal changes under way in Moscow. The overwhelming dangers of the Cold War evaporated as the Soviet Union transformed itself from a totalitarian empire into fifteen new nations with diverse characteristics and entirely different futures. The architects of Soviet diplomacy toward the West in the period of perestroika, glasnost, and democratization were President of the USSR and General Secretary of the Communist party Gorbachev and Foreign Secretary and Politburo member Eduard A. Shevardnadze. Until the end of 1990, they exercised enormous power in both government and in the ruling circle of the Communist party to bring about the peaceful rapprochement between East and West. The effort to end the Cold War, attempted by so many from both sides during the previous four decades, was finally achieved by the last president and foreign minister of the Soviet Union.

During 1991, Gorbachev and the president of the Russian republic, Boris N. Yeltsin, waged a great internal power struggle. At issue was the fate of the Communist party, the Soviet economic system, control of political and social life, and the culture the Soviet system had created. The USSR itself and its continued sovereignty over fifteen constituent republics were also at stake. The battle for power between the communists and the democrats, and between the enormous bureaucracy and its challengers, many of them young outsiders, was over fundamental questions: human rights, property, obligations of the state to serve the needs of individual citizens, and a rule of law. The aspirations, grievances, and discontent of distinct nationalities and ethnic groups were all factors at play in the drama that the world witnessed in the struggle for power between Gorbachev and Yeltsin.

United States Is Cautious, Reactive

In the face of this epic struggle, the tenor of American diplomacy was cautious, watchful, and largely reactive. It was difficult for American policymakers to conduct or even plan diplomatic initiatives because they could not be certain who had power, whether some other entity was gaining power, and when fluid power arrangements would stabilize. The arms-control agenda was not at issue. In fact, Yeltsin's view was to reduce nuclear weapons at the fastest possible rate, and he supported Gorbachev and Shevardnadze in their diplomatic efforts to conclude arms-control agreements with the United States. At issue was which man would prevail and whether counterrevolutionary forces would reverse the push toward political and economic reform and democratization.

Gorbachev, Yeltsin, and US policy constituted a "triangle of uncertainty" according to Vladimir Lukin, Russian ambassador to the United

States.[1] First there was the growing uncertainty within the USSR and in Washington about the stability and strength of Gorbachev's leadership. Gorbachev had captured the respect and admiration of American leaders and, despite his mistakes, there was a sentimental, almost nostalgic hope expressed publicly and privately that he would continue as leader of the USSR. Uncertainty about Gorbachev first arose in fall 1990 when he allowed party hard-liners to oust his reform group from key positions in the government. His choice of successors was viewed as a dangerous step back from reform. The following January, Gorbachev faltered badly and miscalculated the impact of his policy toward the Baltic states (Estonia, Latvia, and Lithuania). Still later, having won a resounding, affirmative vote for a Treaty of Union in a national referendum, he hesitated and did not press forcefully for approval of the new treaty. Gorbachev also vacillated during the four months after the August 1991 coup and failed to implement economic reforms put forward by Stanislav Shatalin, Grigory Yavlinsky, Nikolai Petrakov, and others. With fateful consequences, he vacillated again in the final negotiations on a confederation of independent states.

Another set of uncertainties surrounded Yeltsin: His inner group of supporters was engaged in bureaucratic struggles between Russian and Soviet officials—both government and party—over control of resources, buildings, offices, and local jurisdiction. Yeltsin supported the effort to achieve a Treaty of Union until well after the August coup, believing that a union, even in a looser confederative form, was desirable as long as it had a center that would be limited to defense, foreign affairs, financial, and communications responsibilities. Yeltsin believed that such a structure would enable economic reform to proceed rapidly and would mitigate ethnic and national frictions—he was well aware that a union structure was necessary to protect the interests of Russia and the well-being of the 38 million Russians who live and work in other republics. Ignoring this responsibility would created intolerable pressure and criticism from nationalist groups within Russia. Without a union structure, old supply patterns for raw materials and parts would be disrupted, making it more difficult to move the economy from a command system. For example, how could the textile mills of Russia survive or be modernized if cotton were no longer supplied by Uzbekistan? These were the arguments of nationalistic bureaucrats.

There was also an iconoclastic group of bureaucrats who believed that destruction of the Soviet system was necessary if the Yeltsin government was to survive and real reforms were to take place. After the coup, the view that the Soviet system had to go coupled with the fear that the Communist party would mount future coup attempts. Irresistible pressure built on Yeltsin and his government to allow the USSR to collapse.

The third leg of the triangle—uncertainties in US policy—was a direct reflection of the instability created by the power struggle between Yeltsin and Gorbachev in Moscow. It was perhaps only natural that in the face of these complicated and contending internal forces, Washington representatives tended to support the leaders they had become accustomed to dealing with and who represented formal structures that had long been in place.

A Two-Track Policy

President George Bush and Secretary of State James Baker followed a two-track policy. Since the USSR was the overarching formal entity in existence by constitutional authority, election, and nominal control of the instruments of statehood and power, Washington throughout 1991 conducted its state-to-state negotiations with the government of President Gorbachev. Secretary Baker worked closely with Foreign Minister Aleksandr Bessmertnykh, who succeeded Shevardnadze. On December 20, 1990, Shevardnadze had delivered an emotional speech at a dramatic session of the Congress of People's Deputies. He warned of groups within the Communist party who threatened to reimpose the old totalitarian order and informed the assembled deputies that he was resigning his post in protest. Bessmertnykh, a career diplomat with considerable expertise in arms-control negotiations, was highly regarded and well known in Washington because of his many years of service in the United States. It became increasingly evident to policymakers in Washington that Bessmertnykh could speak only for the "center" in Moscow. Russia and Ukraine, the Baltics, Moldova, Georgia, and all of the former republics, in varying degrees, were asserting their independence from the old Soviet central structure. It was clear that the United States would soon be required to deal directly with the governments of the separate republics. The movement toward independent governance by the separate republics grew in almost direct proportion to the degree that the Communist party split into contending factions. As the party lost coherence, the democrats increased in power. New groups from outside the Soviet bureaucracy rapidly weakened the formerly unchallenged control of the Soviet "center."

The most important question for US policy was whether the center would hold. It began to be clear after the election of Yeltsin in June, but was not definite until after the coup attempt was defeated, who would emerge as the dominant leader. The year 1991 marked the high point of the "war of laws"—the spate of competitive and sometimes conflicting legislation passed by the parliaments of the USSR and the Russian Federation—which reflected the struggle between the center and the republics. Challenges to Soviet authority were explicit in the many declarations of sovereignty by republics, cities, regions, and even villages. The air of freedom that Gorbachev had created when he came to power in March 1985 was destroying the Soviet system, and with that disintegration, a single US foreign policy became impossible. The two-track diplomatic approach was an unavoidable consequence of the revolutionary process under way in Moscow.

The year 1991 began with a US emphasis on pressing forward, as in the past, on arms-control negotiations with the USSR; it ended with the recognition that Russia had replaced the Soviet Union as the dominant power in the region that was formerly the USSR. It is noteworthy that the powerful, though very different, personalities of Gorbachev and Yeltsin played a crucial role, even in this period of revolutionary change in which enormously dynamic forces were beyond the control of individuals or groups. Yeltsin's blunt, direct manner was exemplified by the physical courage he demonstrated during the August 19-21 coup attempt. Gorbachev was regarded by the citizenry as much less accessible than Yeltsin and given more to words than to action. The Soviet people were able to assess continually the behavior and character of both men during nightly television coverage of debates in the parliaments of the USSR and Russia.

Foreign Minister Bessmertnykh, reflecting Gorbachev's approach, worked in close cooperation with US diplomats on the issue of forcing Iraq to withdraw from Kuwait. Bessmertnykh continued the policy of his predecessor, Shevardnadze, in the Security Council of the United Nations (UN) and in bilateral discussions supporting the US-led UN action to turn back the brutal aggression against Kuwait. Bessmertnykh, a seasoned arms-control expert, also fostered the joint efforts of the USSR and the United States to reduce their respective arsenals of both nuclear and conventional weapons.

US diplomatic relations with Yeltsin and his Russian government, however, were delicate, difficult, and not always successful. Protocol required that President Bush and Secretary Baker give precedence to the USSR and Gorbachev; Russia was formally still a constituent part of the USSR. But American diplomats tried to execute a diplomatic dance of formal behavior that reflected how power was shifting. Relations between the White House in Washington and the Russian White House in Moscow did improve during 1991 as Yeltsin and his supporters successfully beat off public challenges from his communist opponents and from Gorbachev himself.

Public challenges to Yeltsin's authority were intricately linked to the desperate, hidden efforts of the Communist party to remain in control. The threat to party control had increased rapidly after the decision by the party itself to allow other parties to participate in political life. When Article 6 of the USSR Constitution, which conferred sole and absolute political power to the Communist party, was amended, with Gorbachev's eventual support, party rule was immediately challenged. Already weakened by internal conflicts and divisions and by the rise of democratic forces outside the party, the Communist party rapidly lost power. The coup de grâce was administered in the aftermath of the putsch of August 19-21, 1991, when Yeltsin banned the party from further activities.

Shevardnadze had warned his country and the world of the coming militant effort by the hard-line communists to regain power. A few months before his warning, in fall 1990, Gorbachev had given key posts in the USSR government to hard-line communists. The Gorbachev reform wing of the Communist party, represented by Politburo members Shevard-nadze, Aleksandr Yakovlev, and Vadim Bakatin, was pushed out of power. Gorbachev, by design or perhaps as a result of inescapable pressure from the dominant right wing of the party, replaced the reformers with such individuals as KGB (secret police) head Vladimir Kryuchkov; party bureaucrat Gennadi Yanayev, who was made vice president, and former Minister of Finance Valentin Pavlov, who was made prime minister. This new hard-line leadership group mounted efforts to curb the democrats, blaming the loss of empire on reform leaders. They stoked the fires of xenophobia, slowed the pace of economic reform, and tried to prevent the breakup of the Soviet Union. President Gorbachev did not resist the hard-liners' attempt to subdue the independence movement in the Baltic states of Estonia, Latvia, and Lithuania. He seemed to be caught in too many crosscurrents: the contest with Yeltsin, the desire to hold the USSR together, a fear of radical economic reform, and a drastic loss of popular support.

Soviets Press the Baltics

In January 1991, the maneuvering to compel the Baltic states to back down from their independent stance began in earnest. On January 13, KGB and military forces were unleashed in Vilnius, Lithuania. The resulting bloodshed and violence shocked people in the Soviet Union and throughout the world. The immediate outcry, both within the USSR and from abroad, probably contributed to the sudden decision by Gorbachev to halt the KGB and military action against the Baltics. Many at the time saw the attacks on the Vilnius government as the beginning of a coup, evidence of the validity of Shevardnadze's warnings voiced less than a month earlier. The events in the Baltics and the massive public demonstrations in Moscow and throughout the world to protest the brutal acts there compelled President Bush to speak out publicly. On January 21, he urged President Gorbachev and the Soviet leaders to "resist the use of force." On the right to self-determination, particularly in the Baltic states, the United States and Gorbachev clearly were in conflict.

The United States has always considered the Baltic states to be independent and never officially recognized the Soviet takeover in 1940. Americans of Baltic origin have kept the hope for independence alive and have always had influence in American political circles. The brutal military actions in Vilnius only reinforced American popular sympathy for the independence movements in Lithuania and the other Baltic states.

On the question of Baltic independence, Yeltsin and the United States were in agreement, directly challenging Gorbachev and the central government. After the brutality in Vilnius, Yeltsin went to Lithuania, denounced the actions, and once again made clear he supported the independence of the Baltic states if that was what the Baltic people wanted. On February 6, 1991, the Bush administration authorized the dispatch of emergency medical aid to the Baltics and Ukraine.

It is widely believed that the military action in Vilnius was undertaken because the right wing of the Communist party—perhaps with Gorbachev's awareness—had calculated that the democrats were in a weakened state of confusion and dissension. In retrospect, it seems that the hardliners had equated a variety of views expressed in public debate and legislative disagreement with a political incapacity to resist a challenge to their existence. In the political maneuverings of late fall 1990 and winter 1991, the Politburo and Central Committee of the Communist party urged Gorbachev to reject the assertions of sovereignty made by the republics, particularly the Baltics and Russia, and to take the steps necessary to bring down Yeltsin as the leader of the Russian republic. When tanks, paratroopers, and KGB goons were sent into the streets of Vilnius, the right-wing leaders expected that the Communist party-sponsored "Committees of National Salvation" would take over, and that the governments of the Baltics would be forced to accede to Gorbachev's demands.

Yeltsin's denunciation of the use of military force in the Baltics did indeed cost him some degree of popular support. The ultranationalist Russian groups such as Pamyat protested vociferously against his support of the Baltic states. Communist party conservatives believed Yeltsin was now vulnerable and pressed for the execution of a two-stage political action designed to undermine and remove him. The first step was a national referendum on the Treaty of Union. The second was a vote of confidence on Yeltsin's leadership in the Russian parliament where Yeltsin and the democrats had a margin of only a handful of votes. It was believed that the referendum would result in an overwhelming affirmation of support for the Treaty of Union and that Yeltsin's actions regarding the Baltics would lead to a vote in the legislature that would remove him from office. In the parliamentary maneuvering that took place on the wording and conduct of the voting on the referendum, however, the democrats were successful in inserting a rider that called for direct popular election of a president for Russia. The democrats knew that if elections were held, Yeltsin as the most popular leader of Russia would become president and gain an independent political base apart from the parliament—a legislative body that had been elected during the period of Communist party dominance and still reflected strong party influence.

The result of the referendum showed popular support for the idea of a new Treaty of Union and for an elected president of the Russian Federation as well. The efforts to topple Yeltsin had failed. In fact, he emerged from these tests of popular support in an even stronger position. Military forces sent into Moscow and other Russian cities in an unsuccessful effort to restrict political demonstrations held in support of Yeltsin and the democrats raised Yeltsin's popularity to even higher levels and united the contending democratic factions. Nonetheless, during this period, the sense of crisis continued. The contention between the two leaders and the power stalemate the struggle produced seemed to make it increasingly possible that both Yeltsin and Gorbachev might be replaced by leaders of a very different kind, perhaps by generals. Rumors of coups and military takeovers were rampant.

Questions for US Policy

All of these maneuverings took place in the open, in the full view of the Soviet people, whose future and very lives were at stake, and to the amazement and fascination of the world. The tasks for American diplomats, as they sought to balance relations with both Gorbachev and Yeltsin and to maintain USSR support in the UN Security Council for efforts to bring Saddam Hussein to heel in the Persian Gulf, were formidable. Fortunately, both Gorbachev and Yeltsin fully supported the American role and the mission of the UN forces. But by now, serious doubts were being raised in Washington about the course and the future of Gorbachev's leadership. Would he be able to control the forces of the right that he had put in power and whose purposes had been revealed in the aggressive military actions in Vilnius?

An even more fundamental question confronted US policymakers: Should the United States support those who wanted to preserve the Soviet Union, or was it in the American interest to support Russia and the republican independence movements? The policy debate in the United States was almost as complicated as disagreements within the Soviet Union. One school of thought believed that supporting independence movements would result in a democratic Russia and a relatively weak collection of independent states that would offer no threat to the West, militarily or economically. On the other side of the argument, some policymakers believed that preserving the union under Gorbachev, even with a much reduced reform program and continued Communist party dominance, would lessen the chances of ethnic conflict and violence and offer a predictable and stable situation.

The official American view seemed to favor Gorbachev's efforts to maintain as much of the old Soviet Union as possible, although ethnic domestic pressures from within the United States as well as human rights concerns led the Bush administration also to champion the rights of Russia, the Baltic states, Ukraine, and those who wished to exercise the right of self-determination. Under any circumstances, it was believed by all parties that the outcome would not be significantly influenced by the United States or any outside forces. It was a matter that would be determined by powerful, dynamic internal forces and the will of the Soviet people. US diplomacy was guided by caution. Its posture was an uneasy straddle of support for both contending leaders who seemed locked in a symbiotic, inescapable sharing of power.

A series of plebiscites in favor of independence was held in the Baltics in February 1991. At the same time, political activity intensified as the Yeltsin prodemocracy forces held massive rallies in Moscow, Leningrad, and other major Russian cities. The "war of laws" between the parliaments of the center and the republics, and the increasingly fierce battle between the Communist party and the democratic forces (wryly described by one observer as "no political picnic") deepened the strong sense of urgency that reflected the growing unpopularity of the Soviet regime and Gorbachev himself. The miners' strikes that erupted throughout the Soviet Union in late winter 1990 and early spring 1991 forced Gorbachev to continue efforts to work with Yeltsin to salvage any remaining economic stability. The miners, eager to rid themselves of communist control, were behind Yeltsin, but there were still crucial political reasons for Gorbachev and Yeltsin to attempt to work together. The country was in a political stalemate. Substantial constitutional and economic reform required a two-thirds majority vote in the legislature. Yeltsin had a working majority but not the two-thirds required for constitutional amendments. In order to achieve support for radical reform, Yeltsin had to depend on the left-center Communist party deputies in the Russian Supreme Soviet—particularly the groups of Afghan war veterans led by Aleksandr Rutskoi. At the same time, the Yeltsin-led Russian Federation was under increasing pressure from constituent autonomous republics to give them greater independence and even sovereignty.

For a period of a few months in the spring and early summer, both the center under Gorbachev and the Yeltsin-led Russian Federation believed that a centrist majority could govern, at least for the time being. The two leaders were then of the view that the centrist coalition had broken the extreme right's hold on Gorbachev and the far left's hold on Yeltsin and freed them to take joint action. Through a series of legislative acts in both governments, privatization was legitimized in the republics and control of natural resources was ceded to the republics. The beginnings of pluralist, democratic government with a new economy and a substantial private sector seemed possible in Russia—and perhaps with it some form of a new union of republics. Policymakers in Washington urged the two leaders to make every effort to work together.

On May Day 1991, the coal mines were transferred from the USSR to Russia, and privatization of industry formerly under control from the center was under way. The long-expected Free Travel and Emigration Law was passed by the USSR Supreme Soviet on May 20, and shortly thereafter, President Bush extended the waiver of the Jackson-Vanik Amendment of the 1974 Trade Act that had curbed trade with countries restricting emigration.

On June 12, Yeltsin was elected president of Russia in the first round, with a 6 percent majority. USSR Prime Minister Ryzhkov received only 18 percent of the vote. The election made it clear that Yeltsin was firmly in control of the Russian government and supported by the Russian people. Polls taken at the time showed that Gorbachev's popularity among the Russians had fallen to below 20 percent. Power clearly was passing from Gorbachev to Yeltsin. Although Yeltsin was the dominant personality, both men continued to work together in attempts to fashion a new Treaty of Union.

US Support of Union Treaty

The earlier "nine-plus-one" negotiations (nine republics plus the USSR), based on long-standing economic relationships between the center and the republics, seemed to be a formula that could result in a new workable Treaty of Union. It would give to separate republics considerable autonomy and reserve for the center foreign affairs, defense, and control of currency. On this expectation, negotiations on a new union treaty continued. The United States supported these efforts and, at least on this subject, it was not necessary to choose between Gorbachev and Yeltsin. President Yeltsin traveled to Washington on June 20 and was received warmly by the White House and the Congress as the leader of Russia and as a possible successor to Gorbachev. The trip was a diplomatic and political success for Yeltsin, in marked contrast to his previous trip to the United States in September 1989.

On June 21, the Supreme Soviet of the USSR approved the new head of government, Valentin Pavlov. Gorbachev, as president of the USSR, would in fact be in charge of the USSR and could negotiate in the role as president with Yeltsin. But the conflict between the democrats of Russia and the Communist party was coming to a head once again. Just the day before, on June 20, Yeltsin had outlawed party activity within the government. This action, by law, removed the Communist party from direct participation in the Russian government. The election of Yeltsin confirmed to party leaders that he would be a powerful, continuing threat.

On a sunny July morning, Yeltsin was inaugurated in the Kremlin as the first directly elected president of Russia. The brilliant weather of the day was taken as an auspicious omen for a ceremony full of rich symbolism marking the change from communist control to a new democratic system of government with directly elected leaders. The inauguration on July 10, 1991, was the third great symbolic moment in the history of perestroika: The first was the breaching of the Berlin Wall; the second was Yeltsin's overwhelming election victory when the Russian people said "no" to communism.

At Yeltsin's inauguration, many people noted that in an earlier Russian election, in 1917, only 20 percent of the voters supported the Bolsheviks. Remembering the reaction of the Bolsheviks the last time the Russian people had said "no" to communism, some people were asking, "Are there Bolsheviks waiting to take over now?"[2] The historical parallels and the resonance of past revolutionary events made the occasion deeply symbolic. The huge portrait of Lenin that had always occupied the center of the stage of the Hall of Congresses in the Kremlin was replaced by a map of Russia. The contemporary emblems of legitimacy—the Russian Constitution and the Declaration of Sovereignty—were placed on the lectern where Yeltsin took the oath of office. Yeltsin and the Russian government were blessed by the leader of the Russian Orthodox Church, the patriarch of all Russia. The flag of the Soviet Union was lowered and the Russian flag was raised in its place. Yeltsin and Gorbachev met at the center of the stage, shook hands, and walked into the audience side by side, revealing once again the symbiotic relationship they shared throughout the six years of perestroika—but they were no longer equals: Yeltsin was in the ascendancy.

Shortly thereafter, a summit meeting took place between Presidents Gorbachev and Bush in London during the meeting of the leaders of the most powerful industrial nations of the world, the so-called Group of Seven. Discussions largely centered on questions of arms control and the Middle East peace conference. The summit, for all of its accomplishments, was far outweighed in the minds of people in Russia and in the other republics by their immensely complicated political and economic problems.

On July 31 in Moscow, Presidents Bush and Gorbachev signed the START treaty. Having been negotiated for over a decade, it significantly reduced nuclear arsenals. The treaty represented a diplomatic milestone in the new relationship between the formerly hostile powers and was an achievement of great distinction for President Bush and Secretary Baker, but it did not solve or even address the new problems that now faced the United States and the disintegrating Soviet Union. It was beginning to become clear to diplomats in both Washington and Moscow that the managed formal relationship between wary adversaries characteristic of the Cold War would not serve the present needs of the two superpowers in forging a new creative relationship. The Soviet Union was engaged in the monumental task of rebuilding a nation and society. The transformation of a multinational empire into fifteen new democratic states, based on rule of law and with a sizable market economy, was clearly an immense undertaking that dwarfed all previous concerns, including arms control.

During the summer of 1991, the US ambassador to Moscow, Jack Matlock, was replaced by a high-profile personality, Robert Strauss, a well-liked, influential Texas Democrat—a businessman, a lawyer, and a politician. Ambassador Strauss arrived on the scene just as the coup attempt unfolded at the end of August. His actions left no doubt about US views. As the coup collapsed, Ambassador Strauss addressed the crowds that had surrounded the Russian White House to protect Yeltsin and his government. Strauss praised Yeltsin's courage and expressed relief that Gorbachev had survived because Yeltsin had successfully resisted the coup attempt.

The coup attempt undertaken August 19-21 by the members of the State Committee for the State Emergency, the so-called Gang of Eight,[3] collapsed in the face of a divided military and KGB and the resolute courage at the barricades of the democrats led by Yeltsin. The right wing's failure resulted in the removal of the Communist party from government—a victim of its own internal differences.

It is quite evident from the interrogation of the coup plotters that the Gang of Eight and their party associates believed they had to act if the process of disintegration of both the Soviet Union and the party had any chance of being stopped. The complicity of the party in the coup attempt and its subsequent removal from legitimate political activity hastened the end of the Soviet state and system of government that had been shaped and governed by the Communist party for seventy-four years.

The Coup Alters the Balance

Yeltsin and his supporters now tended to view the center—the crumbling structure of the USSR—as the last shelter for those who would use any means to regain command of the former authoritarian one-party state. It could not happen again. After the coup attempt, Yeltsin and his democratic reform group saw no other course than to move ahead as rapidly as possible with radical change in Russia. They could no longer wait, while Gorbachev temporized, for the creation of a new political union based on the structure of the former USSR. Other ideas, such as a loose confederation or an even looser commonwealth, now seemed more promising and, unless and until a new structure could be formed, Russia would proceed on its own.

Up until August 19, serious, sustained efforts were made by both Gorbachev and Yeltsin to pursue a controlled evolutionary transition from a USSR based on the Communist party to a new union of politically sovereign republics with strong economic ties. But the possibilities for a controlled gradual transition were destroyed by the putsch. Time had run out.

On August 20, Yeltsin called President Bush and British Prime Minister John Major from the Russian White House in Moscow, which was then surrounded by tanks. The US embassy compound, located just across the street from the Russian White House of the Russian Federation, was also reporting to Washington fully what was happening. The coup plotters had not cut the phone lines. Telephone calls and faxes poured out of the Russian White House offices to government offices, news bureaus, and friends throughout the world. CNN television coverage was also remarkably detailed. The United States formally denounced the coup attempt, voiced its support of Yeltsin, and urged the restoration of Gorbachev to his rightful position as president of the USSR.

During the coup and in its immediate aftermath, events moved quickly. On August 20, Estonia and Latvia declared independence; the next day Lithuania reaffirmed its independence. President Bush recognized the Baltic states' independence on August 24. Foreign Minister Bessmertnykh was dismissed and Soviet Ambassador to Prague Boris Pankin, who denounced the coup, was named in his place. Ironically, a Treaty of Union signing ceremony among the republics had been scheduled for August 20. Under the direction of President Yeltsin and the Russian democrats, negotiations proceeded among the republics of the former Soviet Union. After August 24, Gorbachev resigned his post as head of the Communist party, and all property, records, and assets of the party were seized by the constituent republics. Ivan Silayev, who had been prime minister of Russia under Yeltsin, replaced Pavlov as prime minister of the USSR. The Ukraine, Belarus, Moldova, Azerbaijan, and Kyrgyzstan voted for independence between August 24 and 31. The Soviet Union was unraveling, a process propelled by the failed coup.

On September 1, the Congress of People's Deputies of the USSR approved the formation of an interim confederation of sovereign states; a council of heads of state for questions of foreign affairs; an executive council of all the republics for foreign policy, security matters, and currency issues; and an interrepublican economic council. Only seven of the fifteen republics participated in this interim structure, which from the outset had little chance of success and, in the end, accomplished nothing.

At the end of August, a delegation from the Supreme Soviet of Russia, led by the chairman of the Human Rights Committee, Sergei A. Kovalev, came to Washington. Kovalev met with leaders in the Bush administration, in Congress, and in the media and described the plans of the Yeltsin government to push forward economic and political reforms. In response, administration and congressional leaders expressed the desire to provide humanitarian assistance and to work closely with Yeltsin and the interim USSR government.

In Washington on September 11, President Bush received envoys from the three Baltic states and, in a tangible symbolic gesture, released funds that had been frozen when the Baltic states were occupied by the Soviet Union in 1940. Secretary Baker, in an effort to show US support for the Gorbachev and Yeltsin governments, visited the USSR between September 12 and 16. The ostensible purpose was to attend the CSCE (Conference on Security and Cooperation in Europe) International Conference on Human Rights, which was then under way in Moscow. Soon after arriving, Secretary Baker met privately with former Foreign Minister Shevardnadze to gain his assessment of the situation and conferred with Foreign Minister Pankin, reaching agreement to halt the supply of arms to Afghanistan. Baker also met with military Chief of Staff General Vladimir

Lobov on steps to remove tactical nuclear weapons from Europe. After the conferences in Moscow, Secretary Baker flew to the Baltic states, where he announced a $14 million aid package for the newly independent states.

Between the end of September and the formal demise of the USSR, a series of economic reform plans and union treaties were drafted. None proved successful. The boycott of the Treaty of Union negotiations by Ukraine, Georgia, Moldova, and Azerbaijan continued, and it was evident as time passed that the only possible relationship among the republics would be the loosest possible kind, in which all meaningful, substantial powers would remain with the separate republics. Concern grew in Washington about the disposition of nuclear weapons. It was becoming clear that separate protocols on START and other arms-control matters would have to be negotiated with each of the nuclear-weapon-holding states.

US Attempts to Address Economic Situation

As the economic situation worsened in Russia and in other republics, radical steps were taken in order to meet the crisis. On November 1, the Russian parliament gave Yeltsin sweeping powers for economic reform, including the end of price controls, the privatization of industries, the cutoff of all foreign aid, and the elimination of seventy ministries. On November 15, the Russian parliament declared that Russia had control over all natural resources and economic production within its borders. It then rejected the jurisdiction of the USSR central bank and freed the ruble. The USSR was now only a structural shell. Formal protocol required recognition of the USSR as the overarching political entity, but pinpointing real power required careful attention to Russia and the other republics. The two-track policy would not last much longer.

On November 19, Shevardnadze was reappointed foreign minister by President Gorbachev, bringing the two great leaders who ended the Cold War together once again as the USSR entered its last days. The interim USSR government, led by Gorbachev, and the post-August coup interim Supreme Soviet of the USSR were unable to negotiate agreements with the governments of Russia or the other republics on questions of political or economic jurisdiction. Despite the governmental impasse, and because both Yeltsin and Gorbachev fully supported START and other nuclear weapons reduction agreements, the US Senate on November 25 voted

$500 million to be taken from the FY 1991 defense budget to be used for dismantling Soviet nuclear weapons and for humanitarian and technical assistance.

The Nunn-Aspin Amendment, which authorized the expenditure of these funds, was a new departure in US foreign assistance. The amendment was intended as a form of military conversion and as such was highly controversial. The authors had originally proposed that several billion dollars be taken from the defense budget, because the expenditure would protect American security interests. Negotiations between the White House and Capitol Hill on this proposal were complicated because the upcoming election made candidates nervous about explaining such a large foreign expenditure to voters suffering through the recession at home. In the end, it was possible to agree only on a much smaller amount. Private humanitarian assistance, however, was generous and forthcoming and reflected deep popular concern and sympathy for the people enduring hardships in Russia and the other republics.

Two days later, on November 27, anticipating the inevitable, President Bush announced that the United States would recognize Ukraine if it chose to sever ties with the USSR. A referendum was held in Ukraine on December 1. It affirmed Ukraine's independence, and Leonid M. Kravchuk was elected president.

On December 8, Russia, Ukraine, and Belarus declared that the USSR ceased to exist and proclaimed a new Commonwealth of Independent States (CIS) open to all the former Soviet republics. This preemptive move was explained by President Yeltsin in a telephone call to President Bush and to other Western leaders. Despite Gorbachev's rejection of the new commonwealth, the Ukrainian and Belarussian parliaments ratified the agreement on December 10. Russia did so on December 12.

In Washington, the State Department announced that it was ready to conclude agreements with the commonwealth, but that it would also continue to work with the USSR. At the same time, American political leaders began to express openly the view that the Russian government was clearly the dominant power. On December 15, Secretary Baker visited Moscow and met with Russian Foreign Minister Andrei Kozyrev, who asked the United States to recognize the independence of Russia, Belarus, and Ukraine. Baker said an answer would be forthcoming and in the meantime met with the heads of republican governments, including President Nursultan Nazarbayev of Kazakhstan, particularly on the troubling remaining questions of the control and elimination of nuclear missiles.

Bowing to the inevitable, on December 17, President Gorbachev announced that by the new year, the USSR would cease to exist. Presidents Yeltsin and Gorbachev then agreed on the transfer of the banking, foreign ministry, legal, legislative, and security structures from the USSR to Russia. On December 21, eleven republics of the former Soviet Union inaugurated the CIS. The final chapter of the history of the USSR came to a close when Gorbachev delivered his farewell speech on Christmas Day.

A New Kind of Russian Diplomat

The end of the Soviet Union and the new democratic leadership shaping the foreign policy of Russia and the other independent states brought a new kind of diplomat as well as a new kind of diplomacy. In the past, ambassadors to the United States from the USSR Foreign Ministry were men like Anatoly Dobrynin, Yuri Dubinin, Viktor Komplektov, Aleksandr Bessmertnykh, and Yuli Vorontsov. These were all seasoned diplomats—well trained, competent in arms-control negotiations, masters of the art of managing the Cold War. Men like Dobrynin were powerful politicians of the old Soviet system, had risen through the system to become members of the Central Committee of the Communist party, and had served as bright young men in the International Department of the Committee Secretariat.

The Russian Foreign Ministry retains a core of diplomats from the USSR Foreign Ministry with backgrounds similar to those of the ambassadors of the Soviet period, but this contingent has been drastically reduced in size and is beginning to include people from outside the bureaucratic system. The new breed, led by men like Russian Foreign Minister Andrei Kozyrev and Ambassador Vladimir Lukin, although they come from traditional party ranks, are democrats and intellectuals from a younger generation. Lukin, for example, was formerly chairman of the Supreme Soviet Committee on International Relations and Foreign Economic Ties. In 1968, Lukin was posted in Prague and supported the Czech reform efforts there. He lost his job and narrowly escaped imprisonment for signing a letter of protest against the Soviet military intervention. A member of the USA-Canada Institute until his election as a people's deputy to the Russian parliament, Lukin pursued analytic work consistent with his training as a historian.

Building a Stable Peace

The highest priorities for Russian diplomacy are to promote good working political and economic relations among the republics of the former Soviet Union; to develop close ties with the United States and the West; and to support efforts to strengthen the United Nations, particularly the peacekeeping role of the Security Council. The Yeltsin government has abandoned the policy of aggressive intervention in the Third World pursued by the USSR and has cut off direct assistance to former client states. It has supported the dismantlement of the Warsaw Pact and other military alliances characteristic of the Cold War. In almost every respect, the foreign policy of Russia and the other republics is now designed to foster peaceful relationships with the nations on the periphery of the former Soviet Union and to promote beneficial ties with all nations, where possible. Because the highest priority is to establish a stable political situation at home, foreign political, economic, and military policies are all subordinated to domestic needs. Emblematic of the new foreign policy is Russia's partnership with the United States in working within the UN Security Council on peacekeeping in the Persian Gulf and its efforts to develop the closest possible ties between the two nations in every area of human endeavor through formal diplomatic agreements, extensive business relationships, and people-to-people exchanges from every profession.

On the US side, the disintegration of the Soviet Union in 1991 has required a fundamental change in the nature of American diplomacy in that part of the world. Russia and Ukraine, as the two largest new nations, will receive special attention. The United States intends to maintain formal relationships and open embassies in all of the republics. The area that makes up the former Soviet Union, though less of a military threat, may require more diplomatic resources to understand well enough to protect and pursue US interests.

The revolution brought about the end of the Soviet system, but the new democratic governments of Russia and the other republics have a very difficult course to run before political and economic stability can be achieved. The end of the Cold War has halted the arms race, proxy wars, and struggles in the back alleys of the globe by intelligence services. Export controls and sanctions, travel restrictions, ideological propaganda, and a whole range of Cold War antipathies are rapidly fading into the past. The problems of constructing a stable peace remain.

Notes

1.   Author's interview with Ambassador Lukin at the embassy of Russia, Washington, DC, May 25, 1992.

2.   Conversations at the Yeltsin inauguration ceremony between the author and a group of deputies, July 10, 1991.

3.   The Gang of Eight was in fact more than eight. The emergency committee consisted of: Gennadi Yanayev, Valentin Pavlov, Boris Pugo, Dmitri Yazov, Vladimir Kryuchkov, Valery Boldin, Oleg Baklanov, Anatoly Lukyanov, Vassily Starodubtsyev, Alexander Tizyakov, and others.

2

Nuclear Arms Control After
the Moscow Coup

Ivo H. Daalder

WHEN THE STRATEGIC ARMS Reduction Treaty (START) was signed in Moscow on July 31, 1991, it was widely regarded as the last arms-control accord of its kind.[1] The rapid pace of political change in the eighteen months preceding the Moscow summit had emphasized the growing irrelevance of negotiating the minutiae of weapons characteristics and force ceilings in long, drawn-out deliberations. The START negotiations had begun in 1982 at a time of deep crisis in US-Soviet relations, marked by differences over the deployment of intermediate-range nuclear forces (INF) in Europe. They were completed after Soviet military forces had largely withdrawn from Eastern Europe and German unification had become an accomplished fact.

Nothing underscored this change more dramatically than the August 1991 coup in Moscow. Its failure signaled not only the end of communism in Europe but also the end of the Russian empire that was the Union of Soviet Socialist Republics (USSR). In the weeks following the failed putsch, communism was banned throughout the vast Soviet territories, and power shifted from Moscow to the capitals of the fifteen Soviet republics. On December 8, 1991, the three Slavic republics—Russia, Ukraine, and Belarus—disbanded the Soviet Union, creating in its stead a Commonwealth of Independent States (CIS). Two weeks later, eight of the nine remaining republics formally joined the CIS.[2] On Christmas Day, Mikhail Gorbachev resigned as the last president of the USSR.

These rapid and historic events dramatically altered the course of American nuclear diplomacy. Strategic nuclear arms control negotiations had for over a quarter of a century concentrated on managing nuclear competition. Now, the primary concern became to ensure continued and effective control over the vast Soviet nuclear stockpile, which consisted of some 27,000 weapons spread out over much of the former Soviet Union. With conflict over territory, resources, and power rising within the former superpower, the need to prevent a nuclear civil war—a "Yugoslavia with nukes," as US Secretary of State James Baker termed it[3]—began to drive US diplomacy, first with the Soviet Union and then with the CIS.[4]

Three goals dominated American nuclear diplomacy after the Moscow coup:

- Preserving agreed arms-control undertakings.
- Avoiding the emergence of new nuclear weapons states and preventing the proliferation of weapons and know-how.
- Securing additional nuclear force reductions.

The means to these ends consisted of securing START ratification and insisting on adherence to existing international obligations, as well as encouraging central control over nuclear weapons, preferably by removing all weapons from non-Russian republics. In addition, the United States offered incentives for further nuclear reductions by proposing drastic, unilateral, and reciprocated cuts. It also offered technical and financial assistance to ensure the secure control, safe transportation and storage, and sound disablement and eventual dismantlement of nuclear weapons.

The essence of American nuclear diplomacy, including arms control as the means of that diplomacy, was consequently transformed almost overnight. The key objective was to ensure secure command and control over the former Soviet Union's nuclear forces, not to search for some abstract notion of crisis stability. The speed of implementation became more important than concern with effective verification. Residual nuclear force levels on the US side could be drastically reduced, with only the timing and extent of reductions remaining a matter of debate. And cooperation in implementation replaced long-winded, tedious, and often competitive formal negotiations.

The transformation of American nuclear diplomacy becomes fully apparent when one examines developments in three areas:

- START ratification efforts, which were made more difficult by the uncertainty about the nature of the US treaty partner once the Soviet Union collapsed.
- New initiatives designed to ensure continued, effective, and central control over nuclear weapons.
- Cooperative steps aimed at securing implementation of agreed measures.

Developments in these three areas demonstrate the degree to which nuclear diplomacy in the post-Soviet world has been irreversibly transformed.

Struggling with START

The basic framework of the START agreement had emerged from the ill-fated Reykjavik summit in October 1986 between Presidents Ronald Reagan and Gorbachev and was further refined during the Washington summit a year later.[5] At that time, it was agreed that US and Soviet accountable nuclear warheads would be limited to 6,000 each, with no more than 4,900 on ballistic missiles. These could be deployed on no more than 1,600 strategic nuclear delivery vehicles. Warheads on heavy missiles were further limited to 1,540 and the missiles themselves to 154. Nuclear weapons on heavy bombers were to be discounted against the overall warhead ceiling. In the nearly four years of additional negotiations necessary to complete the treaty, the two countries concentrated on overcoming differences on a host of issues—including how to limit sea- and air-launched cruise missiles (SLCMs and ALCMs), whether to limit mobile missiles, the details of the verification regime, and the relation of strategic offensive force reductions to strategic defensive deployments.

Each of these issues was resolved by the time of the June 1990 Bush-Gorbachev summit in Washington.[6] SLCMs were limited to 880 on each side, but only in a politically binding side agreement. ALCM deployments were initially to be discounted against the 6,000 warhead ceilings. Up to 1,100 warheads could be deployed on mobile missiles. An intricate verification system, including twelve different types of on-site inspection arrangements, was constructed. And there would be no formal link between START and strategic defenses, although Moscow insisted on an informal and unilateral link.

During the endgame in 1991, Linton Brooks and Yuli Vorontsov, who headed the US and Soviet START negotiations in Geneva, spent months resolving a number of minor issues. Three of these issues proved particularly nettlesome and were resolved only in a marathon ministerial session in Washington two weeks before the July 1991 summit.[7] First, there was disagreement on the extent to which nuclear warheads could be removed or "downloaded" from land- and sea-based missiles to meet agreed ceilings. A compromise was agreed to that allowed each side to download a limited number of missile types, but not by more than 4 warheads per missile or 1,250 warheads overall. Second, the two sides debated for months how to distinguish a "new type" of strategic missile from a "modified" missile, finally agreeing that to be considered a new type, a strategic missile must meet any of the following criteria: a different number of stages; a different type of propellant; a 10 percent change in either length or launch weight; a 5 percent change in diameter; or a 5 percent change in the length of the first stage combined with a 21 percent change in throw-weight. Third, there was the issue of telemetry—the data transmitted during missile flight tests. Both sides had agreed not to transmit these data without encryption, but differences in how telemetry is transferred held up agreement on how the encryption ban could be enforced. In the end, they agreed to exchange tapes from all strategic missile flight tests and the information necessary to interpret the data.

During the four years it took to hammer out these and other compromises, the world around the negotiators began to change with remarkable speed. The events of 1989 pushed START—long the mainstay of US-Soviet relations—to the sidelines; headlines instead told of the Berlin Wall coming down, a velvet revolution in Czechoslovakia and a violent one in Romania, free elections throughout Eastern Europe, German unification, and the battle in Moscow between hard-liners and reformers for Mikhail Gorbachev's political soul. Not surprisingly, therefore, when Presidents Bush and Gorbachev met in Moscow in July 1991, the signing ceremony of START (by this time a 280-plus page document) was relegated to the inside pages of the daily press.

Nevertheless, the START treaty remains a major accomplishment.[8] Not only does it mandate drastic reductions in US and Soviet strategic forces (although less than the oft-repeated 50 percent), but it also puts into place an intrusive monitoring regime that could form the basis for verifying additional reductions should these be agreed. Even after the Moscow coup and the subsequent disintegration of the Soviet Union, START remains the basic framework within which further reductions can be negotiated.[9] Its rules and procedures can apply to further reductions, and its verification provisions provide confidence that agreed undertakings will, in fact, be implemented. In addition, START provides a hedge if, however unlikely, events lead to a resurgent threat emanating from the territory of the former Soviet Union. For all these reasons, ratification remains a high priority for the Bush administration.[10]

But this is easier said than done. The United States signed the START agreement with a country that no longer exists.[11] The treaty covers nuclear forces and facilities located on the territory of not one but four newly independent states. More than twenty deployment, production, and other sites covered by the treaty are located outside Russia. Of the actual weapons, 72 SS-25s are deployed in Belarus, 104 SS-18s and 40 Bear-H bombers are deployed in Kazakhstan, and 46 SS-24s, 130 SS-19s, 14 Bear-Hs, and 16 Blackjacks are deployed in Ukraine. The remaining forces are deployed in Russia.[12] In December 1991, all four countries pledged to submit the START treaty for ratification to their parliaments.[13] US officials have repeatedly been reassured on this score, and in January 1992, they were told by leaders of the three non-Russian republics that all strategic forces on their soil would be eliminated as a result of START implementation.[14]

But these pledges and statements leave a central question unresolved. With whom has the United States signed the START treaty, and who is responsible for its implementation? In theory, the treaty could be amended to make all four states party to the treaty. In practice, however, this would be undesirable, since in so doing the three non-Russian republics would be accorded the status of nuclear-weapons states, something two of the three have openly declared they do not want, and the third, Kazakhstan, has privately indicated it does not seek. Also, the recognition of Ukraine, Belarus, and/or Kazakhstan as nuclear-weapons states would violate US and Russian undertakings in the nuclear Non-Proliferation Treaty (NPT) not to transfer nuclear weapons or control there over them to nonnuclear-weapons states. So how is this issue to be resolved?

The principles guiding US policy in this area were outlined by Reginald Bartholomew, under secretary of state for international security affairs, in February 1992. Testifying before Congress, Bartholomew stressed these points:

■ Appropriate responsibilities to the relevant states be set down in legal documents.

- Ratification and implementation support the unified command and control arrangements over nuclear weapons of the former Soviet Union.
- The approach be compatible with the obligations that the states assume under the NPT.
- The agreement reflect a consensus among all four states.[15]

These principles were reflected in the approach being considered by the four states in January 1992—an approach that consisted of Russia ratifying START, the other three states seeking parliamentary approval of the treaty, and all four states concluding a quadripartite agreement that would provide for its implementation.[16]

In late February, Secretary of State Baker told the House Appropriations Committee that the United States had accepted the Russian approach to START ratification.[17] In mid-March, however, Ukraine challenged the approach when it announced it would halt shipments of tactical nuclear weapons on its soil to Russia.[18] Although the ostensible reason for the decision related to Kiev's desire to verify the dismantlement of weapons that had been transferred, the announcement highlighted an aspect of Ukrainian policy that until then had not been clear. Although Kiev had agreed to a joint *command* of nuclear weapons on its soil, and this would not change, to its mind Ukraine *owned* the weapon systems. Such reasoning called into question not only Ukraine's pledge to sign the NPT as a nonnuclear-weapons state[19] but also whether a US-Russian agreement affecting the former Soviet Union's strategic forces would *legally* apply to Ukrainian (or, for that matter, Kazakh or Belarussian) nuclear weapons.[20] Moreover, to admit that these were Ukrainian (or Kazakh or Belarussian) nuclear weapons was to admit that these countries were nuclear-weapons states— something Washington was striving to avoid.

Ukrainian insistence on being treated as a full partner to the START treaty stalemated discussions among the four states to resolve the issue.[21] The United States had no objections to according the three non-Russian states a role in the treaty ratification process consistent with their newly gained sovereignty, but it insisted that the treaty itself remain a bilateral undertaking.[22] Publicly, Moscow continued to maintain that Russia, as the sole legal successor to the Soviet Union, be the bilateral partner of the United States.[23]

The disagreement over START ratification between Russia on the one hand and Ukraine and Kazakhstan—which, like Kiev, insisted that it would retain ownership over some of the nuclear missiles on its soil so long as

Russia, China, and the United States deployed missiles[24]—on the other, forced the Bush administration to become actively involved in the discussions among the four states. Whereas previously the United States had sat back and allowed the new states to devise an acceptable formula for ratifying START, by late March Washington took a proactive course by directly suggesting what approaches it would find both reasonable and acceptable.[25]

One such approach was for the United States and the four former Soviet republics to sign a new protocol to the treaty that would (1) identify the four states as the bilateral treaty partner of the United States; (2) include a commitment by Belarus, Kazakhstan, and Ukraine to sign the NPT as nonnuclear-weapon states; and (3) ensure the elimination of all strategic weapons outside Russian territory by the end of the seven-year START implementation period.[26] Under this approach, the concerns of all parties would appear to have been met: The United States would gain START ratification and a legally binding pledge that the non-Russian states would become NPT members; Russia would gain its desired status as the sole nuclear power to emerge from the Soviet Union; and the three other states would be formal parties to the START treaty, a status that would thereby confirm their newly gained sovereign-state status.

The idea of a five-party protocol to the START treaty gained the favor of Ukraine and Kazakhstan when their respective presidents visited Washington in May.[27] On May 23, 1992, representatives of the four new states and the United States signed the protocol to the START treaty, paving the way for the treaty's ratification later in the year.[28]

The five-nation protocol to the START treaty would appear to have addressed successfully one of the main dangers resulting from the break-up of the USSR—the prospect of instantaneous nuclear proliferation. The protocol not only secures START ratification, thus mandating significant cuts in strategic forces and intrusive on-site inspections, but also represents an appropriate political vehicle for ensuring that, aside from Russia, no new nuclear-weapon states will emerge. It therefore fulfills one of the three goals—ensuring centralized control and avoiding nuclear proliferation—set by the Bush administration in the aftermath of the Moscow coup.

Concerns About Nuclear Command and Control

Among the more immediate issues raised by the failed August coup was growing concern about the degree of control over the Soviet nuclear arsenal. Reports surfaced in the immediate aftermath of the coup that the nuclear "football" containing electronic codes for transmitting launch orders had been taken away from the Soviet president.[29] In part because of these reports, the media concentrated on the possibly precarious state of control over Soviet strategic nuclear forces.[30] The Bush administration minimized the danger and released intelligence information indicating that Soviet nuclear commanders had taken precautionary measures to ensure effective control over strategic forces.[31]

The same sense of confidence was absent, however, with respect to control over tactical nuclear weapons, some 15,000-17,000 of which were deployed in all Soviet republics outside the Baltics and the Caucasus. Secretary of Defense Richard Cheney noted in late August, for instance, that "tactical nuclear weapons are much more widely dispersed than strategic systems. Will they still be controlled from the center? Or will they come under the control of the respective republic governments?"[32] These questions reflected issues raised by an interagency committee inside the Bush administration that for months had been studying the question of nuclear command and control within the Soviet Union. Even before the coup, the committee had concluded that tactical nuclear weapons posed the gravest risk in terms of control.[33]

Finally, there was the worry, already raised by Secretary Cheney, about the possible devolution of command authority over the entire Soviet nuclear arsenal. In early September, Secretary of State Baker set out the key principles that would guide US Soviet policy following the coup. Among these was the admonition that the United States did "not want to see the transformation that's taking place in the Soviet Union either create or add to the problems of nuclear proliferation." He also expressed the US preference "that it would be probably on balance best if not necessarily [nuclear weapons] ended up all in one republic, but that they ended up under one central command authority."[34]

These two concerns, involving tactical nuclear weapons and central control, topped Baker's agenda when he traveled to Moscow in early September 1991. In talks with Soviet officials, Baker suggested possible steps Moscow might take—including withdrawing nuclear weapons from places of potential or present conflict, removing from operational units older weapons lacking or having only primitive fail-safe devices, and concentrating tactical weapons on as few bases as possible to enhance their security.[35] He also sought a commitment from Moscow that it would match any unilateral US reductions in tactical nuclear weapons that Washington might announce in the future.[36]

In Moscow, Baker appeared to preach to the converted. The new Soviet defense minister, General Yevgeny Shaposhnikov, told Baker that keeping track of tactical weapons was difficult, particularly in times of chaos. The new chief of the Soviet General Staff, General Vladimir Lobov, urged Baker to agree to negotiate the elimination of all US and Soviet tactical nuclear weapons, in part because "they are deployed across the vast territory of Europe, which is a risk, especially in the unstable political situation that took shape in the Balkans, on a part of Soviet territory, and in Germany."[37]

In another reflection of these concerns, the president in late August ordered the Pentagon to develop new initiatives on nuclear weapons designed to provide the Soviet Union with incentives to consolidate and reduce their tactical nuclear stockpile. Working in customary secrecy, the Pentagon and other top administration officials developed a bold plan "to step down the thermonuclear ladder," as the US chairman of the Joint Chiefs of Staff, General Colin Powell, would later put it.[38] The initiative, announced by President Bush in an address to the nation on September 27, 1991, included the following steps, which, though undertaken unilaterally, the United States asked the Soviet Union to match (Table 2.1):[39]

- Elimination of all ground-based tactical nuclear missile warheads and artillery shells.
- Removal of tactical nuclear weapons (including SLCMs) from surface ships and attack submarines, destroying some and consolidating the remainder.
- Standing down from alert all strategic bombers and those intercontintental ballistic missiles (ICBMs) scheduled for elimination under START.
- Cancellation of the mobile MX missile, the mobile portion of the Midgetman program, and the short-range attack missile.

President Gorbachev responded to the US initiatives on October 5 by matching the unilateral US moves and, in some cases, extending them to other areas.[40] Specifically, Gorbachev's response included

- Elimination of ground-based tactical nuclear weapons.
- Removal of tactical nuclear weapons from naval vessels (destroying some) and a proposal for their elimination on a reciprocal basis.
- A proposal to remove tactical bombs and missiles from active air force units.

Table 2.1 US and Russian Nuclear-Weapons Initiatives

UNITED STATES   RUSSIA
TACTICAL NUCLEAR WEAPONS
Deployment

- Withdraw all 1,700 land-based weapons from Europe and South Korea, all 500 sea-based weapons "usually at sea" from surface ships and attack submarines, and all air-based weapons from South Korea; cut air-based weapons in Europe by 50 percent.

- Withdraw all tactical nuclear weapons from non-Russian republics by July 1, 1992. As of March 1, 1992, tactical nuclear weapons were deployed only in Russia and Ukraine.

Land-based weapons

- Destroy all 1,300 artillery shells and 850 short-range missile warheads.

- Destroy all artillery shells, short-range missiles, and nuclear mines. Remove all nuclear warheads for air-defense missiles from deployment areas and destroy half.

Sea-based weapons

- All nuclear depth bombs aboard ships and land-based naval aircraft to be eliminated (approximately 50 percent of 2,175 naval weapons). Nuclear SLCMs and tactical bombs to be placed in secure storage.

- Eliminate one-third of all weapons removed from surface ships, "multipurpose" submarines, and land-based naval aircraft, and place remainder in secure storage. Halt production of SLCMs.
- **Propose**, on a reciprocal basis, the elimination of all long-range SLCMs.

Air-based weapons

- Remove all weapons from South Korea, cut those in Europe by 50 percent to about 600-800 weapons.
- Halt development of the short-range attack missile-tactical (SRAM-T) for the tactical air-to-surface missile role.

- Half of bombs and missile warheads to be eliminated.
- **Propose**, on a reciprocal basis, to remove from combat units of frontline tactical air forces all nuclear bombs and missiles and place in central storage.

Table 2.1 continued

UNITED STATES	RUSSIA

STRATEGIC NUCLEAR WEAPONS

Deployment

- Stand down from alert 450 single-warhead Minuteman II missiles, 10 Poseidon submarines with 160 ten-warhead C-3 missiles, and all strategic bombers, moving weapons to secure storage.

- Remove from operational readiness 600 land- and sea-based missiles (with 1,250 warheads) and all strategic bombers, with weapons placed in secure storage.
- Eliminate all strategic missiles outside Russia within 7 years.

Strategic Weapons

- **Propose**, on a reciprocal basis, to eliminate MIRVed ICBMs. If accepted, US will reduce to 4,700 warheads.

- Reduce strategic warheads unilaterally to 5,000—1,000 below the START limit.
- **Propose**, on a reciprocal basis, to cut strategic warheads to 2,000-2,500 on each side.

Intercontinental Ballistic Missiles

- Terminate MX and Midgetman missile programs.
- **Propose**, on a reciprocal basis, to eliminate MIRVed ICBMs.
- **Propose** that both sides limit ICBM modernization to one type of single-warhead missile.

- Freeze deployment of rail-mobile ICBMs at current levels (36), halt modernization, and keep all rail-mobile missiles in garrisons.
- Halt development of follow-on road-mobile missile.
- Destroy 130 ICBM silos.

Sea-Launched Ballistic Missiles

- Stand down from alert 10 Poseidon submarines with 160 ten-warhead C-3 missiles.
- Halt production of W-88 warheads for Trident D-5 missiles.
- **Propose** to cut warheads by one-third if CIS accepts agreement eliminating all MIRVed ICBMs.

- Decommission 6 nuclear submarines and halve the number of submarines on routine combat patrol.
- **Propose**, on a reciprocal basis, to renounce the practice of combat patrols by nuclear submarines.

Strategic Bombers

- Halt development of the SRAM-II missile, stop production of the advanced cruise missile, and terminate B-2 bomber program at 20 aircraft.
- **Propose** to convert "substantial portion" to conventional use if CIS accepts ban on MIRVed ICBMs.

- Halt production of Bear and Blackjack strategic bombers, long-range ALCMs of existing types, and nuclear short-range missiles.
- Terminate exercises involving more than 30 bombers at the same time.
- **Propose**, on a reciprocal basis, to halt development of new tpes of ALCMs.

34

Table 2.1 continued

UNITED STATES   RUSSIA

OTHER INITIATIVES

Strategic Defenses

- **Propose** that Russia join US in taking immediate steps to deploy limited defenses to protect against small-scale ballistic missile strikes.

- **Propose** to create "a global defense system for the world community" by removing SDI and making use of high technologies developed by Russia.
- **Propose** elimination of antisatellite systems.

Nuclear Weapons Safety

- Explore cooperation on warhead security and safety, and safe and environmentally sound storage, transportation, dismantling, and destruction of nuclear weapons.

- Explore the development of safe and ecologically sound technologies for storing and transporting nuclear weapons and of methods for recycling weapons.

Nuclear Testing

- No proposal.

- Begin one-year unilateral moratorium, paving way to complete ban on nuclear testing.

Production of Fissile Materials

- No proposal. US has halted production of weapons-grade uranium and plutonium.

- **Propose** agreement with the US on the "verified cessation of production of all weapons-grade fissionable material."
- **Propose** the creation of an international agency to take gradual control of "the whole nuclear cycle from the mining of uranium and the production of deuterium and tritium, to the storage of waste."

Doctrine

- No proposal.

- **Propose** that all nuclear powers sign a declaration promising not to be the first to use nuclear weapons.

A summary of the nuclear-weapons initiatives announced by President Bush on September 27, 1991, and January 28, 1992, by President Gorbachev on October 5, 1991, and by President Yeltsin on January 29 and 31, 1992.

Source: Adapted and updated from President Bush's State of the Union Address printed in the *New York Times*, January 29, 1992, p. A-16, "Gorbachev's Remarks on Nuclear Arms Cuts," *New York Times*, October 6, 1991, p. A-12, and President Yeltsin's speech on Moscow television, January 29, 1992, printed in *UN Conference on Disarmament*, CD/1123, January 31, 1992.

■ Standing down from alert all strategic bombers and those ICBMs to be eliminated under START and confining rail-mobile missiles to their garrisons.

■ Halting development of multiple independently targeted reentry vehicle (MIRV) mobile missiles, the follow-on SS-25 missile, the short-range attack missile, and deployment of rail-mobile ICBMs.

■ A unilateral cut of 1,000 warheads below START levels and a proposal to negotiate a 50 percent cut in post-START strategic force levels.

■ A reciprocal ban on fissile material production and a one-year moratorium on nuclear testing to encourage agreement on a complete test ban.

The positive Soviet response to the Bush initiative signaled the emergence of a new era in arms control. Quite apart from the inherent significance of these steps, four factors in Bush's initiatives stand out as powerful evidence of the radical transformation of the arms-control agenda.

First, the initiatives underscored a fundamental shift in American thinking about the role of nuclear weapons in a post-Cold War era marked by the ascendancy of true reformers in Moscow and the discrediting of the old line as a result of the failed coup. This shift was apparent in the decision to stand down from alert all strategic bombers, a move that signaled to Moscow that the United States no longer feared a bolt-out-of-the-blue attack.[41] But it was most obviously present in the unilateral elimination of all ground-based tactical nuclear weapons, which had long been the key to US extended deterrence policy in Europe and Northeast Asia.[42] With the disappearance of the Soviet military threat, ground-based nuclear weapons had become a liability rather than an asset. The same was true with regard to sea-based tactical nuclear weapons—the US Navy finally accepted the wisdom of removing these uncontrollable weapons from sea.[43] At the same time, the shift in thinking was not extended to its logical conclusion: Air-based tactical nuclear weapons, even if at sharply reduced levels, would remain in Europe (though not in South Korea) to "provide an essential political and military link between the European and the North American members of the Alliance," as NATO's new strategic concept put it.[44]

Second, the fact that the administration concentrated its unilateral reductions in the tactical nuclear area but left strategic forces largely untouched underscored the degree to which the United States was concerned about a loss of control over these smaller weapons. The idea was that fewer weapons posed fewer problems for effective control; thus, the initiative emphasized incentives for consolidating and eliminating Soviet weapons, both to reduce command and control problems and to remove nuclear weapons as a source of friction in the emerging power struggle among Soviet republics. As US Under Secretary for Defense Paul Wolfowitz stated, the "real agenda is to get rid of 10,000 to 17,000 tactical nuclear weapons in the Soviet Union which nobody needs." He also said that the United States was appealing to "anyone who has any power to take a decision" in the Soviet Union to agree to their destruction.[45] For this reason, US officials traveling to Moscow in early October to explain the Bush initiatives insisted that representatives of the four Soviet republics with strategic arms on their territory be included in the discussions.[46]

Third, the administration emphasized that speed was of the essence. Reciprocal, unilateral steps became the new arms-control game. This represented a fundamental shift in US policy, as Secretary Cheney emphasized: "We clearly, in moving unilaterally, have taken a different approach than I would have advocated even a few months ago."[47] The reasons for the new approach were twofold. Previous arms-control experience suggested that negotiations could end up delaying agreement on the required steps. Arms control by example had the advantage of achieving immediate results.[48] In addition, Soviet disarray put the onus on Washington for breaking the internal deadlock in Moscow. As a State Department official explained, "We know from them that tactical nukes are a political problem for them, given the changing political makeup. The president's proposal gives them the political cover to do what they want to do anyway."[49]

Finally, in emphasizing speed over negotiations, the administration deliberately decided to forgo verifying implementation and to rely instead on an exchange of information.[50] Cheney offered four reasons for this development. He cited the START treaty as a framework for monitoring tactical weapons cuts, the new degree of openness in Soviet society, the engagement of the republics in the arms-control dialogue, and the dire straits of the Soviet economy—all of which suggested that the likelihood of cheating had been drastically reduced.[51] A fifth and more likely reason—an increasing US reluctance that had become apparent in previous nuclear, chemical, and conventional arms control negotiations to allow Soviet and other foreign inspectors to check US facilities and capabilities—remained unstated. Whatever the reason, however, verification—long the bone of contention in arms-control negotiations—was clearly less important in an era of growing trust between Moscow and Washington.

The extent to which political change in the Soviet Union was forcing a transformation of the nuclear arms control agenda was underscored by a new round of unilateral and reciprocal measures proposed in late January 1992, after the USSR had formally ceased to exist. In back-to-back statements, President Bush and Russian President Boris Yeltsin proposed significant additional reductions in strategic nuclear arms, announced the termination of almost all nuclear modernization programs, and suggested new areas of cooperation (Table 2.1).[52]

Bush's proposals focused narrowly on strategic arms. They included halting the B-2 program after 20 aircraft had been procured, canceling the Midgetman missile program, terminating the advanced cruise missile, and ending production of the W-88 warhead for the Trident D-5 missile. The president further proposed that in exchange for a mutual ban on land-based MIRVed missiles, the United States would eliminate all MX missiles, reduce the number of warheads on all the remaining 500 Minuteman missiles to one, cut the number of submarine-launched ballistic missile (SLBM) warheads by one-third from planned levels under START, and convert "a substantial portion" of its strategic bombers to primarily conventional use. According to General Powell, if Russia and the other CIS states were to accept this proposal, US strategic forces would be cut by about 50 percent from post-START levels, to 4,700 warheads overall.[53]

Yeltsin's statements were more wide-ranging, covering not only nuclear but also conventional, chemical, and biological weapons and arms control. Regarding the former, Yeltsin committed Russia to all the steps enunciated by Gorbachev the previous October and added some significant initiatives on his own. Among the more noteworthy of these were

- An end to production of the Bear and Blackjack strategic bombers and of existing types of long-range ALCMs and SLCMs.
- A proposal to reduce strategic offensive warheads to 2,000-2,500 on each side.
- A suggestion to create an international agency to ensure the reduction of nuclear weapons and place gradually under its control the entire nuclear fuel cycle of all countries.
- A proposal to create a global defense system for the world community based on a reorientation of the US Strategic Defense Initiative and Russian defense technology.

Yeltsin's statements were followed two weeks later by even more far-reaching proposals put forward by Russian Foreign Minister Andrei

Kozyrev to the UN Conference on Disarmament in Geneva. In his speech, Kozyrev (1) reiterated an earlier proposal to end the targeting of each other's territory; (2) suggested the adoption of a "zero alert status" for nuclear forces by removing warheads from ICBMs, bombs and cruise missiles from bombers, and SLBMs from missile-carrying submarines, which would remain in port; (3) proposed that the five nuclear powers exchange data on the number and type of nuclear weapons, the amount of fissile material in them, and the installations for their production, storage, and destruction; and (4) recommended that countries take a new look at earlier ideas to place control over nuclear weapons under an international organization like the United Nations.[54]

A fundamental shift in nuclear arms control had emerged. Unilateral, though coordinated public announcements, coupled with ministerial-level talks, replaced the competitive negotiating game. Agreements would no longer be formalized in treaty language drafted by international lawyers talented in rendering simple steps and obligations in convoluted and obscure language. Instead, an exchange of letters or an agreed short document spelling out reciprocal obligations would suffice.[55] Formal verification provisions, other than those already accepted under START and other agreements, would be noticeably absent. Most remarkable, however, was the new strategic question guiding arms-control negotiations. Rather than asking "How much is enough," both sides asked "How low can we go?"

In ministerial talks between Baker and Kozyrev in the months following the Bush-Yeltsin initiatives, the United States and Russia sought to arrive at a common answer. Though more amicable, collegial, and cooperative than in previous years, discussions still underscored a number of differences. First, there were differences over the mix of reductions. The United States insisted not only on deMIRVing all land-based missiles, but also on retaining multiple warheads on its sea-based missiles, even if it was willing to reduce these from the present eight warheads per missile to between four and six. Since Russia had long emphasized its land-based missile capability and the United States its sea-based missile force, Moscow argued that deMIRVing apply to all missiles, whether land- or sea-based.[56]

Second, the two sides differed on the scope of any post-START reductions. The Pentagon, in particular, maintained that the Bush-proposed reductions to 4,700 warheads on the US side were as low as the United States could go and rejected any notion of decreasing to the 2,000-2,500 level proposed by the Russians. Thus, Secretary Cheney has said that his "basic instinct is [that] there's a level there that we want to hold at," in part because any further reductions would cut into the US SLBM force:

"It's important to preserve an adequate level in terms of the numbers of submarines we have. I think that's stabilizing, not destabilizing."[57]

In the end, however, both sides compromised on the issue. During the Washington summit between Presidents Bush and Yeltsin June 16-17, a joint understanding was reached under which the two sides agreed to reduce their strategic nuclear inventory to 3,000-3,500 warheads on each side. The agreement also banned MIRVed ICBMs and reduced sea-based warheads to 1,750, or half the planned post-START US force.[58] Once implemented, these radical reductions will have gone a long way to ensuring effective control over Russian nuclear forces.

Cooperative Disarmament

The concern about control over the Soviet nuclear arsenal that had led to the bold unilateral reductions announced by the United States was also manifested in a second major departure from traditional American diplomacy—the provision of direct technical and financial assistance in the nuclear destruction process. Even before the August coup, US and Soviet officials had worried about the security of the Soviet stockpile. Since early 1991, a US interagency committee had studied the matter in detail, and in early August General Powell received a letter from his Soviet counterpart suggesting that nuclear security be added to the regular military-to-military talks.[59]

It was the August coup, however, that propelled the issue to the top of the agenda. In his September 27, 1991, initiative, President Bush suggested new avenues of cooperation in three areas:

> First, we should explore joint technical cooperation on the safe and environmentally responsible storage, transportation, dismantling, and destruction of nuclear warheads. Second, we should discuss existing arrangements for the physical security and safety of nuclear weapons and how these might be enhanced. And third, we should discuss nuclear command and control arrangements, and how these might be improved to provide more protection against the unauthorized or accidental use of nuclear weapons.[60]

In his response, President Gorbachev announced his readiness to engage in a dialogue with the United States on these issues.[61]

During their meeting in Madrid at the opening of the Mideast peace conference in late October, Presidents Bush and Gorbachev agreed to establish two working groups, including one group that would examine how to implement their initiatives while discussing modalities of nuclear-weapons safety, dismantlement, and control.[62] At its first meeting in Washington in November, the working group on safety, security, and dismantlement (SSD), which included representatives of the four republics with strategic weapons on their soil, the United States, according to Bartholomew, "made a major push for the Soviets to disable and to consolidate in secure locations the widely dispersed tactical nuclear weapons."[63] The United States also briefed the Soviet participants on the particulars of American safety, security, and command and control arrangements, on how weapons could be disabled quickly, and on the dismantlement methods used by the United States. Unfortunately, however, the Soviet participants did not reciprocate information. According to Bartholomew, there "was a general reluctance to engage with us across the board, or to describe their systems and procedures in the detail that we described ours."[64]

In part as a result of disappointment and in part because of the deteriorating political climate, it was left to the US Congress to address the issue.[65] Moving without any support from the administration, the Congress voted in late November 1991 to amend the Arms Control Export Act in order to allocate $400 million of Defense Department funds to assist in the destruction of Soviet nuclear and chemical weapons (another $100 million was designated for humanitarian assistance).[66]

It took the overwhelming Ukrainian vote for independence in early December, however, to get the Bush administration to act forcefully to deal with a disintegrating Soviet Union. In a speech at Princeton University on December 12, 1991, Secretary Baker made three central points in regard to nuclear issues. First, he stressed the need to avoid the emergence of new nuclear-weapons states as a result of the Soviet transformation. Second, he announced that the SSD talks that had begun in November would be accelerated. Third, he declared that the administration was prepared to draw on the $400 million appropriated by Congress to assist in the destruction of Soviet weapons of mass destruction.[67]

Immediately after his speech, Baker flew to Moscow, Minsk, Alma-Ata, and Kiev to talk with the leaders of the four republics that had strategic weapons on their soil. In his discussions, Baker stressed four points:[68] First, he urged them to maintain existing arsenals in a safe, secure, and responsible manner and under reliable control, with one single collective authority; all four agreed to do so. Second, he urged them to join the NPT; Russia pledged to fulfill the former Soviet Union's obligations as a nuclear-weapons state, while Belarus, Kazakhstan, and Ukraine privately declared their readiness to join as nonnuclear-weapons states and to submit to full-scope International Atomic Energy Agency (IAEA) safeguards. Third, all states agreed to accept visits and advice from US experts on disabling and dismantling nuclear weapons. Finally, Baker pressed the leaders to adopt stringent export control legislation to prevent the proliferation of nuclear technology and materials.

Parts of these commitments were confirmed in agreements signed by these and other members of the new CIS. Thus, in the Alma-Ata agreement, the three non-Russian states agreed to remove all nonstrategic forces to Russian facilities by July 1, 1992, for eventual dismantlement. Belarus and Ukraine also declared they would join the NPT and conclude safeguards agreements with the IAEA. Noticeably absent from this provision was a commitment by Kazakhstan to do the same. In addition, the four countries undertook commitments not to transfer nuclear weapons or other explosive devices and technologies or in any other way encourage a state not possessing nuclear weapons from acquiring them.[69] Finally, in the Minsk agreement on strategic forces, the CIS members declared the "need for joint command of strategic forces and for maintaining unified control of nuclear weapons of mass destruction."[70]

In order to follow up on Baker's commitments and to ensure that the Alma-Ata and Minsk agreements would be implemented, President Bush wrote the presidents of the four new states in late December proposing to send a US delegation "to discuss practical steps on nuclear safety, security, disabling, and destruction, as well as controls to prevent proliferation."[71] The delegation would also discuss how the United States could assist in these efforts. The proposed agenda for the SSD talks included command and control; safety, security, disabling, and accelerated destruction of tactical nuclear weapons; START, CFE, and NPT obligations; and export controls, including arms transfers.

The American delegation, which was led by Under Secretary of State Bartholomew, traveled to the four capitals in mid-January and generally found cooperative audiences.[72] The delegation was reassured about the security of command and control arrangements, which remained physically in the hands of the Russian president and the head of the CIS armed forces, General Shaposhnikov. Significant progress had been achieved in transporting tactical nuclear weapons to storage and dismantlement sites in Russia.[73] By late January, ground-based short-range nuclear forces (SNF) remained deployed only in Ukraine and Russia, and some air-based weapons were also still in Belarus.[74] Finally, all tactical nuclear weapons remaining outside Russia had been removed from operational units.

The main problem the US delegation confronted concerned the pace of dismantlement efforts inside Russia and the degree and scope of possible US assistance in this process. According to Bartholomew, the Russians believed it would be difficult to meet the schedule outlined by Gorbachev earlier to dismantle all weapons by 2000. The problem they confronted was not the destruction process itself but rather the absence of storage facilities for recovered plutonium and enriched uranium.[75] Russian officials suggested that the $400 million appropriated by Congress be used to construct such facilities.[76] Rather than endorsing the suggestion to construct elaborate facilities, the Bush administration proposed a number of alternative and cheaper ways to store the recovered materials.[77] At the same time, the administration did not consider the option of storing fissile materials recovered from dismantled weapons under either international or joint supervision, an option suggested both by the Russians and by the IAEA.[78]

In mid-February 1992, Secretary Baker traveled to Moscow prepared to settle this and other questions. He carried with him seven proposals dealing with transportation, storage, disablement, and dismantlement of nuclear warheads. These included information on US warhead storage containers, fissile material containers, special rail cars, and "bullet-proof" blankets for warhead protection during transit; nuclear-accident response planning; an accounting system for inventory management; and civil use of fissile materials.[79] Baker proposed that these items, as well as the question of long-term storage of recovered fissile materials, be discussed in subsequent meetings by US and Russian experts.[80]

In early March, a sixty-seven-person expert team, led by William Burns, the former director of the Arms Control and Disarmament Agency, traveled to Russia to discuss these various items with their Russian counterparts. During these meetings, the Russians agreed to make available to the United States engineering diagrams on special containers and rail cars the Russians used for transporting weapons to determine whether it might be cheaper to build additional containers and rail cars than to convert US equipment to Russian use, as the United States had initially proposed. From information provided by Russian officials, the United States believed that some 45,000 containers were needed to transport weapons and fissile materials in a safe and secure manner. Building these to Russian rather than American specifications was believed to be both cheaper and quicker.[81]

As a result of the March SSD talks, the United States was able in April to certify Russia, Ukraine, and Belarus as being committed to the courses of actions prescribed in the Soviet nuclear-risk reduction legislation passed by Congress in November 1991, thus releasing funds for assisting in the nuclear safety, security, and dismantlement process.[82] Current plans are to spend the $400 million Congress appropriated in the following manner: $25 million for a scientific clearing house in Moscow; $10 million for a scientific clearing house in Kiev; up to $20 million to help in nuclear-accident planning; $10-20 million for a computer system to track fissile materials; $10-20 million for safety and security improvements to railroad cars; and $80-100 million for constructing containers to transport individual weapons and components. The remainder will probably be spent on building a facility for the long-term storage of fissile materials.[83]

Since January 1992, therefore, the Bush administration has concentrated on developing cooperative efforts with the Russians to secure the rapid implementation of the Bush-Gorbachev initiatives announced the previous fall. The scope of these efforts, involving both financial commitments and a detailed exchange of highly sensitive and critical information, would have been unthinkable a year or even months ago. By spring 1992, cooperation on nuclear-weapons matters was in many respects becoming routine as officials traveled between Moscow and Washington to determine the best ways in which the process could be completed both rapidly and safely.

At the same time, the administration has been criticized for neglecting the other CIS states, particularly Kazakhstan and Ukraine, where large numbers of strategic and, in the case of Ukraine, tactical nuclear weapons remained deployed.[84] Although US officials have repeatedly been assured by Alma-Ata that the 104 SS-18s in Kazakhstan would be dismantled as part of the START agreement, no Kazakh official has ever said so publicly. Rather, President Nursultan Nazarbayev has said repeatedly that Kazakhstan will retain "parity" with other nuclear powers, arguing that only "if these nuclear weapons are destroyed by the United States, the former Soviet Union, and our neighbor—the PRC—then we are prepared to destroy them."[85]

Ukraine posed a similar, if not more difficult, problem. On March 12, 1992, President Leonid Kravchuk announced a halt to the transfer of tactical nuclear weapons to Russia. "We cannot guarantee that weapons transported to Russia will be destroyed or that they will not fall into undesirable hands," Kravchuk said.[86] He argued that Russia had failed to provide Ukraine with access to the nuclear dismantlement process to verify that the weapons being withdrawn were in fact destroyed. He also criticized the absence of any verification mechanism—whether involving the United States, an international body, or even inspections among the CIS states themselves.

Although weapons shipments from Ukraine to Russia resumed in April,[87] the episode highlighted the uncertain state of affairs in the former Soviet Union. The solution is self-evident: Instituting an international monitoring regime—preferably under IAEA auspices but possibly involving the CIS states and the United States—would help build confidence on all sides that commitments are being met.[88] So far, Washington has resisted, arguing that START verification provisions, coupled with detailed information exchanges, will suffice. However, START is yet to be ratified, and as noted, even the modalities for doing so remain uncertain. One cannot escape the suspicion that the real reason for the Bush administration's opposition to verification measures is the requirement that these be reciprocal, allowing Russian inspection of US installations.[89] The old fear that American secrets might somehow fall into the wrong hands is obstructing measures that could verify that nuclear weapons will be dismantled and recovered materials will not be reused. Most important, the absence of adequate inspection provisions raises the specter of "loose nukes" in the former Soviet Union.

Conclusions

This overview of American nuclear diplomacy since the August coup demonstrates that although the nuclear arms control agenda has been unalterably transformed by the disintegration of the Soviet Union, some old habits die hard. It is true, however, that the Bush administration should be credited with a degree of boldness in its vision of where it wanted to go in the nuclear realm. It effectively seized the moment, particularly in late September 1991, to take steps eliminating weapons that had grown increasingly obsolete and whose deployment was slowly becoming politically untenable. In so doing, it provided the fragile leadership in the Kremlin the political cover necessary to take actions necessary to control the widely dispersed arsenal of thousands of tactical nuclear weapons. In addition, by embarking on the new road of arms control by example, the administration clearly demonstrated that the United States no longer feared the Soviet Union in the way it once did. Relaxing the alert status of strategic bombers, slashing modernization programs, and proposing deeper cuts in strategic forces—all these steps manifested the changing political climate and the new military conclusions that could be drawn from it.

But at the same time, there remained instances in which the vision was more bold in appearance than reality. Two examples stand out. First, although eliminating ground-based SNF and removing tactical nuclear weapons from sea, the Bush administration, this time supported by some important European allies, insisted on maintaining a residual air-based nuclear force in the conviction that nuclear weapons embodied the shared interests of the two sides of the Atlantic. This is old thinking, plain and simple. At a time of an overwhelming, offensively structured and forward-deployed Soviet military threat to Western Europe, American nuclear weapons on the continent were a welcome symbol of the US commitment to distant allies in the nuclear age. In the post-Soviet world, such symbols are outdated, and imparting nuclear weapons with values that they do not possess—not merely symbols but the embodiment of the transatlantic link—is potentially dangerous and may become self-fulfilling.

Second, there is the strange case of verification. Throughout the Cold War, the United States insisted on adequate and effective verification as the condition for arms control. This insistence became the hallmark of the Reagan administration, as intrusive on-site inspections were demanded for INF, confidence- and security-building measures, strategic arms reductions, chemical weapons, and conventional force negotiations. The sincerity of this insistence was put in doubt, however, after Mikhail Gorbachev came to power and the Soviet Union then accepted the principle of on-site inspections on a reciprocal basis. In the endgame of each of these arms-control negotiations, it was the Soviet Union that held out for more intrusion and the United States that resisted. Now, the United States relies on a Russian free press and data exchanges, having more confidence in compliance by Russia than in its ability to safeguard a few clandestine programs. The costs of granting access are today believed to outweigh the benefits from gaining it.

This turnabout conveys a narrow approach to the benefits of verification, focused singly on the likelihood of cheating. But verification is beneficial not just because it can detect or deter cheating; it has many other benefits as well. Verification is crucial to transparency, which is the source of information about all kinds of activities and thus a crucial confidence builder. It may also aid to reassure third parties, which, as the case of Ukraine demonstrates, promotes security for all. Finally, verification adds legitimacy to agreed undertakings, assuring not only parties to agreements but also nonparties that commitments are abided by. In these and other ways, verification is a tool for building security, not a threat to maintaining it.

The transformation of American nuclear diplomacy has been far-reaching, indeed. Steps taken to date would have been unimaginable a few years ago. But this is only the beginning, not the end of the road. Nuclear stockpiles remain vast in size, and participants have little if any idea concerning the purpose for which they are maintained at this or any other level. Fortunately, we now know that the road to arms control need not be tortuous, tedious, or time-consuming. Reciprocal unilateral measures, followed by simple, formal agreements setting out the terms and the manner in which these will be verified, point the way to more far-reaching steps in the future.

Notes

The author would like to thank Dunbar Lockwood, Andrew Winner, and a number of US government officials for their helpful comments on an earlier draft.

1. See, for example, Michael Gordon, "The Last Arms Accord?" *New York Times*, July 16, 1991, pp. A-l, A-9; and R. Jeffrey Smith, "Comprehensive Arms Pact May Be Last of Its Kind," *Washington Post*, July 18, 1991, p. A-29.

2. "Accord on Creation of Commonwealth," *Washington Post*, December 10, 1991, p. A-32; and "Text of Accords by Former Soviet Republics Setting Up a Commonwealth," *New York Times*, December 23, 1991, p. A-10. The three Baltic states had gained formal independence earlier; Georgia refused to accede to the commonwealth.

3. Cited in Dunbar Lockwood, "Commonwealth Leaders Pledge Arms Cuts, Central Control," *Arms Control Today*, Vol. 21, No. 10 (December 1991), p. 25.

4. Thomas Friedman, "US Hopes Moscow Can Retain Control of Soviets' Nuclear Arms," *New York Times*, September 5, 1991, pp. A-1, A-12; and Andrew Rosenthal, "Arms Issue Drives US Soviet Policy," *New York Times*, December 12, 1991, p. A-13.

5. For a concise overview of the START negotiations since that time, see International Institute for Strategic Studies (IISS), *Strategic Survey*, 1987-1988, (London: IISS, 1988), and subsequent editions.

6. "Joint Statement on the Treaty on Strategic Offensive Arms," *Arms Control Today*, Vol. 20, No. 5 (June 1990), pp. 22-23.

7. Dunbar Lockwood, "START Treaty Signed; Brings Historic Cut in Strategic Warheads," *Arms Control Today*, Vol. 21, No. 7, (September 1991) pp. 25, 32-33.

8. For an early assessment, see IISS, *Strategic Survey*, 1989-1990 (London: IISS, 1990), pp. 194-201.

9. Indeed, Senators Claiborne Pell and Joseph Biden, respectively chairman and ranking majority members of the Senate Foreign Relations Committee, have suggested that prior to ratification, START be amended to incorporate lower force

ceilings. See R. Jeffrey Smith, "Russia to Be Sole Nuclear Republic," *Washington Post*, February 6, 1992, p. A-20.

10.   See, for example, the comments of Secretary of Defense Richard Cheney and Secretary Baker in Bill Getz, "Russia Inherits Role in START," *Washington Times*, January 31, 1992, p. A-3; and Smith," Russia to Be Sole Nuclear Republic," p. A-20, respectively.

11.   On the legal implications of the Soviet collapse for arms control, see John B. Rhinelander and George Bunn, "Who's Bound by the Former Soviet Union's Arms Control Treaties?" *Arms Control Today*, Vol. 21, No.10 (December 1991), pp. 3-7.

12.   *Treaty Between the United States of America and the Union of Soviet Socialist Republics on the Reduction and Limitation of Strategic Offensive Arms* (Washington, DC: Arms Control and Disarmament Agency, 1991), pp. 150ff; and "Soviet Strategic Nuclear Weapons Outside the Russian Republic," *Arms Control Today*, Vol. 21, No. 10, (December 1991), p. 29.

13.   "Agreement on Joint Measures on Nuclear Weapons," *Pravda*, December 23, 1991, p. 2, reprinted in *Joint Publication Research Services—Proliferation* (hereafter *JPRS*), January 16, 1992, pp. 35-36.

14.   See Thomas Friedman, "US Says 4 Soviet Republics Vow to Carry Out Nuclear Arms Cuts," *New York Times*, December 19, 1991, pp. A-1, A-14; "Statement by Reginald Bartholomew Before the Senate Armed Services Committee," February 5, 1992, p. 8 (hereafter "Bartholomew Statement").

15.   "Bartholomew Statement," p. 9.

16.   *Ibid.*

17.   See Baker's statement, as quoted in *Arms Control Reporter*, 1992, p. 611.B.724.

18.   Serge Schmemann, "Ukraine Halting A-Arms Shift to Russia," *New York Times*, March 13, 1992, p. A-3.

19.   See "Agreement on Joint Measures on Nuclear Weapons," p. 36.

20.   See also Senators Sam Nunn, Richard Lugar, John Warner, and Jeff Bingaman, "Trip Report: A Visit to the Commonwealth of Independent States," Washington, DC, Senate Committee on Armed Services, March 6-10, 1992, p. 15.

21.   See, for example, Steven Erlanger, "Russian Legislature Votes to Curtail Yeltsin's Powers," *New York Times*, April 12, 1992, p. A-10.

22.   "Testimony of Secretary of State Baker Before the Senate Foreign Relations Committee," April 9, 1992, *Federal News Services*, transcript, p. 12-1.

23.   John Lloyd, "Russia Brushes CIS Partners Aside on START Treaty," *Financial Times*, April 18-19, 1992, p. 2.

24.   See, for example, Fred Hiatt, "Commonwealth Faces Unstable Future," *Washington Post*, March 22, 1992, pp. A-1, A-30.

25.   George Leopold, "U.S. Raises Urgency Level on START," *Defense News*, April 20, 1992, p. 10.

26.   See M. Mayorov and I. Porshnev, "START Treaty: 1+4?" *Interfax*, April 13, 1992, reprinted in *Foreign Broadcasting Information Services—Soviet Union* (hereafter *FBIS-SU*), April 14, 1992, pp. 4-5.

27.   Don Oberdorfer, "Ukraine Agrees to Eliminate Nuclear Arms," *Washington Post*, May 7, 1992, pp. A-1, A-38; and Don Oberdorfer, "Kazakhstan Agrees to Give

Up A-Arms," *Washington Post*, May 20, 1992, pp. A-1, A-31.

28.   Barbara Crossette, "4-Ex-Soviet States and U.S. in Accord on 1991 Arms Pact," *New York Times*, May 24, 1992, pp. A-1, A-12.

29.   David Remnick, "I Want to Breath the Air of Freedom in Moscow," *Washington Post*, August 23, 1991, p. A-25.

30.   See, for example, Patrick Tyler, "Troubling Question of Coup: Whose Finger Was on Soviet Nuclear Trigger?" *New York Times*, August 24, 1991, p. A-9; Bill Gertz, "Soviet Nuclear Arsenal Watched," *Washington Times*, August 27, 1991, p. A-8; Fred Hiatt, "Soviet Official Questions Nuclear Arsenal's Security," *Washington Post*, August 28, 1991, pp. A-1, A-18; John J. Fialka, "Soviet Chaos Upends Strategies for Averting Nuclear Miscalculation," *Wall Street Journal*, August 20, 1991, p. 1; Douglas Waller, "Nuclear Codes and the Coup: Weapons in the Wrong Hands?" *Newsweek*, September 2, 1991, p. 57; and Michael D. Lemonick, "What About the Nukes?" *Time*, September 9, 1991, p. 45.

31.   See, for example, the comments of Secretary Cheney and Brent Scowcroft on NBC's "Meet the Press" and CBS's "Face the Nation" on August 25, 1991, as reported in Jessica Lee, "US Didn't Fear Nuclear Threat," *USA Today*, August 26, 1991, p. A-3. See also Barton Gellman, "General Withdrew Missiles to Shelters During Coup," *Washington Post*, August 28, 1991, p. A-18.

32.   Quoted in John Lancaster and Barton Gellman, "Citing Soviet Strife, Cheney Resists Cuts," *Washington Post*, August 30, 1991, p. A-32.

33.   See Strobe Talbott, "Towards a Safer World," *Time*, October 7, 1991, p. 20.

34.   Quoted in Friedman, "US Hopes Moscow Can Retain Control of Soviets' Nuclear Arms."

35.   William Beecher, "US to Seek Talks on Control of Soviet Nuclear Arms," *Minneapolis Star-Tribune*, September 6, 1991, p. 7.

36.   David Hoffman, "US, Soviets Sign Afghan Arms Halt," *Washington Post*, September 14, 1991, p. A-1.

37.   Quoted in Serge Schmemann, "Soviets Hail US Arms Plan and Signal Their Own Cuts," *New York Times*, September 29, 1991, p. A-1. Shaposhnikov's comments were cited in "Can We Trust the Russians to Go Along?" *Newsweek*, October 7, 1991, p. 22.

38.   "Press Briefing by Secretary of Defense Richard Cheney and Chairman of the Joint Chiefs of Staff Colin Powell," *Defense Issues*, September 28, 1991, p. 4. For background to the initiative, see also John Yang, "Bush Plan Emerged After Failed Coup," *Washington Post*, August 28, 1991, p. A-23; and Andrew Rosenthal, "Back-Porch Plotting and Secret Meetings Leading to Arms Cut Denouement," *New York Times*, September 29, 1991, p. A-14.

39.   "Remarks by President Bush on Reducing US and Soviet Nuclear Weapons," *New York Times*, August 28, 1991, p. A-4.

40.   "Gorbachev's Remarks on Nuclear Arms Cuts," *New York Times*, October 6, 1991, p. A-12.

41.   See, for example, R. Jeffrey Smith, "Initiative Affects Least Useful Weapons," *Washington Post*, September 28, 1991, pp. A-1, A-22.

42.   For a detailed examination of this issue in the European context, see Ivo H. Daalder, *The Nature and Practice of Flexible Response: NATO Strategy and Theater Nuclear Forces Since 1967* (New York: Columbia University Press, 1991).

43.   This step had first been proposed by Paul Nitze in the early 1960s. As the Reagan administration chief arms-control adviser, Nitze had again pressed the idea in the late 1980s, but to no avail. See Michael Gordon, "Nitze Suggests A-Arms Trims for the US and Soviet Navies," *International Herald Tribune*, April 7, 1988, pp. 1-2. See also Ivo H. Daalder and Tim Zimmermann, "Banning Nuclear Weapons at Sea: A Neglected Strategy," *Arms Control Today*, Vol. 18, No. 9 (November 1988), pp. 17-23.

44.   "The Alliance's New Strategic Concept," Brussels, NATO Information Services, November 7, 1991, p. 15. General Powell justified the retention of air-based weapons in Europe in similar terms and also pointed out that "the increased capability associated with conventional weaponry in recent years has to some extent inclined us in the direction of getting rid of tactical nuclear weapons. We can now do conventionally much more efficiently things we thought we could only do with tactical nuclear weapons." See "Press Briefing by Secretary Cheney and General Powell," p. 8. For arguments to the contrary, see Ivo H. Daalder, "Abolish Tactical Warheads," *New York Times*, September 10, 1991, p. A-19; and Daalder, "The Future of Arms Control," *Survival*, Vol. 34, No. 1 (Spring 1991), p. 56.

45.   Quoted by Neil Buckley and Lionel Barber, "Moscow Will Act on N-Arms," *Financial Times*, October 1, 1991, p. 1. See also David Hoffman, "Bush Attempting to Capitalize on Major Changes in Moscow," *Washington Post*, September 28, 1991, p. A-19.

46.   "Bartholomew Statement," p. 3.

47.   "Briefing by Secretary Cheney and General Powell," p. 9. However, the extent of Cheney's acquiescence to the new approach was put in doubt when, a day later, he said that if Moscow did not reciprocate, "then obviously there are certain steps we've taken we could reverse. We can put the bomber force back on alert, we can redeploy our sea-based tactical nuclear systems," thus putting into doubt the unilateral nature of at least some of the announced measures. See "This Week with David Brinkley," Reuter Transcript, September 29, 1991, p. 1.

48.   See, for example, Richard Perle, "Bush's Jump Start," *New York Times*, September 30, 1991, p. A-17; and R. Jeffrey Smith, "Cutting Arms Unilaterally: A Different Approach for a New Era," *Washington Post*, September 29, 1991, pp. A-33, A-37.

49.   Quoted in "Will Bush's Plan Work?" *Newsweek*, October 7, 1991, p. 25. See also Doyle McManus and Michael Parks, "At Summit Arms Discussions, It Will Be a Whole New Ballgame," *Los Angeles Times*, October 28, 1991, p. A-4.

50.   In a statement released the day after the president's announcement, the Pentagon argued that with respect to "the SNF and naval systems, we do not envision any formal verification regime, although we are willing to discuss possible confidence-building measures with the Soviets. It will also be very important to use the increased openness that currently exists between the US and the new Soviet leadership to further enhance the transparency of both sides' actions." Department of Defense, "Fact Sheet on the Strategic Arms Reduction Treaty," September 28, 1991, p. 2. This

approach was acceptable to the Soviet Union. See, for example, the statement by Soviet Deputy Foreign Minister Aleksey Obukov in *Moskovskiye Novosti*, October 27, 1991, p. 12, reprinted in *JPRS-Proliferation*, December 11, 1991, p. 13; and Michael Parks, "Leaders Approve Ways to Verify Arms Cutbacks," *Los Angeles Times*, October 30, 1991, p. A-1.

51.   "Press Briefing by Secretary Cheney and General Powell," p. 9. See also Michael Gordon, "A New Era: Trust Without Verification," *New York Times*, September 29, 1991, p. A-12.

52.   For President Bush's proposal, see his State of the Union Address in *New York Times*, January 29, 1992, p. A-16. Yeltsin's proposals were contained in three statements: "Russia's Policy in the Field of Arms Limitation and Reduction," speech on Moscow Television, January 29, 1992, in UN Conference on Disarmament, CD/1123, January 31, 1992; "Statement by President Yeltsin before the United Nations Security Council," January 31, 1992, excerpted in *New York Times*, February 1, 1992, p. 5; and "Letter by President Yeltsin to UN Secretary-General Boutros Ghali," *Rossiyskaya Gazetta*, January 31, 1992, pp. 1, 3, reprinted in *JPRS-Arms Control*, March 3, 1992, pp. 16-20.

53.   Of the 4,700 warheads, Powell indicated that 500 would be deployed on ICBMs, 2,300 on SLBMs, and 1,900 on bombers. Of the latter, 800 would be START-accountable. See "Briefing on the FY1993 Budget for Defense Programs," Department of Defense, January 29, 1992, Reuter Transcript, p. 6.

54.   UN Conference on Disarmament, *CD/PV.611*, February 12, 1992, pp. 4-5.

55.   On these new modalities, see the statements by Secretary Baker in Thomas Friedman, "US and Russia See New Arms Accord for a July Summit," *New York Times*, February 19, 1992, pp. A-1, A-6; David Hoffman, "US, Russia Seek to Create Missile Warning Site," *Washington Post*, February 19, 1992, p. A-24.

56.   Barry Schweid, "Russian Deal Possible on Multiple Warheads," *Philadelphia Inquirer*, March 11, 1992, p. 4. If accepted, the Russian proposal would still leave both sides with about 1,000 warheads on their ICBMs and SLBMs. Specifically, assuming that SLBMs (but not ICBMs) could be downloaded by as many warheads as necessary, the United States would have to remove 944 ICBM warheads and 3,968 SLBM warheads from its post-START forces, leaving 500 single-warhead Minuteman missiles and 24 single-warhead Trident missiles on each of 18 boats, for a total of 932 remaining warheads. Russia (and other CIS states) would have to eliminate 2,460 ICBM warheads and 1,416 SLBM warheads from its post-START forces, leaving 568 single-warhead SS-25s, and 456 single-warhead SLBMs on 27 boats. These calculations are based on data in "Fact Sheet: Impact of President Bush's Proposals," Washington, DC, Arms Control Association, January 30, 1992.

57.   Quoted in Kathy Sawyer, "Cheney Dismisses Yeltsin Offer on Bigger Arms Cuts," *Washington Post*, February 3, 1992, p. A-5. See also the statements by Cheney and Powell in "US Defense Skeptical on Yeltsin's Proposals for Strategic Weapons Cut," *Aviation Week and Space Technology*, February 10, 1992, p. 21; and by General Lee Butler, Commander of US Strategic Command, in "Former Soviets Continue to Modernize Nuclear Forces—SAC Chief," *Defense Daily*, April 9, 1992, p. 53.

58. "Joint Understanding on Strategic Arms Reductions," Washington, D.C., White House, Office of the Press Secretary, June 17, 1992. For an attempt to justify retaining 5,000 warheads "plus or minus 20 percent" in the post-Cold War era, see Thomas Reed and Michael Wheeler, "The Role of Nuclear Weapons in the New World Order," declassified report to the Commander in Chief of the Strategic Command, December 1991.

59. Talbott, "Towards a Safer World," p. 20; and Associated Press, "State of Soviet Weapons Unclear," *Washington Times*, August 28, 1991, p. A-8.

60. "Remarks by President Bush on Reducing US and Soviet Nuclear Weapons," p. 4. For the French proposal, see Alan Riding, "Mitterrand Urges Talks on A-Arms," *New York Times*, September 12, 1991, p. A-3.

61. "Gorbachev's Remarks on Nuclear Arms Cuts," p. 12.

62. Parks, "Leaders Approve Ways to Verify Arms Cutbacks," p. A-1.

63. "Bartholomew Statement," p. 3.

64. *Ibid.*, p. 4.

65. See Sam Nunn and Richard Lugar, "Dismantling the Soviet Arsenal," *Washington Post*, November 22, 1991, p. A-25; and Les Aspin, "Memorandum on Legislation to Reduce the Soviet Nuclear Threat," Washington, DC, House Committee on Armed Services, December 2, 1991.

66. The amendment, known as the "Soviet Nuclear Threat Reduction of 1991," is reprinted in *Arms Control Reporter*, 1991, p. 611.E-3.27. See also Don Oberdorfer, "First Aid for Moscow: The Senate's Foreign Policy Rescue," *Washington Post*, December 1, 1991, p. C-2.

67. James Baker, "America and the Collapse of the Soviet Empire: What Has to Be Done," address at Princeton University, December 12, 1991.

68. David Hoffman, "Quick Recognition Seen for Former Soviet States," *Washington Post*, December 20, 1991, pp. A-35, A-39. See also Thomas Friedman, "US to Delay Post-Soviet Recognition," *New York Times*, December 20, 1991, p. A-10.

69. "Agreement on Joint Measures on Nuclear Weapons."

70. "Text of Strategic Forces Agreement," TASS, December 31, 1991, reprinted in *JPRS-Arms Control*, January 30, 1992, p. 23.

71. "Bartholomew Statement," p. 4.

72. For details, see *ibid.*, pp. 5ff.

73. On this process, see also William Broad, "Moscow Begins Withdrawal of Nuclear Weapons from Ukraine," *New York Times*, December 21, 1991, p. A-1; R. Jeffrey Smith, "Ukraine Rigs A-Weapons to Ensure Safe Transfer," *Washington Post*, December 25, 1991, pp. A-1, A-26; and R. Jeffrey Smith, "Ukraine Minimizes West's Nuclear Fears," *Washington Post*, December 25, 1991, p. A-26.

74. See also the statement by President Yelstin in Paul Lewis, "World Leaders, at the UN, Pledge to Broaden Its Role to Achieve a Lasting Peace," *New York Times*, February 1, 1992, p. A-4.

75. "Bartholomew Statement," p. 7.

76. See William Broad, "Soviets Say Arms Scuttling Will Take 10 Years," *New York Times*, December 18, 1991, p. A-20; Stanislav Kondrashov, "Dollars for Nuclear

Disarmament Seek Employment in CIS States," *Izvestiya*, January 25, 1992, p. 5, reprinted in *FBIS-SU*, January 29, 1992; Fred Hiatt, "A-Arms Chief Says Russia Needs Help," *Washington Post*, February 5, 1992, p. A-22.

77.   "Bartholomew Statement," p. 7.

78.   See R. Jeffrey Smith, "Soviets Suggest Giving US Keys to Nuclear Sites," *Washington Post*, December 19, 1991, p. A-42; "IAEA Seeks to Guard Soviet A-Fuel," *Washington Post*, January 16, 1992, p. A-22; and Hiatt, "A-Arms Chief Says Russia Needs Help."

79.   Nunn, et al., "Trip Report," p. 14. Baker also presented a plan to address the "brain-drain" problem, involving the establishment in Moscow of a US-German-Russian—financed international center for employing weapons scientists in non-weapons-related work. Thomas Friedman, "Baker and Yelstin Agree on US Aid in Scrapping Arms," *New York Times*, February 18, 1992, pp. A-1, A-6; and David Hoffman, "Ex-Soviet Scientists to Get Aid," *Washington Post*, February 18, 1992, pp. A-1, A-10.

80.   See *Arms Control Reporter*, 1992, p. 602.B.216.

81.   "Opening Statement of the Honorable William F. Burns," House Armed Services Committee, March 26, 1992.

82.   "Certification Pursuant to the Soviet Nuclear Risk Reduction Legislation," US State Department, April 8, 1992.

83.   R. Jeffrey Smith, "3 Former Soviet Republics Meet US Arms Terms," *Washington Post*, April 27, 1992, p. A-13.

84.   See, for example, Nunn, et al., "Trip Report," pp. 17-18; and Graham Allison, Ashton Carter, and Philip Zelikow, "The Soviet Arsenal and the Mistaken Calculus of Caution," *Washington Post*, March 29, 1992, p. C-3.

85.   "President Sets Conditions," Moscow Television, February 16, 1992, reprinted in *JPRS-Arms Control*, March 18, 1992, p. 45.

86.   Quoted in Eleanor Randolph, "Kiev Halts A-Weapons Transfer," *Washington Post*, March 13, 1992, pp. A-1, A-21.

87.   Reuter News Service, "Ukraine Says It Is Resuming Transfer of A-Arms to Russia," *Washington Post*, April 15, 1992, p. A-33.

88.   On these points, see Daalder, "Abolish Tactical Warheads"; Francois Heisbourg, "Subsidize Soviet Disarmament," *New York Times*, October 10, 1991, p. A-27.

89.   According to American scientists engaged in long-standing and detailed discussions with Soviet and, now, Russian officials, Russia will accept verification of the transportation, dismantlement, and storage process if the United States reciprocates. See Christopher Paine and Thomas B. Cochran, "Kiev Conference: Verified Warhead Controls," *Arms Control Today*, Vol. 22, No. 1, January-February 1992, pp. 15-17.

3

The European Community and the Yugoslav Crisis

John Zametica

THIS IS THE HOUR of Europe," declared Luxembourg Foreign Minister Jacques Poos as he and his Dutch and Italian colleagues arrived in Yugoslavia soon after the shooting began in Slovenia at the end of June 1991. The European troika of ministers, representing the European Community (EC), had embarked on a dramatic mission aimed at stopping the Yugoslavs from further fighting. Poos's near-triumphant words went around the world, inspiring hope in many quarters that an energetic external intervention would defuse a potentially terrible conflict.

But as events played out, the arrival of the EC proved to be too late. The much-predicted secessionist war in Yugoslavia had already begun. Sucked into the Yugoslav imbroglio as a conflict manager, the EC battled valiantly against formidable odds to pacify Yugoslavia—but cease-fire after cease-fire was broken because the warring factions had discovered they could treat the international community with contempt. As its failures multiplied, the EC began to draw heavy criticism. In the end, toward the close of 1991, the United Nations (UN) replaced the EC in the estimation of both the Yugoslavs and the rest of the world as the only credible—indeed, impartial—organization able to influence events. The EC, meanwhile, fell into considerable disarray over the question of extending diplomatic recognition to the secessionist republics of Slovenia and Croatia. Any observer would have been forgiven for concluding that the EC effort in the Yugoslav crisis was, from the beginning, a mistake. What went wrong?

The Background

The outbreak of hostilities in Yugoslavia caught the Western world still celebrating the end of the Cold War and the recently concluded Gulf War. A "new world order," the phrase in vogue, did not seem to be an unreasonable proposition. In Europe, the EC had its own new agenda, having earmarked 1992 as the turning point in its movement toward deeper integration. This translated, inter alia, into attempts to enact a joint foreign policy platform for the twelve members of the EC. Calls were also being made, not without attracting controversy, to develop a separate EC security system complete with a defense force. In general, the EC had good reason to contemplate these major steps with self-confidence. Through its example of economic prosperity and democratic government, it had contributed enormously to the 1989 revolutions in Eastern Europe. It appeared more a question of "when" than "if" some, perhaps all, of the newly liberated countries in the east would join the EC. The collapse of the Warsaw Treaty Organization and the fact that the Soviet Union was in turmoil, soon to fragment, left the North Atlantic Treaty Organization (NATO) searching for a new role and wondering whether it would have one at all. The EC seemed to be the most likely candidate to fill the European vacuum: politically, economically, and even militarily.

Early hopes invested by the East Europeans in the Conference on Security and Cooperation in Europe (CSCE) as the basis for a continental security system had proved unfounded as it gradually dawned on them that the CSCE could offer only "soft" security. Moreover, East European overtures to NATO were being politely rejected. In the shifting sands of post-1989 Europe, the EC stood anchored as a model of success, about to enlarge itself physically and widen its role. It was an alluring and dynamic component of the transition from the past occurring in both the east and west on the continent of Europe.

The International Community and the Yugoslav War

The war in Yugoslavia quickly demonstrated that the traditional instruments available to the international community were singularly ill-suited for intervention. But this opened a window of opportunity for the EC. Each of the existing, well-established international organizations—the

UN, NATO, and the CSCE—faced apparently insurmountable obstacles with regard to involvement in Yugoslavia.

The problem for the UN was that Yugoslavia presented a case par excellence of a member state's internal affairs. The recent precedent set by the UN in Kurdistan could not be applied to Yugoslavia where, for the time being, no similar grounds existed for humanitarian intervention. Thomas Pickering, the US ambassador to the UN, stated bluntly that the UN had no role in Yugoslavia unless other international organizations failed.[1]

The problem for NATO concerned the simple question of mandate. Yugoslavia borders Italy and Greece, but the fighting was unlikely to spread into these two NATO countries. As a strictly defensive alliance, NATO had no business in Yugoslavia. Even if NATO could conjure up some grounds for intervention, it would be faced with the necessity of making a series of *political* choices in the conundrum of Yugoslavia's internal quarrels. Since there was no peace to keep, what exactly would NATO be doing in Yugoslavia? Protecting the country's integrity on behalf of the federal government? Or helping the secessionist republics of Slovenia and Croatia to establish their independence? And how, in any event, would the international community react to an extension of NATO's role at a time when its speedy demise seemed desirable to many? NATO involvement was never in the cards.

On the face of it, the CSCE appeared much better equipped, indeed authorized, to intercede in Yugoslavia than was any other international body. Here, after all, was an organization specifically designed to deal with matters of European security. But there was a fatal flaw as far as the Yugoslav situation was concerned: the sacrosanct principle of unanimity among CSCE members. Except for the question of human rights, the CSCE sphere of competence had traditionally related to problems between rather than within states. Admittedly, this began to change somewhat after the November 1990 Paris summit of the CSCE with the establishment of an office for free elections and a conflict-prevention center.[2] Moreover, at the June 1991 Berlin meeting, the CSCE ministers agreed to adopt an emergency mechanism conceived to address the internal affairs of member states. It would be fair to observe that the ever-deepening crisis in Yugoslavia had served as a catalyst for this move. And yet the emergency mechanism was only a half measure at best. The CSCE defined emergencies as either human rights violations or a "major disruption endangering peace, security and stability." All of this, however, amounted to empty words and a mechanism without punch. The CSCE could now assemble for an emergency meeting called by a member state backed by twelve other members to consider such questions, but any decisions could be taken only with the unanimous consent of all members. In other words, the CSCE had merely agreed to continue as a debating forum that could now meet at short notice. Its impotence could thus be demonstrated more quickly—and it was. Austria, perhaps the country most keen to see the breakup of Yugoslavia,[3] invoked the emergency mechanism after the war broke out in Slovenia to discuss "unusual military activities" in Yugoslavia. It was a farce that worsened over time. Eventually, early in July 1991, the CSCE breathed a sigh of relief when the EC began to take over.

The Initial Response

It is in many ways surprising that the EC had stood idle as the crisis in Yugoslavia deepened. It took a strong, behind-the-scenes US intervention early in 1991 before the EC was fully alerted to what was happening in the country.[4] It was not as though the situation was totally unclear. There were widespread public predictions in the West that a violent conflict in Yugoslavia was likely unless the international community could prevent it. Already in November 1990, the CIA had leaked to the press a report predicting war in Yugoslavia within eighteen months.[5] Even if the EC was not quite sure whether it had a mandate to intervene, it certainly had an interest in doing so. Yugoslavia bordered on two EC countries, Italy and Greece. Another two, Austria and Hungary, were likely to become EC members in the medium to long term. Violence in Yugoslavia had the potential to destabilize the whole region of southeastern Europe, involving Albania, Bulgaria and Hungary, and perhaps Greece. Though the actual fighting was unlikely to spill over into an EC country, trade routes would be affected and refugees could create major problems. For reasons of self-interest alone, the need for the EC to act was more than apparent.

There was certainly no dilemma for the EC as to what its general approach would be in the Yugoslav crisis. A key judgment among most EC members was that any breakup of the country could not take place peacefully. This meant that the EC was not going to encourage secession. The EC formula was stated repeatedly in public—a "single and democratic Yugoslavia"—but the formula contained the proviso that it depended entirely on the Yugoslavs themselves to hammer out a form of future coexistence. The crucial point for the EC was that any change should be arrived at peacefully and democratically.

The EC position was widely misunderstood and led to an avalanche of criticism once the war began in Yugoslavia. Accusations were that the EC was conducting a shortsighted policy, that it was hell-bent on preserving a Yugoslavia that was clearly on its last legs, and that this approach had given comfort to the central (and neo-Bolshevik) authorities in Belgrade who then responded with force to the Slovene declaration of independence in June. Such was the criticism of those who were sympathetic to Slovene and Croat separatism.

The EC can be criticized more fairly with regard to two other points. The first is that it had continued to embrace the unjustified hope that the Yugoslavs would somehow resolve their differences without violence. As late as April 1991, an EC ministerial mission, which included Italian Foreign Minister Gianni de Michelis, visited Yugoslavia and gained the "positive feeling" that the country would solve its crisis.[6] This was not just polite diplomatic language. The EC ministers were so unconcerned about the situation that "there was no time" for them to meet the leaders of the six republics—the real power in the land.[7] Instead they met federal Prime Minister Ante Markovic (at this stage thoroughly ignored by all the republics), the president of the collective presidency, Borisav Jovic (widely seen as the extended hand of Serbia's President Slobodan Milosevic and distrusted by non-Serbs), and federal Foreign Minister Budimir Loncar (a man at the helm of a superfluous foreign policy in light of the fact that all six republics were running their own external affairs). But the EC liked Prime Minister Markovic because it approved of his economic reform program. Sadly, the EC had overlooked the fact that no one in Yugoslavia had the same appreciation for Markovic or his policies. Incredibly, too, the EC received and believed intelligence that Markovic was fully backed by the federal armed forces—which, if true, would make him the most formidable player in Yugoslav politics.[8] So strong was the belief in Markovic within the EC that the ministerial visit in April was preceded by the approval of a $1 billion loan to Yugoslavia, for which a financial protocol was formally signed on June 24, only a day before Slovenia and Croatia declared independence.

The EC approach was characterized by wishful thinking rather than a desire to preserve a single Yugoslavia at any cost. This also accounts to a large extent for a second legitimate criticism of EC policy: its belated response to the developing crisis. In one sense, this may have been a deliberate act. "The Soviet Union played a part in the EC 'wait and see' attitude towards Yugoslavia," one EC official admitted. "The EC saw a parallel with the Soviet Union, and there was a fear that if something was done in Yugoslavia, it would have to be repeated in the Soviet Union. This the EC didn't want to do."[9]

By the time the war started in Slovenia, the EC still "had no plan of action."[10] But what exactly could the EC have done to halt the Yugoslavs on their path toward war? Its principal weapon was economic leverage. Yugoslavia conducted 53 percent of its total trade with the EC and had a cooperation agreement that was signed in 1980 and came into force in 1983. It gave Yugoslavia preferential trade treatment, allowing free entry of most of its goods into the EC market. Economic leverage and the fact that the EC had a long-standing formal relationship with Yugoslavia (since the first trade agreement in 1970) legitimized EC diplomatic activity in Yugoslavia.

A sense of urgency finally developed in May when Yugoslavia was plunged into a constitutional crisis following the failure to elect Stipe Mesic, a Croat, to the post of president of the collective presidency. In an unprecedented move, the EC sent to Yugoslavia its Commissioner Jacques Delors and Prime Minister Jacques Santer of Luxembourg, the country that held the EC presidency. This was not a mediating attempt but an expression of the great anxiety felt by the EC about the ever-deteriorating situation in Yugoslavia. At the same time, however, Delors and Santer (who now took the trouble to meet all the republican leaders) read the riot act to the Yugoslavs. If they were interested in further aid from the EC and wanted to begin negotiating an association agreement, they would have to

- Agree on the new head of state and end the leadership crisis.
- Resolve in a peaceful fashion all other differences.
- Back more vigorously Markovic's reformist policies.
- Immediately and dramatically improve the human rights situation in Kosovo, an ethnic Albanian province of Serbia.

All these admonitions fell on deaf ears. The Yugoslavs were no longer thinking about economic matters. Delors and Santer were shocked not only by the worsening economic situation but also by the hard-line attitudes held by the republican leaders. Douglas Hurd, the British foreign secretary, stated that the EC message to Yugoslavia had struck a balance between "our desire not to see disintegration" and "the inadmissibility of the use of force."[11] He could have added that the EC had at last woken up to the the reality of a terrible tragedy about to unfold. But it was too late.

Conflict Management: From Brioni to The Hague

As the Yugoslavs went to war in late June, with the ineffectiveness of the CSCE instruments in full view, the EC rapidly took over the task of managing the conflict. Yugoslavia in effect came under a form of EC tutelage. It so happened that an EC summit meeting was taking place in Luxembourg on June 28. This enabled the assembled leaders to coordinate their efforts, immediately dispatching to Yugoslavia the troika of foreign ministers: Gianni de Michelis of Italy (previous holder of the EC presidency), Jacques Poos of Luxembourg (current holder), and Hans van den Broek of Holland (next holder). They arrived equipped with the "Luxembourg formula" consisting of three points:

- A cease-fire and withdrawal of troops into barracks.
- The suspension of the Slovene and Croat declarations of independence for a period of three months.
- The reestablishment of the collective presidency.

After a dramatic series of meetings with the Yugoslavs during the night of June 28-29, the troika was satisfied on all the points—and the three men were rather pleased with themselves. "It shows that on the political level, we already have a rapid reaction force," de Michelis announced.[12] And Poos could not resist summing up his view of the situation: "If the Yugoslavs want to enter the Europe of the 20th century, they have to follow our advice."[13]

Forty-eight hours later, this rapid reaction force had to fly back into the country. The Yugoslavs had elected not to follow EC advice and continued fighting in Slovenia. The euphoria was over, and the EC had discovered that international fire fighting was not the easiest of jobs.

The returning troika threatened the suspension of EC aid to Yugoslavia and demanded written guarantees that its interim peace plan would be implemented. A success of a kind was recorded on July 1 when Stipe Mesic was at last confirmed as the president of the collective presidency. Yet the fighting went on, with Croatia emerging as a separate and potentially a much larger battlefield. The EC foreign ministers, meeting at The Hague on July 5, decided to suspend aid and embargo arms deliveries. The CSCE had already agreed to endorse an EC civilian observer mission to help stabilize a cease-fire and monitor the implementation of the EC peace plan. Continuing its shuttle diplomacy, the troika went to Yugoslavia for a third time; the group now included the Portuguese foreign minister because the Italian mandate had expired. On July 7, on the Adriatic island of Brioni, the troika managed to get the agreement, though not the signatures, of the main Yugoslav protagonists to a joint declaration consisting of five main points:

- It was up to the people of Yugoslavia to decide their future.
- A new situation had arisen in the country that required close monitoring and negotiations among different parties.
- Negotiations should begin not later than August 1 on all aspects of Yugoslavia's future.
- The collective presidency should play its full political and constitutional role with regard to the federal army.
- All parties were to refrain from unilateral action, particularly from acts of violence.

In addition, the Slovene federal army was to return to the barracks, and the Slovene territorial defense force was to be deactivated and returned to quarters. A controversial aspect, a three-month moratorium on further moves toward independence by the secessionst republics, was also agreed upon.

Undoubtedly, the Brioni deal would not have been possible without active EC involvement. The trouble was that the agreement proved completely worthless. The Slovenes, in particular, cheated immediately. Convinced (correctly) that they had won the propaganda war in the West, they failed to demobilize, to lift the blockade on all the federal army barracks, or to stop the harrassment of federal army officers and their families living in Slovenia. They were helped by the fact that the Serbs and the army had lost all interest in keeping Slovenia within the federation. Much to the amazement of the world, and to Slovenia itself, the collective presidency decided on July 18 to pull out all the army units from the breakaway republic. In other words, the Yugoslavs themselves, not the EC, were shaping conditions for the next round. Slovenia was now out of the way, which de facto finally brought an end to the old Yugoslavia. There remained, however, a mountain of unfinished business. The center of the crisis shifted to Croatia, where the Serbian-populated enclaves had already witnessed months of sporadic violence.

The conflict between Croatia and its Serbian population was always going to be the decisive one in the manifold Yugoslav crisis. Croatia, having just invoked the right to self-determination, wished to impose its state sovereignty on all of its territory. But the Serbs of Croatia, regarding themselves not as a minority but as a nation—and a threatened one at that— were also invoking the right to self-determination. In this, they had the full support of the republic of Serbia. In effect, therefore, the two largest republics in the federation were pitted against each other in what was becoming an increasingly merciless struggle for territory.

There was nothing political or ideological about this contest. It was purely ethnic in character. Many in the West had swallowed the simplistic notions about Croatian "democracy" and Serbian "bolshevism." The truth was somewhat different. Neither of the regimes was particularly attractive by Western standards; both of them leaned toward authoritarianism. Technically, the conflict amounted to a secession within a secession: the Serbs of Croatia seceding from the republic that was itself seceding. In any case, the outbreak of large-scale hostilities in Yugoslavia confronted the EC with a series of problems much larger in importance than the immediate task of stopping the war: secession, self-determination, minorities, and borders. It was these questions that, perhaps inevitably, were going to transform the role of the EC in Yugoslavia from that of conflict manager to arbiter. Already at the beginning of July, France's President François Mitterrand argued for the introduction of new European legal norms to help resolve Yugoslav-type conflicts. Of course, in the continued absence of any such guidelines, the EC was always likely to pursue improvised policies, hastily laying down the laws based on the pressures and requirements of the moment and on compromises reflecting its internal balance of forces.

During July, August, and September 1991, as the violence in Croatia escalated to reach the proportions of a major, sustained war, the EC found that all its efforts to broker cease-fires bore fruit that lasted only days, sometimes hours. Quite simply, neither the Croats nor the Serbs had any interest in complying with cease-fires that would freeze an unacceptable situation. The Croats did not want to be prevented from imposing the sovereignty of their new state in the Serbian enclaves. The Serbs, on the other hand, were still busy consolidating their authority over large tracts of Croatia. The EC was powerless. At the end of July, the EC foreign ministers decided to triple the size of the monitoring force (fifty observers hitherto based in Slovenia) for duties in Croatia—to monitor cease-fires that existed only on paper. On the same occasion, the ministers ruled out any European armed intervention.

The idea of sending some kind of European force into Yugoslavia was voiced early on, but it lacked clear definition. Would it be a peacekeeping force even though there existed no durable peace to keep? Or would it be a peacemaking one, involving a higher level of activity and suggesting military intervention? The French in particular appeared keen on sending a Euro-force into embattled Yugoslavia. In late July and early August, the media in Western Europe indulged in an orgy of conjecture about this issue. It amounted to a lot of hot air. As long as the Yugoslavs kept fighting, there was never a serious possibility that the EC could mount a military operation because that would entail fighting at least some of the Yugoslavs—in all probability the Serbs, who had made plain their opposition to the idea of any foreign military presence. France argued that the Western European Union (WEU) could be used as an "interposed" force in Yugoslavia. But this said more about the French attitudes toward European military integration than about the EC policy toward Yugoslavia. France was the most enthusiastic supporter in the EC of the "joint foreign and security policy," which the approaching EC summit at Maastricht in December was meant to codify as an integral part of the European union treaty. Not all EC members, however, desired to establish a defense arm to provide some teeth to the joint security policy. Britain was the chief skeptic, willing to promote WEU in terms of strengthening the European pillar of NATO, but fearing the implications for NATO if the EC acquired a distinct defense identity.

Yugoslavia thus supplied a relevant context for an internal EC debate about the security aspect of its future development. During September, as the war raged on in Croatia, noises were again made within the EC concerning Euro-troops for Yugoslavia. In part, this reflected the despair felt by many in Western Europe about the EC's impotence in stopping the Yugoslav bloodletting. On this occasion the French position was supported by Germany, Italy, and Holland. Speculation suggested a figure of 30,000 troops. It is known that the WEU had engaged in contingency planning for a Yugoslav operation. Again, however, Britain was adamantly opposed. Citing its Ulster experience as an example, Britain argued that it was incomparably more difficult to extricate a force from a troubled area than to send it there. In any case, with Germany unable for constitutional reasons to back its rhetoric with concrete action in Yugoslavia involving German troops, Britain's attitude was crucial.

At a tense meeting of the EC foreign ministers on September 19, Britain's Douglas Hurd finally put a stop to the debate that had so fired the imagination of some of his colleagues. But it is difficult to imagine that the EC would have, at this point, staged some kind of military action in Yugoslavia had Britain not resisted. President Milosevic of Serbia warned that foreigners were welcome as tourists, businesspeople and diplomats, but they would not be welcomed as soldiers. He meant it. Any EC military-type push into Yugoslavia, even if it gained CSCE mandate, would force political choices. In other words, the EC would have to take sides in the Yugoslav war. No agreement existed on the part of the warring factions for external involvement. This was the critical criterion that, when met, eventually led the UN to decide on the deployment of peacekeeping blue helmets in Yugoslavia. The risks attendant in the process of peacemaking, as opposed to peacekeeping, were too great, with every likelihood that such peacemaking would escalate rather than defuse the conflict. The EC did not, collectively, have the political will to flex its muscle in this way. Jacques Delors, the European Commission president, lamented: "The Community is like an adolescent facing the crisis of adulthood. If the Community were 10 years older there would have been an intervention force."[14]

The Peace Conference Fiasco

By the time the British had buried the Euro-army plan for Yugoslavia, the EC was already taking important steps on the diplomatic front. This amounted to a peace conference on Yugoslavia, sponsored by the EC Twelve, under the chairmanship of retired British diplomat Lord Carrington. Convened hastily early in September, the conference was an attempt to build a modest momentum toward political dialogue amid the chaos and bloodshed of the Yugoslav conflict. Attached to the conference was a five-member arbitration commission headed by the French constitutional lawyer Robert Badinter. It was a success in itself that the conference began work on September 7 at The Hague, bringing together the Yugoslav collective presidency, the federal government, and the presidents of the six federal republics. Predictably, however, the Yugoslavs used The

Hague as a platform for an exchange of insults. Such was their intransigence that the conference stood virtually no chance of making any progress. It duly collapsed and the fighting in Yugoslavia continued.

In October, on the point of despair, Lord Carrington made a last effort to salvage something out of the wreck. The initiative he took appears to have been entirely his own. On October 18, he reconvened the peace conference, presenting the Yugoslavs with a document (Arrangements for a General Settlement) consisting of four important proposals:

- Sovereign and independent republics with international personality for those that wish it.
- A free association of the republics with an international personality.
- Comprehensive arrangements, including supervisory mechanisms, for the protection of human rights and special status for certain groups and areas.
- In the framework of a general settlement, recognition of the independence, within existing borders, unless otherwise agreed, of those republics wishing it.

The Carrington plan, of course, amounted to a recipe for the breakup of Yugoslavia, although it may be said that the country was already crumbling. Carrington, admittedly, had put forward only a working document. Even so, it lagged hopelessly behind developments. To propose a special status for "certain areas" (i.e., the Serbian enclaves in Croatia) missed the fundamental point about the war in Yugoslavia—namely, that the Serbs of Croatia wished to *secede* from Croatia. No amount of international guarantees concerning their status would change the fact that they would still be in the position of a minority, precisely what they did not wish to become. Indeed, while the other republics broadly accepted the Carrington plan, Serbia rejected it on the grounds that it presupposed the extinction of Yugoslavia and did not address itself to the question of national self-determination. Serbia's objections spelled the end of the peace conference in 1991. But it was remarkable that Carrington's proposals had not been seen by the EC foreign ministers before they were submitted to the Yugoslavs.[15] This was yet another indication of the ad hoc style the EC had adopted toward Yugoslavia.

There existed, clearly, a deliberate reluctance on the part of the EC to address itself directly to the most burning issue in Yugoslavia: national self-determination. The EC proceeded on the assumption that it was *republics* that were in conflict rather than *nations*. Logically, therefore, it argued that the internal, republican frontiers were inviolable except where a change occurred through peaceful agreement. The trouble was that, except in the case of Slovenia, those frontiers did not—and could not because of various ethnic mixes—represent clear ethnic lines. The EC found itself supporting the insupportable: a breakup of Yugoslavia along mostly artificial frontiers that were fueling the war in the first place. The internal frontiers in Yugoslavia were always meant to delineate the administrative competence of the republics and nothing else. They made sense only as long the federation existed. They were not even codified in any legal documents, having been established arbitrarily by a small group of Tito's communist colleagues at the end of World War II. But there they were, and the EC clung to them. The reason, if any, was that there were too many overlapping ethnic groups in Yugoslavia, all of them invoking self-determination. Had the EC seriously attempted to examine the issue of self-determination in Yugoslavia, it would have begun a walk through a political minefield. Not only Croatia but Bosnia-Herzegovina, Kosovo, Vojvodina, Sandzak, and other regions would have presented conflicting cases for self-determination. It was much easier for the EC to stick to the existing republican borders. But this, it has to be said, did nothing to tackle the causes of conflict in Yugoslavia.

Diplomatic Recognition

The EC had, in the preconflict stage, supported the idea of preserving some kind of Yugoslav entity essentially on the grounds that a breakup would entail violence. This view, of course, proved to be an overwhelmingly correct assessment. Paradoxically, as the violence spread and showed no signs of stopping, some EC members began to develop the argument that the only way to halt it was to endorse the breakup of the country by extending diplomatic recognition to the secessionist republics. This argument, moreover, was paraded under the cover of the right of nations to self-determination. Almost from the very start of the fighting in Slovenia, Germany in particular stood out as the self-appointed champion of national self-determination. In practice, this would translate into German backing of secession. Other EC members disagreed. On June 28, British Prime Minister John Major said that "the first prize is to keep the Yugoslav federation together."[16] President Mitterrand held the same view.

But Germany's Chancellor Helmut Kohl took the position that "it is unacceptable that today in Europe people are being shot or that suddenly the rights of self-determination should no longer play a role."[17] German Foreign Minister Hans-Dietrich Genscher went even further, stating that the Yugoslav federal army "had gone mad," that it was "running amok."[18] By the beginning of July, Germany was already sending unmistakable signals that Slovenia and Croatia should be recognized as independent countries.

Perhaps the most striking aspect of Germany's championship of secession was the total capitulation of the government in Bonn to public opinion. The grass-roots feeling in the Christian Democratic party, the majority partner in government, was strongly in favor of the breakaway republics. The Catholic lobby naturally sided with the Catholic Slovenes and Croats, and the bulk of 600,000 Yugoslav guest-workers in Germany was made up of Croats and represented a significant pressure group. In addition, with Germany only recently reunified, the whole country was according the highest esteem to the principle of national self-determination. Genscher, moreover, was badly shaken when the Bundestag foreign affairs committee voted unanimously to investigate his alleged policy of "appeasement" toward the federal government in Belgrade.[19] But all these were internal political factors: Germany was supposed to coordinate policy with its partners in the EC. Increasingly, it did not. The greater the violence in Yugoslavia, the more Germany threatened unilateral action, meaning diplomatic recognition of Slovenia and Croatia. During the summer, Germany's partners, notably France, Britain, and Spain, succeeded in holding it back. This, it turned out, was only a delaying action.

In November, the EC imposed economic sanctions against all six Yugoslav republics, only to lift them in December from all but Serbia and Montenegro, the two republics widely and simplistically perceived as the principal culprits in the conflict. Germany was the leading force behind the imposition of sanctions. By this time, Bonn was arguing that diplomatic recognition of Slovenia and Croatia constituted the only means of putting an end to the war in Yugoslavia.[20] The Badinter Arbitration Commission had argued against early recognition of Croatia, but this did not impress the Germans. Under enormous pressure from Bonn, the rest of the EC agreed in December to recognize the two breakaway republics by the middle of January 1992. Germany, too, was meant under this agreement to withhold recognition until that date. But it did not, going ahead unilaterally in December. A long, bitter aftertaste remained in several EC countries that would have preferred recognition to follow a general political settlement in Yugoslavia.

Conclusions

The diplomatic recognition of Slovenia and Croatia closed a chapter in the involvement of the EC in the Yugoslav conflict. It coincided with the first robust cease-fire to hold on the battlefields since fighting started in June. But the cease-fire had been brokered by the UN, not the EC, and there is precious little evidence to support the German view that its drive for recognition yielded the positive results. In the eyes of the Serbs, the EC had become a discredited, less than impartial third force, an opinion that led Serbia to turn to the UN. At the same time, the Serbian government thundered against the "Fourth Reich" with considerable domestic propaganda success. Consternation over Germany's aggressive attitude was very much in evidence in some EC quarters as well. "We are not talking about the recognition of Croatia," said a Dutch diplomat privately. "We are talking about the recognition of Germany as a superpower."[21] German dominance in the recognition debate will not be forgotten soon.

It may be argued that in 1991 the EC failed, almost spectacularly, its first major test of addressing itself to an external crisis. Given its stated ambition (codified in the Maastricht treaty on European union) to develop a joint foreign and security policy, the EC record in Yugoslavia is abysmal. It failed completely, in the first place, to react decisively in the preconflict stage. Yugoslavia, of course, was never going to be an easy problem to solve, and perhaps no external force could have dissuaded the Yugoslavs from war. Yet the EC did not seriously attempt to prevent conflict until it was too late.

In its role as a conflict manager, the EC cannot be blamed for a string of broken cease-fires. More significant is the fact that the EC had in Yugoslavia transformed itself from mediator to arbiter.[22] The Hague peace conference on Yugoslavia and the economic sanctions imposed were two expressions of the arbitrating nature of EC involvement. In this self-appointed role, however, the EC overlooked the fundamental causes of the Yugoslav conflict—national self-determination and borders. It opted for simple solutions and outdated formulas. The decision to recognize Croatia, for example, overturned completely the standard diplomatic practice of recognizing only those governments in control of their territories. The

whole character of EC efforts in Yugoslavia had by the end of 1991 acquired political undertones, which was either unnecessary or plainly coun-
terproductive. The EC, in short, mismanaged the Yugoslav conflict, and as
the subsequent events in Yugoslavia demonstrated in spring 1992, it failed
to stop it once it had begun. If the EC truly intends to develop a common
security policy, the mistakes made in Yugoslavia will need to be understood and avoided in the future.

Notes

1. *Washington Post*, July 4, 1991.
2. However, as far as the conflict-prevention center was concerned, the
"Charter of Paris for a New Europe" implies interstate problems relating to military
affairs. But it does mention "the conciliation of disputes as well as broader tasks relating to dispute settlement."
3. The Austrian delegation at the CSCE Berlin meeting included among its
members Dimitrij Rupel, the Slovene foreign minister.
4. Private information from a Dutch government official.
5. *International Herald Tribune*, November 29, 1990.
6. *Danas* (Zagreb), April 9, 1991.
7. *Vreme* (Belgrade), April 8, 1991.
8. Private information from an Italian government official.
9. Private information from a Dutch government official.
10. *Ibid.*
11. *Financial Times*, June 4, 1991.
12. *Wall Street Journal*, July 1, 1991.
13. *Financial Times*, July 1, 1991.
14. *Daily Telegraph*, September 3, 1991.
15. Private information from EC officials.
16. *Financial Times*, June 29, 1991.
17. *International Herald Tribune*, July 1, 1991.
18. *The Times*, July 4, 1991.
19. *Financial Times*, July 5, 1991.
20. *Daily Telegraph*, December 16, 1991.
21. *Daily Telegraph*, December 17, 1991.
22. Ranko Petkovic, "Role of the European Community and the United Nations
in Solving the Yugoslav Crisis," in *Review of International Affairs* (Belgrade), Vol. 43,
March 1992.

4

A North American Community: "From the Yukon to the Yucatan"

Alan K. Henrikson

D URING 1991, PRESIDENT George Bush joined the president of
Mexico, Carlos Salinas de Gortari, and the prime minister of
Canada, Brian Mulroney, in initiating a complex process designed to bring about a North American Free Trade Agreement (NAFTA) on the continent. The idea was described variously by
commentators as leading to a worldwide "strategic alliance" among the
three partners, a business-based "North America Inc." to compete with
the European Community and Japan, and even an economic "Fortress
North America."

That the NAFTA scheme did implicitly threaten a new regional trade
bloc, on the basis of which the United States, Mexico, and Canada could
bargain collectively with Europe and Japan, is unmistakable. It clearly had
coercive connotations as well as more constructive intent. US State Department Counselor Robert Zoellick, while denying that NAFTA would
contribute to "the promotion of regional blocs," stressed that a NAFTA arrangement would "strengthen the hand" of the country's foreign economic policy. "The signal the United States wants to send the world," he
stated, "is that we are committed to opening markets and that we will extend a hand to others who share that commitment"—and not, he seemed
to imply, to others.

In August 1992, the continental free-trade negotiations were successfully concluded with congressional action expected in 1993. By negotiating
a free market with both Canada and Mexico, the US government demonstrated that it had not abandoned "its leadership role" in the field of trade,

thus answering critics who wondered if the "new world order" outlined by President Bush had a place for economics.[1]

Apart from international power connotations, the NAFTA project, though focused on economics, seemed to prefigure what could be characterized as a "North American community"—that is, a new and positive identity shared by the peoples of the three North American countries. For the first time in their histories, Mexicans, Americans, and Canadians could come to feel that they had more in common with each other, despite cultural and other differences, than with any nonneighbor outside the hemisphere—notably their parent societies in Europe, where a new identity also is rapidly forming. A NAFTA particularly could contribute to overcoming the estrangement between the Hispanic and *norteamericano* peoples in the New World. A greater inclusion of the continent's widespread, increasingly self-aware native groups—the continent's "first nations"—into a feeling of North American community, or family of peoples, also might result.

The notion of a North American community implicitly challenges the politically established concept of a "North Atlantic community," informally built around the *North* Atlantic Treaty Organization (NATO).[2] It is not today widely remembered that the first suggestion of a "NAFTA," dating from the early 1960s, was for a North *Atlantic* Free Trade Agreement. This transatlantic NAFTA would have joined Canada and the United States with the United Kingdom, and perhaps other members of the European Free Trade Association (EFTA), formed in 1960 in part in reaction to the 1957 Treaty of Rome establishing the European Community (EC) on the European continent. Today's concept of a westward-oriented NAFTA is similarly, though less intentionally, an alternative to the larger "Pacific Basin community" concept. Some thought was given during the 1980s in the United States to concluding a free-trade pact with Japan.

Today's *North American* Free Trade Agreement is premised on the formal fact and the economic "success" of the 1988 bilateral US-Canada Free Trade Agreement (USCFTA), which went into effect at the beginning of 1989.[3] A further, trilateral pact, to include Mexico, could have competed with the USCFTA, complemented it, or completed it. The Canadian government had to decide what position to adopt toward, and what part to play in, trade talks between the United States and Mexico.[4] Whatever the form of a new continentwide trading relationship, a NAFTA was sure to do more than merely include a further economic partner with its own resources and needs. A three-way North American continental trade bond has ideological and even geopolitical significance.

"Right now," as President Bush stated in April 1991 to a group of Hispanic-American businesspeople at a meeting in Houston, "we have the chance to expand opportunity and economic growth from the Yukon to the Yucatan. Think of it: The North American Free Trade Agreement would link us with our largest trading partner, Canada, and our third-largest partner, Mexico. It would create the largest, richest trade zone on earth—360 million consumers in a market that generates $6 trillion in output a year." Observing that there are some doubters who seem to "oppose letting our neighbors enjoy the benefits of progress," the president said pointedly: "Ask them what is wrong with increased productivity throughout the continent. And ask them what's wrong with a more stable Mexico."

The NAFTA will be good for the entire neighborhood. "A unified North American market would let each of our countries build on our strengths," the president said. "It would provide more and better jobs for US workers. It would stimulate price competition, lower consumer prices, improve product quality. The agreement would make necessities such as food and clothing more affordable and more available to our poorest citizens. It would raise productivity and produce a higher standard of living throughout the continent." Both America's neighbors, Mexico perhaps even more than Canada, would share in this overall progress. "A free trade pact would encourage investment, create jobs, lift wages, and give talented Mexican citizens opportunities they don't enjoy today." The development would have much larger, international importance: "A stronger Mexico, in turn, means a stronger United States and a stronger North American alliance."[5]

One can see in President Bush's concept of a Mexican-American-Canadian "alliance," though ostensibly a political concept, a broader community ideal—a notion of bringing together North America's nations on a basis of moral parity. The differences between the United States and both Canada and Mexico are, of course, vast. A decade ago, these were cited as reasons, among others, why a tripartite commonwealth would never work.[6]

Indeed, the disparity between the United States and the others in economic strength and demographic size cannot be ignored. The Canadian economy, heavily resource-dependent though its industry is fairly modern, is one-tenth the size of the US economy. Canada's population of 26.6 million is about the same fraction of that of the United States with its 250 million people. The Mexican economy, although its population is sizable and growing (86.2 million and soon to reach 100 million), is barely more than one twenty-fifth the size of that of the United States.[7]

Besides the obvious problem of finding a way to balance these three unequally weighted countries in a North American negotiation, there is the related problem, hardly less difficult, of overcoming the deep-seated alienation between Americans and their neighbors, especially those to the south. Historical tensions that have existed between US citizens and their culturally nearer cousins to the north must also be overcome. And between Mexicans and Canadians (viewed from a southern perspective as "gringos from the far north"), a lack of mutual knowledge—a veritable cultural void—has long prevailed. A bond must be formed where virtually none has ever existed, either positive or negative.[8] The long-term success or failure of even a limited free-trade agreement among the three may well depend on whether the process engenders a harmonious feeling of a shared social identity.

Negotiation, Legislation, and Adjudication

The interplay of diplomatic *negotiation*, *legislation*, and, more prospectively, *adjudication* in completing a NAFTA and, beyond this, in creating a North American community is the central theme of the following analysis. Fundamental to success is finding a basis of equality among the three national parties that are so unequal in national product and in population size. Normally, the equalization of unequal nations is achieved through the formal processes of diplomacy. In the North American context, international negotiation has often taken place on two distinct planes—that of national leaders at what now are called "summit" meetings, and that of ministers and officials conferring at lower levels of government. Usually all of these encounters and conferences—Canadian-American, Mexican-American, and Canadian-Mexican—have been bilateral.[9]

The leaders' meetings, often occurring at the beginnings of administrations or on special commemorative occasions, have tended to be symbolic. Such manifestations of equality and expressions of cordiality, nonetheless, have performed the vital function of preserving international comity among the nations involved.[10] On a more day-to-day basis, this is the function of the ambassadors, the surrogates of the heads of state, in the capitals. The exchanges between cabinet ministers and other departmental representatives usually are mainly substantive. Special task forces of various kinds also address practical problems of common interest. Taken together, the intergovernmental connections between the United States and Canada and between the United States and Mexico have in recent years become much more regularized. A "consultative" process, going beyond ordinary diplomacy, serves as a support system, and the medium, for the current North American trade discussions.[11]

President Bush has carried the habit of North American consultation further than ever. An informal leader who does not hesitate to pick up the telephone (his chosen instrument), he occasionally has discussed NAFTA and other matters with Prime Minister Mulroney and President Salinas in three-way conference calls. Trilateral telephone diplomacy is now a feature of North American international relations. Although it conveys a sense of familiarity and thus engenders a feeling of community, summitry by telephone does not fully meet the symbolic requirements of contact between national leaders. Nonetheless, for doing business, such as negotiating the free-trade pact, the new form of leaders' communication has its utility.

Most substantive discussion of trilateral trade occurs at the cabinet level or below. In the case of the NAFTA talks, there are, beneath the plane of American, Canadian, and Mexican leaders and foreign ministers, three layers of meetings. First, there are the "ministerials," involving US Trade Representative Carla Hills, Canadian International Trade Minister Michael Wilson, and Mexican Commerce Secretary Jaime Serra Puche. Second, there are meetings of the "chief negotiators," Julius Katz, John Weekes, and Herminio Blanco Mendoza. Third, there are sessions of "working groups"—some nineteen in number—dealing with particular economic sectors and technical issues.

Most of this multilayered diplomacy is conducted in camera—in the time-honored, traditional way. There is, however, a "new diplomacy," as it has been termed by one of its most adroit and innovative practitioners, Allan Gotlieb, Canada's ambassador to Washington during most of the 1980s.[12] His successor, Derek Burney, has continued and developed the novel practice. Such is the interpenetration now of the political systems of the United States and Canada and also of the United States and Mexico that outright "lobbying" in one another's capitals is needed and accepted in order to get things done. The Mexican government, currently represented in Washington by Gustavo Petricioli Iturbide, is a more recent convert to the more aggressive, intrusive diplomatic approach, and he and his colleagues seem to be adept at using them. "Public diplomacy," reaching far beyond the capital communities to influence opinion, is also being employed.[13]

The scope of public contact among the United States, Canada, and Mexico is being expanded further by state and provincial governments and even by many city governments.[14] Mostly located in border zones, numerous local and state authorities have taken strong stands on the subject of North American free trade, usually in favor of it. Such transboundary "micro-diplomacy," as it has been termed, is a major factor in moving the process forward, partly through its influence on the work of federal legislators from those areas.

This brings us to the role of legislation. Currently, US-Mexican as well as US-Canadian relations are being powerfully shaped by legislative activity, and even by some direct contact between national legislators. On the American side, those involved include not only senators and representatives from border states but also other members of Congress who sit on key substantive committees—especially the Senate Finance Committee (chaired by Lloyd Bentsen, D., Texas) and the House Ways and Means Committee (chaired by Dan Rostenkowski, D., Illinois). Despite participants' efforts to communicate, however, American, Mexican, and Canadian legislative processes are essentially disconnected, and independent action by any of the three legislatures is capable of disrupting important relationships established by diplomacy.[15]

To make the operation of a NAFTA permanent—and thus more predictable and reliable—it is necessary to institutionalize the new relationship through court processes and other third-party procedures. Like the earlier US-Canadian agreement, the NAFTA is to be protected by judicial arrangements. The main beneficiaries of "judicialization" are Canada and Mexico, as they are relatively more vulnerable to external shocks, including sudden shifts in US trade policy and behavior. Ambassador Gotlieb in particular has proposed that the "fragmentation" of political power and growing influence of "special interests" in US policymaking, and the general decline of "respect for political authority" everywhere, will cause others increasingly to turn to "the rule of law" and also to institutions—that is, "supranationalism"—to safeguard their interests.[16] Mexicans, observing how the US-Canadian dispute-settlement system has worked, also have come to see judicial-institutional protections as a guaranteeing counterbalance to be used if necessary against their powerful neighbor.

The model for the NAFTA dispute-settlement mechanism, although not a perfect one, was established in the dispute-settlement mechanism provided for in the 1988 USCFTA.[17] This pioneering system merits brief description, for it will influence the working of NAFTA dispute settlement. Chapter 18 of the USCFTA, its general dispute-settlement chapter (not covering trade remedies), required of the parties mandatory notification of measures, mandatory provision of information, and also consultation upon request. If consultation failed to resolve a particular matter, referral to the United States-Canada Trade Commission was provided for. Should the commission fail to reach a satisfactory resolution of an issue, then it could be settled either by arbitration or through recommendations by binational panels to the commission—which, in turn, was mandated to resolve the dispute.

Chapter 19 of the USCFTA provided for further institutionalization by calling for establishment of a secretariat to assist the binational panels, composed of five members—two Canadians, two Americans, and a fifth member chosen jointly. The thought of the negotiators was that the secretariat would develop in knowledge and expertise along the lines of the Secretariat of the General Agreement on Tariffs and Trade (GATT).

The difficult issue of trade remedies (antidumping and countervailing duties), or "contingency protection," was addressed in a separate and temporary regime. This feature, however, generally was regarded as an integral part of the USCFTA's dispute-settlement package. Under this transitional scheme, Canada and the United States allowed themselves seven years to negotiate a comprehensive, permanent set of rules governing subsidies and anticompetitive pricing. In the interim, producers in both countries retained the right to seek redress from subsidized or dumped goods. Any relief granted was subject to challenge and review by a binational panel charged with determining whether existing laws were being applied correctly and fairly. These panels took on, it has been said, the "judicial review function" of the Court of International Trade in the United States and the Federal Court in Canada.[18]

Canada and the United States further agreed in 1988 to consult each other regarding any new trade legislation affecting the other. Moreover, either side could ask a binational panel to review such legislative changes in light of the "object and purpose" of the USCFTA and the applicable rights and duties of the antidumping and subsidies code of the GATT. The offending party's failure to make those modifications that might be recommended would allow the aggrieved side the right, after consultation, to pass comparable legislative measures or take equivalent executive steps—or to terminate the trade agreement. By these means, an emergent "supranationality" was delicately balanced with national sovereignty, "interdependence" was intricately adjusted to independence, and "North America" was judiciously integrated with the separateness of the two countries.

The relevance to the three-way NAFTA negotiation is obvious and direct. The Canada-US-Mexican agreement establishes a three-member Trade Commission comprising ministers and cabinet-level officers designated by each country. A NAFTA secretariat also is provided for. Dispute settlement will involve consultation and also panel proceedings, with the third NAFTA country able to join if it wishes. Alternative dispute settlement for private commercial disputes also is to be encouraged.

The Origins of the Trilateral Concept

The idea of a North American economic arrangement (as distinct from a US-Canadian or US-Mexican trade pact) is historically recent and traceable. It originated during the 1979-1980 presidential campaign in the United States. On November 13, 1979, the former governor of California, Ronald Reagan, announced his candidacy to be the Republican nominee for the US presidency in a televised speech from the New York Hilton, and expressed this vision:

> We live on a continent whose three countries possess the assets to make it the strongest, most prosperous and self-sufficient on earth. Within the borders of this North American continent are the food, resources, technology, and undeveloped territory which, properly managed, could dramatically improve the quality of life of all of its inhabitants.
>
> It is no accident that this unmatched potential for progress and prosperity exists in three countries with such long-standing heritages of free government. A developing closeness among Canada, Mexico, and the United States—a North American accord—would permit achievement of that potential in each country beyond that which I believe any of them—strong as they are—could accomplish in the absence of such cooperation. In fact, the key to our own future security may lie in both Mexico and Canada becoming much stronger countries than they are today.

In somewhat more practical terms, Reagan continued: "No one can say at this point precisely what form future cooperation among our three countries will take." But if elected president, he said, he would "invite each of our neighbors to send a special representative to our government to sit in on high-level planning sessions with us, as partners." He further would "immediately seek the views and ideas of Canadian and Mexican leaders" and "work tirelessly with them" to develop closer ties. He then declared, in words that, probably unwittingly, make clear the difference between a "community" model for North America and the more traditional "international" pattern of US-Canadian and US-Mexican relations: "It is time we stopped thinking of our nearest neighbors as foreigners."[19]

An even more holistic "North American" vision was offered by the California governor at the time, Edmund G. (Jerry) Brown, Jr. His was an ecological and anthropological, no less than an economic, perspective. Speaking to the Democratic National Convention at Madison Square Garden in New York on August 13, 1980, Brown stated:

> I have a dream that all Americans can advance together, but that we do so in a form of regional interdependence. I see a type of common market or economic community that will bring along with us our brothers and sisters who share this land of North America. Mexicans, Canadians, Native Americans—North and South—all are a part of our destiny and it is time that we recognize that we are a part of theirs.[20]

The distinctive emphasis of Governor Brown's continental model—a "North American Community" plan to be governed by rules such as those codified by the Organization for Economic Cooperation and Development (OECD)—was not on "securing" the continent—the Reagan keynote— but on "saving" it.[21] By transforming our "part of the planet," as Brown liked to refer to the continent, into an ideal ecological niche—North America the Beautiful, let us call it in contrast with Reagan's North American Bastion image—the citizens of the United States and their neighbors could once again elevate the imagination of the world. "Frontiers are closing," Brown had speculated in New York, "but others are opening up."

The simultaneity and similarity of these North American expressions, also made by former Texas Governor John Connally and by other presidential aspirants, indicate that common forces probably were at work.[22] Some of these factors were external to North America; others were internal to it. Together, these forces generated a surge of continentalism in US policy, against a doctrinal surface of globalism.

The outside forces then at work included, first, the Arab oil embargo directed against the Western economies during the 1973 Middle East war. A true historical watershed, the embargo focused Americans' concern on their access to resources—notably, their country's reserves of oil and gas. These both Canada and Mexico were known to have in underused abundance. The 1979 energy crisis compounded American anxieties, and interest grew in the continent's reserves of petroleum. A second external factor was the political frustration the United States had experienced in Vietnam, coinciding with the start of talks in Europe about mutual and balanced force reduction (MBFR). Both events presaged at least a partial withdrawal of US military forces from overseas back to the North American continent. A third was the example, seen mainly in a negative light, of "a world regionalizing all around us," in the phrase of Governor Brown's economic-planning director, Andrew Safir. "We see OPEC, we see the EEC, and we see less formal regions like the Latin American free trade association," Safir said. "This bloc-to-bloc bargaining tendency could be dangerous to non-member countries. That's another reason for forming a North American economic unit."[23]

Developments inside the continent also increased interest in "North Americanism." First, there was the slump in industrial productivity in the United States. A spate of proposals—investment tax credits, urban enterprise zones, worker training problems, and other such incentives—intended to "reindustrialize America" was the result. The maintenance of external tariffs, at least against North America's extrahemispheric trade partners, would shield its uncompetitive industries as they retooled for global competition once more. A second internal development was the appearance—or in some cases reappearance—of self-conscious regions within the territories of the United States, Canada, and Mexico.[24] Some of these were transborder regions, an aspect giving rise to the idea of an inclusive continental identity overarching them all. A third development within the North American context, related to the passage of generations and a demographic shift from the Northeast to the Southwest, was the emergence of a "new agenda" in American politics. Functional North American issues such as pollution of the Colorado River and transboundary acid rain, as well as social problems related to cross-border labor migration, could most appropriately be dealt with in a continentwide context. Mexico, the United States, and Canada seemed increasingly to be parts of a systemic whole.

Despite occasional North Americanist statements by Ronald Reagan during the first years of his presidency, however, little or nothing was done within the US government to fill in his 1979 continentalist vision. The Reagan administration's closely related scheme of a Caribbean Basin Initiative received far more attention from the federal bureaucracy. This

perhaps seemed more truly to be foreign policy rather than extended domestic policy. Another major reason for this discrepancy, surely, was the
distinct lack of enthusiasm on the parts of Canadian Premier Pierre Elliott
Trudeau and Mexican President José López Portillo. One informal trilateral meeting took place in 1982, within a larger gathering, at the opening
of the Gerald R. Ford Presidential Library in Grand Rapids, Michigan. But
nothing substantial came of that brief, ceremony-dominated encounter.
Neither Canada nor Mexico wanted anything to come of it.

Having broached the idea of North American cooperation, the US
government—led by President Reagan who in truth did not yet have anything specific to propose—did not press further the thought of an accord.
A diplomatic precondition developed: Officials in either Ottawa or Mexico
City had to say, first, that they wanted an agreement. Given the political
and economic preponderance of the United States, it was assumed in
Washington, the actual request for talks, had to come from the smaller
countries—at least formally. Only thereby could Canadians or Mexicans be
able to maintain their equal national dignity, it was thought. This order of
precedence seemed unbreakable, and it negated official thought.

Comprehensive Trade with Canada

A partial breakthrough occurred late in 1983 when Canada's minister for
international trade, Gerald Regan, announced the effective end of the
Trudeau government's "Third Option" policy of trying further to diversify
Canada's economic relations. Canada's vaunted contractual link with the
European Community (EC) in 1976 had proved almost fruitless. So, too,
had a similar agreement of 1976 with Japan.[25]

A further development shaping Canada's policy was the apparent
futility of working only through the GATT, as was made evident at a
GATT ministerial session in 1982. This meeting, which Canada's External
Affairs Minister Allan MacEachen chaired, failed to achieve agreement on
any of the major issues before it. Some of these, notably the criticism by
most non-European GATT participants of the protectionist EC Common
Agricultural Policy, are still before the GATT in its Uruguay Round. The
frustrations of multilateralism remain a powerful incentive today for continental cooperation or region-based solutions.

The upshot was a considered decision, resulting from an internal trade-
policy review directed by Derek Burney (then Canadian Department of
External Affairs assistant under secretary for trade and economic policy),

to open discussions with the United States regarding possible bilateral agreements for particular economic sectors. The prototype for this sectoral approach was the 1965 US-Canada Automobile Pact, through which the two countries managed a free market in automobiles. To this important Canadian overture, the US trade representative at the time, William Brock, responded most enthusiastically. A joint search began for appropriate sectors for possible further agreements.

It gradually became evident to Washington and Ottawa that the asymmetries between the two national economies were such that overly elaborate cross-sectoral trade-offs would be necessary. Not enough balanced compromises within individual sectors could be found. For example, the lack of American productive activity in the urban transit sector (light rail systems) meant that any opening of the US market in that field would have to be compensated by Canadian concessions in some other area (opening government procurement in provincial hydroelectric and telecommunications utilities was suggested as the quid pro quo). Cross-sectoral deals, besides being difficult to justify politically (to those whose interests were being sacrificed), would not necessarily expand overall bilateral trade.

The conclusion reached was that only a comprehensive trade pact between the two countries would make economic and also political sense. An across-the-board trade pact also would be less likely to run into international legal difficulties under the GATT, Article 24 of which required that free-trade areas not be cartel-like discriminatory arrangements against others.

There was no serious thought given in the early 1980s to including Mexico in a US-Canada trade agreement.[26] The US government was, however, beginning to contemplate a general framework agreement for the liberalizing of bilateral economic transactions of all kinds with Mexico. The Canadian government, by now working with the United States more or less in parallel on its Caribbean Basin Initiative, was starting to think of the Western Hemisphere as a new field of business endeavor as a means of offsetting earlier disappointments in Europe and Asia. A bilateral US-Canadian trade agreement, Ottawa reasoned, could both safeguard Canada's interests within a partial continental market and prepare the way for wider hemispheric and global trade discussion.

Not until 1985, following the election in Canada in September 1984 by an unprecedented majority of a Quebec-born, pro-American businessman, Brian Mulroney, did things really begin to move. The new Progressive

Conservative cabinet under Mulroney abolished the Liberal government's defensive Foreign Investment Review Agency and National Energy Policy. When meeting with President Reagan at Quebec City on March 17 and 18 (the "Shamrock summit")—the first of the regularly scheduled annual US-Canadian summits—Mulroney committed himself publicly to a process of considering the broadest possible ways of liberalizing US-Canada economic relations. A Declaration on Trade in Goods and Services gave expression to the two leaders' intentions. By the end of 1985, Mulroney had given formal notice that his government would pursue a new trade agreement with the United States, and President Reagan had notified Congress of the same.[27]

Presidential notification of Congress triggered the fast-track procedure of the trade law of 1974 and also the Omnibus Trade and Competitiveness Act of 1988. The legislation provides for a waiting period before formal negotiations can begin. Then, when an agreement is negotiated and submitted, Congress has ninety legislative working days (which could extend to eight months) within which to vote for or against the proposal in its entirety. Amendments are not allowed. Under these strict legislative provisions, designed to strengthen US trade diplomacy and make it reliable, the negotiations commenced on May 21, 1986, in Ottawa, the location symbolizing Canada's formal initiative and equal responsibility for the talks. On January 2, 1988, after more than a year and a half of exceedingly difficult and high-powered old and new diplomacy, President Reagan and Prime Minister Mulroney, in contact by telephone, agreed to sign the US-Canada Free Trade Agreement.

The key to this final achievement, much of which was the handiwork of Peter Murphy on the US side and Simon Reisman on the Canadian side, was the strong presidential and prime ministerial stake in achieving success. The decisive involvement during the final phase of the negotiation of the two finance ministers, US Treasury Secretary James Baker and Canadian Finance Minister Michael Wilson, also contributed significantly to a conclusion. Secretary Baker was, in a sense, the "super-negotiator" the Canadians, confused by the indeterminacy of the American political system, had been looking for from the beginning. Subsequently ratified following approval by the Canadian Parliament and the US Congress, the USCFTA came into force on January 1, 1989.

A massive text consisting of 151 articles, numerous annexes and schedules, and explanatory notes totaling more than 2,400 pages, the USCFTA, when fully implemented in 1998, will have eliminated by progressive stages (depending on the sensitivity of particular sectors) all tariffs between the two countries. The agreement preserved the structures of the 1965 Automobile Pact and removed tariffs on tires and auto replacement parts. Safeguards remained in the new 50 percent "North American local-content" requirement for cars. The USCFTA also broke important new ground, beyond the scope of any previous agreements in the GATT, in covering trade in financial services and telecommunications.

Probably most important from Canada's perspective was the fact that the new agreement provided for increased security of market access to the United States through the dispute-settlement mechanism already described. "If Canada had to abandon its traditional strong reliance on multilateralism to achieve its trade agenda with the United States," one of the Canadian negotiators, Michael Hart, has written, "the new agreement had at a minimum to contain strong rules and institutional provisions to overcome the much feared disparity in power between Canada and the United States." If, in reality, "the disparity may not be so great when it comes to individual issues," Hart explained, "strong dispute settlement procedures were essential to making the agreement acceptable to Canadians."[28] The same could prove true for Mexico.

The Inclusion of Mexico

From the conceptual point of view of Washington, the possibility of forming a larger North American trade arrangement including Mexico was logically implicit in the conclusion of the Canadian agreement. The appropriate next step, however, could not be a sudden trilateral negotiation but, rather, a bilateral exploration based on recognition of the many special characteristics of the US-Mexican relationship. There may have been some strategists in Washington who imagined advantages in a hub-and-spoke or divide-and-rule procedure by which only the United States, at the controlling center, would have privileged bilateral access to the economies of each of its neighbors. In the end, however, a wider, plurilateral arrangement, extendable eventually to the rest of the Western Hemisphere and even continents beyond, carried the day in the US capital.

From the perspective of Mexico City, a trade pact with the United States, within whatever US strategic design, was becoming an increasingly attractive idea by the late 1980s. The repayment of Mexico's colossal external debt depended on revenues from the export of oil and gas. The price of petroleum remained too low, however, to be sufficient to that task. The market for Mexican oil was global; the market for Mexican manufactured goods, which perhaps could command higher prices, was regional. This divergence placed a premium on modernizing and expanding Mexico's manufacturing industries and targeting North America. The United States was already Mexico's main customer for manufactured exports, taking fully 85 percent. The efforts of Miguel de la Madrid to secure greater access to the US market during his presidency (1982-1988), through a Trade and Investment Framework Understanding (1987), initiated a process that, in the phrase of one analyst, made some kind of NAFTA "a logical culmination."[29]

Without the decision of de la Madrid's successor as President, Carlos Salinas de Gortari, to initiate trade-agreement discussions with Washington, this geoeconomic logic might never have been acted upon. Soon after assuming office, Salinas, a Harvard-trained, free-market-oriented professional economist, concluded, somewhat as Canadian officials had done earlier, that economic relations with Western Europe or Japan would not counterbalance a naturally developing economic relationship with the United States on the North American continent.

More than two-thirds of Mexico's overall trade was with the United States, and that proportion was growing. A trip to Europe in January 1990, to attend the World Economic Forum in Davos, led the Mexican president to complain of Western Europe's obsessive "fascination" with events in Eastern Europe and its "relative lack of attention" to other parts of the world. European investment capital seemed less likely to come to Mexico. This sobering experience helped cause Salinas in March of that year, despite continued strong nationalist and protectionist sentiments in his country, to approach the US government about negotiating a bilateral free-trade pact, similar to the US-Canada FTA.[30] In June, Presidents Salinas and Bush announced their mutual goal of pursuing a comprehensive trade agreement between their two countries. In August, the Mexican government formally requested negotiations.

To the Bush administration, some of whose most prominent figures were either native or naturalized Texans (Secretary of State Baker, Secretary of Commerce Robert Mosbacher, and President Bush himself), the overture from Mexico was almost irresistible. They and others sensed that a historical window of opportunity had opened. The Canadian government under Brian Mulroney, however, was somewhat taken aback by the sudden development—a virtual elopement—in the US-Mexican trade romance. This was especially so as the purported goal of the US-Mexican talks was a larger Yucatan-to-Yukon market. Somewhat embarrassed, personally and politically, Prime Minister Mulroney denied that he had been left out. "I don't feel like a wallflower at all," he insisted defensively. "We take part when we decide we are going to take part, but don't assume we weren't invited."[31]

It quickly became apparent to all three parties that separate bilateral trade relationships—US-Canada, US-Mexico, and, prospectively, Canada-Mexico—would be much less efficient than a consolidated trilateral arrangement. Accordingly, in September 1990, the Canadian government requested that it participate in the negotiations.[32] Initial Mexican feelings that Canada was "barging in" were quickly overcome, as the two smaller trade partners realized that perhaps they could help themselves by helping each other as allies on certain issues.

On February 5, 1991, the three countries' leaders jointly announced "their intention to pursue a North American free trade agreement creating one of the world's largest liberalized markets." American, Canadian, and Mexican trade ministers would proceed as soon as possible, "in accordance with each country's domestic procedures," with trilateral negotiations. These would be aimed at a "comprehensive" agreement. The broad goal of the talks would be to "eliminate obstacles to the flow of goods and services and to investment, provide for the protection of intellectual property rights, and establish a fair and expeditious dispute settlement mechanism."[33]

President Bush, though he must have been preoccupied with the Persian Gulf crisis at the time, opened his press conference on February 5 with his announcement of the NAFTA initiative, indicating its significance for his administration. The proposed agreement, he said expansively, would be "a dramatic first step toward the realization of a hemispheric free trade zone, stretching from Point Barrow in Alaska to the Straits of Magellan."[34] This was an allusion to his earlier Latin America-oriented Enterprise for the Americas Initiative of June 27, 1990.

On March 1, the president asked Congress for an extension of fast-track authority to negotiate a NAFTA as well as to complete the long-continuing GATT Uruguay Round. In explaining his request—virtually a demand—he made clear his conviction that "refusing to extend the fast track would end negotiations before they have even begun."[35] He explained: "Fast track really is another term for 'good faith.'" Congress had its constitutional responsibilities, and the administration duly would consult it, as it would the relevant parts of the private sector, as Bush acknowledged. But the legislative attachment of amendments to an agreement—that is, if fast-track authority were not continued—could force the negotiators of a NAFTA text "to call off talks or start again from square one."[36]

There was at that time considerable bipartisan support within the congressional leadership group for extending free trade to Mexico in exchange for a more open Mexican economy. Given the force of President Bush's leadership in the wake of Operation Desert Storm, one might have thought that continued fast-track authorization by Congress would have been almost a foregone conclusion. It was not. There was, however, enough support. Congressional permission was given on May 23 and 24: The vote in the House was 231-192, and in the Senate 59-35. The real support level probably was even higher. Some members, having determined that the administration was going to win, probably voted against fast track in order to please certain concerned constituents and for partisan reasons.[37] Trilateral trade negotiations on the fast-track basis duly got under way in Toronto on June 12. Soon, however, the movement forward began to slow.

Slow Motion on the Fast Track

Some of the hindrances to speedy action on the NAFTA were internal to the United States. Opposition came mainly from three sources. The most powerful was big labor, ever-fearful that free trade would "export American jobs" to low-wage-paying Mexico. The AFL-CIO, wholly opposed to the NAFTA concept, estimated that some 50,000 jobs would be lost. The second source of opposition was the environmentalist movement, some elements of which were worried that a shift of industrial activity to Mexico, with its lower environmental standards, would turn that country into a "pollution haven." The third source was the human rights community, some of whose members were concerned about the social welfare and political rights of Mexicans in any headlong rush into a North American economy. Highly critical of the corruption-ridden Institutional Revolutionary party (PRI) that had long governed Mexico, some human rights organizations wanted to make democratic reform a necessary condition of concluding a NAFTA.

The Bush administration at first offered assurances. Its spokespersons never tired of citing estimates by respected economists (e.g., Rudiger Dornbusch of MIT) of the long-term gains to the American economy that would result from a trade pact including Mexico. They emphasized as well the antipollution programs currently being initiated by President Salinas. And they predicted the further inevitable triumph of democracy in Mexico, as elsewhere throughout Latin America. Besides these public-relations efforts, the White House then devised, in consultation with the party chiefs on Capitol Hill, an "action plan."

Basically, the strategy was to break up the anti-NAFTA coalition that was forming into component parts. The issues raised by critics thus could be dealt with in separate but parallel negotiations. For example, there would be discussion of a fund for retraining displaced workers. There would be talks with Mexican officials about labor standards and practices. There would be further discussion of a comprehensive border agreement dealing with matters such as environmental issues. The approach—an adroit political maneuver—contributed to winning further support from Congress, and it assuaged many private organizations that opposed the NAFTA concept as well.

The onset of the 1991-1992 presidential election campaign generated new problems, making the debate over the NAFTA a much broader one. Within President Bush's own party, an "America First" contender for the nomination, Patrick Buchanan, warned of a sellout through the NAFTA of America's economic interests. The imaginative and acerbic Buchanan even proposed constructing a barrier—dubbed by the press "the Buchanan Fence"—along the US-Mexican border to keep out unwanted immigrants.

The Democratic party initially was in even greater disarray over the NAFTA issue. One candidate, Tom Harkin (D., Iowa), preached the labor union gospel before he dropped out of the running. Another, Paul Tsongas, technocratic in outlook, embraced the basic NAFTA concept, provided that an agreement was of the "right kind." But he, too, ceased campaigning. The Democrat with the strongest views was one of the progenitors of the pan-American idea, former California Governor Jerry Brown. Despite his dream of all Americans "advancing together," he finally decided that he was against the NAFTA plan on the grounds that it was too probusiness. The Democratic party's politically sensitive frontrunner, Bill Clinton, was initially in favor of NAFTA (with environmental safeguards and a workers' adjustment program added), but he wavered between thinking that the idea still was great statesmanship and no longer good politics. His winning the Democratic nomination, however, has basically stabilized his support for it and narrowed the gap between Republicans and Democrats on the subject.

In Mexico and Canada, the furor in the United States over NAFTA was disconcerting to the political leaders, whose opponents found encouragement for their own criticisms. President Salinas, obviously worried, came to see President Bush at Camp David on December 14 in order to reaffirm continued mutual support for their goal. "I am convinced that the negotiations do not merely involve adding or subtracting amounts and figures," he declared. "We are also talking about a vision for the future of this region at the end of this century and the beginning of the 21st."[38]

The Mexican and American presidential teams at Camp David reportedly differed significantly over some features of the NAFTA text the negotiators were then drafting. Numerous lines remained bracketed or undecided. The Mexican side stressed, in particular, the need for increased market access to the United States for agriculture, textiles, and automobiles. No Mexican avocado, to illustrate one issue, has been marketed legitimately in the United States for decades, owing to sanitary and public health restrictions that seemed, to Mexicans, to constitute nontariff barriers. American officials, clearly pursuing a "USCFTA-plus" strategy, stressed the need for American banks and other financial institutions to be able to expand their operations into Mexico. They also sought the opportunity for American oil companies to break into Mexico's huge constitutionally reserved, state-owned energy sector. The line between "basic" petrochemicals and "secondary" petrochemicals (in which outsiders could invest to some degree) still had to be clarified. US Trade Representative Hills, present at the Camp David meeting along with other senior Bush administration officials, reminded the Mexicans that an agreement had to be "comprehensive," covering such further matters as intellectual property rights.[39]

The Canadian leader, Brian Mulroney, was by this time under severe pressure at home. Only in part were his political difficulties a result of internal controversy over the NAFTA idea as such, or even over the USCFTA and its effects. However, with his popularity at an all-time low, the Canadian economy in recession, and the province of Quebec involved with the rest of the country in a profound debate about national unity, Mulroney was understandably sensitive to any irritations in Canada's trade relationship with its American neighbor.

Free trade simply was no longer viewed favorably by most Canadians. Beer, cars, and lumber were some of the particular issues in contention. A summary account can provide a glimpse into the real world of US-Canadian and, by extension, US-North American trade relationships, and also of the statesmanship and the diplomacy needed to protect them. No mechanical legal arrangement can by itself suffice.

Just after Christmas 1991, US Trade Representative Hills issued a notice that Washington intended to impose punitive duties on Canadian beer, on the basis of a GATT report that beer imported into Canada was not being distributed freely. The Canadians had a countercomplaint, also made at the GATT, regarding tax credits given to some American brewers—especially Anheuser-Busch, which controlled nearly half the US market and did not seem to merit help in the Canadian view. As beer had not been included in the original USCFTA, the issue was not a direct test of that agreement, but the dispute that erupted called post-USCFTA trade comity into question.

A second issue arose in February 1992 when the US Customs Service declared that some 90,000 Honda Civics assembled in Alliston, Ontario, failed to meet the 50 percent "North American content" requirement for duty-free entry into the United States. The engine blocks of the cars had been built at a factory in Anna, Ohio, but other high-value components had been imported from Japan. This administrative action seemed another case warranting Prime Minister Mulroney's complaint at the time: "We are getting sideswiped by American Japan-bashing." The Canadian (and also Mexican) deeper fear was that Japan might shift its investment directly to the United States.[40]

Canadian indignation rose to the level of high dudgeon when early in March 1992 the US Commerce Department ruled that Canadian provincial timber policies in effect subsidized softwood lumber exports by an average of 14.48 percent. This finding foreshadowed American countervailing duties against Canada in the equivalent amount. Prime Minister Mulroney was furious. "We are their biggest market and their best customer, so we won't sit idly by and allow low-level functionaries to exercise retribution and harrassment." He added, "I'm not big on gunboat diplomacy, but we are not without our own resources."[41]

A range of retaliatory measures was contemplated in public. One option was to impose Canadian duties on US fruits and vegetables, particularly produce from California. The argument was that farmers in that state gained an advantage from the low rates charged them for irrigation water. The tax-supported Mississippi River system was another target. Items benefiting from cheap river transport could be penalized because they were subsidized. Such talk was mostly bluff. Canada's Trade Minister Michael Wilson publicly counseled that it would not be in Canada's interest to get into a tit-for-tat battle with its largest trading partner.[42] This reflected the accepted wisdom in official Canadian circles that it is foolish to link issues in dealing with the United States because Canada, being smaller and less diversified, could always be "out-linked." Issues should be dealt with on their merits.

The American ambassador in Ottawa, then Edward Ney, openly addressed Canadians' hurt feelings, even as he confronted critics of the United States on the issues themselves. Through the editorial pages of the Toronto *Globe and Mail*, he addressed "a word from the bully to the boy scout." Ney rejected the widespread attribution of recent US trade decisions to current politics at home ("election-year bluster"). The particular matters in dispute had long histories, he observed, and the issues involved were neither simple nor one-sided. He noted that the EC as well as the United States had won GATT cases against Canada's provincial marketing restrictions on beer. Regarding automobiles, he insisted upon the US government's right to audit foreign companies, such as Honda, that claimed benefits under the USCFTA. As for softwood lumber, he pointed out that the current US-Canadian dispute would not have arisen at all had the Canadian government not recently terminated a 1986 memorandum of understanding on that subject.

Most fundamental, Ambassador Ney counseled that resolution of these and similar problems would not come through "talk of retaliation and trade wars" but instead through "thoughtful and serious negotiation and consultation." The two countries should continue to try to reach agreement on subsidies and rules of origin, which were central issues in the softwood lumber and Honda cases. The GATT Uruguay Round had made some progress on the subsidies question already. In addition, the trilateral North American free-trade talks provide "an excellent opportunity" to address the whole question of rules of origin and North American content. The USCFTA, which had "softened the effects of the recession and contributed modestly to Canada's economic growth," was never expected, Ney emphasized, to "eliminate" trade disputes. What it did do was to "provide a framework" for dealing with them.[43] His effort, however, showed the inadequacy of dispute-settlement procedures alone for the management of US-Canadian trade problems. Active diplomacy was needed.

Conclusion

Despite opposition that has slowed the development of a North American political consensus on NAFTA, if not necessarily the actual NAFTA negotiations, an agreement has been concluded and must now be signed, drafted into legal form, and submitted to the legislatures in the three countries. So great are the historic forces moving these three economies toward some form of integration that it is difficult to imagine the NAFTA process ending in failure. The momentum began in 1979 and 1980, gained in 1983 and 1985, accelerated with the USCFTA in 1988, shifted direction with Mexico's decision to negotiate in 1990, and broadened in force with Canada's entry into trilateral talks in 1991. Enthusiasm seemed to decline somewhat in early 1992, but officials pressed ahead and were able to announce the conclusion of negotiations in August 1992.

After formal submission, Congress has ninety working days—which could stretch out as long as eight months—in which to approve the agreement, without amending it. Assuming that the necessary implementing legislation is promptly submitted, one could imagine fairly expeditious consideration by Congress. Approval, however, will not take place without committee hearings and a full debate. The upshot could be a delay of congressional consent until sometime in 1993. By that point, a change of government in both Canada and the United States might have occurred, complicating but probably not wholly confusing the transnational politics of NAFTA approval.[50]

The attitude of Canada's Parliament as well as the Mexican Congress toward trilateral North American trade, though the agreement surely will be criticized in those bodies, should follow the policies of Canada's and Mexico's leaders. Opposition in both countries—in the business community and labor unions as well as in political circles—should be reduced somewhat by the North American dispute-settlement mechanism, including the Trade Commission.[51] Experience with the USCFTA, however, has shown that providing adjudicative measures for trade relations does not end the task of diplomacy, which now involves peoples as well as governments. Both old and new diplomacy are needed to form a trinational consensus, such as Governors Reagan and Brown and others imagined in 1979 and 1980. A sense of North American community must be engendered. Without it, a North American market, no matter how well negotiated, cannot truly thrive.

Notes

1.   Robert B. Zoellick, "North American Free Trade Agreement; Extending Fast-Track Negotiating Authority," prepared statement before the Senate Foreign Relations Committee, April 11, 1991, *US Department of State Dispatch*, Vol. 2, No. 15 (April 15, 1991), pp. 254-263. Zoellick developed this theme further in "The North American FTA: The New World Order Takes Shape in the Western Hemisphere," address before the Columbia Institute's conference on "NAFTA: Impacts of a Borderless Economy on North American Regional Competitiveness," Tucson, Arizona, April 3, 1992, *US Department of State Dispatch*, Vol. 3, No. 15 (April 13, 1992), pp. 290-295.

2.   See, e.g., Christian A. Herter, *Toward an Atlantic Community* (New York: Harper & Row, 1963).

3.   The question of the USCFTA's economic benefit is, of course, a matter of great controversy, particularly in Canada where many plant closings have occurred. The Canadian government considers that Canada's vulnerable economy would be in worse shape without the agreement, in part because of the security of access to the US market that the USCFTA provides. For assessments, see Ronald Wonnacott, "Canadian Adjustment to the 1989 Canadian-US Free Trade Agreement: Some Broad Observations," *Business in the Contemporary World*, Vol. 3, No. 1 (Autumn 1990), pp. 15-24; Maude Barlow (National Chairperson, Council of Canadians), "The Free Trade Agreement Fails Canada," *American Review of Canadian Studies*, Vol. 21, No. 2/3 (Summer/Autumn 1991), pp. 163-169, and Allan R. Taylor (Chairman, Royal Bank of Canada), "Canada-US Trade Agreement: Second-Year Review," *American Review of Canadian Studies*, Vol. 21, No. 2/3 (Summer/Autumn 1991), pp. 171-179.

4.   One expert defined Canada's options as follows: Canada could (1) stand aside, (2) request official observer status, (3) engage actively in the negotiations from the outset, or try to (4) reach its own bilateral free-trade agreement with Mexico—which could create a "Rube Goldberg contraption." The wisest course seemed to be for Canada to join US-Mexican discussions while these were still at an exploratory stage. "If the negotiations were trilateral from the outset, then the current Canada-US agreement could be the starting point." Sidney Weintraub, "The Canadian Stake in US-Mexico Free Trade Negotiations," *Business in the Contemporary World*, Vol. 3, No. 1 (Autumn 1990), pp. 127-130.

5.   President George Bush, "Fast Track and Trade Opportunities," address before the Hispanic Free Trade Breakfast, Houston, Texas, April 8, 1991, *US Department of State Dispatch*, Vol. 2, No. 15 (April 15, 1991), pp. 253-254.

6.   Herbert Meyer, "Why a North American Common Market Won't Work—Yet," *Fortune*, Vol. 100, No. 5 (September 10, 1979), pp. 118-120, 122, 124.

7.   "North American Economic Overview, 1990," *US Department of State Dispatch*, Vol. 3, No. 7 (February 17, 1991), p. 113. The gross domestic product figures for the three were $5,423.4 billion (US), $575.6 billion (Canada), and $237.7 billion (Mexico).

8.   On these relationships, see Alan Riding, *Distant Neighbors: A Portrait of the*

Mexicans (New York: Vintage, 1986): "Probably nowhere in the world do two countries as different as Mexico and the United States live side by side" (p. ix). See also Andrew H. Malcolm, *The Canadians* (New York: Bantam, 1986): "Americans look north toward their Canadian cousins and are often puzzled and perplexed by a people who can simultaneously seem so similar yet somehow strangely different" (p. 5). On Canadians and Mexicans, see J.C.M. Ogelsby, *Gringos from the Far North* (Toronto: Macmillan, 1976).

9.   The first trilateral meeting took place in March 1956 at White Sulphur Springs, West Virginia, where the Canadian and Mexican leaders—Louis St. Laurent and Adolfo Ruiz Cortines—joined President Dwight D. Eisenhower, then recovering from a heart attack and wishing to demonstrate his statesman's abilities before the November elections.

10.   This function is implicitly demonstrated in Lawrence Martin's skeptical *The Presidents and the Prime Ministers: Washington and Ottawa Face to Face: The Myth of Bilateral Bliss, 1867-1982* (Toronto: Doubleday Canada Limited, 1982).

11.   In 1982, the Canadian and American foreign ministers, George Shultz and Allan MacEachen, personal friends since their postgraduate-student days at the Massachusetts Institute of Technology, began a pattern of quarterly meetings. In 1984, Prime Minister Mulroney and President Ronald Reagan agreed to hold annual meetings at the summit level. "These practices have become, in effect, new mechanisms for better management of the relationship," as a former Canadian ambassador to the United States, Allan Gotlieb, has characterized them. Allan Gotlieb, *"I'll Be with You in a Minute, Mr. Ambassador": The Education of a Canadian Diplomat in Washington* (Toronto: University of Toronto Press, 1991), pp. 140-142. US-Mexican discussions across a broad range of subjects are conducted by a cabinet-level binational commission.

12.   Gotlieb, *"I'll Be with You in a Minute, Mr. Ambassador."*

13.   Damian Fraser, "New Links Across the Border," *Financial Times*, December 13, 1991, describes the Mexican government's lobbying activities and also its appeals to the "Mexican diaspora." Moreover, Mexico effectively has been making a broader appeal through cultural diplomacy. Perhaps the most remarkable expression of this is "Mexico: A Work of Art," a four-month celebration in New York City of Mexicans' cultural heritage. Glenn Collins, "From Mexico, Dance, Theater, Music and 30 Centuries of Art," *New York Times*, September 11, 1990, pp.C-13, C-14.

14.   The best theoretical treatment is Ivo D. Duchachek, *The Territorial Dimension of Politics: Among, Within, and Across Nations* (Boulder: Westview, 1986). On "subnational" diplomacy and the USCFTA, see Earl H. Fry, "Canada-US Economic Relations: The Role of the Provinces and the States," *Business in the Contemporary World*, Vol. 3, No. 1 (Autumn 1990), pp. 120-126.

15.   In 1959 a Canada-US Interparliamentary Group was formed, but it has not developed enough strength to be able to harmonize the two countries' legislative processes.

16.   Allan Gotlieb, *The United States in Canadian Foreign Policy*, O. D. Skelton Memorial Lecture, Toronto, December 10, 1991 (Ottawa: Department of External

Affairs and International Trade, 1992), p. 17. See also his *"I'll Be with You in a Minute, Mr. Ambassador,"* pp. 145-153.

17.   For an authoritative analysis by one of the Canadian USCFTA negotiators, see Michael Hart, "A Lower Temperature: The Dispute Settlement Experience Under the Canada-United States Free Trade Agreement," *American Review of Canadian Studies*, Vol. 21, No. 2/3 (Summer/Autumn 1991), pp. 193-205. See also the useful account in *The Canada-US Free Trade Agreement: Synopsis* (Ottawa: Supply and Services Canada, 1988).

18.   Hart, "A Lower Temperature," p. 200.

19.   Mimeographed text obtained from Reagan campaign headquarters in 1979. Robert Lindsey, "Reagan, Entering Presidency Race, Calls for North American 'Accord,'" *New York Times*, November 14, 1979, pp. A-1, A-24.

20.   Text obtained from the Office of the Governor, Sacramento, California in 1980.

21.   See the elaboration by Brown's associates, Mark S. Adams and Barry Steiner, "Energy and the North American Community: Canada, Mexico and the United States," *Hastings International and Comparative Law Review*, Special Edition, Vol. 3, No. 3 (Spring 1980), pp. 369-434.

22.   The following analysis is based on papers given by the author: "The Rediscovery of North America," Organization of American Historians 74th Annual Meeting, Detroit, Michigan, April 1-4, 1981, and "American Rediscovery of North America," panel on "Future of North American Cooperation: Canada-US-Mexico," 24th Annual Conference, Western Social Science Association, Denver, Colorado, April 21-24, 1982.

23.   Alan Richman, "2 Nations Are Cool to Reagan Plan," *New York Times*, November 15, 1979, p. B-16.

24.   This phenomenon is brilliantly evoked by Joel Garreau in *Nine Nations of North America* (Boston: Houghton Mifflin, 1981).

25.   J. L. Granatstein and R. Bothwell, "Missing Links: The Contractual Links with the European Community and Japan," in *J. L. Granatstein, ed., Towards a New World: Readings in the History of Canadian Foreign Policy* (Mississauga, Ontario: Copp Clark Pitman, 1992), pp. 158-179.

26.   One of the earliest discussions in Washington, DC, of this further possibility was the symposium, organized by the author, "The North American Concept: Issues That Affect Canada, the United States, and Mexico, and How They Are Internationally Managed," under the sponsorship of the Center for the Study of Foreign Affairs, Foreign Service Institute, US Department of State, Arlington, Virginia, on April 15, 1987.

27.   The political-strategic issue of whether to begin trade discussions with Canada first and only later go to Congress—given by the US Constitution (Article 1, section 8) power to regulate commerce—or to seek congressional authorization from the beginning produced a division, and caused some delay, within the US government. The "active diplomacy"—that is, the lobbying—of the Canadian embassy helped to tip the scales in favor of seeking congressional authorization. See Gotlieb, *"I'll Be with You in a Minute, Mr. Ambassador,"* pp. 101-107.

28.   Hart, "A Lower Temperature," p. 197.

29.   M. Delal Baer, "North American Free Trade," *Foreign Affairs*, Vol. 70, No. 4 (Fall 1991), p. 133.

30.   Larry Rohter, "Free-Trade Talks with US Set Off Debate in Mexico," *New York Times*, March 29, 1990, pp. A-1, D-30; Zoellick; "The North American FTA," p. 290.

31.   "Mulroney to Decide When to Join Talks," *Globe and Mail*, June 13, 1990.

32.   As Prime Minister Mulroney later explained: "It's important that we be part of the [three-way] negotiation. Otherwise, you'd have had a situation where the United States could become the centre of a series of deals where we'd all be spokes in a wheel. This is going to be trilateral all the way." Interview with Brian Mulroney, "'The Basics Are Right,'" *Maclean's*, Vol. 105, No. 1 (January 6, 1992), p. 70.

33.   Joint statement issued by the United States, Canada, and Mexico, February 5, 1991, *US Department of State Dispatch*, Vol. 2, No. 6 (February 11, 1991), p. 96.

34.   President Bush, opening statement at news conference, February 5, 1991, in *ibid.*, p. 96.

35.   President Bush letter to Congress (Chairman of the Senate Committee on Finance Lloyd Bentsen, Chairman of the House Ways and Means Committee Dan Rostenkowski, and House Majority Leader Richard Gephardt), May 1, 1991, *US Department of State Dispatch*, Vol. 2, No. 18 (May 6, 1991), p. 317.

36.   Excerpts from the president's remarks to the Society of Business Editors and Writers, Washington, DC, May 1, 1991, in *ibid.*, pp. 320-321.

37.   "The Fast Track West," *Economist*, Vol. 319, No. 7709 (June 1, 1991), p. 32. Support for fast track was strongest in the West. The "textile belt" in the South probably was more against GATT than against Mexico—i.e., global market liberalization rather than a regional opening. Most members of Congress from the Northeast and the upper Middle Western "rustbelt" also voted against fast track. California, though in the West, was mixed in its response. Most of the California Democrats in Congress were opposed; almost all the California Republicans were in favor.

38.   "President Salinas Meets President Bush During a Working Trip to the United States," *Mexico On the Record*, Vol. 1, No. 2 (January 1992), p. 1.

39.   Author's telephone discussion with a knowledgeable member of the Mexican embassy in Washington, April 27, 1992. Rita Beamish, "Bush, Salinas Vow Pact Soon on Free Trade," *Boston Sunday Globe*, December 15, 1991, p, 2. Besides Hills, other US officials present at Camp David were Commerce Secretary Robert Mosbacher, Treasury Secretary Nicholas Brady, National Security Adviser Brent Scowcroft, and Robert Zoellick from the State Department.

40.   Hugh Winsor, "US Honda Ruling 'Low-Level Politics,' PM Says: Canadian Ambassador in Washington Ordered to Begin Appeal Process," *Globe and Mail*, February 14, 1992; Clyde H. Farnsworth, "US-Canada Rifts Grow over Trade," *New York Times*, February 18, 1992, pp. A-1, D-4. During the NAFTA negotiations, the US negotiators have tried to raise the North American-content requirement for automobiles from 50 percent to 60 percent or even higher. Both Canada and Mexico have resisted for fear of losing valuable Japanese and other foreign investments. A further way by which the American Big Three automakers (General Motors, Ford, and Chrysler)

could secure a privileged position in the North American market, though only temporarily, would be through a two-tier scheme phasing out tariffs and nontariff barriers faster for their products than for those of new, extracontinental investors. Robin Dunnigan, "The North American Free Trade Agreement Negotiations: A Case Study of the Automobile Working Group," paper prepared for the Institute for the Study of Diplomacy, School of Foreign Service, Georgetown University, 1992.

41.   Graham Fraser and Alan Freeman, "Cabinet to Discuss Retaliation for US Lumber Duty," *Globe and Mail*, March 10, 1992. Gordon Ritchie, a former Canadian ambassador in Washington and the deputy chief negotiator of the USCFTA (currently serving as an adviser to the Canadian Forest Council) demanded in the US press that the Bush administration give the Canadian industry a fair hearing under the agreement. "Canadians are asking no more. They will accept no less." Gordon Ritchie, "US Protectionism Claims Canadian Casualties," *Wall Street Journal*, March 6, 1992, p. A-8.

42.   Drew Fagan, "Aid Possible for Exporters Hurt by US: Ottawa Ponders Slapping Duties on American Fruit, Vegetables," *Globe and Mail*, March 11, 1992.

43.   Edward N. Ney, "'We're No Protectionist Bully,'" *Globe and Mail*, March 17, 1992.

44.   Author's telephone conversation with press officer, Office of the United States Trade Representative, April 23, 1992.

45.   Keith Bradsher, "Bush Eases Cold-War Trade Curb: Sees a Mexico Pact Before Fall Election," *New York Times*, April 24, 1992, pp. D-1, D-2.

46.   A study by Gary Hufbauer and Jeffrey Schot, for the Institute for International Economics, projects losses mainly by Canadian auto-parts makers, textile producers, and some fruit and vegetable farmers. These would be more than offset, however, by gains from the expansion of two-way trade between Canada and Mexico. In employment terms, between 5,000 and 6,000 jobs might be lost, but about 12,000 jobs could be created by 1995. See Colin MacKenzie, "Gains Will Offset NAFTA Losses: Study," *Globe and Mail*, February 28, 1992.

47.   Bernard Simon, "Mulroney Fears US Will Delay Trade Pact," *Financial Times*, March 9, 1992.

48.   Farnsworth, "US-Canada Rifts Grow over Trade."

49.   Bernard Simon, "A Free Trade Disagreement," *Financial Times*, March 13, 1992.

50.   "Liberals Would Seek New Talks on Free Trade, Chrétien Says," *Globe and Mail*, February 13, 1992.

5

The Maastricht Negotiations

Jenonne Walker

ON DECEMBER 10 AND 11, 1991, leaders of the twelve European Community (EC) countries reached agreements of vast potential importance not only for themselves but also for America's future role in Europe. If ratified and fully implemented (by no means certain after the treaty was rejected in Denmark's referendum and only narrowly approved in France), the agreements reached in Maastricht, the Netherlands, will be as important as the 1957 Treaty of Rome in moving EC members toward new forms of shared sovereignty and common action. They could make the Community a major player in international financial, foreign, and security affairs. The two most important agreements are discussed in this essay: First, the Community fixed a timetable for full economic and monetary union, including the creation of a single currency controlled by a European Central Bank and the granting of some powers to the EC to enforce economic and fiscal discipline on member states. Second, the EC established a "political union" that is to include common foreign and security policies.

It would be a serious mistake to consider the Maastricht agreements anti-American. But one motive in the drive toward both economic and political union has been to enhance the collective clout of EC members, not least in their relations with Washington. Indeed, the European Monetary System—monetary union's predecessor—was created in 1979 to insulate Community members from the dollar's instability, and the 1985 decision to complete the Community's single market was largely inspired by belief that only a Community-wide base could enable European firms to compete with their American and Japanese counterparts. Monetary union is seen by most Community members as the logical, even necessary, next step in creating a single market.

More recently, the end of the Cold War has made West Europeans hope that by acting together, they can achieve more influence on international issues affecting their vital interests. The Community's painfully obvious disarray during the Persian Gulf crisis drove home to most members the inadequacy of existing mechanisms for coordinating member governments' foreign policies.

At the same time, the prospect of a united Germany at the heart of Europe made most of its neighbors—and especially the French—eager to limit German freedom of action by locking Germany even more tightly into a European Community. Views in France differ (as they do in all Community member states) but one of the most striking developments culminating at Maastricht was the willingness of the present French government, and apparently much of the political class, to accept limits on French sovereignty in financial and foreign policy in order to place limits on Germany.

The second key reason for Maastricht's success is that German Chancellor Helmut Kohl shares that French aim. He and Germany's other current leaders want to reassure their neighbors that Germany has no ambitions for an independent foreign, much less military, role. Indeed, Kohl sometimes gives the impression that he wants to set limits on German freedom of action while that still is acceptable to the citizenry.

Formally, the Maastricht treaties are the result of two year-long intergovernmental conferences—one on economic and monetary union and one on political union—launched in tandem at the EC's December 1990 summit in Rome. But in fact most Community members already had agreed to move toward economic and monetary union and common foreign and security policies before the conferences began. Many of the specific issues in the year-long process known as "Maastricht" were about how to make Community decisions—in other words, about the balance of power and influence in post-Cold War Europe.

Debates about the Community's security role in particular were less about Europe's security needs than about power, including the role of the United States, which saw a threat to NATO's position and therefore to US influence in Europe. As a case study in diplomacy, one of the most interesting things about the Maastricht process is how Washington tried to influence a negotiation to which it was not a party, including its efforts to use NATO communiqués as tacit "treaties" about what would or would not happen at Maastricht.

The Road to Maastricht

Mechanics. The intergovernmental conference (IGC) on economic and monetary union was conducted by senior officials from member states' finance ministries meeting every other week and finance ministers themselves meeting monthly. The IGC on European political union was conducted by member states' permanent representatives at Community headquarters in Brussels meeting weekly, with results reviewed by foreign ministers at their monthly meetings. Because the political-union conference covered environmental, energy, research, education, social, home, and judicial policies and reform of Community institutions as well as foreign and security policies, a wide range of other ministries participated. Final decisions on both conferences were taken by heads of governments (in France's case, the head of state) meeting frequently as the European Council as well as in intense bilateral exchanges. Drafts were submitted by the EC Commission, by a committee of national central banks (on economic and monetary union), and by member states or groups of states (most notably rival Anglo-Italian and Franco-German drafts on common foreign and security policies). It was the task of the country holding the rotating EC presidency (Luxembourg for the first half of 1991, the Netherlands the second half) to reconcile these conflicting suggestions into successive drafts that were the papers officially on the table.

The two conferences never were as separate as a description of their structure makes it seem. The range of issues involved provided ample fodder for cross-bargaining. Germany, for instance, tried to condition its agreement on economic and monetary union not only on ensuring that a European Central Bank would inherit the Bundesbank's commitment to price stability but also that there would be major strides toward political union. One key negotiation took place within the German government itself, with the Bundesbank and Finance Ministry trying to extract the highest possible price for acceding to Kohl's desire, as they saw it, to sacrifice German fiscal stability on the altar of his broader political goals.

Issues of Economic and Monetary Union. Economic and monetary union (EMU) had been rhetorically embraced as a goal by most Community members for nearly two decades, but it became a live issue in the late 1980s. Europe's businesses wanted to end the costs and uncertainties of constantly changing currencies as they tried to take advantage of the single market. Central bankers chafed at a situation in which their exchange rate and other key policies were effectively set by the Bundesbank, with no voices outside Germany influencing the decisions. The Community therefore decided at its summit in Strasbourg, France, in December 1989 to launch EMU negotiations before the end of 1990. The first of three stages of progressively tighter coordination of monetary policies in fact began in July 1990, and that October all but Britain agreed that stage two should begin in 1994. (Chancellor Kohl reportedly wanted this agreement in October, before formal opening of the intergovernmental conference, because he could not be sure his domestic political situation would permit him to make it later.)[1]

Key questions left for the IGC were

- Whether to set a firm date for stage three—full monetary union.
- When a European Central Bank (ECB) would begin operating.
- What EC discipline to impose on member state economies to ensure convergent antiinflationary policies.
- Whether the ECB would be as independent of political control as the Bundesbank is now.

On all issues, results at Maastricht closely followed the draft prepared by the committee of bankers and was strongly supported by the German government.

Several of Germany's partners had wanted an ECB to be established in stage two to give them an earlier voice in some of the decisions now made by Germans alone. And many were uneasy with the notion that monetary policy would be put beyond reach of politicians. But Bonn knew it had what the others wanted and used that position to bargain hard. It agreed to a January 1, 1999, deadline for stage three—full economic and monetary union—but with no ECB established until then. In return, Germany's partners agreed that

- Beginning in stage two, the EC Commission will monitor members' efforts to bring government budget deficits down to agreed levels.
- Tough "convergence criteria" will be established for participation in stage three: National inflation rates, government budget deficits, public debt, and interest rates will have to conform with those of the best-performing Community partners.
- The ECB will put price stability above all else.
- The ECB will be independent of instructions by member governments or the EC Commission.

Once stage three begins, any Community member with "excessive" budget deficits that rejects recommendations for change made by vote of the other Community finance ministers will be subject to financial penalties.

How this will work in practice remains to be seen. Will a government facing a tough election raise taxes or slash spending to stay within EC convergence criteria? Will a hard-pressed prime minister's peers help him or her by creatively interpreting the convergence criteria? What would the political effect be on the Community if Italy, for instance, is denied charter membership in stage three? No one can know the answers. But the extraordinary feature is that negotiations on this unprecedented transfer of sovereignty were relatively easy. By January 1999 at the latest, all EC members except the United Kingdom (discussed more later) that meet the convergence criteria are pledged to forsake national currencies in favor of a single European currency. They must transfer power over monetary policy to a European Central Bank that, in theory at least, will be insulated from political pressure.

Most of this was agreed, at least in broad outline, during the Luxembourg presidency that ended July 1, 1991. Holdouts were the Community's "poor four"—Spain, Portugal, Greece, and Ireland, whose worries about the effect of monetary union on their economies were assuaged by promises of additional assistance, including a "cohesion fund" for states with per capita GNP less than 90 percent of the Community average *if* their economic policies are deemed conducive to meeting EC convergence criteria.

Former British Prime Minister Margaret Thatcher hates any suggestion of transferring sovereignty, and even if her successor John Major plans, as most believe, to bite the EMU bullet in time to make the United Kingdom (UK) a charter member of stage three, he was not willing to risk her ire and that of other Tory party diehards before the April 1992 election. While still chancellor of the Exchequer, Major had floated the notion of fixing the value of the European currency unit (ECU) relative to EC members' national currencies and seeing whether it ever might become a single Community currency by natural choice of users rather than by imposition of a deadline. This was called a proposal for a "hard ECU."

Only Spain saw any merit in what most perceived as an effort to prevent monetary union from ever happening. The issue was resolved in October 1991 when all agreed to an "opt-out clause" suggested the previous May by Commission President Jacques Delors.[2] A separate protocol stipulates that the UK—and the UK alone—will not have to join stage three of EMU unless its government and Parliament take a separate decision to do so. The protocol also provides that the United Kingdom cannot prevent the other EC members from moving to full EMU, and the others cannot block British membership if the United Kingdom decides to join and meets the convergence criteria.

Issues of Political Union. In April 1990, French President François Mitterrand and Chancellor Kohl jointly proposed that an IGC on political union be held concurrently with the one already planned on economic and monetary union. Community members agreed at their December 1990 Rome summit that a future political union should extend to security and defense policies.

Negotiations on the common foreign and security policy aspects of political union were grouped around two broad questions. The first had to do with how the Community would make decisions and therefore involved the relative power and influence among EC members. The second was to determine what issues would be subject to joint decisions and therefore affect in part the balance of influence between the EC and the United States.

On the first set of issues, France and Britain wanted decisions to be made entirely by the councils of prime ministers and foreign ministers usually dominated by larger Community members. The Netherlands and other smaller states wanted a role for the Community's supranational Commission, which they traditionally have expected to protect their interests. A related issue was whether some council decisions could be taken by majority vote and, if so, whether voting should be weighted in favor of larger members. Bonn was willing to defer to French opposition to a significant Commission voice, but wanted a role for the European Parliament where unification may swell German ranks.

The decisionmaking issue was played out through rival concepts that came to be known as the "tree" and the "temple." The former would have brought all Community business into one treaty with one set of procedures (thus making the Community a tree with many branches). Applying standard Community procedures to foreign and security policies would have (1) given the EC's supranational Commission sole right to propose policies, (2) extended whatever powers the European Parliament might acquire to those policies, and (3) let the European Court of Justice make binding judgments about members' compliance. The latter approach would create a policymaking mechanism parallel to but different from standard EC procedures; these different procedures would form the pillars of a temple called the European union.

Even most of the Community members that would have preferred a "tree," including Bonn and Rome, knew that Paris and London would never accept it. Certainly that was the assumption of Luxembourg in April 1991 when, as holder of the EC presidency, it tabled an initial "temple" draft. The Commission mounted a rearguard action and reports that it had the support of most EC members emboldened the Dutch, who assumed the presidency in the second half of the year, to table an entirely different "tree" draft in September. That sparked a major revolt. Even those who preferred the Dutch approach knew it was too late to change course. And critics of the Dutch move found themselves so staunchly defending the earlier Luxembourg draft that backsliding from it—including its provisions for some majority voting in foreign and security policies—became difficult.[3]

Paris would accept the possibility of being outvoted—in some carefully limited circumstances—by other EC governments, but would not accept a transfer of foreign policy powers from national governments to a supranational Commission or European Parliament. Germans and other advocates of a greater parliamentary role could and did complain about the Community's alleged democratic deficit. But President Mitterrand was quoted as saying of an EC summit that "true democracy is in this room."

Thus, neither the EC Commission nor the Court of Justice is mentioned in the treaty articles about foreign and security policies (although the Commission almost certainly will have the observer role it has played in past efforts to coordinate members' foreign policies). The EC Parliament will only be "consulted" and "informed" and its views "duly taken into account." Heads of government will decide three important things by unanimity: which issues should be subject to common policies; the broad outline of those policies; and whether some implementing decisions can be taken by weighted majority voting among the foreign ministers.

Britain objected until very late in the day to any majority voting, but finally gave in. Prime Minister Major's government may have been uncomfortable about its isolation on so many other issues. It had failed to get face-saving language applying the EMU opt-out clause to all EC members. And when it refused to let the Community move even gingerly into social policy—in this case on workers' rights—the other eleven members made a separate pact without UK participation. Probably more important, however, London knows that it can, if it wishes, use the unanimity rule to deny foreign ministers permission to take majority votes on any given issue.

It may prove important that Maastricht has enshrined the principle of majority voting, limited and hamstrung as it may be, for foreign policy-making. Most ambitious ideas for deepening European integration have to be around a good while before Community members are comfortable with them. But the press of events will determine whether the Community does shift from being a means of virtually constant consultation by which sovereign states try to coordinate foreign policies to a union with majority voting or some other mechanism to resolve differences and permit timely action. Only when and if major Community members become convinced that they need a more efficient way of collective decisionmaking to advance their interests in the world will a common foreign policy worthy of the name become a reality.

The second level of debate—about the scope of EC joint action and especially how much responsibility the EC should take for its members' security—was more complex and less tangible. The Community is only beginning a process that will be the work of a generation or more. Its evolution will depend more on reactions to a changing Europe than on anyone's grand design.

In 1990, Italian Foreign Minister Gianni de Michelis and Commission President Delors each had separately proposed that the EC take on the mutual defense obligation of the Western European Union (WEU) and commit to merger of the two organizations when the WEU's mandate expires in 1998.[4] No other Community member was ready for that. During 1991, therefore, disagreements over near-term steps were quite minor. Those minor issues, however, became surrogates for a more fundamental clash about the longer-range future of Europe.

The debate that emerged was as much about NATO's future—and thus, many Americans believe, America's role in Europe—as about the European Community. It therefore was played out in the development of NATO communiqués defining the alliance's role in post-Cold War Europe and in discussions about whether to give the WEU a military capability, as well as in negotiations about a new EC treaty.

France and Britain most vividly illustrate the two extremes of opinion within the EC; other members' views fell somewhere between. Although not eager to see the US Army leave Germany, most current French leaders believe the Americans will go soon and are disinclined to defer French ambitions for Europe in order to fight what they see as inevitable. They insist that a European political union could not forever abjure a role in defense of its own territory, leaving that entirely to an American-led NATO. Ideally, these French leaders say, a WEU force would one day share responsibility for Europe's defense with the United States in a NATO transformed to be an alliance of two genuinely equal partners. That transformation should include peacetime replacement of NATO's Integrated Military Command (symbol in French eyes of European military subordination to the United States) with a committee to oversee joint training and contingency planning. When or if the US Army leaves, a WEU force would be prepared to take on the job alone. In the meantime, the French hope to see America's influence in Europe reduced, even while substantial US forces remain on the continent.

The British vision is very different. The United Kingdom sees its de facto second-in-command role in the Atlantic alliance as one of its few remaining symbols of big-power status and is, if anything, even more intent than Washington on NATO's primacy. Like other EC members, the UK wants a bigger European role within NATO, which requires Europeans to act in concert. And like them, it favors using the WEU as NATO's European pillar. But it wants the WEU to be as nearly as possible a subcommittee of NATO—or at least equidistant between it and the EC—and never part of the European Community. London wants WEU's membership to be open to all European members of the alliance (including Turkey, thus probably making EC-WEU merger impossible). European ambassadors to NATO should double as ambassadors to the WEU. The WEU could have its own planning staff, but it should be a "cell" at NATO's military headquarters. Some of NATO's European units might be joined by French units and call themselves a WEU force for action with the United States beyond the NATO area. But this would be largely a cosmetic device to enable NATO to act beyond its territory. And the current British government does not want the WEU ever to have any role in defense of its members' own territory.

Continental EC members believe that a political union should eventually have a defense component, although they have not written off a continued American military role in Europe and want to avoid making the French expectation of a total American troop withdrawal a self-fulfilling prophecy. Germany shares this view. The Persian Gulf crisis dramatized differences over what policies to adopt, but current German leaders believe that a political union must have the means, including military means, to implement foreign and security policies. Germans want to begin putting structures in place now even if they remain fairly hollow shells for some time. They also see a specifically West European defense identity as a way to draw France into closer military cooperation with its neighbors and to avoid German "singularization" on military issues. In sum, Germany hopes that participation in a military force labeled "European" will overcome the citizenry's aversion to military action beyond the country's borders—a role for which Germany deems NATO inadequate because of America's dominant position.

Thus, although the actual language proposed at Maastricht on foreign and security policies was quite modest, EC members knew they masked profoundly different visions of the future. So did Washington.

When the original Franco-German proposal for foreign and security policy aspects of European political union was launched in April 1990, French government spokespersons were quick to say they did not intend a substitute for NATO: "For us the Atlantic alliance is absolutely essential."[5] Paris and Bonn further elaborated their intent in a second joint paper on December 6, 1990, that called for extending coordination of security policies "to all spheres"—meaning beyond the economic aspects of security already put under the EC's domain by the 1986 Single European Act. They proposed agreement at Maastricht that

- Common EC security policy would "eventually lead to a common defense."
- The WEU would have an "organic relationship" to European political union and eventually form part of it.
- Links should "gradually" be strengthened between the WEU and EC states not members of it.

The Franco-German paper also laid out arrangements for majority voting that eventually were adopted at Maastricht. The same paper, however, stipulated that Maastricht decisions must "respect the commitments made to the Atlantic alliance allies" and expressed conviction that "the whole Atlantic alliance will be strengthened by the increase in the Europeans' role and responsibility and the establishment of a European pillar within it."[6]

The American Role

Most of the Franco-German proposals seemed consistent with what senior American officials had been saying. When asked about the initial April

1990 Franco-German proposal to move the EC into security policy, President Bush professed to see no threat to NATO. And Secretary of State Baker told NATO foreign ministers in December of that year that Washington welcomed a strengthened European security identity and use of the WEU both for European military action beyond NATO's area and as the European pillar of NATO, so long as it operated within and strengthened the alliance rather than undermine it.[7]

In short, although Washington clearly was following the Maastricht process carefully, even with some concern, its initial reaction was cautiously supportive. Early in 1991, however, caution turned to alarm. One version of what happened is that NATO's Supreme Commander General John Galvin grew worried about what the parallel development of the EC and WEU could do to NATO unity and especially to his ability to count on NATO troops when he wanted them. Galvin, according to this story, persuaded Joint Chiefs of Staff Chairman Colin Powell to help him try to dilute even Secretary Baker's cautious initial endorsement of EC ambitions. Another possibility is that some Europeans—almost certainly including Britons—warned Washington that its attitude was being seen as indifferent, giving credence to the French contention that the United States was losing interest in Europe and that Europeans needed to make their own arrangements. Some civilian American officials also were beginning to worry about what EC coordination of security policies would do to America's leading position in NATO. That role, as one American diplomat told the *New York Times*, traditionally had let Washington "tell the Europeans what we want on a whole lot of issues—trade, agriculture, you name it."[8]

For whatever mix of reasons, Washington changed signals from, as one observer put it, "green to blinking amber."[9] But in doing so, it faced two problems: One was the rhetorical support successive American administrations had given to EC political as well as economic union. The second was that Washington found itself objecting less to the specific language being proposed for the Maastricht treaty than to where the process might eventually lead.

The American position was most explicitly spelled out in a February 1991 message to all WEU capitals that became known as the "Bartholomew demarche" after Under Secretary of State for Security Policy Reginald Bartholomew. Although reaffirming US support for European unity and a strengthened European identity within NATO, the communication warned that anything that seemed to diminish NATO's centrality or to create a monolithic bloc of certain members would weaken domestic US support for an American role in Europe's security.

The so-called Bartholomew demarche tried to lay down the law on what subjects must be the sole province of NATO. It insisted that the WEU could not be subordinated to the European Community and that it must be open to all European members of NATO but not include EC members that were not also in NATO. It also said that the WEU should not duplicate NATO's tasks or contemplate independent European military action in Eastern Europe outside the NATO context. Only WEU action beyond Europe would be acceptable. (Some senior US officials were quoted as saying that Washington adamantly opposed any WEU military action, even beyond Europe, except in concert with the United States.)[10] Other American officials about this time said it was acceptable for EC members to "consult" on security issues prior to NATO meetings, but that "decisions" could only be taken in the full Atlantic alliance. And preserving NATO's Integrated Military Command was called the sine qua non of the Atlantic alliance.

The telegram conveying these views to American embassies in Europe was particularly harsh in tone and was not intended to be left with foreign ministries. It was a set of instructions for embassy representatives delivering the message. But the cable failed to make that clear, and soon all EC capitals had the written product.

The French reaction was, not surprisingly, the most vehement. The tone of the demarche reportedly was considered so insulting that the Élysée (the president's residence) at first refused to accept it;[11] one senior French official privately termed it the "Brezhnev-Bartholomew Doctrine of Limited Sovereignty."[12] Even some Europeans sympathetic to American worries privately called it a tactical mistake. At least some American officials, however, believed that Washington's strong stand, even though resented, would have a salutary long-term impact.

No words on paper can resolve such questions as whether NATO is "central" to European security or whether EC members act as a "monolithic bloc" in it. And neither Washington nor most other NATO capitals want to extend the NATO guarantee to Eastern Europe to resolve the issue of what Western force if any might be used there. Debate over the spring and summer therefore revolved around a few concrete issues and some deceptively trivial words that were codes for deeper differences. The chief issues on the Maastricht agenda were whether a new EC treaty would provide for a formal link between the EC and the WEU and whether it would cite "common defense" as an eventual possibility for the Community.

It was Paris, whose ambitions for a European security identity arguably are greatest, that wanted the least decided at Maastricht—simple acknowledgment that "common defense" is an eventual possibility for the Community. London, the least enthusiastic about a common European defense, argued for specific decisions setting the limits of a potential EC security role. For a time, the United Kingdom threatened to hold agreement on political union hostage to agreement on those limits.

Meanwhile, London and Washington were using NATO ministerial or summit communiqués to try to define the alliance's future and thereby to limit that of any other European security institution. In drafting NATO communiqués, negotiators deliberated not only concrete issues such as the alliance's military structure and how to develop its liaison arrangements with countries in Central and Eastern Europe but also whether NATO would be termed "the" or "a" forum for security consultations and decisions. Other key words were "transparency" (by which the United States meant that EC deliberations should be open to influence by Washington and NATO's other non-EC members such as Turkey) and "complementarity" (code for the EC/WEU's not poaching on NATO's turf).

At the same time, both Washington and Paris were busy trying to "create facts." Some Americans were delighted that NATO could reach agreement in May 1991 on command arrangements for its Rapid Reaction Corps before the WEU had begun discussing details of a similar force of its own—thus, US officials hoped, making any WEU force that eventually emerged seem a pale copy. Paris was equally pleased about organizing back-to-back EC-WEU meetings during the Persian Gulf and Yugoslav crises, not only because it made substantive sense but also because it highlighted to Anglo-Saxon sensitivities the fact that the two organizations already were acting as part of the same entity.

The Endgame

Key compromises were reached in the process of drafting the communiqué for NATO's June 1991 foreign ministerial meeting in Copenhagen. Washington accepted that "it is for the European allies concerned to decide what arrangements are needed for expression of a common European foreign security policy and defense role." American officials confirmed that this meant Washington would cease objecting to a formal EC/WEU link or even eventual merger.[13] The Copenhagen communiqué registered NATO's first acknowledgment of the legitimacy of a security, including defense, role for the European Community. And although NATO was called "the" essential forum for agreeing on policies related to NATO commitments, it was given only equal billing with the EC, WEU, and CSCE as "key institutions" for European security more broadly.

At the same time, the allies reaffirmed their commitment to NATO and to its "core functions." Those who participate in the Integrated Military Command promised, contrary to French wishes, to preserve it. The "core functions" were defined to include "consultations on any issues that affect [its members'] vital interests" (i.e., not limited to East-West security issues, as France sometimes had argued) and "to deter and defend against any threat of aggression against the territory of any NATO member state" (i.e., not just from the former Soviet Union). European allies also promised "transparency" and "complementarity" between their own evolving security and defense identity and NATO.[14]

London, Paris, and Washington nonetheless each continued vying to give its favorite European security organization prominence; Bonn strove to keep all its fences mended. During Foreign Minister Hans-Dietrich Genscher's early October visit to Washington, he joined the United States in proposing that Central and East European states join NATO in a new North Atlantic Cooperation Council, which NATO's (German) Secretary General Manfred Woerner said would make NATO "the" Pan-European security forum. Bonn's chief aim was to open NATO as much as possible to Europe's new democracies in the east, but it also liked being able to give NATO a boost at the height of Franco-German efforts to enhance the EC's security role.

Throughout the summer, London and Rome worked on a joint paper that was presented in October as a compromise between British views and those of the continental European states. NATO once again was called "the" key component of a European security system; WEU's purpose was described as reinforcing the Atlantic alliance and its functions spelled out to seem equidistant between the EC and NATO. WEU also, however, was called the defense component of the European union and a 1998 review was foreseen of links between the two.

Paris and Bonn, however, seemed to ignore the Anglo-Italian effort later that month when issuing an elaboration of their own December 1990 proposal. The Franco-German draft language for Maastricht made explicit that the WEU "is" an integral part of European union, should have troops answerable to it, and "will" help implement EC security policies. The Anglo-Italian draft spoke of WEU military action only outside the NATO area; the Franco-German draft imposed no such limits. But it also was more detailed about WEU-NATO cooperation than earlier Franco-German papers, calling for closer military cooperation, transparency and complementarity of roles, and cooperation between the WEU and NATO secretariats.

These Franco-German affirmations of loyalty to NATO were scarcely noted by the American press, which focused only on a footnote added at the last minute and not proposed for agreement at Maastricht. The footnote said "for the record" that the two countries planned to expand their joint brigade and hoped that other WEU members would contribute units so it could become the nucleus of a WEU force.

London initially professed to see its olive branch rejected. Significantly, however, the American reaction to this iteration of the Franco-German position was cautiously positive. Several factors were probably responsible for the changed American tone in Copenhagen and subsequently: the criticism the Bartholomew demarche in February had received, not least in the United States; allied willingness to reaffirm commitment to NATO; and possibly a desire to end a transatlantic dispute that otherwise might mar President Bush's claim to foreign policy mastery during the US election.

A growing expectation that Congress will slash American troop strength in Europe—and perhaps the administration's own recognition that when the Yugoslav chips were down, it had not wanted leadership, or even involvement, in Europe's new security problems—also played a role. The political editor of London's *Financial Times* believes that Prime Minister Major was persuaded by his talks with President Bush that the United States could only be counted on to complement, not substitute for, security arrangements among the Europeans themselves, and that Major therefore decided to go along with what his EC peers wanted at Maastricht.[15]

In any case, NATO's November summit in Rome seemed finally to lance the transatlantic boil. The summit communiqué reaffirmed the essential points agreed by foreign ministers in Copenhagen the previous June, including the professed belief of all that a European security and defense identity would be good for the Atlantic partnership and that it is up to the Europeans to decide how to develop it. WEU was described as both the defense component of the European integration process and a means of strengthening NATO's European pillar. At the same time, NATO was given a potentially important new role by agreement to turn its liaison arrangements with the countries of Central and Eastern Europe into the more formal and institutionalized North Atlantic Cooperation Council (NACC). American and European officials alike seem to agree that the Rome NATO summit cleared the way for relatively easy agreement on foreign and security policies at Maastricht.

Winners and Losers

The Maastricht treaty on political union includes just about everything that Washington and London initially found objectionable. WEU is made an integral part of the union process and will implement decisions taken by EC ministers. All EC members will be invited to join the WEU, but European NATO allies not in the EC can have only associate status. WEU thus is subordinate to the European union, pledged to cooperate with NATO but not equidistant between it and the EC. The political-union Treaty specifies that common EC foreign and security policies will include the "eventual" framing of a common defense policy (that is, the military aspects of security) and perhaps in time a common defense (that is, its own military capability). No limits are set on the geographic scope of that common defense. There will be some limited possibilities for majority voting on "implementation" of common policies but not, for now at least, about "issues having defense implications." The Maastricht result, in short, almost precisely parallels the Franco-German papers of December 1990 and October 1991.

Many American and British officials nonetheless insist that their efforts paid off and were worth the bad blood spilled in the process. They claim credit for Maastricht treaty language about the European union's respect for NATO obligations and compatibility with alliance policies (although similar language was in Franco-German proposals from the outset) and for a separate WEU pledge to be NATO's European pillar as well as the EC's defense arm (although if NATO endures and the WEU becomes the forum for coordinating its members' defense policies, both of which Paris has always said it wants, the WEU can hardly be anything else).

Washington and London may have received "compensation" for Maastricht outside the treaty: French acknowledgment, in NATO's Copenhagen communiqué, that the alliance can discuss any issue affecting its members' security and that there is a potentially important new role for NATO in Pan-European security cooperation if the NACC develops as its champions hope. Key US officials acknowledge that the Maastricht result was not what they wanted, but say the Copenhagen and Rome NATO communiqués set a broader "context" in which Maastricht is "acceptable."[16]

Maastricht was not the end of the debate. Washington will continue trying to squeeze the broadest possible range of decisions into NATO and to influence the WEU's evolution. London hopes to interpret Maastricht language about the WEU elaborating and implementing EC decisions as meaning that the EC will simply defer to a still-separate WEU on defense issues.[17] But one thing NACC, the Atlantic alliance, and the European Community all have in common is that no one can now know what their roles and responsibilities or the relationships among them will be as Europeans and Americans alike adjust to a changing Europe. Many of Maastricht's architects acknowledge that on common foreign and security policies, they have set out only chapter headings and given a broad sense of direction. For the content, as used to be said about German unification, "history will decide."

Notes

1. *Economist*, London, November 3, 1990, p. 55.
2. *Economist*, London, May 10, 1991, p. 84.
3. *Financial Times*, October 2, 1991, p. 14.
4. The Western European Union groups nine EC states that also are members of both the EC and NATO (the United Kingdom, France, Federal Republic of Germany, Italy, Belgium, Netherlands, Luxembourg, Spain, and Portugal) in a mutual-defense alliance whose original purpose was largely to provide a framework for German rearmament. Moribund for years, it began to revive in the 1980s as a forum for coordinating its members' security policies; on two occasions, members have used it to coordinate their military deployments in the Persian Gulf.
5. *Washington Post*, April 10, 1990, p. A-19.
6. *Declaration of the Member States of Western European Union Which Are Also Members of the European Union on the Role of WEU and Its Relations with the European Union and with the Atlantic Alliance*, Maastricht, the Netherlands, December 11, 1991.
7. *Financial Times*, December 18, 1990, p. 2.
8. *New York Times*, June 9, 1991, p. E-3.
9. Hans Binnendijk in *International Herald Tribune*, April 2, 1991, p. 6.
10. *International Herald Tribune*, March 14, 1991, p. 1.
11. *Washington Post*, June 11, 1991, p. 25.
12. Private conversation, April 1991.
13. Private conversations with American officials, June-July 1991.

14.   Final Communiqué of the North Atlantic Council ministerial meeting in Copenhagen, Denmark, June 7, 1991.

15.   *Financial Times*, October 10, 1991, p. 10.

16.   Private conversations, January-February 1992.

17.   Private conversations, February-March 1992.

6

The Improvised Diplomacy of German Unification

Flora Lewis

THEY MET ON OCTOBER 7, 1989, in the formal, rather stodgy Schloss Niederschönhausen instead of in the huge, gleaming Central Committee building downtown in order to mark the ceremony of the occasion—the Politburo of the German Socialist Unity party (communist) receiving the chairman of the Communist party of the Soviet Union, Mikhail Gorbachev. Erich Honecker, the East German party chief, was celebrating on a grand scale the fortieth birthday of his state.

"It was a dialogue of the deaf," participants said later. But it set in motion a critical change in the map of Europe, the withdrawal of the Soviets from the center of the continent to their own borders, a political tidal wave in the streets of the East, and a year of diplomacy that confirmed the end of the Cold War and opened a new era. For two generations, the partition of Germany and of Europe had been recognized as unnatural, unacceptable, and dangerous. But there seemed no way to overcome it without the much greater danger of provoking World War III, so it was accepted and began to seem immutable. Suddenly, the end of division, demanded by the peoples of the East, was coming into sight. But it was not inevitable.

The crisis that did not happen was resolved by an extraordinary diplomatic triple play—Bonn to Washington to Moscow—against the noisy background of millions throwing out their communist masters in search of democracy and prosperity. And it ended the partition of Germany, erasing the line where Soviet and allied troops met in 1945 in victory, a line that soon became the front between the two most heavily armed camps the world had ever seen. After two generations of confrontation, "the German question" was resolved without a single shot, and its symbol, the Berlin Wall, was pulled down.

The annals of diplomacy contain nothing like it. There was no contingency plan in any chancellery or foreign ministry, although one man, Bonn's Hans-Dietrich Genscher, had been nourishing the vision most of his life and working to make it possible for his sixteen years as foreign minister of the Federal Republic. Events drove the diplomats despite themselves, step by step, and yet they managed to guide developments and bring them to an amicable fruition.

Gorbachev Hopes to Preserve East Germany

All the evidence shows the result was far from Gorbachev's intention when he gave the East German leaders a long account of his troubles trying to reform and revive the Soviet Union that day in the East Berlin suburb of Pankow. He was careful not to give them any orders or instructions, but his purpose was clear enough. Several of his German hosts at the table understood it. There were two key points. One was to blunt what had come to be called "the red rejection front," the Stalinist coterie in the Soviet bloc working with the hard-liners in Moscow to undermine the plans of perestroika and, if possible, oust Gorbachev from the leadership. The other was to preserve the East German state—and thus Moscow's hold on the bloc—which Gorbachev believed required a reform movement parallel to his own.

Egon Krenz, a hulky, long-faced Politburo member, then age fifty-two, had been secretly leading a fight for liberalizing measures in East Germany for some time. Honecker had been ill, though rumors that he was dying turned out to be false. Members of the Russian delegation later said he was sprightly enough in meeting Gorbachev and reviewing the mammoth parade with him. But his ideological arteries, never flexible, had hardened to granite. He had cut himself off from the country's life behind the walls reserved for the privileged leadership, and he refused to listen to arguments that any kind of change was needed.

The night before the meeting at the castle, which had been the residence of East Germany's first president, Wilhelm Pieck, huge crowds had gathered to greet Gorbachev in Berlin's main square and celebrate the opening of festivities. Communist youth, 100,000 of them organized in a torchlight parade, filed by for three hours, but surprisingly, they did not cheer the German Democratic Republic (GDR), according to prescribed form. They chanted "Gorbie, Gorbie, Gorbie." Krenz said, after that, the Soviet leader felt the tension—he could sense things were different. Both the German leadership and the Soviets expected Honecker's speech to give some signal that reforms were coming. But there was nothing, just the same old hollow boasts and exhortations. "We were all disappointed," Krenz said. "Our goal was to work more closely with the Soviets on re- form, some openness. We wanted to make a better [GDR], a better socialism."[1]

Gorbachev delivered his message to Honecker carefully, working by in- direction. He heaped praise on the East German state for what it had done in forty years and then launched into an impassioned lecture about the problems of the Soviet Union and the need for perestroika and glasnost. "There was no sense of meddling in our affairs," Krenz said, "but we un- derstood his point quite well. It wasn't clear whether Honecker didn't un- derstand or didn't want to. He came back with an even worse speech than before. Gorbachev got no echo from him. That was the background for Gorbachev's remark that he who is late in keeping up with history gets left behind. For me, and several of us, it was a signal that we have to act now, but what to do?"[2]

Both Krenz and Günther Schabowski, another Politburo member, in- sisted that there was no direct intervention or plotting from the Soviets. They contrasted Gorbachev's method with the way Leonid Brezhnev or- chestrated and directed down to the merest details the maneuver to oust the first East German leader Walter Ulbricht and replace him with Ho- necker in 1971. But the Soviets knew what was going on. Valentin Falin, a Soviet Central Committee official who had served as ambassador to West Germany and is a specialist in German affairs, told *New Perspectives Quar- terly* a few months later: "In 1989 alone, both in Moscow and Berlin, we put it to Honecker four times straight on the table. If the party doesn't take the initiative, changes will go on in an organic way and you will be left out in the cold. . . . But he didn't listen. . . . It caused alienation and bitterness between us."[3]

The Soviets also knew about the fights with Krenz and took it for granted that he would be the one to succeed Honecker if a break came. Falin said that after the jubilee Honecker planned to oust Krenz from the Politburo and send him to Leipzig. Krenz was opposed to the use of force but Honecker insisted on it although he knew the Soviets did not intend to back up the German army. "We never made it a secret to anybody in the East German leadership that, whatever the developments, our forces were not stationed in the [GDR] to be a judge in domestic events," Falin said. "Soviet troops would not intervene."[4]

On the evening of October 7, there was a big reception at the Palace of the Republic. "You could see by his expression that Gorbachev was upset," Schabowski said later. "But he didn't say anything. There were two encounters at the party, Krenz and Falin, and myself and [Gennadi] Gerassimov [then Soviet Foreign Ministry spokesman.] Without telling each other beforehand, we both told the Russians you can be sure there will be change soon."

In fact, along with a third Politburo member, Peter Lorenz from Karl-Marx-Stadt (now again called Chemnitz) they had begun planning how to move Honecker. "He had told us that after the anniversary, he would be ready to discuss some questions of principle. But he also ordered us not to have any contact with Gorbachev. When we heard that, we began the conspiracy on our own," Schabowski said.[5]

The infighting in the Politburo was not known outside, but it reflected the deep turbulence that had developed in the country. In May, Hungary had announced that its citizens were free to cross the Austrian border without hindrance and had even torn down some of the barbed wire to show it had opened the Iron Curtain. Some East Germans began to slip across. By late summer, many thousands who had gone on vacation in Hungary or countries further east were gathering in camps near the border to demand the right to leave as well.

Hungary Lets East Germans Go

The Hungarian communist government decided to let them out. Prime Minister Miklós Németh and Foreign Minister Gyula Horn flew secretly to an American base in West Germany to meet Chancellor Helmut Kohl on August 24 and tell him the news. (They quarreled later about who deserved the credit.) The two governments arranged almost daily meetings in Vienna after that to make detailed plans.[6] The Hungarians informed Moscow, but did not ask permission and said nothing to East Berlin. The East German leadership was furious when it learned from the Soviets that "a brother socialist country" was simply tearing up the agreement against letting citizens go west without permission of their own government.

They realized it amounted to opening a back door around the Berlin Wall. Honecker ordered his foreign minister, Oskar Fischer, to persuade Moscow to take special action. But the Soviets, with an air of regret, East Berlin thought, said the time was past when they could force anyone to do "what members of the socialist community need."

The Hungarians did delay opening the border for a week or so to give East Berlin time to persuade the refugees to return. None agreed. So the GDR stopped giving any more exit permits for Hungary. Then, on the evening of September 11, Budapest television announced that the refugees would all be free to leave starting at midnight.

By October, 45,000 East Germans had fled west. Thousands more had crammed into the gardens of the West German embassy, a handsome old palace in the Mala Strana section of Prague, and also into the much smaller modern villa that is the residence of Bonn's ambassador in Warsaw. Honecker wanted to clear them out before the jubilee, but insisted they must first return to the GDR and would be given permission to leave from there. Of course, they did not believe him. The physical and hygienic conditions in the embassies were getting desperate. Genscher met with Foreign Minister Fischer at the UN and they worked out a plan to bring the refugees to the west in trains across East Germany, so they could be said to have left from there.

It was another incredible blunder by the East Germans. Genscher flew to Prague and, his face glowing with pride, announced the news from an embassy balcony to the crowd below. Before he got beyond "I am happy to tell you . . . ," he was drowned out by cheers. The trains were scheduled to go through Dresden. There, more thousands stormed the railway station to push their way on board. Security forces had to be used to keep them out and seal the trains. After that, refugees were evacuated through neutral countries, and they kept arriving. A new slogan appeared in the mounting crescendo of East German demonstrations calling for reforms—"We want to stay." Krenz and his friends took it to confirm their belief that permission to travel and visible reforms would surmount the crisis.

Krenz Makes a Move

Gorbachev flew home from the jubilee on October 8, and Krenz launched his maneuver. The Soviets had no intention of giving up East Germany, nor any suspicion they might have to. Their leader had been enthusiastically received by the public. Polish party leader Mieczyslaw Rakowski turned to Gorbachev at one point on the reviewing stand and said, "It looks like they want you to liberate them again."[7] A few days later in Warsaw, Polish President General Wojciech Jaruzelski, who had also been present at the jubilee, said he saw no reason to worry about developments in East Germany. "I have seen many demonstrations," he said, "and I know which ones are real and which are made to order. From what I saw in East Berlin, I know these people are patriots, they are loyal to their state."[8]

Krenz thought so too. He drafted a paper on reforms and, against Honecker's will, forced it to a debate at the Politburo meeting October 10. "I would laugh reading it today," he said later. "There was nothing fundamental, just promises of more openness, travel, consumer goods." But there were two days of fierce argument before it was watered down enough to gain consensus, and by the time it was published, he and his friends realized Honecker would not implement it anyway. "We made our decision to push too late, so we had to try to change the leadership," Krenz said.[9]

Krenz did not use the word "conspiracy," but Schabowski did several times, and that is what it was. The plotters decided it would have to be done inside the Politburo, which met on Tuesdays. There were twenty-six members, including alternates, and they could count on only five or six votes against Honecker. The key, they felt, was Prime Minister Willi Stopf. His relations with Honecker and his main hard-line ally, Klaus Mittag, had been strained for a long time. They asked the Soviet ambassador to get Stopf on their side. Stopf agreed to propose the motion and persuaded most of the others. With traditional communist discipline, when the overwhelming majority was clear, the members adopted it unanimously. Even Honecker voted against himself.

But the leaders were still concerned not to let the public know of their fight. Honecker was to announce his resignation on grounds of health and age (he was seventy-seven) at the Central Committee next day. Schabowski did not trust what he might say extemporaneously. That afternoon, Schabowski wrote out the statement on his computer. "But I didn't include 'My successor will be. . . .' Just that it's time for a younger man, with no name. I was astonished the next day when he said 'Egon Krenz.' We had never discussed that. I don't know who put the name in. It was meant for the public, a way of saying Krenz wasn't in opposition to

Honecker but was recommended by him. That was a big handicap for Krenz in what turned out to be his forty days of interregnum."[10]

The leadership was getting seriously worried abut Leipzig and its swelling demonstrations. Krenz said that, contrary to later reports, Honecker never issued orders to put them down by shooting, but Schabowski said orders were considered. The Defense Ministry, the security police, and the local authorities had prepared for massive force, which would have brought a massacre, in case the orders came. According to Krenz, he was worried enough to call all the officials involved and explicitly give orders not to use force, a move he feels proud of now. He rejects reports that the Leipzig orchestra leader Kurt Mazur was the key. "A mere musician couldn't have stopped the soldiers from shooting if they'd been told, but he did help calm the people," Krenz said.[11]

But that was only one Monday, and the demonstrations had been occuring regularly at the start of each week. More had to be expected, and they were spreading to other cities. Krenz took over as first secretary after the Central Committee meeting October 18. His aim, he said, was to "sustain the sovereignty of the [GDR]" by improving relations with Bonn, including by granting the right to travel and by showing close support for Gorbachev's program. He also sought to provide "a better socialism for the [GDR]. I believed we could start at the same point as Gorbachev did in 1985. But now I see it was an illusion. Society was already in too deep a crisis. We introduced the *wende* [turn] to improve the [GDR] not to bring unification."[12]

That weekend, Genscher attended a conference of the Institute for East-West Security Studies at Frankfurt, West Germany. The news of Honecker's replacement by Krenz came as a bombshell, stunning the high-ranking East Germans present. I was sitting next to Genscher as the speeches droned on. At one point, he leaned toward me and whispered, eyes aglow with excitement, "Aren't I lucky to be in office in this period? I was right."

Genscher's comment was primarily in reference to the speech he had made at Davos, Switzerland, in February, 1987, when he argued, "We must take Gorbachev seriously, we must take him at his word." Most allied officials then were still highly skeptical, suspicious that Gorbachev's "new thinking" was just a trap to fool the West. As late as May 1989, White House spokesman Marlin Fitzwater called the Soviet leader "a drugstore cowboy, all talk and no action." But Genscher was also referring to his long and patient efforts to improve relations with the East so as to bring about German unity. He sensed very quickly the historic importance of accelerating events, though the only person who had said publicly that Moscow was getting ready to jettison its satellite empire, including East Germany, was Vernon Walters, US ambassador to Bonn. That summer, he had predicted unification within five years. Walters was officially reprimanded for his "provocative" remarks.

In East Berlin, Krenz and his team hurriedly worked on a new program, keeping Gorbachev closely informed through the Soviet embassy. They had made no detailed plans. They spoke of a "contractual agreement" and a "security partnership" with the Federal Republic. "We were looking for ways to put the German question on the agenda," Krenz said later, a momentous switch for the GDR, which had always insisted that the question was closed with the permanent existence of two German states. West German President Richard von Weizäcker had said in June 1987, "The German question will be open so long as the Brandenburg gate is closed," and President Bush had spoken of unification as a strategic goal. But this was standard diplomatic language and was taken as the traditional incantation.

Berlin Wall Falls

On November 1, Krenz went to Moscow and told Gorbachev that the GDR would change its laws and make permits for travel to the West easily available, though he did not give a date. On November 6, the proposed act was published, but it was complex and still full of restrictions. The public took it as a minor sop. Then, on November 9, the Politburo decided to permit the people to travel as much as they wanted, effective November 10. Schabowski reported it to a press conference, but in ambiguous terms, without details. Tens of thousands of people began streaming toward the Berlin Wall, to test the news. Erich Mielke, the security chief, called Krenz at 9 PM to say a dangerous situation was building and orders had to be issued to the guards. Krenz's version is that he phoned around and then ordered the crossing points opened. People began pouring through, but Krenz saw that most were first requesting the still-necessary permits, so he felt relieved. "Our authority was holding," he said.

There are other versions, all incomplete. The outpouring just happened. Krenz resented being blamed for a "disorganized operation." He said later, "There are people who think revolutions are played out by a scenario. These events are not to be foreseen." He was convinced in any case that an attempt to stop the joyous outpouring westward by force would have been a disaster. "A military solution at that time would have brought not just the death of the leader, as in Romania later, it would have been civil war," Krenz said.[13]

Suddenly, the wall was breached for good. People started to talk of German unity. Nobody other than the Soviet and East German leaders had been sure what the Soviet troops would do. Now it was clear—they did not lift a finger. Vladimir Grimin, a senior official said to be the KGB station chief at the Soviet embassy in East Berlin, said later, "It was an important test of our credibility. It showed the West we really had new thinking in our foreign policy."[14]

It also showed the East. A week later, on November 17, students massed in Prague to demonstrate against the rigid Czechoslovak regime. The police put them down with much brutality, though without shooting. But the people had seen that Soviet forces had not intervened in Germany, and they suddenly realized they too could get rid of the regime. That was the start of Czechoslovakia's "velvet revolution." It was followed by the bloody upheaval in Romania and ambiguous change in Bulgaria. Then Poland and Hungary, which had been on the reform path already, dumped their communists. In a few months, the whole Soviet bloc built by Stalin had collapsed, and the Warsaw Pact was an empty anachronism.

But the new East German rulers still thought they could somehow preserve the state. They started talks with dissident leaders and promised free elections at the end of 1990. The people thought differently. More and more of them used the newly open border to flee west. By the end of the year, 300,000 had gone, disrupting production, hospitals, and services.

Kohl Plans for German Unity

Kohl decided he must act to get ahead of events. In great secrecy, a handful of people working under his foreign affairs adviser, Horst Teltschik, prepared a speech for him to deliver to the Bundestag. Kohl had brought Teltschik with him to Bonn from Mainz, where he had been state president of the Rhineland-Palatinate, instead of taking an expert from the Foreign Ministry. There were constant strains between the chancellery and the ministry. Genscher had become Foreign Minister in the coalition government under the previous socialist chancellor, Helmut

Schmidt, and he retained the post when his Free Democratic party decided to switch coalition partners, bringing Schmidt down.

Kohl the Rhinelander—the provincial, slow, sometimes bumbling but always calculating politician—was never quite at ease with Genscher, who came from Halle in East Germany and was nimble, worldly, and publicity-conscious. An adviser said Kohl felt that if he told Genscher what his speech would say the night before, the foreign minister would break the news on the radio at six the next morning. So nobody was told. The chancellor startled everybody with his ten-point plan for German unity on November 28.

Governments in East and West were outraged. Shortly after, when Genscher was in Moscow to see Gorbachev, the Soviet leader denounced him angrily and said, "I don't like being taken by surprise." Genscher had to admit that he had been just as surprised by his own government and he was livid.[15]

President Bush, who was to meet Gorbachev at the "seasick summit" in Malta on December 2-3, said nothing, but Washington was annoyed. French President François Mitterrand made his fury known and arranged to see Gorbachev in Kiev and Prime Minister Margaret Thatcher in London to talk of ways to slow down the Germans. On November 18, Mitterrand had convoked a special summit of the European Community (EC) at the Élysée palace to discuss events in the East. In a press conference that day, he said firmly, "German reunification is not on the agenda."

But of course it was—put there not so much by Kohl but by the people in the streets of Leipzig, Dresden, Berlin, and elsewhere. When diplomatic tempers cooled, Kohl's plan was seen to be rather mild. He spoke of reunification only as an ultimate "goal" and of readiness to establish "confederal structures between the two German states" that could lead to a "federation." He offered aid to the GDR on condition of economic and democratic reform.

Moscow flatly rejected Kohl's plan. There was still little sense of how fast things would move. But West Germany's allies began to realize that the direction was inevitable and they must rally to work with Bonn if they were not to be left helplessly behind. The EC summit at Strasbourg December 8-9 supported the principle of unity. Meanwhile, Krenz fell, and free elections in East Germany, already moved forward from the end of 1990 to May, were definitely scheduled for March 18. It was the only way to produce a valid negotiating partner and the only orderly way to let the East Germans speak for themselves. Otherwise, the street would decide chaotically.

There was a frenzy of consultations and bilateral summits, everybody flying off to see everybody else (when possible, on a tropical island). Washington, which did not feel the atavistic fears of a big Germany that gripped Europeans east and west, began to plan strategy and procedures for dealing with the issue.

US Insists That Germany Remain in NATO

Secretary of State James Baker, from the beginning, worked with a small team of advisers he had brought into the department, virtually shutting the bureaucracy out of policymaking. It had serious disadvantages in some ways and provoked resentment from the career foreign service. But on the German issue, it enabled the administration to move fast, without the endless insider quarrels that had marked the Reagan years. One official involved said afterward, "We spent 3 percent of our time on interagency arguments and the rest on substance. It was about the reverse before."[16]

The approach of excluding State Department regulars also blocked the effect of their suspicions and dislike of "Genscherism." Many were convinced Bonn's foreign minister wanted reunification and a deal with the East so badly he would take it on any terms, selling out Western interests. They considered him a devious waffler. The inner team did not share these fears, accepting Genscher's often-repeated thesis that settlement with the East could come only to a Germany firmly anchored in the West.

The key players were Robert Zoellick in the State Department, a young aide Baker had brought with him from Treasury as counselor, and Robert Blackwill, a fifty-one-year-old former diplomat who had left to teach at Harvard but returned with the Bush administration to head Europe Affairs at the National Security Council. Zoellick relied on Dennis Ross, head of State's Policy Planning staff for expertise on the Soviets. National Security Adviser Brent Scowcroft, a cautious former general who had been deputy to Henry Kissinger in that post, always took part in sessions with President Bush. But it was the two Roberts who drafted most of the papers and planned the strategy, keeping most of officialdom out of it.

Focusing on the president's committed positions and Baker's crisis-avoidance approach, they worked out some basic principles and began looking for procedures. The ideas were not complicated:

■ The Germans were to determine their own fate and therefore required close coddling.

- They should remain in NATO.
- The Soviets must be persuaded that their interests were taken fully into account.
- Britain and France, particularly, must be brought in to assure allied solidarity and help bring Moscow around.

But the tactics were tricky. President Bush threw himself enthusiastically into the game of constant phone calls, letters, and summits to cultivate warm personal relations with the foreign leaders. Secretary Baker became one of the world's most frequent travelers. Zoellick called it a "multiring circus," trying to keep everybody involved with a sense of being heard.

The crucial diplomatic decision was to go public with a clear demand that a united Germany must remain in NATO. Baker did it in a speech in Berlin in late December, in the context of changing East-West relations and a new role for the alliance. The effect was to change the issue. From that point on, the nub question was Germany in the alliance. Whether it should be united took second place, though gradually became accepted as inevitable.

Moscow Reacts

Moscow was shocked at the idea. The Warsaw Pact was falling apart. It began to focus on the NATO plan as an even worse prospect than losing the GDR. But it was not until the end of the winter that Moscow came to realize the GDR could not be saved; the task had to be to assure the best possible deal for the Soviets.

Ironically, it was probably not so much increasing calls for unity from the East German crowds that convinced Moscow but increasing talk from Bonn about a single currency. It is a historical error to hold, as many claim, that the partition of Germany was decided in Yalta or even at the three-power summit of victors in Potsdam in July 1945. Occupation zones were established, but they were not intended to split the defeated country permanently. It was the Western currency reform in 1948, designed to revive the economy, that led the Soviets to cut off their zone and the Americans, French, and British to unite theirs. The deutschemark split Germany in two parts—two generations later, it united them.

Washington and Bonn began to push the pace in January. They were the only governments not intent on dragging things out, but the two capitals had somewhat different reasons for being in a hurry.

Bonn worried about the exodus of East Germans, still running at about 2,000 a day. Kohl's aide, Teltschik, leaked a report that the GDR was going bankrupt and Bonn thus must step in quickly with economic measures. It is hard to tell whether that analysis was premature or a self-fulfilling prophecy. The opposition Social Democratic party (SPD) charged the chancellery with a deliberate scare tactic to promote its Christian Democratic allies in upcoming East German elections. Polls gave the SPD the lead, and Kohl was running scared.

But later, a Bonn official revealed another reason for the chancellor's sense of urgency. Gorbachev's position in the Soviet Union was steadily worsening. Bonn worried that he might lose out any day and that a major switch in policy might follow before any agreements had been achieved. There was an even more dire nightmare: If civil war broke out in the Soviet Union, what would the nineteen Soviet divisions in East Germany do? They had nuclear weapons.

Washington was not thinking in those terms, but it saw speed as a strategic objective, concerned that the longer complicated issues were debated, the more likely the Soviets would find a way to stick on Four Power rights, the remaining provisions from the 1945 accord that gave Moscow and the other three powers occupation rights. A chaotic transition was envisaged, in which the Germans united but failed to regain sovereignty and the Red Army remained. Washington wanted a "clean" finish and understood that meant bringing the Soviets to feel they would not be excluded from Europe or their security endangered.

In January, Genscher, constantly airborne, went again to Washington. He settled down in Baker's office, "putting our feet up and half lying in our chairs," and discussed a procedure that would leave "internal" unification to the two Germanies but link their talks with the four occupation powers. To stress that the Germans were deciding essentials for themselves, Baker called it "two-plus-four," not four-plus-two. At first Genscher resisted any inclusion of the four because it could limit Bonn's freedom of action, but in the end, Baker's explanations convinced him.[17]

Then Baker took the idea to Moscow, stopping off at Shannon Airport to sell it to French Foreign Minister Roland Dumas. The British were also consulted. It turned out to be a magic formula. On February 10, Kohl went to Moscow, with Genscher, and got Gorbachev to say publicly that the Soviets accepted the right of the German people to decide if they wanted a single state. He ceded the principle of unity.

Genscher worked the personal relations approach as assiduously as Bush. He told how he had once said to Leonid Brezhnev, "We divided

German history. The [GDR] got Marx and we got *Das Kapital*." He drew laughs from Eduard Shevardnadze with a good-news-bad-news joke that the Soviet foreign minister relayed to the Politburo's delight: The good news—Lenin's mother is still alive. The bad news—she's pregnant. It paid off later in the two-plus-four talks when the earnest young East German Foreign Minister Markus Meckel, a pastor from the dissident peace movement, talked at length about the need to denuclearize all of Germany. Genscher tried to hide his wince, but Shevardnadze cut Meckel off. "You don't know what you're talking about," the Soviet official snapped. "Let Genscher speak."[18]

All the NATO and Warsaw Pact foreign ministers had long been scheduled to meet in Ottawa on February 13 to launch the "Open Skies" conference, a plan for mutual aerial inspection. But the program was quickly overshadowed by special meetings to set up two-plus-four. It had to be put to all the NATO ministers, the others fuming at having been left out. It was an angry session. The excitable Italian Foreign Minister Gianni de Michelis complained vociferously. "It's none of your business, be quiet," Genscher told the representative of Nazi Germany's former Axis partner.

The Poles were particularly upset. They wanted in. Although Genscher had repeatedly given assurances that there would be no claims on Germany's border with Poland (moved westward at Stalin's demand after World War II to compensate for Poland's eastern territories seized by the Soviets), Kohl had refused a clear commitment. To assuage politically active ex-refugees for electoral reasons, Kohl insisted a binding pledge could be given only by a united German government.

That brought mounting pressure on Kohl from all his allies. The Poles were told they could be present when two-plus-four began discussing the border. Genscher came close to threatening to break up the Bonn coalition, which could have dumped Kohl. Finally, on March 2, the chancellor agreed to twin resolutions by the two German parliaments accepting the border after East Germany's March 18 election. Poland was also promised a special treaty on friendly relations.

Genscher, who has a keen sense of symbolism unlike Kohl's tendency toward insensitivity, took pains to appease the Polish foreign minister when Shevardnadze set a bilateral meeting for June 11 at Brest. The city (formerly Brest-Litovsk) is on the Polish-Soviet border, where Lenin made the 1917 treaty with Germany taking Russia out of World War I. Shevardnadze's brother had died there when Germany attacked in 1941, and he wanted Genscher to join him in laying a wreath on the grave. The

German told the Pole, Krzysztof Skubiszewski, that it was an important gesture of reconciliation between Bonn and Moscow.

NATO and the New Germany

On the issue of Germany in NATO, Genscher came up with a compromise that would allow the Red Army to stay on GDR territory for a few years and a pledge that no NATO forces would enter, although Washington arranged to include a provision that NATO treaty guarantees would cover the whole of the new Germany. It was awkward and impractical but critical, because it meant that when a West German ambassador turned up at NATO after unification, he would automatically represent the entire country—another way of boxing the Soviets.

After having insisted that German unity was for distant "history to decide," then that it should be arranged slowly and deliberately, then that the principle was acceptable but Four Power rights must be maintained, and then that there should be a Europe-wide referendum, Moscow was floundering. It launched a series of what it should have known were unworkable ideas. There was talk of neutrality for Germany, then of being in East and West alliances at the same time, then of being in NATO on "French terms" (a political member but not integrated in the military command).

Poland had a useful influence on the NATO issue. At first, it said it would remain in the Warsaw Pact with Soviet troops on its territory—not at all the position of Hungary and Czechoslovakia, which insisted on withdrawal. Poland did not want to be left facing an unknown Germany. But when the prospect of Germany staying in NATO looked serious, it came out with strong support. The Soviets called a Warsaw Pact meeting in an attempt to present a solid front of their allies on Moscow's line. It was not possible. The East Europeans as well as the West wanted Germany in NATO, and Moscow was no longer in command.

The visible Soviet uncertainty strengthened the conviction of both Washington and Bonn that Moscow would come around. Gorbachev kept saying that Germany in NATO was "unacceptable" and would offend all the Russian people who had sacrificed 20 million in the war. At one point, he told a French visitor that if he agreed, "there will be a Soviet marshal in this chair [Gorbachev's] the next day."[19] It was taken as an empty bluff. He was obviously weakening.

The East German elections produced poor results for the Social Democrats, whose leader had been arguing against early unity. Kohl and Genscher triumphed. Diplomacy went into high gear. Gorbachev flew to a Washington summit held May 30 to June 3. Bush went to considerable lengths to maintain the appearance of equal superpower status for the Soviets, including signing a trade agreement. Just before, Baker had delivered to Moscow "nine assurances" responding "to Soviet concerns regarding German unification." There were no new concessions, but the paper was drafted to impress the Soviets with how sincerely the United States kept their interests in mind.

No gloating, no shoving—but Washington was pressing on its goals. One participant said there was a point in an extended summit meeting when the Russian Falin took the floor and delivered a stinging speech: "You cannot trust the Germans. You and we are two big powers. We have a responsibility from World War II to keep the Germans under control, and that's why we must be together. While the Germans are technically uniting domestically, we have to keep sovereignty in our hands and troops in the country at least another five years," Falin said.[20]

The Americans noticed, however, that Gorbachev and Shevardnadze were ostentatiously chatting with each other throughout Falin's performance, as though they had nothing to do with it. Bush and his staff did listen carefully. The response was that the United States would have nothing to do with such a deal, that it was banking on a strong alliance with the Germans in NATO.

The incident seemed even more peculiar when Bush, according to plan, told Gorbachev that under Helsinki self-determination principles, the German people should have the right to choose their alliance. Without argument, Gorbachev said, "I agree." The Soviet aides were visibly startled. Bush said it again, to make sure Gorbachev had not misunderstood, and got the same reaction. Still wondering if they had a breakthrough, the Americans put the point in the press conference declaration Bush was to make and, the next day at Camp David, showed the paper to the new Soviet ambassador, Aleksandr Bessmertnykh, later Shevardnadze's replacement as foreign minister. He said, "No problem."

But three weeks later, when the two-plus-four ministers had their second formal meeting in East Berlin, Shevardnadze reverted to the Falin approach, taking a harder line than he had at the first meeting in Bonn May 7. It turned out, as Genscher had suspected, that the Soviets considered this a domestic necessity to get Gorbachev through his difficult Twenty-seventh Party Congress scheduled for early July.

On July 1, the West German deutschemark was introduced to replace the now nearly worthless East German mark, at a politically generous rate of one-for-one despite the financial complaints of Karl-Otto Poehl, head of the West German Central Bank. Bonn had debated constitutional procedures for unification earlier in the year and had settled on using Article 23—which provided simple accession by any "land" requesting it. That avoided elaborate constitutional negotiations. The Federal Republic would simply swallow up East Germany.

Some were distressed. West German writer Günter Grass, a socialist who still dreamed of some kind of "third way" between the models of the two societies, was later quoted in the press as saying that "the [GDR] lost an ideology and gained a currency, but Germany has lost its soul." The leaders who had emerged so suddenly to sweep away the East German communist regime were submerged again and all but forgotten.

Seeking Soviet Acceptance

The next step was to overcome Moscow's reservations. The US team drafted a resolution for Bush to present to the NATO summit July 5-6 in London. It was not distributed to the allies until just a week before, with strictures that it should not be given, as would be usual, to the NATO bureaucracy. Bush and Baker began the cajoling, persuading routine again. Baker got agreement at 2 AM the night before the session. Giving NATO a new look to adjust to the "loss of the enemy" and to project an important review of its missions had been envisaged well before. There were many voices predicting that NATO was bound to fall apart once the Warsaw Pact collapsed, and the allies were determined not to let that happen.

But the new point was to find ways to console the Soviets and give Gorbachev a perch on which to alight. A key sentence was, "The Atlantic Community must reach out to the countries of the east which were our adversaries in the Cold War, and extend to them the hand of friendship." Proponents promised an enhanced role for the Conference on Security and Cooperation in Europe (CSCE), which Moscow now considered vital for its future status in Europe, and invited Gorbachev to address the NATO Council and all the Warsaw Pact members to establish regular liaison.

That was another important building block, but nobody expected it would bring immediate results. Gorbachev then surprised them all, in the sudden intuitive way he sometimes made decisions, shucking off the hesitations of advisers once he concluded he needed a deal and had won the best he could get. He met Kohl July 16 at the resort of Zheleznovdsk, near Stavropol where he had begun his rise in the Soviet party. Citing the July London declaration, he said it was now a changed NATO and he had no objection to Germany's membership.

In the meantime, the situation inside the Soviet Union was deteriorating badly. Moscow had not foreseen that keeping its troops in East Germany would become a tribulation, not an asset, as desertions and harassment from the population mounted. It had foreseen the trouble it faced bringing them home, without housing or jobs for them. Indeed, it was above all the disaffection of army officers who had no place to go when large numbers were demobilized that had brought Nikita Khrushchev's downfall.

Kohl was ecstatic. He promised $10 billion for housing and retraining for the troops when they went home and hard-currency pocket money while they were still in Germany. There were assurances of further economic aid and promises that established trade patterns with the GDR would not be broken abruptly.

At the beginning of the two-plus-four process, the American team had pushed through the idea that it would be a "steering group." The point was to block any Soviet effort to have the Four Powers decide on the future size and deployment of German forces and other measures, so that the eventual treaty would have no clauses limiting German sovereignty. Such issues were to be negotiated in other contexts, in the Conventional Forces in Europe negotiations or in the CSCE. The Soviets wanted everything in the same bag, a way of preserving certain rights. But Gorbachev accepted Kohl's pledge to reduce all German forces to 350,000, keep NATO out of the East, and make a separate treaty on withdrawal of all Soviet forces by 1994.

Genscher flew directly to Paris for the final two-plus-four session guaranteeing the Polish border. French Foreign Minister Dumas presided, but a French commentator noted that Paris had contributed nothing to the diplomacy but champagne to celebrate. There was some truth in the remark. London and Paris had tried fitfully to brake developments. But the Americans kept them on board when it came to facing Moscow, arguing that allied solidarity was important to the Soviet turnaround. There were no cracks to be exploited in the allied front when it mattered, though there had been plenty of friction, personal irritation, and moments of risk.

The deal was almost done. There remained formal completion of what came to be called the Treaty on the Final Settlement with Respect to Germany. Early in the process, the idea of finishing with a peace treaty that had been considered necessary for some forty years was discarded. It would involve too many countries and rake up too many bad memories when the point was to bury them. Even the intention of submitting the treaty for endorsement to the CSCE summit in November was dropped.

East Germany held further elections and reorganized itself into five new "länder" instead of a unitary state so that they could apply for inclusion in the Federal Republic under Article 23 of Bonn's Constitution.

But there was a last-minute hitch on the treaty that could have stalled everything. In what the Americans and other allies considered Kohl's careless excitement when Gorbachev surprised him with agreement, the chancellor had accepted provisions that no NATO forces or command structures could ever enter former GDR territory. That would leave a permanent demarcation line in a united country and might pose unforeseen future problems, the allies felt. There were tough negotiations in Berlin for four or five days in early September. The Germans were torn: They did not want to break with the Americans, who called it a "life or death issue," and they did not want to lose the treaty.

Once again, diplomacy found a winning formula by reference to the acceptable principle of self-determination. The restrictions would last until all Soviet troops had been withdrawn, by the end of 1994 at the latest, and "upon German request," Western allied forces would stay in Berlin during that period. But afterward, German forces under NATO could be stationed in the east as elsewhere in the country, "but without nuclear weapons." No foreign forces or nuclear weapons would be stationed or deployed there. The Soviets accepted that the compromise met their needs.

The treaty was signed in Moscow September 12. Unity and sovereignty were proclaimed at midnight October 3, with an emotional celebration and fireworks at the Brandenburg gate, now open to all. An elderly Berliner who had lived through it all—the war, the blockade, the Berlin Wall—summoned her son and grandchildren from the west for the occasion. In the jostling crowd from all parts of Germany, she heard an eastern-accented voice say with teary awe, "Jetzt bin ich Bundesburger" (Now I'm a citizen of Federal Germany). She smiled. After all, it had come in her lifetime. Hans Modrow, former communist party chief of Dresden who became prime minister to save the GDR after the fall of Honecker, chose the date for a trip to Japan—as far as one can get from Berlin without going into space.

The long-scheduled West German elections on December 2 were instead the first free all-German elections since Hitler took power. Kohl and Genscher triumphed. The SPD, which had kept warning against haste and the costly problems of unification, was punished by the voters. The old "German question" was history. New questions, arising from the disproportionate size and economic strength of the new country in the center of Europe, were on the horizon. But there were good reasons to feel confident that history would not repeat itself.

Not the least of these reasons was the smoothly successful diplomacy that guided and cemented the change. There had been arguments and temper tantrums, hurt feelings and misgivings. But no force and no crisis marked the settlement of an issue that had threatened the world with nuclear war for two generations. It had, essentially, been done in seven months. Many factors brought it about, but the approach that led to the feeling of "no losers, only winners," as President Mitterrand said at the CSCE summit in Paris, was not inevitable. It had to be managed with lucid skill and a clear sense of priorities, sober respect for both realities and appearances.

And the speed turned out to have been critical. Less than six months after the proclamation of unity, with war in the Gulf and Gorbachev stiffening at home and relying increasingly on hard-liners in the military and the KGB, it might have been impossible to complete the agreement.

A new Europe and, perhaps, a new diplomacy were arising from the result. The exercise showed it can be done, without any enemy to galvanize interests and overcome reluctance. Many other parts of the world could benefit from such an achievement of the old political art.

Notes

1. Interview with author at Krenz's villa in Pankow, outside Berlin, November 9, 1990.
2. *Ibid.*
3. Interview conducted in Moscow by Nathan Gardels, January 18-19, 1990, *New Perspectives Quarterly*, Spring 1990.
4. *Ibid.*

5.　Interview with author at Schabowski's apartment near the former Berlin Wall, November 10, 1990.

6.　Author's interviews with Németh, Horn, and ex-Premier Károly Grósz in Budapest in November 1990.

7.　Interview with author in Rakowski's office in Warsaw, December 1990.

8.　Interview with author in Jaruzelski's office in Warsaw, December 1990.

9.　Interview with Krenz, November 9, 1990.

10.　Interview with Schabowski, November 10, 1990.

11.　Interview with Krenz, November 9, 1990.

12.　*Ibid.*

13.　*Ibid.*

14.　Author's interview with Grimin at Soviet embassy in East Berlin, November 9, 1990.

15.　Author's interview with Genscher during CSCE summit, Paris, November 15-16, 1990.

16.　Author's interview with US official who requested nonattribution.

17.　Author's interviews with Genscher and US officials.

18.　*Ibid.*

19.　Author's interviews with Élysée and US officials who requested nonattribution.

20.　Author's interview with US official who requested nonattribution.

7

US-Japan Trade:
The Never-Ending Negotiations

Alan William Wolff and Thomas A. Kalil

US-JAPAN RELATIONS DETERIORATED significantly in 1991 and early 1992. The year began with a fight over Japan's contribution to the US-led effort in the Gulf, continued with a host of bilateral sectoral trade disputes, and culminated in President George Bush's trip to Japan. Japan's political leadership, apparently forgetting the adage that "the customer is king," infuriated the US public by stating that American workers are lazy, illiterate, and really work only three days a week. The US response was immediate. A new flurry of trade legislation aimed at Japan was introduced in the Congress, and private corporations and local governments initiated "Buy America" programs. By March 1992, the *Washington Post* would claim that "US-Japanese relations have suffered their most serious downturn in decades."[1]

This downward spiral led some analysts to predict a rupture in the relationship: an abrogation of the US-Japan security treaty, an abandonment of the multilateral trading system, a move toward regional trading blocs, and a trade war that would significantly reduce trans-Pacific flows of goods, services, and capital. But veteran observers of the US-Japan relationship are skeptical of doomsday scenarios. The United States and Japan have always managed to muddle through past trade disputes, usually after eleventh hour, highly publicized concessions from Japan made to an increasingly skeptical America. At least some Japanese elite now heavily discount warnings that Japan is on a collision course with the outside world.[2] Japan's business leadership also questions whether America's consumers are willing to forgo Japanese consumer goods and whether American man-ufacturers are able to do without Japanese components and capital goods.[3]

The Political and Economic Context

It is impossible to interpret the US-Japan economic and trade relation-ship in 1991 and 1992 without reference to a broader political and eco-nomic context. The end of the Cold War, the length and severity of the US recession, and US election-year politics stand out as three factors hav-ing had a large impact on the relationship.[4] Despite the premonitions of Japanese pollsters, who continually questioned US decisionmakers about what effect the fiftieth anniversary of Pearl Harbor would have on US public opinion, the date triggered only a flurry of "anniversary" stories in the US media. The effect of Japan's initial reluctance to support the US-led alliance in the Gulf was also transitory.[5]

Certainly, the most important event of 1991 (and of the postwar era) as the Cold War waned was the collapse of the Soviet Union. Policymakers began to discuss deep cuts in nuclear and conventional arms, a reduction in the US military presence in Europe, Western economic and technical assistance to the Commonwealth of Independent States (CIS), and partici-pation by the CIS in such Western institutions as NATO, the Interna-tional Monetary Fund, and the World Bank.

There was no shortage of theories as to how this transformation in the geopolitical environment would ultimately affect the US-Japan relation-ship. For example, some predict that America's economic competitiveness will improve as a result of reductions in defense spending and thus estab-lish the foundation for more balanced economic ties. Others believe that a common interest in containing Soviet power was the glue that held the al-liance together and that the elimination of this threat will allow conflict over economic issues to dominate the US-Japan agenda. Still other ana-lysts point to a post-Cold War agenda that both the United States and Japan could embrace: nonproliferation, regional security, global environ-mental issues, basic science, and economic development in the Third World, Eastern Europe, and the former Soviet Union.

Politics and recession were tandem problems. As the 1992 presidential election approached in the United States, Japanese officials became concerned that American politicians would "blame Japan" for the poor performance of the US economy.[6] Then-Commerce Secretary Robert Mosbacher suggested in December 1991 that Japan's closed markets had contributed to the length and severity of the recession. President Bush's decision to recast his trip to Asia and Japan by inviting twenty business leaders and putting "jobs, jobs, jobs" at the top of his agenda was clearly driven by domestic political concerns.

Japan's political and business elites overwhelmingly prefer Bush to his political opponents on the left and right. Since the Democratic party as a whole is viewed as protectionist, the Japanese government believes it has a stake in helping Bush get reelected.[7] Indeed, in private conversations with the Japanese, top Bush administration officials reportedly portrayed the US-Japan trade conflict as a political problem as opposed to an economic one. The argument was that Japan must make enough trade concessions to help the Bush administration keep the protectionists at bay.

In the primaries, Patrick Buchanan had questioned the economic patriotism of two top Bush political advisers who had Japanese clients by calling them "geisha girls of the New World Order." Democratic candidates Bill Clinton and Paul Tsongas had put some distance between themselves and the most hawkish trade policies. For example, in his commercials, Tsongas stated that while "others just blame the Japanese, Paul Tsongas will beat them, the American way, by making quality come first again."[8] Despite the attention it received on a sporadic basis in the primaries, there was no indication that trade would emerge as a central issue in the 1992 general campaign.

The State of the Debate

The events of 1991 and 1992 must also be placed in the context of the debate over the nature of US-Japanese economic competition. Participants in the debate (academics, members of Congress, administration officials, journalists, industry executives) disagree about the seriousness of Japan's economic challenge, whether Japan's political economy is "different" in ways that matter, and how the United States ought to respond to the Japanese challenge.

One issue is how serious that challenge is. US-Japan trade and competitiveness issues are obviously more important to the extent that one believes American industry is in deep trouble. Pessimists point to America's loss of market share in such key industries as semiconductors, automobiles, flat-panel displays, and machine tools. Massachusetts Institute of Technology's Charles Ferguson predicts that "If US and European [electronic] companies continue business as usual, they will either fail outright or become, in effect, local design and marketing subsidiaries of Japanese companies that will dominate a $1 trillion world hardware industry."[9] Economists such as Kenneth Courtis (Deutsche Bank) note that in 1990, Japan invested $660 billion in plant and equipment, as compared with the US investment of $510 billion.

Japanese businesses and commentators are also highly confident about the competitiveness of Japanese industry. As a roundtable discussion on the auto industry in the magazine *Shukan Toyo Keizai* illustrates, many are worried primarily about the political reaction to the expansion of Japanese industry:

> If Japanese car makers decide to maintain the same growth that they are now experiencing they will devour the competition. There is no discernible weak spot in the competitive strength of Japanese car makers. [automotive magazine publisher]

> Few segments of Japan's main industries are inferior to US or European industries, and if there was a determination to do so, any of those segments could become superior. However, in doing so the industry in the other country would become wiped out. [business commentator]

> Properly winning means absolutely no announcement of the victory.[10] [automotive magazine publisher]

Other analysts believe that the decline of the United States and the ascendance of Japan have been exaggerated. Optimists note that US exports have more than doubled since 1985; that the United States still maintains a commanding lead in industries such as aircraft, pharmaceuticals, software, and chemicals; and that the value of US capital goods exports has increased from 1.4 percent of GDP in the late 1960s to 4 percent today.[11]

In "Who Is Us?" Harvard professor Robert Reich adds a new dimension to the debate by questioning the linkage between the competitiveness of US corporations and America's standard of living. Reich argues that given the globalization of the US economy, "we should be less interested in opening foreign markets to American-owned companies (which may in fact be doing much of their production overseas) than in opening those markets to companies that employ Americans—even if they happen to be foreign-owned."[12]

Defining the Problem

Japan's economic success has sparked a heated debate as to its causes. Some believe that Japan's economic performance can easily be explained by Japan's high rates of savings and investment, a well-educated and motivated work force, and superior management skills.

As for Japan's current account surplus and America's current account deficit, most economists believe these are a function of savings/investment imbalances and real exchange rates in the two countries. In a recent review of the adjustment experiences of the advanced industrial countries, Paul Krugman notes that the US current account deficit declined from 3.6 percent of GNP in 1987 to 1.8 percent in 1990, while Japan's surplus declined from 3.6 percent to 1.7 percent during the same period. Krugman concludes:

> Exchange rate adjustment did and does work. Because of the substantial lags in adjustment, all major exchange rate adjustments are followed by a period of confusion and doubt about the adjustment mechanism. In the end, however, the depreciation of the dollar and the appreciation of the yen have had just about the effects that conventional wisdom would have predicted.[13]

This mainstream view has come under attack in recent years. "Revisionists" such as Chalmers Johnson, Jim Fallows, Karel von Wolferen, and Clyde Prestowitz claim that Japan's success in world markets cannot be understood without reference to Japanese institutions and practices. These include

- A "capitalist developmentalist state" that actively promotes Japanese industry through "visions," home market protection, research and development (R&D) subsidies, public corporations, tax incentives, low-interest loans, forced technology transfer, administrative guidance, and tolerance or encouragement of anticompetitive practices.
- A unique industrial organization that includes a dominance of the Japanese economy by six bank-centered industrial groups (*kinyu keiretsu*), a 70 percent rate of cross-shareholding by Japanese corporations, hierarchical relationships between leading manufacturers and their subcontractors (*kigyo keiretsu*) and distributors (*ryutsu keiretsu*).
- Public policies that systematically favor producer interests over consumer interests.

Revisionists argue that this environment allows Japanese companies to make large investments in R&D and plant and equipment with minimal regard to short-term profit and loss considerations. It also permits Japanese companies to charge higher prices for goods in the Japanese market and "dump" in overseas market, while restricting foreign investment and limiting access to the Japanese market. Revisionists also argue that this industrial system is effective, if not efficient, and that, if unchecked, Japan will eventually dominate most high value-added markets.

Although disagreeing with the policy recommendations of revisionists, economists such as the late Bela Balassa, Edward Lincoln, and Robert Lawrence have concluded that (1) Japan's imports of manufactured goods are some 25 to 45 percent lower than one would expect; (2) *keiretsu* may reduce Japanese imports by as much as $35 billion; and (3) Japan's level of intraindustry trade (exports and imports in the same commodity) is extraordinarily low by international standards.

Although some elements of the revisionist case have won broader acceptance, there is by no means a consensus on how the United States should respond. The "free trade" versus "managed trade" debate does not do justice to the range of options that have been proposed:

- The United States should stop its "aggressive unilateralism," "defang" Section 301 of the Trade Act, and concentrate on multilateral trade liberalization through the GATT.[14]
- The United States should continue the Bush administration policy of pursuing process-oriented, bilateral negotiations in specific sectors where Japanese trade barriers can be identified.
- The United States should continue negotiations on Japanese policies and practices (land use, savings/investment imbalances, enforcement of the antimonopoly law, *keiretsu* relationships, transparency of government policy) through the Structural Impediments Initiative, pursued by the Bush administration.
- Japanese corporations should voluntarily set goals for increases of imports of autos, auto parts, and other goods. The achievement of these goals should be supported by the United States and Japan (Bush/Miyazawa action plan).[15]
- Advanced industrial countries should work together to develop international rules and norms where they currently do not exist, such as in the areas of competition and innovation policy.[16]

- Where informal barriers exist, the United States should "insist on appropriate sectoral import levels that properly reflect the international competitiveness of US suppliers."[17] The Reagan and Bush administrations have used this approach with the 1986 and 1991 semiconductor trade agreements.
- The United States should insist that Japan's total imports of manufactured goods increase by 15 percent per year.[18]
- The United States should recognize that Japan is either unable or uninterested in becoming "more like us." The United States and Japan should negotiate ranges of acceptable outcomes, using international airline negotiations and agreements on capital-adequacy ratios for banks as models.[19]
- Japan should eliminate its bilateral trade deficit with the United States over the next five years, a proposal of House Majority Leader Richard Gephardt.

The debate over US-Japan trade policy is also closely linked to the "strategic industries" debate. Prying open the Japanese market or responding to Japanese industrial targeting, dumping, patent flooding, and acquisition of high-technology companies becomes much more important if one believes that certain industries and technologies will have a disproportionate impact on America's economic welfare. This premise is self-evident to US trading partners and provides an internal compass for their trade and technology policies. The comment that the United States should be indifferent as to whether it produces potato chips or computer chips may be apocryphal, but it does reflect the thinking of much of the economics profession and certain segments of the US government.

If the United States adopted a more activist technology policy, as has been suggested by groups such as the private-sector Council on Competitiveness, trade policy would not bear the burden that it currently does. This is perhaps most clear in the recent flat-panel display case. An antidumping petition, brought by a coalition of small US flat-panel display manufacturers, was vigorously opposed by America's largest computer manufacturers. IBM complained that the imposition of duties of up to 62.67 percent was "an eviction notice from the US government to makers of portable computers, the fastest growing part of the US computer industry."[20] If the United States had policy instruments in addition to trade remedies, the US display industry might not have filed this highly controversial antidumping case.

The Events of 1992: Déjà Vu

Many of the bilateral trade issues that were on the US-Japan agenda in 1991 and early 1992—auto parts, semiconductors, financial services, and construction—had been the subject of prior negotiations. Depending on one's views, this was proof that (1) the original agreement was worthless; (2) the Japanese government or private sector had not worked to fulfill the agreement; (3) the US private sector had failed to take advantage of the agreement because of low-quality products or lack of effort; or (4) the Americans are never satisfied and will continue to demand trade concessions as long as the Japanese government is prepared to dole them out.

Auto parts, for example, have been on the US-Japan agenda since the late 1970s. A Trade Facilitation Committee on auto parts, which was supposed to meet twice a year, was disbanded after Japan agreed in 1981 to restrain its auto exports to the United States. This committee was re-established in 1985, and auto parts were the subject of the 1986 market-oriented sector-selective talks in transportation machinery. The agreement reached in 1987, however, was little more than a call for cooperation in the collection of trade statistics.[21]

Although one would have thought that auto parts was a likely candidate for designation under "Super 301" in 1989 or 1990,[22] disagreements between the two major associations (the Automotive Parts and Accessories Association and the Motor Equipment Manufacturers) prevented this from occurring. In June 1991, the congressionally mandated Auto Parts Advisory Committee (APAC) released a report calling for the administration to "begin preparation" of self-initiated Section 301 and antidumping cases against Japan. APAC had also commissioned a study by the University of Michigan, which predicted that the US auto-parts deficit with Japan (which had increased from $4.4 billion in 1985 to $10.5 billion in 1990) would reach $22 billion by 1994.

Members of Congress were also incensed by revelations from a US Customs Service audit of American Honda Motor Company. Auditors determined that Honda had been significantly inflating its North American content—"of approximately $775 of materials or parts for the engine assembled in Ohio . . . only three parts ($9.06) and $42.69 of raw materials are sourced from US-based companies that do not have an equity relationship with Honda." This finding reinforced fears that Japanese auto manufacturers in the United States would maintain their exclusionary relationships with their Japanese suppliers.

Although administration officials did not embrace the APAC recommendations, they did negotiate an agreement with Japan to conduct a joint study of the sourcing of auto parts by Japanese auto manufacturers in Japan and in the United States. More important, as part of the US-Japan Global Partnership Plan of Action, Japanese manufacturers agreed to increase their imports of US auto parts by $2 billion and their purchases of auto parts in the United States by $8 billion. Although these pledges were regarded with skepticism by some,[23] representatives of APAC indicated that they would not press for a Section 301 case as long as Japanese companies delivered on their commitments.

A similar story can be told in semiconductors. US-Japan conflict in semiconductors began in the middle to late 1960s, when the United States began to put pressure on Japan to allow US companies such as Texas Instruments to establish foreign subsidiaries in Japan. The Japanese Ministry of International Trade and Industry (MITI) eventually did so, but only after requiring that US firms form joint ventures with Japanese companies, license their patents at reasonable prices, and accept limits on their production of integrated circuits. In the early 1970s, the Nixon administration pressed Japan to relax its tariff and quota barriers on semiconductors and even threatened to take Japan to the GATT. Japan agreed to formal liberalization, but also announced liberalization "countermeasures," such as subsidies, administrative guidance, and encouragement of cartel arrangements.[24] Japan's covert protectionist measures were successful at keeping the market share of US firms at roughly 10 percent. A 1983 agreement of the US-Japan High Technology Working Group on semiconductors was once again unsuccessful in providing meaningful market access to US companies.

In 1986, the United States and Japan signed a five-year agreement that called (in a secret side letter) for the foreign share of the Japanese market to reach 20 percent by June 1991. After President Reagan imposed sanctions against Japan in 1987 for failing to comply with the agreement, Japanese government and industry started to take it seriously. Japanese companies began to design US chips into Japanese autos, compact-disc players, telecommunications switches, and high-definition television sets.

In March 1990, when it was clear that the goals of the 1986 agreement would not be met, the chief executive officers of the major US semiconductor and computer companies began to develop a joint proposal for a new agreement. By October 1990, the Semiconductor Industry Association and the Computer Systems Policy Project had submitted a common position that called for less-intrusive antidumping measures against Japanese semiconductors and continued efforts to expand access to the Japanese market. Although elements of the US trade-policy community would have been happy to see the agreement lapse, the consensus agreement between the users and producers of semiconductors eventually served as the basis for the US government's negotiating position.

It was also fairly close to what the United States and Japan agreed to sign in June 1991. The system of "fair market values" (individual company minimum prices based on company-specific cost and price data) was replaced by an agreement that enabled rapid response to any future allegations of dumping. The last of the sanctions imposed against Japan in 1987 were lifted. The government of Japan agreed to recognize the US industry's expectation that foreign market share would reach 20 percent by the end of 1992, a seventeen-month extension of the goal contained in the 1986 agreement. The major stumbling block was the methodology for calculating market share—MITI insisted on a formula that in the US view artificially inflated foreign market share.[25] In the end, the United States agreed to a "two-formula" approach, but insisted that the first formula was the only relevant one.

It now appears that the semiconductor issue will be on the US-Japan bilateral agenda for some time to come. In early 1992, US semiconductor companies became increasingly unhappy with the lack of progress made under the agreement. Foreign market share, which had increased steadily in the 1988-1990 period, showed no signs of improving. Absent progress, renewed conflict on the issue of semiconductor market access seemed likely as the December 31, 1992, deadline approached.

A New Approach: The Structural Impediments Initiative

Frustration with endless sector-specific negotiations led to a search for a new mechanism to manage the US-Japan trade relationship. In 1989, in addition to initiating negotiations on wood products, satellites, and supercomputers under the Super 301 provision of the 1988 Trade Act, the US administration announced that it would begin talks on "structural impediments" that prevented the reduction of US and Japanese trade imbalances. After a year of wide-ranging discussions, the United States and Japan both announced a series of commitments designed to "contribute to further reductions in external imbalances" and promote "efficient, competitive and open markets." Japan made commitments in six areas: savings and investment imbalances, land policy, the distribution system, exclusionary business practices, *keiretsu* relationships, and pricing mechanisms. The US commitments were essentially a recitation of the administration's economic program, covering savings and investment, improvement of US competitiveness, corporate behavior, government regulation, research and development, export promotion, and work-force education and training.[26]

As Kozo Yamamura has pointed out, the Structural Impediments Initiative (SII) report is "replete with promises of laws to be drafted and passed, studies to be made, surveys to be conducted, administrative procedures to be changed, and data to be gathered."[27] Key members of Congress are skeptical of the exercise. Senator Max Baucus, chairman of the Senate Finance International Trade Subcommittee, has pressed the administration to develop benchmarks for measuring the results of the SII or to drop the SII process entirely and renew the Super 301 provision of the 1988 Trade Act.

The administration argues that the issues the SII is addressing will not produce immediate results and that Super 301 is not an appropriate instrument for negotiations on wide-ranging domestic reform. Although they profess to be unsatisfied with the pace of Japan's reform process, US officials point to a number of "noteworthy" Japanese actions since the release of the SII joint report:[28]

■ Japan has agreed to spend 430 trillion yen (roughly $3.3 trillion) on a ten-year public infrastructure program to reduce its savings-investment gap, the counterpart to its current account surplus.

■ Tax benefits for farmland in urban areas have been curtailed.

■ Japan's Large-Scale Retail Store Law has been amended to streamline approval procedures for store openings.

■ Japan's Fair Trade Commission has been somewhat more aggressive in taking formal action against violators of the antimonopoly law.

■ Japan has agreed to increase the transparency of government-business relations by, for example, putting administrative guidance in writing.[29]

■ Japan is requiring greater disclosure of *keiretsu* relationships—including stock holdings, related-party transactions, and major customer sales and purchases.

With an agreement by George Bush and Kiichi Miyazawa to reenergize the SII, US negotiators are considering whether to lengthen the list of

Japanese commitments. For example, one area of interest is corporate governance. The administration has noted that "*keiretsu*-affiliated firms, unlike firms based on traditional economic models, are not necessarily short-term profit maximizers. Often their main objective is to increase market share while preserving a domestic economic *status quo*." US negotiators plan to explore with the Japanese government measures that would increase the ability of shareholders to influence the management of *keiretsu*-affiliated companies, such as by making improvements in the proxy voting system.

These issues do go to the heart of the differences between US and Japanese industrial societies. It is not at all clear, however, that Japan is eager to make changes. Many Japanese believe that "corporate liberation from shareholder control" has been the sine qua non of Japan's economic success.[30] Others, most notably Akio Morita, argue that Japanese companies must stop their single-minded pursuit of market share if they wish to avoid a backlash from the United States and Europe. Japanese companies, Morita insists, should increase the salaries of their workers, raise their dividends to levels comparable to those of European and American companies, and contribute more to the environment and to their communities.[31] Genuine movement in this direction would help diffuse trade friction between Japan and the rest of the world, and the United States should participate in this debate to the maximum extent possible.

Low Politics No Longer: President Bush in Japan

Clearly, the most important event in US-Japan relations in 1991 and early 1992 was the president's trip to Japan. This trip was originally billed as a diplomatic mission to strengthen political ties with Asia, particularly with Japan. The president abruptly postponed the trip on November 5 after Senator Harris Wofford's surprise victory over former Attorney General Richard Thornburgh in the Pennsylvania Senate election. Bush's political advisers were also concerned by polls showing that 70 percent of Americans agreed that President Bush "spends too much time on foreign problems and not enough time on problems in this country."[32]

When Bush's trip was rescheduled for December 30 to January 10, the emphasis had shifted from diplomacy and the architecture of the post-Cold War era to "jobs, jobs, jobs." To underscore that point, the president invited twenty-two business executives to accompany him, including the chief executive officers of the Big Three auto manufacturers.

Critics charge that the president's trip was an unmitigated disaster, symbolized by his dramatic illness at a state dinner. Columnists accused him of abandoning his belief in free trade and embracing "managed" trade and of cynically attempting to blame the recession on Japan's unfair trade practices. His political opponents claimed that Japan's trade concessions were inadequate and that the voluntary pledges affecting Japanese companies lacked the enforceability of a government-to-government agreement. Others questioned why the executives accompanying President Bush were earning such large salaries, given the enormous financial losses of their companies. US auto manufacturers were soundly criticized for failing to close the gap between US and Japanese productivity and for failing to make cars with steering wheels on the left-hand side.

The media, however, did a poor job of reporting the accomplishments of the president's trip. It did represent the first time that trade issues with Japan had been publicly raised to the presidential level, which the US business community had advocated for years. It is now no longer the case that trade constitutes "low politics," as opposed to the "high politics" of national security and diplomacy. The level of cooperation between government and business on trade issues in preparation for and during the trip was also unprecedented. Furthermore, the US-Japan Global Partnership Plan of Action agreed to by President Bush and Prime Minister Miyazawa contained several trade agreements, which, if implemented, would lead to an improvement of the US-Japan trade relationship:

■ Japanese auto manufacturers agreed to increase their purchases of US auto parts from $9 billion in FY 1990 to $19 billion in FY 1994.

■ Japanese auto dealers' associations "reconfirmed their willingness to undertake dual dealerships to sell US automobiles." Japanese auto manufacturers set as a target the importation of 20,000 US autos.

■ Both governments agreed to support the plan's "Business Initiatives for Global Partnership." MITI had asked major Japanese companies to prepare voluntary plans for increasing imports, expanding local procurement by Japanese overseas subsidiaries, and increasing cooperation between Japanese and foreign firms. Twenty-three major Japanese companies had announced plans to increase imports by $10 billion from FY 1990 to FY 1993.

- A new agreement was reached on Japan's $5 billion public-sector market for computer products and services. The Computer Systems Policy Project, a coalition of the major US computer manufacturers, had raised the profile of this issue by commissioning a study on the relative performance of US firms in the private- and public-sector markets. The study found that US companies had 41 percent of the private-sector market for mainframe computers and 0.4 percent of Japan's national government market for mainframes.
- The United States and Japan agreed to "re-energize" the Structural Impediments Initiative.
- Progress is said to have been made on other issues as well, including market access for paper products and flat glass, the 1991 US-Japan Semiconductor Trade Arrangement, and standards and certification problems.

Unfortunately, the administration did an inadequate job of setting reasonable objectives for the trip and communicating those goals to the media and the public. The trip might not have been such a public relations disaster if the administration had communicated that

- Japan's trade barriers remain a serious problem that the administration is committed to addressing over a long-term period.
- Opening the Japanese market is only one of the measures the United States needs to take to revitalize the American economy.
- The trip would not (and could not) result in trade concessions sufficient to jump-start the US economy.

The War of Words

Both Japanese and Americans saw a sharp increase in harsh rhetoric in 1991 and 1992 that reflected hardening attitudes on both sides of the Pacific. A 1991 study sponsored by the Central Intelligence Agency (*Japan 2000*) warned that the Japanese were "creatures of an ageless, amoral, manipulative, and controlling culture," bent on world economic domination. In *The Coming War with Japan* (St. Martin's Press, 1991), two American academics, George Friedman and Meredith LeBard, wrote that Japan would attempt to force the United States out of the western Pacific and that the United States would either have to respond militarily or be content to be a "hemispheric" power. The book became a bestseller in Japan, although it received much less attention in the United States.

In the aftermath of the president's trip, several Japanese politicians made comments that further heightened tensions. On January 19, 1992, Speaker of Japan's Lower House Yoshio Sakurauchi said that American workers were lazy and illiterate, and that whereas IBM and the Big Three automakers once dominated global markets, "now the roles are reversed. America is saying to Japanese companies, 'Buy parts from us.' It's Japan's subcontractor." On February 3, Prime Minister Miyazawa commented on the "lack of a work ethic" in the United States.[33]

These remarks reflected Japan's increasingly negative views toward the United States. Japanese commentators coined new terms such as *kenbei* (dislike for America) or *bubei* (contempt for America) to capture this mood. Japanese began to talk of the need for a "Marshall Plan for America" to help the United States tackle AIDS, homelessness, drugs, and poorly run companies. The head of the Stanford University Japan Center in Kyoto noted that current Japanese public opinion "reminds me of the fall of 1941, when the Japanese were saying that America is decadent because it's filled with other races and falling to pieces."[34]

As a result of rising unemployment and unhappiness with the US-Japan trade relationship, some in the United States called for initiatives to "Buy American." The Los Angeles County Transportation Commission canceled a $122 million railcar contract with Sumitomo. Companies began to offer their employees significant incentives to buy American cars. A February 1992 *Washington Post*-ABC News survey found that two out of three Americans questioned were making a "conscious effort to avoid buying Japanese products."[35] Finally, in an incident that attracted even more attention, Senator Ernest Fritz Hollings told South Carolina workers on March 2, 1992, that they "should draw a mushroom cloud and put underneath it: Made in America by lazy and illiterate Americans and tested in Japan."

A "Meltdown" in the Relationship?

Although the US-Japan relationship was superficially calm in early 1991, this proved to be the quiet before the storm. There are plenty of reasons to be pessimistic about the US-Japan relationship during the remainder of the 1990s. Japan's trade surplus, which had started on a downward path in

1987, is expected to reach record levels in 1992. (This is occurring despite a significant shift of Japanese production to Southeast Asia, North America, and Western Europe.) Japanese overcapacity in some sectors, a result of heavy capital spending in the late 1980s, could trigger export drives and renewed dumping. US-Japan friction has expanded from traditional sectoral disputes. Many in the United States are concerned about Japanese purchases of high-technology companies, "glass ceilings" for American managers in Japanese subsidiaries in the United States, allegations that Japanese companies investing in the United States are maintaining their *keiretsu* relationships, and structural differences between the US and Japanese economies.

Given the downward spiral in the US-Japan relationship, it is no wonder that there are calls for "a return to normalcy." This is not the right course of action. Clearly, US political leaders must avoid pandering to the baser instincts of popular opinion. Xenophobic attitudes are unacceptable, as is "blaming Japan" for America's economic deficiencies. But it is also unacceptable to ignore genuine trade problems with Japan.

Thoughtful observers should recognize that the neoclassical model is often inadequate for analyzing the Japanese economy.[36] Although the revisionists can be overly polemical, their analysis of US-Japanese economic competition cannot be ignored. Japan's imports of manufactured goods, its level of inward direct investment, and its level of intraindustry trade are all extraordinarily low in comparison to other advanced industrialized countries. Japan has often used denial of foreign access to its market as a tool for creating competitive advantage. The United States should be alarmed by the loss of US market share to Japan in the industries of the twenty-first century, its sluggish productivity growth, and its inability to match Japan's rate of investment in plant and equipment and R&D. These underlying problems must be addressed before the US-Japan relationship can be genuinely improved.

Notes

1.   Don Oberdorfer, "US-Japan Relations Seen Suffering Worst Downturn in Decades," *Washington Post*, March 1, 1992, p. A-1.

2.   See, for example, Bill Emmott, *The Sun Also Sets* (New York: Times Books, 1989), p. 220. "Makoto Kuroda, who became the Ministry of International Trade and Industry's top trade official in 1986, summed up the real Japanese attitude in an interview when he told me that congressmen and other Americans were always claiming

that a trade crisis was looming and that time was running out. Yet, as Kuroda said, 'The earth still turns.'"

3.   T. R. Reid, "Japan's Premier-Apparent Talks Tough on US Trade Disputes," *Washington Post*, October 19, 1991, p. A-16. "Japanese exports are so closely integrated into America's economic structure," Miyazawa said, particularly citing Japanese microelectronic components used by US weapons makers. "If Japanese exports are stopped, there will be problems in the US economy."

4.   A full discussion of Japanese political and economic developments (for example, the possible gridlock triggered by recent political scandals) is beyond the scope of this essay.

5.   The United States complained about Japan's indifference to Iraqi aggression in Kuwait; Japan's attitude seemed to be that whoever controlled the oil would have to sell it. Japan was annoyed by US lack of appreciation for its large financial contribution to the Gulf War effort. Japan's unwillingness to send even noncombatants might have been a more significant issue if US casualties had been higher.

6.   The Japanese government tracked the results of the 1992 presidential primaries closely. MITI, for example, decided to postpone its decision on the extension of the voluntary restraint agreement on automobiles pending the outcome of the Illinois and Michigan primaries.

7.   In the 1988 campaign, one prominent financial analyst stated that the central banks of Japan and Germany should be registered as Republican political action committees, given their role in providing short-term assistance to the dollar.

8.   David E. Rosenbaum, "Candidates Playing to Mood of Protectionism," *New York Times*, January 26, 1992, p. A-1.

9.   Charles H. Ferguson, "Computers and the Coming of the US Keiretsu," *Harvard Business Review*, July-August 1990, p. 55.

10.   Trends in International Automobile Industry," *Shukan Toyo Keizai*, May 4, 1991, pp. 56-59.

11.   Lawrence B. Lindsey, "America's Growing Economic Lead," *Wall Street Journal*, February 7, 1992, p. A-14.

12.   Robert B. Reich, "Who Is Us?," *Harvard Business Review*, January-February 1990, p. 60.

13.   Paul R. Krugman, "Has the Adjustment Process Worked?," in C. Fred Bergsten, ed., *International Adjustment and Financing* (Washington, DC: Institute for International Economics), p. 313.

14.   Jagdish Bhagwati, "Aggressive Unilateralism," in Jagdish Bhagwati and Hugh T. Patrick, eds., *Aggressive Unilateralism: America's 301 Trade Policy and the World Trading System* (Ann Arbor: University of Michigan Press, 1990). Section 301 of the 1974 Trade Act provides the president with the authority to retaliate against "unjustifiable, unreasonable, or discriminatory" foreign trade practices that burden or restrict US commerce.

15.   "US-Japan Global Partnership Plan of Action," *Bureau of National Affairs Daily Executive Report*, January 10, 1992, pp. M-1–M-8.

16.   Sylvia Ostry, *Governments and Corporations in a Shrinking World* (New York: Council on Foreign Relations, 1990).

17.   Advisory Committee for Trade Policy and Negotiations, "Analysis of the US-Japan Trade Problem," Washington, DC, February 1989.

18.   Rudiger Dornbusch, "Give Japan a Target and Say 'Import!'" *New York Times*, September 24, 1989, Sec. 3, p. 2.

19.   Clyde V. Prestowitz, Jr., *Trading Places: How We Allowed Japan to Take the Lead* (New York: Basic Books, 1988).

20.   Jack Robertson, "ITC Finds US Display Firms Hurt," *Electronic News*, August 19, 1991, p. 1.

21.   For example, on the issue of relationships between auto manufacturers and their parts suppliers, the final report notes that "the US and Japanese Governments exchanged views regarding relations between vehicle makers and their parts suppliers in each country. As a result, it was revealed that the vehicle makers emphasize the importance of parts suppliers in the design and development of parts, the just-in-time systems, and the long-term and stable relationships between vehicle makers and parts suppliers. There are indications that the procurement policies of the US and Japanese industries are converging." Auto Parts Advisory Committee, "Overview of US Automotive Parts Trade with Japan: An Interim Report to the Secretary of Commerce," Washington, DC, 1990, Appendix 4.

22.   "Super 301" was a provision of the 1988 Trade Act that required the US trade representative to identify "trade liberalization priorities"—foreign trade barriers whose elimination has the greatest potential to increase US exports.

23.   The *Yomiuri Shimbun* noted that, at MITI's request, Japanese auto companies padded their targets by including items other than auto parts. Mazda's plan, for example, listed as US products the canned food used in company restaurants. *Yomiuri Shimbun*, November 28, 1992. The Economic Strategy Institute (headed by former US trade negotiator Clyde Prestowitz) pointed out that Japan's targets were contingent on a 50 percent increase in the production of Japanese transplants, which could put additional pressure on American-owned parts manufacturers.

24.   "In view of the worsening situation of domestic makers' profitability owing to the low-price offensive by US capital on the integrated circuit, the Ministry of International Trade and Industry began to deliberate a step toward the designation of the IC industry as a subject of cartel formation. . . . MITI's aim in this move is to lower the production cost, to prevent excessive competition, and to stabilize price through a unified and concentrated production." *Nihon Kogyo Shimbun*, January 8, 1972.

25.   MITI, for example, wanted to include chips produced in Japan for internal consumption by companies such as IBM.

26.   These commitments were spelled out in the Joint Report of the US-Japan Working Group on the Structural Impediments Initiative, June 28, 1990.

27.   Kozo Yamamura, "Will Japan's Economic Structure Change? Confessions of a Former Optimist," in Kozo Yamamura, ed., *Japan's Economic Structure: Should It Change?* (Seattle: Society for Japanese Studies, 1990), p. 54.

28.   See "Structural Impediments Initiative Joint Statement for the Record," Subcommittee on International Trade, Committee on Finance, United States Senate, March 13, 1992. This statement was jointly submitted by the office of the US trade

representative, the Departments of the Treasury, State, Commerce, Justice, and the Council of Economic Advisers.

29.   But see Yamamura, "Will Japan's Economic Structure Change?" He notes that "the vacuousness of this paragraph is evident to all familiar with administrative guidance, even without the qualifying causes." The *Asahi's* reaction to this paragraph was to the point: "When the report itself appears to depend on administrative guidance for carrying out much of what it promises, can all of that be done in writing?" Even if guidance is conducted in writing, "what are the chances of foreigners understanding what is really said in a document?" April 15, 1990.

30.   Koji Matsumoto, *The Rise of The Japanese Corporate System: The Inside View of a MITI Official* (London, Kegan Paul International, 1991).

31.   "Why Japan Must Change," *Fortune*, March 9, 1992, pp. 66-67. This is a summary of Morita's February 1992 *Bungei Shunju* article. Morita also notes, however, that "a company would hesitate to make even minor reforms in this regard, however, if it wants to remain competitive."

32.   Democrats, seeking to capitalize on this vulnerability, distributed "Anywhere But America Tour" T-shirts, highlighting the president's extensive foreign travels.

33.   Read in their entirety, however, Miyazawa's remarks were eminently reasonable. He stated that too many US university graduates had gone to Wall Street to perform leveraged buyouts and issue junk bonds as opposed to becoming engineers. The timing of his remarks was, at best, ill-advised.

34.   Michael Hirsh, "1992 Looks Like a Grim Year for US-Japan Relations," Associated Press, January 24, 1992.

35.   Richard Morin, "US Gets Negative About Japan," *Washington Post*, February 14, 1992, p. B-1.

36.   As Chalmers Johnson recently observed, "It is more likely that history will come to judge English-language academic economics as having the same relationship to Asian capitalism that academic Marxism-Leninism taught in the USSR had to the Soviet economy." Chalmers Johnson, "History Restarted: Japanese-American Relations at the End of the Century," paper delivered at the Economic Strategy Conference sponsored by the Economic Strategy Institute, Washington, DC, March 1992.

8

The Philippine Base Negotiations

*Richard L. Armitage**

ORMAL NEGOTIATIONS ON THE FUTURE of US military facilities on Philippine bases lasted from September 1990 until
August 27, 1991, when a Treaty of Friendship, Cooperation, and
Security was signed in Manila by Ambassador Frank Wisner for
the United States and Secretary of Foreign Affairs Raul Manglapus for the
Philippines. The treaty, which the United States planned to bring into
legal force as an executive agreement, was rejected by the Senate of the
Philippines on September 16, 1991. Subsequent discussions in Manila focused on establishing a three-year time frame for US forces to withdraw
from Subic Naval Base, the only installation containing a US facility in the
wake of Mt. Pinatubo's June 1991 eruptions. These discussions foundered. On December 31, 1991, the government of the Philippines issued a
formal notice that the 1947 Military Bases Agreement (MBA) would terminate in one year. US forces are now scheduled to be withdrawn completely
from Subic by December 31, 1992.

The formal talks had been preceded by an exploratory round in Manila
in May 1990 to determine whether there existed a mutually acceptable
basis for replacing the MBA. The need either to replace it or terminate the
American presence had, from the perspective of Manila, a sense of urgency dictated by the following provision of the Philippine Constitution:

XVIII.25 After the expiration in 1991 of the Agreement between the Republic of
the Philippines and the United States of America concerning Military Bases, for-

---

*The author served as the principal US negotiator.

eign military bases, troops or facilities shall not be allowed in the Philippines except under a treaty duly concurred in by the Senate and, when the Congress so requires, ratified by a majority of the votes cast by the people in a national referendum held for that purpose, and recognized as a treaty by the other contracting State.

The United States took the view that this provision misrepresented the intent of the MBA as amended in 1966, which provides:

XXIX Unless terminated earlier by mutual agreement of the two governments, this Agreement and agreed revisions thereof shall remain in force for a period of 25 years from September 16, 1966, after which, unless extended for a longer period by mutual agreement, it shall become subject to termination upon one year's notice by either government.

The US position was that the earliest the government of the Philippines could present a one-year notice of termination was September 16, 1991, with the legal sanction for the US military presence expiring no earlier than September 16, 1992. On May 14, 1990, the Philippines presented the United States a notice of termination effective September 16, 1991, one year earlier. Despite the confusion and false sense of emergency created by imprecise language in the Philippine Constitution and what the United States considered a premature deadline, the US delegation assured its Philippine counterpart that the notice of termination need not preclude the complete replacement of the MBA before September 16, 1991. From the vantage point of May 1990, there appeared to be sufficient time for negotiations, drafting, debate, and ratification. Indeed, the initial target date for completing the new agreement (exclusive of Philippine Senate action) was the end of January 1991.

As 1991 dawned, however, it was clear that the United States was very far indeed from an agreement with the Corazon Aquino government. The Philippine negotiating panel, nominally headed by Secretary of Foreign Affairs Manglapus but in fact dominated by Secretary of Health Alfredo Bengzon, was clearly in no hurry to come to terms. Bengzon, a longtime opponent of an American military presence in the Philippines, had succeeded in recruiting staff for the panel consisting of activists with similar views who were drawn from various government departments and agencies. Under the effective direction of Bengzon, the panel had exhausted calendar year 1990 with repeated acts of political theater. They apparently hoped to increase the likelihood of one of two outcomes: the complete removal of US forces from Philippine bases by September 1991 or soon thereafter; or the creation of new arrangements permitting an extension of the US tenure to perhaps June 12, 1998 (the centenary of the Constitution promulgated by Filipino patriot Emilio Aquinaldo) accompanied by operational restrictions and massive US remittances in the form of annual "compensation."

The key elements of the 1990 drama directed by Bengzon and his aides centered on the following:

- Serving the MBA termination notice as mentioned earlier without prior consultation one would have expected between two allies. The action deliberately fed the anti-American frenzy already at work among many of Manila's twenty-eight daily newspapers and increased the security risk to the visiting US delegation.
- Leveling public accusations of US bad faith with respect to an alleged "shortfall" in assistance levels that President Reagan had undertaken to provide (subject to congressional approval) in his letter to President Aquino of October 17, 1988.
- Demanding that the United States remove permanently its F-4 jet aircraft from Clark Airbase by September 1991. A State Department travel advisory issued in September 1990 warned that because of unsettled internal security conditions, US citizens should avoid nonessential travel to the Philippines. The Philippines had been given twenty-four hours' notice that the advisory would be issued. It was the view among US negotiators that the "combat aircraft crisis" was generated by Manila on short notice in order to divert attention from the travel advisory. The government was understandably sensitive about negative publicity concerning the internal security situation and its impact on the public image of the Aquino administration.

The negotiating process did begin to gather speed in 1991, however, and the US side hoped that the theatrical repertoire had been exhausted and serious business had begun. Notwithstanding the accumulation of Philippine grievances (which began with Admiral George Dewey's arrival in Manila Bay in 1898) and in spite of serious concerns about the motivations and objectives of Bengzon and his assistants, US negotiators were reasonably confident that neither President Aquino nor many Filipino senators took the theater seriously or really intended to protract a degenerative crisis with their closest ally and strongest international supporter.

Indeed, US negotiating objectives seemed, in the US view, to be reasonable and, if achieved, an attractive outcome for the Philippines.

US Objectives

The United States sought a ten-year agreement covering US use of facilities on Subic Naval Base, Clark Airbase, and the smaller facilities (Wallace, O'Donnell, and San Miguel) associated with them. A tenure of this nature should have been sufficiently long to encourage the US Congress to appropriate much-needed military construction funds and to allow Manila time to draft realistic plans for the conversion of the facilities to civilian use and to accumulate funds for the implementation of those plans. As a token of seriousness in this regard, the United States agreed that Clark Airbase should be immediately reconfigured to accommodate both Philippine Air Force operations and civilian economic enterprises. A decade, compared with the ninety-nine-year (amended in 1966 to twenty-five-year) duration associated with the 1947 MBA, was viewed by the US side as sufficiently short to attract the acquiescence of Filipinos who desired the eventual complete withdrawal of US forces. The United States was willing to discuss a duration of under ten years, but in light of the parlous economic situation in the Philippines, it seemed unlikely that Manila could offer feasible alternatives to Filipino employees of the facilities and contractors dependent on the facilities in less than a decade. The United States was not willing to play the assigned role of the departing neocolonialists in a June 12, 1998, pageant scripted and choreographed by Bengzon and his acolytes. Finally, the United States was willing to discuss the gradual "phase-down" of US forces over ten years, a process that would make it feasible for the Philippines either to negotiate a long-term access agreement with the United States or ask US forces to withdraw completely.

The United States was also willing to address, within the limits of customary international practices, the concerns expressed by the Philippines in an area denoted by the code word "sovereignty." One of the enduring myths propagated by self-styled "nationalists" in the Philippines is that in 1947, the United States imposed its military presence on an unwilling Philippines by means of an unequal agreement (the MBA) that thoroughly stained both the honor and independence of the republic. In fact, President Manuel Roxas asked the United States to stay in order to forestall the virtually complete abandonment of his prostrate country by the Truman administration.[1] In any event, the United States was quite willing to increase the visibility of Filipino base commanders and to negotiate a new Status of Forces Agreement (SOFA) fully consistent with the more than thirty such agreements the United States has around the world. The complete subordination of US forces and their dependents to Philippine civil and criminal jurisdiction, as suggested by Philippine negotiators, was totally unacceptable to the United States and a significant time-wasting obstacle for several months.

The United States was also willing to subsume the issue of military bases in a broader discussion covering the entire bilateral relationship and thus participated in the Philippine-American Cooperation Talks (PACT). The Philippine side had asked that the discussions be broadened to demonstrate convincingly to the Philippine Senate that the relationship amounted to more than bases, but that bases were an organic part of a relationship that conveyed great benefits to the Philippines in terms of trade, science and technology, and culture and education. The US side agreed to US participation, but cautioned the Philippine panel not to expect US financial undertakings in any of the "nondefense" areas under discussion. The US team's suspicions were later justified when the Philippine side demanded, among other things, trade concessions and official debt relief in return for a new bases tenure.

Two Key Issues

By May 1991, the negotiations had centered on the two key questions of compensation and duration. Technical teams representing the two sides were making very slow progress—but progress nonetheless—on the SOFA and on issues pertaining to the phased drawdown of US forces, the types of units that would be permitted to use Philippine bases, and the precise delineation of US, Philippine, and joint-use areas on Clark Airbase. By February, however, it had become clear that the ability of the United States to resolve to its satisfaction many of the outstanding technical issues had become hostage to the Philippine government's expectations concerning assistance levels. By the same token, the range of assistance levels the United States was willing to consider was dependent not only on satisfactory resolution of the technical issues but also on the actual length of time the United States could continue to operate at the facilities.

The two sides had fundamentally differing views not only about compensation levels but about the nature of compensation itself. A brief summary of the two approaches helps to understand how the negotiations unfolded.

The Philippine government viewed compensation as rent—as a contractual obligation that ought not be a qualified pledge of "best efforts" by the US executive branch to obtain congressional approval of the agreed sum. The Philippine government claimed that the continued use of its bases by US military forces delayed Philippine development activities; thus, compensation was seen as covering, at least in part, opportunity costs allegedly forgone by delaying the civilianization and Filipinization of the bases. The idea of linking significant portions of US assistance explicitly to bases as "compensation" had originated with President Ferdinand Marcos in 1979. As a result of the 1988 MBA five-year review, President Reagan pledged his best efforts to provide the Philippines, over fiscal years 1990 and 1991, a total of $962 million in security assistance, development and commodity assistance, and housing investment guarantees. It was the inability of the administration to provide the prorata 50 percent of the $962 million in fiscal year 1990 that permitted Manila to wage a strident, emotional anti-US propaganda campaign during the May 1990 exploratory talks.

Not surprisingly, the US view of "compensation" was markedly different from that of the Philippines. The United States and the Philippines are allies under the terms of a mutual defense treaty, and as matters of policy and practice, the United States does not pay "rent" for the use of an ally's military facilities. Nevertheless, the United States recognizes instances in which it is difficult for some allies to assume the financial burdens associated with regional security and, in some such cases, provides economic and military assistance in a variety of forms. As a particularly pertinent example, the United States had provided the Aquino government between 1986 and 1989 with (according to US embassy estimates) more than $900 million in financial benefits in excess of the compensation levels agreed to with President Marcos in 1983. Yet in May 1990, the United States found itself being pilloried in a public manner by the Philippine government for an alleged shortfall of some $96 million in the fiscal year 1990 assistance allocation for the Philippines.

During initial "feeling out" conversations about compensation in autumn 1990, the US team had urged Secretary Manglapus to break completely with the Marcos-era practice of linking aid levels to bases arrangements. The US side tried to convince him that although the needs of the Philippines were indeed increasing, the value of the facilities to the United States was decreasing.

US force levels at Clark and Subic would be cut substantially over the next decade even if there were no Philippine pressure to do so. The Cold War seemed very much over in autumn 1990. US domestic base closures were expected to increase pressures in Congress to eliminate overseas bases. Most important, however, Manila itself was depreciating the value of the bases to the United States by conducting a public relations vendetta (in full hearing range of President Bush and the Congress) over the short-fall issue, by having successfully called for the removal of US jet aircraft from Clark, and by insisting upon a dead-end, phase-out agreement of considerably less than ten years' duration. US negotiators would not, under any circumstances, agree to a five-, seven-, or even ten-year compensation scheme that Congress might not uphold, thereby risking more debilitating crises over alleged shortfalls. Neither did the negotiators think it wise for the Philippines to tie significant portions of US assistance to the sinking ship (indeed, the ship Manila seemed positively intent upon sinking) represented by military bases.

In light of the jaundiced view in which a good many key US legislators held the Aquino government, the US team thought it would be politically astute for President Aquino to seize the initiative and denounce the Marcos-inspired linkage between aid and bases as precisely the sort of symbolic dependency the Philippines wished forever to abolish. The US team hoped for a declaration reaffirming the relevance of the US-Philippine alliance and calling upon Congress to view aid levels as a function not of some mean-spirited landlord relationship with a tenant but of traditional friendship and shared democratic values. US negotiators believed such a declaration would have arrested dramatically declining support in Congress for maintaining a Philippine assistance account of over $550 million in fiscal year 1991. Further, it could have frustrated the designs of Bengzon and his friends to forge a tactical alliance between those who wanted US forces out of the Philippines altogether and those who wanted the Philippines to be the permanent ward of the US taxpayer.

It is not known whether these hopes as expressed to Secretary Manglapus were relayed to President Aquino, whose interest in reversing practices initiated under Marcos was, as a general matter, understandably high. In any case, they were never realized.

Philippine Proposal Surprises United States

In February 1991, Manila spelled out its position on compensation. For an agreement of not more than seven years, the Philippines wanted $825 million per year: $400 million in cash grants and $425 million in such non-budgetary assistance as guaranteed trade access through increased export quotas and forgiveness of official indebtedness. Manila also wanted three entire categories of US assistance *not* counted against bases compensation: the contribution of the United States to the Multilateral Assistance Initiative (MAI), development assistance, and food aid under Public Law 480—total support worth some $233 million in the fiscal year 1992 budget request.

The Aquino government's proposal was breathtaking in scope. It completely disregarded US law concerning unrestricted grants of taxpayer funds. It tied more—not less—of the fruits of the overall bilateral relationship to a military bases arrangement. And it desired, within the space of a very few years, to abolish the arrangement itself.

US negotiators were prepared to agree with the Philippine bases panel to exclude the MAI contribution and food aid from the compensation scheme. Japan, a mainstay in MAI, did not wish to see this international effort made contingent on a bilateral bases relationship. Donors of food aid prefer to see it serve solely humanitarian purposes. Although the United States had wanted to abolish compensation completely, it seemed that the other categories of US assistance—foreign military financing grants, economic support funds grants, military training grants, and development assistance grants—were all potentially "countable" if Manila insisted on keeping the linkage between aid and the bases. President Bush, in early February 1991, had requested almost $363 million for the Philippines in these four accounts for the fiscal year beginning in October 1991. The US team advised the Philippine negotiating panel that the United States would seek to sustain an annual appropriation of this size in return for an acceptable ten-to-twelve-year agreement. For a seven-year arrangement, however, the United States would not wish to commit itself to anything beyond $240 million per year in these four categories.

As the February 1991 round in Manila drew to a close, therefore, the US negotiators believed they had at least bracketed the compensation problem. They saw Manila's $825 million proposal as a bargaining ploy; indeed, they saw the $400 million cash grant as the real kernel of the proposal—the essence of bases-related compensation. The US team could not imagine, for instance, that the Philippines would actually wish to link what it hoped would be an expanding trade relationship to a contracting bases relationship. By the same token, the Philippine bases panel might well believe that the US offer of $240 million per year for a seven-year deal was merely an opener. In short, the US team believed the compensation issue was manageable. The last act in the February round was to agree with Manglapus and Bengzon on press guidance for spokespersons on public affairs—parameters that would help them keep in complete confidence the opening discussions on compensation.

Imagine, therefore, the shock when, 40,000 feet over the Pacific en route to Japan, the US negotiating team received a call from the US embassy in Manila informing them that the spokesman for the Philippine panel, Ambassador Raul Rabe, had gone public with the Aquino government's compensation proposal during the joint press briefing. Rabe's revelations were not a slip of the tongue. In a prepared statement, he opened characteristically by caricaturing the US position under the pretext of responding to "recent press reports" (leaks from the Philippine side), and then he spelled out the Philippines' "minimum package for a seven-year duration." He stated that the Philippines proposed "taking $400 million in a cash grant as the first tranche which we can use to support a bond issue we can offer to our regional partners. . . . To close the gap between $825 million and $400 million, we can explore . . . improved trade access and arrangements for debt reduction or condonation."

The Aquino government's decision to advertise its compensation gambit in public established a standard of performance in the compensation arena it had no hope of attaining. Filipino officials who subsequently offered explanations for Rabe's remarkable performance gave conflicting accounts of its genesis. Some claimed it was a signature Manglapus tactic used previously and with very limited success, one that involved floating a number in public and then imploring the other side to spare him the political humiliation of failing to deliver. Others maintained that Manglapus would not have reneged on jointly agreed press guidance, but that Bengzon—in a poison-pill maneuver to set up President Aquino for a stinging rebuke should she ever submit a compromise proposal to the Senate—handed Rabe a statement and ordered him to read it. Regardless of "whodunit" for whatever purpose, the long-term effect of the Rabe statement was to engrave the number "825" in stone and to inject trade and debt forgiveness into a discussion that was supposed to center on military bases.

During March and April 1991, discussions continued via cable traffic and featured a visit by Secretary Manglapus to Washington. It had become clear that Manila's technical panels addressing SOFA and military operating procedures had gone as far as they were authorized to go absent a breakthrough on compensation. Yet no breakthrough seemed imminent.

The US delegation's seventh visit to Manila, which lasted from April 29 to May 3, ended with the gauntlet being dropped by the United States on the compensation issue. The US departure statement, read by the US embassy's counselor for public affairs at a press conference, concluded with the following words:

> The US side is, in sum, satisfied that it has done the best it can under current circumstances with respect to bases-related compensation. It has moved a considerable distance toward meeting the needs of the Philippine side since January of this year, when the issue was first tabled. Although no one will deny that the developmental needs of this country are great, and no one will begrudge the Philippine side for having tried to do its very best for citizens of this country, the US ability to meet these needs has its limit. The limit with respect to bases-related compensation has been reached. The US position contains nonmonetary elements which provide the foundations for a new relationship which will benefit our peoples for many years to come. The ultimate question is not whether the United States is willing to go back to the well to produce more dollars which do not exist, or to tie extraneous economic activities to a basing tenure which, in a few years, may cease to exist. The question is whether or not the Philippines wants this new relationship.[2]

The limit had indeed been reached. It would be difficult to overstate the sense of growing impatience, frustration, and even anger within the US administration and Congress over the dilatory tactics of the Philippine panel. This general feeling of dissatisfaction with the interlocutors stemmed in large part from the realization that bureaucratic mountains had been moved within the United States to accommodate Manila's concerns, with scarcely an acknowledgment, much less a courteous "thank you" in return. Upon departing Manila on May 3, the US team's compensation offer consisted of the following elements:

■ $362.8 million in annually appropriated funds, consisting of military purchase grants, economic support fund grants, development assistance grants, and grants for the training of military personnel. The United States also agreed to shift, over time, funds from the military purchasing account to economic support and development assistance. Manila was also given the right to retire official military indebtedness with new military financing grants.

- Excess defense articles and excess medical equipment would be provided free of charge and transported without cost to the Philippines. Because of uncertainties concerning the precise times when excess stocks would become available, the United States declined to commit to an annual dollar-value figure. US estimates, however, were that the Philippines would take possession of something on the order of $1 billion worth of fully serviceable items over a ten-year period.
- The "Buy Philippines" program, which had pumped $206.6 million into the Philippine economy in fiscal year 1990 through the sale of local goods and services to US forces by virtue of a balance-of-payments waiver, would be reinstituted instead of being terminated along with the MBA.

Assuming the Buy Philippines program produced profits of about $100 million per year, and that excess defense and medical articles would also be worth about $100 million per year, the United States was offering the Philippines more than $560 million annually in compensation. This was a figure exclusive of the MAI contribution ($160 million requested in fiscal year 1992), food aid ($33 million requested in fiscal year 1992), and US assistance to the Philippines in securing access to new lines of credit (valued by the Philippines itself at $50 million per year). Furthermore, the textile agreement with the Philippines contained built-in growth features worth about $70 million per year. The United States also agreed to help Manila raise money (about $2 billion) from regional partners for debt buy-backs and development projects, a "good offices" activity to which the Philippine government assigned a value of $100 million per year. In short, if the name of Manila's game was reaching the number "825," the United States had allowed it to win.

Yet the definition of "winning" seemed to mean different things to different people within the Aquino administration. The rejectionists on the bases panel, having played the compensation card for all it was worth, turned their attention next to the duration issue. The US side had proposed a compromise term of nine years, with one additional year for the complete withdrawal of US forces in the event Manila chose not to renew the agreement or to negotiate a long-term access arrangement. The Philippine panel, which had moved from three years to five years in its previous positions, now (as of late May 1991) offered a seven-year duration *inclusive* of a withdrawal period. Accompanying this new position was a plea from

President Aquino that the United States accept as sincere and accurate her judgment that seven years was the absolute maximum to which the Senate would agree.

The US reaction to President Aquino's apparent predicament was basically sympathetic. As the month of June approached, the US team was becoming increasingly curious as to when, if ever, she might realize that her bases negotiating panel had been hijacked by stridently anti-American elements. US Ambassador Nicholas Platt advised President Aquino that in order for her seven-year proposal to receive serious consideration in Washington, particularly in connection with the level of compensation offered, US military services would need seven good years at the facilities—that is, seven years *plus* a withdrawal period, if needed. On June 11, with Mt. Pinatubo rumbling ominously in the background, Manila offered a duration of "seven plus one." At the same time, however, Secretary Manglapus informed the US team officially that agreements reached several months earlier between the two panel chairmen on criminal-jurisdiction matters within the draft SOFA were no longer operative according to the advice of the Philippine Department of Justice. Clearly Manglapus, whose grip on the panel had always been tenuous, was not in control. More to the point, from the US perspective, the question remained whether President Aquino had any intention of doing something about the various manifestations of official skulduggery brought repeatedly to her attention.

June 1991: Mt. Pinatubo Erupts

The cataclysmic eruption of Mt. Pinatubo rearranged the landscape of central Luzon, and, with it, the agenda of the base negotiations. Within hours, Clark Airbase, Camp O'Donnell, Wallace Air Station, and Naval Station San Miguel were all but off the agenda. Clark, in particular, had been rendered useless by the prospect of future massive mudslides from volcanic ash, hundreds of feet deep, accumulated on the slopes of Pinatubo. Camp John Hay, a rest and recreation center in northern Luzon, was unaffected by the volcano and returned, as previously scheduled, to full Philippine control on July 1, 1991. Subic Naval Base, though not subject to prospective mudflows, was virtually buried in volcanic ash and saddled with reconstitution costs estimated in excess of $250 million.

How to proceed in the wake of Pinatubo presented a real dilemma. The American embassy in Manila was of the view that all the SOFA and operational obstacles might be dismantled in short order if US negotiators were to restate the essentials of the emerging deal in terms of the US compensation proposal of May coupled with the Philippine's "seven plus one" duration proposal of June. Although President Aquino might have accepted such a proposal with alacrity, opponents to a base agreement may well have continued their delaying tactics and prepared themselves for a final showdown in the Senate.

Pinatubo created a new situation for the United States. The Navy would not have been eager to spend money for Subic's complete reconstitution if it could anticipate only a seven-year tenure. Congress and the American people, moreover, transfixed by the images of Pinatubo's destructive fury, might have thought the administration extravagant to offer the same amount of money for the use of one severely damaged installation. It was, after all, the Philippines that had given the negotiations the ambience of a particularly contentious real estate transaction. The US team's negotiating guidance was clear—get more time for Subic in order to amortize the repair costs and lower the amounts explicitly linked to base compensation. Above all, US negotiators were to seek an agreement that would not outrage Congress or inflame American public opinion.

The US approach, therefore, consisted of the following:

- In view of the massive humanitarian problems caused by Pinatubo, the United States would seek to keep intact the entire sum ($362.8 million) in base-related compensation requested by the president for fiscal year 1992.
- The United States would seek a duration of ten years for Subic Naval Base and give up all the remaining facilities.
- From 1993 on, the United States would again try to delink aid and bases. The US delegation proposed that Manila accept something akin to the formulation worked out between the United States and Greece in recent base negotiations—that is, a specific US assistance undertaking would be made for one year only, accompanied by a commitment to seek unspecified "appropriate levels" for the agreement's remaining years. Such an approach would spare the Aquino government the political risk of being seen as accepting a lower compensation amount in the wake of Pinatubo by injecting into the formulation a very large dose of creative ambiguity.

The eighth and final visit of the US delegation to Manila took place in July 1991. An agreement in principle, reflected in a joint statement issued on July 17, was reached. Its major provisions were as follows:

- The government of the Philippines accepted a ten-year duration for US operations at Subic Naval Base.
- The United States agreed to turn over Clark Airbase by September 1992 and the smaller installations by September 1991.
- The Philippines rejected the notion of delinking aid and bases. It accepted instead a "modified Greek formula" that called upon the executive branch of the US government to seek $362.8 million (the combined total of four accounts) in fiscal year 1992, and not less than $203 million in security assistance monies (military purchase grants, economic support fund grants, and training grants) during each year starting in fiscal year 1993. Development assistance funds, set at $100 million by the House of Representatives for fiscal year 1992, were therefore decoupled from base compensation. This had been Manila's preference several months earlier.
- All other nondefense initiatives would remain intact. One of the most important, from the perspective of President Aquino, was the creation of a US-Philippine Program Review Group. The group would meet annually at the beginning of the US budget cycle and would afford Manila extraordinary access to key nodes within the US interagency arena.

Even though Bengzon and his key assistant had left the bases panel several weeks before the key July round, their legacy survived. It took nearly six more weeks of tortuous technical negotiations on operational procedures and SOFA issues before Manila was finally prepared to sign the Treaty of Friendship, Cooperation, and Security on August 27. In fairness, about two weeks were absorbed by US interagency deliberations about whether a document the United States intended to bring into legal force as an executive agreement could, or should, be called a "treaty." Yet even at the eleventh hour, a Filipino under secretary of defense threatened to scuttle the signing ceremony over which President Aquino was scheduled to preside because of a trivial and esoteric issue concerning air space over one of the facilities. The new US ambassador, Frank Wisner, quickly papered over the dispute and spared President Aquino yet another humiliation at the hands of her bases panel.

The treaty itself consisted of eleven articles (Article VII, Defense Cooperation and Use of Philippine Installations being the most important) and three supplementary agreements (Cultural and Educational Cooperation, Installations and Military Operating Procedures, and SOFA). The US commitment to "provide security assistance to the Government of the Philippines to assist in the modernization and enhancement of the capabilities of the Armed Forces of the Philippines and to support appropriate economic programs" was supplemented by a letter from President Bush to President Aquino. The letter spelled out the administration's base-related compensation undertakings (in accordance with the July 17 joint statement) and also summarized many nondefense areas of bilateral cooperation from which the Philippines drew and would continue to draw significant benefits.

President Aquino replied with two letters, both dated August 27. The first praised President Bush's letter as constituting "a basis for cooperation between our two Governments in the areas of security, economic, and other forms of assistance." The second took the president to task for not undertaking to provide excess defense articles valued at "an average of $150 million annually . . . inclusive of 'lethal' articles." Such an undertaking had not been agreed to during the talks. President Aquino then took advantage of a congratulatory telephone call from President Bush to discuss at some length the subject of debt relief. Neither the second letter nor the telephone conversation served to stimulate US interest in the outcome of the ratification debate in Manila.

The Aquino administration nevertheless worked vigorously to secure ratification of the treaty. It could not, however, overcome the legacy of its own negotiating tactics. Within the Senate, a coalition was formed by three or four senators who opposed a continued US presence under any terms and eight or nine senators who professed to be disappointed with the compensation package. The latter group repeatedly baited Secretary Manglapus for allegedly having accepted $203 million instead of $825 million in compensation. Although it was an apples-and-oranges comparison totally unfair to the government, in a way the Aquino administration found itself on the receiving end of tactics and arguments strikingly similar to those it had used against the United States over the previous fifteen months.

Philippine Senate Rejects Treaty

The Philippine Senate's rejection of the treaty in September 1991 was attributable to many causes. The Philippine Senate was a tough audience, consisting in large part of people who suffered under the rule of Marcos, a dictator seen by many in the Philippines as having been propped up by the

United States solely for the sake of military bases. The constituency within the Philippine Senate for continuing to receive US economic and security assistance had been weakened by constant (and essential) US demands for economic reform and the unrelenting US insistence upon aid-reform conditionality. Virtually every one of the senators who voted against the treaty had also voted consistently against economic reform legislation.

Possibly most important, President Aquino never articulated a comprehensive personal view of the overall issue and did not, until after August 27, 1991, demonstrate visible leadership on the bases question. Instead she tried to play peacemaker within her government and between her people and the Senate, thereby leaving the field wide open to anti-American activists on the negotiating panel who subsequently abandoned her. They, at least, had a clear idea of what they wanted.

It is also true that few Filipinos of any political persuasion believed the United States would actually leave the bases under any circumstances. Many important Filipinos have a greatly exaggerated and wholly unjustified view of the strategic importance of their archipelago to the United States, a perspective combined with a crippling sense of powerlessness vis-à-vis their former colonial mentor. In a very real sense, therefore, Filipino negotiators and senators probably felt quite secure in believing that somehow the United States would find a way to stay, to forgive their unruly behavior, to shower them with gifts, and, in general, to patch things up. Several of the senators who voted against the treaty may have regarded their votes as only symbolic or advisory. President Aquino's prevote threat to call a national referendum no doubt encouraged this belief.

A contributing factor to the Senate's decision was that although the United States viewed the bases as important, primarily as training centers and logistical links between California and Kuwait, they were no longer seen as vital. Neither the administration nor Congress was willing to contemplate seriously any of the measures (debt forgiveness, increased trade quotas) that presumably could have wrapped up the talks earlier and perhaps facilitated ratification by the Philippine Senate.

The final act of the negotiating drama began September 17, 1991, and lasted until the end of the year. President Aquino first advised the United States that she would sponsor a popular referendum aimed at nullifying the Senate's vote. The response of the United States was to emphasize its view that the referendum was purely an internal matter for the Philippines. The United States would watch with interest as the process unfolded, but would not attempt to influence its outcome. In order, however, for the United States to regard seriously President Aquino's stated desire to resurrect the treaty via the referendum process, Manila was asked to cancel the MBA termination notice issued in May 1990. President Aquino immediately did so.

Within a few weeks, it become clear that President Aquino was facing both legal and political obstacles to the referendum campaign. Her new executive secretary, former Secretary of Justice Franklin Drilon (a key figure behind the SOFA stalemate of early 1991) proceeded to sound out US Ambassador Frank Wisner about the possibility of pursuing an extended withdrawal period for US forces instead of the referendum. Ambassador Wisner, quite properly, left the matter entirely in Drilon's hands. In the end, the Aquino administration opted to drop the referendum and instead offer the United States a three-year withdrawal from Subic. Significantly, the matter of compensation was not mentioned.

In the course of accepting Manila's offer, however, Ambassador Wisner was presented a request that formal negotiations be initiated in Manila to flesh out the details of the withdrawal. This request was regarded in Washington as a clear danger signal. From the perspectives of interested Washington agencies, a phased, three-year withdrawal from Subic was manifestly in Manila's interest. The Philippines had, after all, nothing resembling a realistic plan to convert Subic Naval Base to non-US use. Had such a plan existed, there were no funds to implement it. If Manila wished to stretch the departure of US forces out over thirty-six months, all that seemed to be required was a termination notice to take effect in September 1994. It was not at all clear to Washington what exactly needed to be negotiated.

Saying "yes" to the Philippine proposal of a three-year withdrawal proved to be insufficient. From Manila's perspective, there seemed to be two obstacles. First, the constitutional provision that any foreign military presence be governed (after 1991) by a treaty led the Aquino government to conclude that as of January 1, 1992, US forces would have to be seen as being in the actual process of withdrawing. Withdrawal, in Manila's view, was different from presence and therefore constitutionally permissible. Second, the Aquino government wanted senators who opposed any bases agreement to believe that the extended withdrawal of US forces was in fact a genuine withdrawal rather than a subterfuge intended to facilitate reconsideration of the rejected treaty by a new president and senate.

Manila's view of its own political constraints ultimately caused Washington to lose interest in the process itself. In an apparent effort to assuage antitreaty senators, Manila attempted to reopen formal negotiations on a wide range of issues. Washington balked at the notion of negotiating the terms of US withdrawal, citing the unfortunate precedent that could inadvertently be set for bases agreements around the world. Key decisions concerning how US forces will depart a given overseas base cannot be left in the hands of other governments. It was, in fact, Manila's demand for a detailed withdrawal plan that convinced the US Commander in Chief, Pacific, that the thirty-six-month withdrawal option was not as attractive as it initially appeared to be.

In late December 1991, President Bush broke the deadlock by proposing to President Aquino that the Philippines issue a new unilateral notice terminating the 1947 MBA. He noted that it would be convenient if US forces were permitted a period in excess of one year to depart. President Aquino nevertheless chose the minimum one-year notice period provided for in the MBA. Accordingly, the deadline for US forces to depart Subic Naval Base was set as December 31, 1992.

Subic could have continued to serve, at least for the balance of this century, as a valuable ship repair, training, and logistical facility for US Pacific forces. The treaty rejected by the Philippine Senate would have protected US interests and conveyed significant, long-term benefits to the people of the Philippines, an overwhelming majority of whom supported its ratification. The Bush administration has moved quickly to assure allies and friends in the Pacific that the inability of the Philippine government to sustain a US presence at Subic does not presage a diminution of the US role as a force for peace and security in East Asia. In the immediate aftermath of Manila's termination notice, President Bush announced the transfer to Singapore of the Seventh Fleet's logistical support headquarters from Subic.

The US-Philippine relationship remains important, and the 1951 mutual defense treaty remains in effect. The challenge for the governing elite in the Philippines is to tackle the daunting problems facing the archipelago without placing the United States squarely in the center of matters. Although US economic and security assistance will continue, it is unlikely that levels anticipated before September 16, 1991, will be realized.

Once US forces have departed Subic, an important element of Filipino nationalist mythology will have been forever removed. Filipinos who have pointed to the US military presence as a source of political fragmentation and societal corruption will no doubt discover that the removal of 6,000 US sailors has little if any salutary effect on these problems. To the extent that the military-bases issue may have presented elements of the Filipino political elite with an excuse for inaction in the face of the country's pressing problems, its elimination may indeed augur well for the Filipino people. This, at least, is the hope of the many American friends of the Philippines.

Notes

1. Fred Green, ed., *The Philippine Bases: Negotiating for the Future* (New York: Council on Foreign Relations, 1988), William E. Berry, Jr., "The Military Bases and Postwar US-Philippine Relations," pp. 133-134.
2. Armitage departure statement read by US panel spokesman Stanley Schrager, Manila press conference, May 3, 1991.

9

Developments in
North-South Korean Negotiations

Robert A. Scalapino

HISTORY MAY RECORD 1991 as the year of the major breakthrough in North-South Korean relations. Given the many
dashed hopes of the past, one must remain cautious. Yet there
can be no doubt that recent events, and especially those occurring between October 1991 and January 1992, constituted the most
promising developments in the troubled history of the postwar Korean
peninsula.[1]

The year did not start on a particularly auspicious note. When President
Kim Il Sung of the Democratic People's Republic of Korea (DPRK) delivered his New Year's address on January 1, he did devote considerable
attention to the issue of reunification, urging that this "historic cause" be
accomplished "within the next several years."[2] But Kim's formula was a
familiar one, encapsulated in the phrase "one nation, one state, two systems and two governments." He had long proposed and the South had
long rejected a confederal republic of Koryo (an ancient name for Korea)
whereby the North and South governments were united through a common state organ based on equal representation, with extensive autonomy
for the two governments, to be reduced gradually as unification became
feasible. The rival proposal of President Roh Tae Woo of the Republic of
Korea (ROK) had been for a commonwealth, a framework for negotiation
and growing interaction between two independent states.[3] In his address,
Kim made clear a gnawing worry: In the light of German unification, did
the South expect to "absorb" the North, with its system prevailing over
communism? Such an idea, he insisted, was absurd, and its opposite, the

communization of the South was a false worry advanced to justify ROK militarism. A unified state could be achieved now, with posterity handling the unification of systems at some future point.

Kim set forth a number of requirements or proposals for progress in North-South discussions, all previously advanced in one form or another. First, he called for a political consultative conference for national reunification with representatives of all parties and organizations to be involved (an example of the long-held "united front" strategy whereby a politically monolithic North could be pitted against a pluralistic South). The South must also abolish laws hostile to the North (anticommunist edicts) and release those imprisoned for visiting the North without permission. The settlement of such issues as visits by members of divided families and economic exchanges could not advance ahead of a settlement of military matters, argued Kim. Among other things, it was necessary to adopt a North-South nonaggression declaration, conclude a peace treaty between the DPRK and the United States, and achieve a phased withdrawal of US troops and nuclear weapons from the South.

Despite a final call to make 1991 "a year of relaxation and peace" and an "historic year of bringing a new phase to national reunification," it is doubtful whether Kim had any premonition of what lay ahead over the next twelve months. In the background, to be sure, lay some unsettling events from the standpoint of the North. Not only had East Germany collapsed, but Leninism was in retreat throughout Eastern Europe and also in the Soviet Union. Most troubling, Moscow had extended diplomatic recognition to the ROK in the fall of 1990. Economic and cultural relations were expanding between China and the ROK, the Tiananmen incident notwithstanding. Finally, after what looked like a promising breakthrough, DPRK negotiations with Tokyo were stalled, and the United States was showing little flexibility toward the North. In sum, the international scene was decidedly unpromising from the perspective of Pyongyang.

There were grave problems on the home front as well. According to statistics of the ROK's National Unification Board, the North's GNP dropped by 3.75 percent in 1990.[4] Weather conditions had been bad for several years, and food was in short supply. Even more important, a severe energy shortage was developing. Trade with the Soviet Union, which had accounted for more than 50 percent of the North's total trade and was the principal source of oil, was dropping sharply. Moreover, Moscow's demand for hard-currency transactions and global market prices was scheduled to take effect on January 1, 1991, although some adjustments were subsequently made. China had reportedly promised assistance as 1990 closed, but its capacity for aid was limited.

In contrast, the South's position was relatively strong as 1991 opened. Roh's "Nordpolitik" policies had been a resounding success, climaxed by official recognition from Moscow. Diplomatic relations had also been established with virtually all of the East European nations and with Mongolia. South Korean trade and investment were flowing into China, and in January 1991, the ROK trade office opened in Beijing, with the Chinese office in Seoul set up a few months later.

At home, economic growth continued, with a GNP increase of 9 percent recorded in 1990. In per capita GNP, the South had reached nearly $5,000 per annum, far ahead of the North, where per capita GNP was variously estimated at between $980 and $1,500. Moreover, due to heavy DPRK military expenditures, the North's private consumption was estimated at less than one-half of GNP in 1989, whereas in the South, it was 65 percent. The differences in trade statistics were awesome. For the North, total trade was $4.8 billion in 1990 compared with $118.2 billion for the South.[5]

ROK politics continued to be fragile, but at the beginning of 1990, the ruling Democratic Justice party had merged with two of the three opposition parties, and under the label Democratic Liberal party (DLP), the coalition had taken a commanding majority of the National Assembly, holding more than 70 percent of the seats. The DLP was weakened by persistent internal factionalism and limited public support as measured by public opinion polls, but it held together. Meanwhile, the radical student movement had ebbed. A combination of violent tactics and an espousal of policies akin to those of Pyongyang had alienated the South Korean citizenry at large, including a majority of the students.

In sum, as 1991 opened, the South could negotiate from greater strength than at any time in its history, whereas the Northern leaders were being forced to consider new options.[6] Yet compromises on both sides were likely to be necessary if advances were to be made, and certain new moves on the part of the major states involved, especially the United States, would be required.

Old Problems Rise Anew

The first months saw limited progress. The North, hoping for a suspension of the Team Spirit military exercises, was bitterly disappointed when the joint US-ROK maneuvers were held (albeit on a more limited scale and of shorter duration than planned), with the main operations held in mid-March. As in the past, the DPRK was invited to be present as an observer and rejected the offer. In protest, Pyongyang canceled participation in the fourth inter-Korean prime ministerial talks, scheduled for February 25, with a stream of invective issued against both the ROK and US governments. The Roh government was accused of militarist, fascist policies and of acting in sycophantic fashion toward certain powers (the USSR) while serving as the puppet of the United States. Washington was charged with hegemonic designs on Asia, sabotage of the peace process through rampant militarism, and "groundless slanders" against the DPRK on the issue of human rights. The decibel level of North Korean rhetoric has always been extraordinarily high.

There was one promising sign. Despite the refusal to attend the high-level talks, the North did continue discussions relating to joint sports teams, and on February 12, it was announced that joint table tennis and soccer teams would be formed to compete in Japan and Portugal respectively, in April and June.[7]

Throughout the spring months, however, very limited advances were made on other fronts. The appointment of an ROK general to be the senior member of the UN forces side on the Military Armistice Commission was denounced by the DPRK on the grounds that the South's military had been denied command by the United States and hence could not head a cease-fire supervising body.[8] The North continued to assert that it would sign the International Atomic Energy Agency (IAEA) nuclear safeguards accord only when an agreement was reached with the United States with respect to American military forces and nuclear weapons in the South. To allow inspection of its nuclear facilities without removal of the nuclear weapons in the South, the DPRK insisted, was manifestly unfair. And Pyongyang steadfastly stated that it would never accept dual representation in the United Nations, since that served to perpetuate two Koreas. Rather, North and South should share a single seat.

Nevertheless, both international and domestic pressures were mounting. At home, the sharp reduction in DPRK-USSR trade was having an adverse effect; even bus schedules were being stretched out to conserve gasoline. Because of energy shortages, various factories were operating on a part-time basis only. Meanwhile, the North was seeking to buy grain abroad, including South Korean grain through indirect sources.

Soviet and Chinese Moves Shake Pyongyang

In April and May, two international diplomatic developments shook Pyongyang's leaders. President Gorbachev traveled to Cheju Island to meet with Roh Tae Woo, a move symbolic of the new relationship between the two countries. The North, stung by this event, angrily denounced Roh for attempting to "isolate and stifle" the North "by wooing the guest who was returning empty-handed from his Japan tour."[9] There can be no doubt that the Gorbachev-Roh meeting served to illustrate the precarious nature of DPRK international ties.

More important, in his late spring visit to Pyongyang, Premier Li Peng told his hosts that China could not veto South Korea's application for UN membership. Having been forced by the Soviets to abandon its opposition to cross-recognition by the major states, given USSR recognition of the ROK, the DPRK was now compelled by China to relinquish its adamant opposition to dual representation in the United Nations. On May 27, the DPRK Foreign Ministry issued a statement saying that the government "had no alternative but to enter the United Nations at the present moment as a step to tide over the temporary difficulties caused by the South Korean authorities."[10] Never had the North's old alliances seemed so limited in value.

On the IAEA front, however, the stalemate continued. Although Northern representatives stated at one point that the DPRK was prepared to enter into negotiations to sign the safeguards agreement by September, at the June 10 meeting of the IAEA board of governors in Vienna, the North Korean delegation walked out when the Japanese raised questions about the North's intentions, subsequently stating that it would not sign the agreement under pressure and reiterating its demand that the United States allow inspection of its bases in the South and that a nonaggression declaration be adopted between North and South.[11]

It was widely believed that the North had made the decision to defer any signing of the safeguards agreement or inspection for as long as possible. International speculation centered upon the reasons. Some believed that years earlier, the North had determined to develop a nuclear-weapons program, realizing that in the foreseeable future, it would not be able to compete with the South in conventional weaponry; military costs already were amounting to over 20 percent of DPRK GNP. Satellite pictures and defector testimony raised suspicions by 1991 that the North might be within one to three years of producing a nuclear device. Some observers thought that the time needed might be even shorter, and given the lessons of Iraq, questions arose about the effectiveness of the IAEA inspection process itself. Yet Northern spokespersons, including Kim Il Sung, continued to insist that the North had neither the capacity nor the desire to produce nuclear weapons and that the issue of inspection was an issue of fairness.[12] Yet another possibility was that, at least in part, the nuclear issue had become a bargaining chip on the DPRK side, since it had very few such chips.

Despite the impasse on the matter, the North and South reopened bilateral discussions in early August and agreed on a fourth round of prime ministerial talks to commence August 27. One week before that date, however, the North asserted that because of a cholera outbreak in the South, it wanted to shift the meetings from Pyongyang to Panmunjom. The excuse for the shift was so ridiculous that it was assumed, probably correctly, that the North wanted a postponement to assess developments in Russia after the abortive coup of August 18-20. It was then agreed that the meetings should be held October 22-23.

Trade and Cultural Ties Expand

Meanwhile, economic and cultural interaction between North and South was accelerating. In the first four months of 1991, two-way indirect trade had totaled $57 million, in comparison with $2.9 million the previous year. By the end of November, such trade had reached $150 million, and the ROK was using moneys allocated to a South-North Exchange and Co-operation Fund to subsidize that trade, since the South, as expected, was incurring a heavy deficit.[13] Moreover, direct trade had commenced with the shipment of five thousand tons of South Korean rice to the North and a subsequent agreement for further direct trade involving a Korean-operated firm in Japan. Despite Pyongyang's reluctance to advance on the economic front prior to political-military agreements, ties were being forged, due principally to the North's severe economic problems.

For the first time, moreover, the DPRK was taking an active interest in the idea of special economic zones, indicating the influence of China. At an international conference held in Ulan Bator, Mongolia, in July, the DPRK announced its intention to set up a special economic zone in its northern region. A second meeting sponsored by the UN Development Program on a possible project relating to the Tumen River area was held in Pyongyang October 16-18, just a few days before the fourth prime ministerial talks, with South Korean representatives among others present on this occasion.[14] The signs were unmistakable that for the North, a "turning out" process had begun, whatever obstacles lay ahead. DPRK representatives to the October conference urged further progress at an early date.

Similarly, in addition to North-South cooperation in international sports meets, academic contacts were expanding in third-country settings, and a meeting of academics in Seoul climaxed the year's intellectual ties. An exchange of musical concerts had also taken place, with North Korean musicians coming to Seoul for the first time since the division of the peninsula. And a delegation of South Korean National Assembly members attended the Eighty-fifth Inter-Parliamentary Union Conference held in Pyongyang at the end of April.

The fourth prime ministers' talks finally opened in Pyongyang on October 22 with political-military issues at the top of the agenda.[15] For many years, the fundamental difference between the South and North on the question of mutual relations had centered on the matter of priorities. The South had insisted that improvements start with economic and cultural exchanges (in the course of which mutual trust could be developed) and then lead to ultimate agreements with respect to political and security matters. The North had taken the position that bold measures regarding the latter issues were required at the outset, with a consultative conference on political reunification convened and the signing of a nonaggression declaration, accompanied by a drastic reduction in military forces that aimed at defense forces of no more than 100,000 on each side. At the same time, the United States was expected to evacuate both its troops and its weapons from the South, and beyond this, there was a demand that its nuclear umbrella over the ROK be removed.[16]

At the October meetings, both sides signaled some willingness to compromise, and the rhetoric was relatively low key. However, the only agreement was that the two sides would hold talks before the next prime ministers' meeting with the aim of drafting an agreement to resolve political and military confrontation and promote exchanges and cooperation. The basic compromise lay in the fact that all facets of the North-South relationship were to be put in the same package.

US Announces Withdrawal of Nuclear Weapons

Before the October meetings, President Bush had made a major announcement that paved the way for subsequent developments in Korea.

He declared on September 27 that the United States was unilaterally eliminating all ground-based tactical nuclear weapons. In October, it was indicated in Washington that the withdrawal would include air-delivered nuclear weapons based in South Korea as well. This action, not a part of the
global agreement, was clearly intended to create incentives for North
Korea to allow inspections. On November 8, President Roh declared that
the ROK would not possess and would no longer store nuclear weapons on
its soil. He challenged the North to take a similar vow. A stick was put
forth amid the carrots when on November 21 the United States announced
that the planned withdrawal of US forces from the South would be frozen
pending some resolution of the nuclear problem.

Four days later, the North announced it was ready to permit international inspection if the United States would also allow inspection of its facilities in the South. This round of exchanges was completed on December 11, when in the course of the fifth prime ministers' meetings, the
ROK offered to open to North Korean inspection any civilian or military
facility, including US installations, if the North would permit reciprocal inspection.[17] The ball had been thrown back into the North Korean court.

Even when the December 11-13 meetings opened, however, many outside observers doubted whether substantial results would take place. It
was known there had been debates within South Korean circles as to how
far to go in reaching an accord if the North continued to stall on nuclear inspection. It soon became clear, however, that a decision had been made,
presumably by President Roh, to move forward and that the way was
being paved through interim negotiations for a far-reaching accord. Working secretly, the two sides had scored a major breakthrough.

Agreement Reached

On December 13, it was announced that both sides had accepted an
Agreement on Reconciliation, Nonaggression, and Exchanges and Cooperation between the South and North.[18] The agreement opened by reaffirming the three principles of unification set forth in the July 4, 1972, joint
communiqué whereby unity was to be achieved without external interference, through peaceful means, and on the basis of "great national unity."

The first eight articles dealt with reconciliation. Both sides pledged to
respect the other's system; not to interfere in its internal affairs; to cease
slander and abuse; to refrain from actions seeking to overthrow the other

side; to undertake efforts to convert the armistice into a durable peace; to discontinue confrontation and build cooperation and make efforts to support national dignity and interests in the international arena; to establish a North-South liaison office at Panmunjom within three months; and to create a North-South Political Subcommittee within one month to discuss means of implementing these provisions.

The next section, composed of six articles, dealt with nonaggression and pledged the two sides to avoid all military action against each other; to seek a peaceful settlement of disputes through dialogue and negotiation; to designate the military demarcation line as defined by the July 27, 1953, armistice as the demarcation line and zone of nonaggression; to create a North-South Joint Military Committee within three months to implement the nonaggression agreement; to promote various confidence-building measures and disarmament; to install and operate direct telephone links between the military authorities of both sides to prevent accidental conflict; and to form a North-South Military Subcommittee within one month to implement both the agreement on nonaggression and the cessation of military confrontation.

The third section had nine articles. These dealt with cooperation and exchange and pledged the joint development of resources and exchange of goods and investments; free travel and contacts between the two regions; free correspondence, meetings, and visits between divided families; the connecting of severed railways and roads and the opening of sea and air routes; postal and telecommunications contacts and efforts to ensure their privacy; cooperation in the cultural realm; and the establishment of a North-South Joint Cooperation and Exchange Subcommittee within one month to effectuate the agreement.

The final section, composed of two articles, stipulated that the agreement would become effective from the date when the two sides each had exchanged its text and had completed the necessary formalities.

Developments continued to unfold rapidly after the conclusion of the December meetings. On December 18, President Roh announced that there were no longer any nuclear weapons in South Korea and again called upon the DPRK to abandon its nuclear-weapons development program.[19] It was also indicated by government spokespersons in Seoul that the accord just signed would not go into force unless the nuclear question was resolved. On December 26, the first inter-Korean nuclear talks took place at Panmunjom, on December 31, an agreement on a nonnuclear Korean peninsula was signed by the two parties.

In his 1992 New Year's address, President Kim devoted the opening portions to talking about the attack upon the nation by imperialists and re-actionaries seeking "to check our forward movement," but insisted that the party and people were of one mind, and socialism had been safeguard-ed.[20] He continued by discussing the domestic situation, indicating that the problem of providing the population with adequate food, clothing, and housing lay ahead as well as that of securing sufficient electricity, coal, and transport facilities. Only in the latter part of the speech did he come to the December accord. Proclaiming it a "great victory" and the product of a nationwide struggle that represented a new landmark, Kim placed the em-phasis upon reunification at the earliest possible date so that foreign domi-nation could be ended and national identity achieved.

With respect to the nuclear question, Kim asserted:

No one should be permitted to put unjust pressure upon us, arguing about the nu-clear inspection. It is our consistent stand that the Korean peninsula should be turned into a denuclearized, peace zone. We have stated more than once that we have no intention or capacity to develop nuclear weapons and that we are ready to accept the nuclear inspection if fair treatment is assured. We mean what we say, we do not say empty words.

In his concluding sections, Kim returned to an earlier theme—that "the imperialists" were seeking to destroy socialism completely so as to revive the colonialist system and bring the world under their domination. He pledged the North's affiliation with the nonaligned movement in the struggle for the independence of all countries.

One week later, on January 7, 1992, a statement was issued by the DPRK Foreign Ministry stating that the government had decided to sign the Nuclear Safeguards Accord "in the near future and have it ratified through legal procedures at the earliest possible date and accept an in-spection at a time agreed upon with the International Atomic Energy Agency."[21] The statement concluded with this sentence: "The DPRK Government will, in the future, too, faithfully fulfill its obligations under the Nuclear Non-Proliferation Treaty and thus make an active contribu-tion to the cause of completely eliminating nuclear weapons from the globe and defending peace and security in Asia and the rest of the world."

On the same day the DPRK made this official statement (and the tim-ing possibly may have been by prior agreement), the ROK Ministry of National Defense announced that it had decided not to conduct Team Spirit exercises in 1992 and that the US had agreed to this decision.[22] The explanation was that North Korea had clearly indicated its intention to abide by the December 13 accord, and, further, that by initialing the joint declaration for a nonnuclear Korean peninsula on December 31, the North had formally pledged its commitment not to possess nuclear fuel reprocessing uranium enrichment facilities as well as indicating that it would sign, ratify, and implement the IAEA safeguards agreement. Consequently, the ROK government wanted to take a further step to improve North-South relations and ease tension.

On January 22, a US team headed by Under Secretary of State Arnold L. Kanter met in New York with North Korean officials for some six hours in the highest-level bilateral meeting since the Korean War. Reportedly, the North Koreans reiterated that they would sign the safeguards agreement very shortly and ratify and implement it as soon as possible.[23] The agreement was subsequently signed in Vienna on January 30.

DPRK on Nuclear Issues: Serious or Stalling?

Certain questions remain. Are reports that a nuclear complex exists at Yongbyon, including a reprocessing facility with the capacity to produce weapons-grade plutonium, exaggerated or incorrect? If not, are the North Koreans busily dismantling or hiding their most advanced operations? Are they prepared to discard reprocessing facilities? And will inspection be permitted going beyond the present IAEA regulations, perhaps by the South and North themselves, as Roh has proposed? Or will the DPRK continue to stall, using whatever excuses can be found?

As of early April 1992, it appeared the DPRK would reach an agreement with the IAEA on on-site inspection in June. On April 3, a high-ranking North Korean official stated that Pyongyang would submit by late May a list of sites the agency may inspect, and that this would include the Yongbyon nuclear facility. He also said the DPRK would comply with any special IAEA inspection of facilities not listed in its original report. He further stated that mutual North-South inspections may also be possible by June. On April 9, the North's Supreme People's Assembly ratified the IAEA accord as the first step. Meanwhile, various reports concerning the removal of certain items from the Yongbyon facilities have been published, but hard facts are impossible to obtain. In any case, whatever difficulties may develop in the course of negotiations, the North appears committed to on-site inspection at this point.

It is important to analyze the factors that made possible the extraordinary developments in North-South Korean relations in the past twelve months. One must start with the two Koreas, since they are the principal players. As has been indicated, the DPRK has been beset with numerous serious problems in the recent past. Domestically, the adverse impact of an autarkic economy has been ever more starkly revealed, augmented by the collapse of the old Soviet Union and the struggle by the People's Republic of China (PRC) to improve its economy. At the beginning of 1990, the North was

- Already in default on foreign debts, some of which extended back nearly two decades.
- Confronted with plant obsolescence and lacking access to scientific-technological advances.
- Hampered by low investment in agriculture as well as industry.
- Facing serious structural imbalances.

Several years of bad weather and the swift decline in Soviet trade and assistance added mightily to the problems.

Meanwhile, a younger group of better-educated, more technologically inclined individuals have been rising within the party and especially within the administrative structure of the DPRK. There is mounting evidence that in internal policy discussions or debates, they are prevailing, with the idea of economic reform—modeled somewhat after the Chinese pattern—being accepted. It appears that this group is clustered around Kim Jong Il, the forty-nine-year-old son of the "Great Leader." And young Kim is now rising rapidly in power, with his succession likely to be made official in the not-to-distant future. It has long been asserted in Pyongyang that in addition to party matters, young Kim has been in charge of domestic policy. More recently, individuals like Kim Yong Sun, a key party figure reportedly very close to young Kim, have stated that the latter is also being given authority over DPRK foreign policy. And as 1992 opened, it was announced that he had been named supreme commander of the North Korean military forces.

Clearly, the plan is to place Kim Jong Il in a position of supreme power in the party, government, and military before his father's death to ensure that the final transition cannot be challenged. The elder Kim, soon to be eighty, will operate in a manner somewhat similar to Deng Xiaoping—as éminence grise behind the velvet curtain—with his imprimatur probably required for truly important decisions, but with others, and most notably his son, in charge. Under these circumstances, it may have been decided that such changes as were required in a foreign policy that had become completely outdated should be made quickly, while the authority of the elder Kim was intact.

Thus, a combination of factors—adverse international trends, critical economic problems on the home front, and the generational changes involved in a succession that is already far advanced—have underwritten major policy adjustments by the DPRK. However, as will soon be noted, these probably would not have taken place, at least in their current form, had important external shifts not been made.

Looking at the South, one is struck by the changes in attitude and policy in Seoul (as well as in Pyongyang). It seems very likely that a key factor has been the domestic political situation. President Roh Tae Woo's term is coming to an end in 1992, and he cannot succeed himself. His Nordpolitik, as indicated earlier, has been a striking success, thanks to its timing in relation to world developments. What would be more fitting, from Roh's standpoint, than to secure his place in history by culminating his presidency with a historic South-North accord that, at a minimum, paved the way for a major reduction in tension on the peninsula and, in the longer run, proved to be the first major step toward unification? In a more immediate sense, moreover, with Roh's popularity having risen sharply among the ROK electorate because of the heightened hopes for South-North peace and cooperation, he could more easily control party politics, including the coming presidential nomination, and possibly ensure victory in the multiple elections that will be held within the next twelve months. Thus, the evidence indicates that Roh personally overrode some doubters within South Korea—and, possibly, reservations among a certain sector of the American government—to authorize a new course. Moreover, he continues to harbor hopes of a summit meeting with Kim Il Sung.

In sum, domestic factors in both North and South, albeit of a radically different nature, meshed in such a fashion as to permit flexibility and some degree of risk taking, at least if the December accord is implemented. Virtually no one expects some parts of that accord to be put into operation soon or in their entirety. The idea that truly free travel, North to South and vice versa, will be allowed, or that all media of one side will have access to the other, especially Southern media to the North, seems unrealistic, at least under current circumstances. At a minimum, a great deal of bargaining and numerous exclusions or qualifications lie ahead. It is relatively easy to lay down broad goals or principles—that is an old Asian tradition. However, to translate words into concrete actions represents a prodigious task, especially in this instance. Nevertheless, certain pledges have been made that now stand as promises against which to measure the sincerity of the participants.

A Changing Environment

Beyond the two Koreas, the actions of the four major states that have been historically involved with the Korean peninsula were also of great importance in shaping recent events. The policies of the old Soviet Union were perhaps the most spectacular—and certainly shook Pyongyang to its core.[24] The idea that the "motherland of socialism"—a state (and party) that had brought the DPRK into existence and nurtured its leader in his youth—would be the first major power to move to a de jure two-Koreas policy in addition to terminating abruptly its special economic relations with the DPRK stung Pyongyang to the quick.

The bitterness was all the greater, moreover, because it could not be fully expressed in public. Despite the severe cutbacks, the North still remains tied to the former Soviet Union in some degree, militarily as well as economically. Indeed, there was brief hope in key North Korean circles that those elements in Soviet society, especially in the military, more favorable to the old relations might prevail. Hence, disappointment was strong when the August coup in Moscow failed.

The Soviet actions were the principal factor in the decision of DPRK leaders to abandon their long-standing opposition to cross-recognition by the major states (Pyongyang had accepted cross-recognition by others for many years) and open negotiations with Japan for diplomatic ties. To be sure, the move was camouflaged by Pyongyang's insistence that the Japanese had made the first overtures—and the necessary initial concession—but the fact was that DPRK leaders decided upon this move after Soviet policies became clear. They hoped that DPRK-Japan negotiations would lead to much-needed Japanese economic assistance.

At first, Japan's actions alarmed both South Korea and the United States.[25] An exploratory diplomatic mission led in fall 1990 by Shin Kanemaru, vice president of Japan's Liberal Democratic Party, seemed to place minimal preconditions in front of the normalization process. Once the Japanese Foreign Ministry took charge of the matter, however, it was made clear that recognition of the DPRK would be contingent upon a satisfactory resolution of the nuclear issue and that there would be regular consultation with the ROK. Moreover, as the negotiations progressed, new issues were raised: the whereabouts of the Japanese woman reportedly kidnapped who had taught Japanese to the Korean saboteur involved in the destruction of the Korean Airlines plane over Southeast Asia; the fate of Japanese wives of Koreans repatriated to the North; and the compensation due the DPRK as a result of Japan's wartime and postwar policies. Pyongyang came to realize that normalization was contingent upon its policies, most especially on the nuclear matter. It could not use a Japan card against the South.

Meanwhile, China remained the one big neighbor that provided public support to the DPRK.[26] High-level visits between the two countries' leaders have been frequent, and on ceremonial occasions, both sides aver their undying friendship and camaraderie, with phrases like "as close as lips and teeth" evoked. The PRC, especially after the Tiananmen incident, had reason to draw closer to the remaining Leninist states of Asia so as to defend the faith and to denounce what it termed "peaceful evolution," interpreted as the efforts of imperialists to subvert socialism by nonviolent means and reimpose control over their nations. The strong nationalist overtones in this message fitted well with North Korean ideological themes, and the idea of a close linkage with China mitigated the sense of isolation in the aftermath of the Leninist collapse in the West.

At the same time, however, as noted earlier, China's friendship did not override its perceived national interests. In effect, the Chinese pursued a de facto two-Koreas policy with almost as much zeal as the Russians pursued a de jure two-Koreas program. Sino-South Korean trade shot up. Investment on the part of the South Korean private sector grew. Visits, especially of ethnic Koreans living in northeast China, to the ROK increased, and a variety of other cultural exchanges took place. Out of deference to the North, the PRC continued to refrain from granting diplomatic recognition to the South, but it signed certain economic agreements official in nature, made it clear to Pyongyang that it could not veto the ROK's UN admission request, and in various other ways treated the South as its favorite concubine while acknowledging the North to be its legal wife. Moreover, Beijing made it clear that it did not favor nuclear weapons, South or North. The DPRK got the message.

The truly crucial actions of a major power in influencing developments in the Korean peninsula, however, were those of the United States.[27] At an earlier point, the North had hoped it could improve relations with the

United States, and to this end, it had undertaken some modest actions, including tendering invitations to key American politicians and to some ex-diplomats and scholars as well. It also sought to cooperate with respect to MIA (missing in action) remains from the Korean War. Subsequently, it welcomed the opening of low-level negotiations out of the two embassies in Beijing. However, these actions had no payoff for the North, at least in an immediate sense.

Yet sentiment in the United States for some modification of policies was gradually building within the government and especially in private circles. Concern over the DPRK nuclear program undoubtedly served to advance this cause, but there were other factors. It was recognized that the presence of American nuclear weapons did not significantly enhance American-South Korean deterrence capabilities, and they were becoming a political issue in the ROK. The political left, and not just the left, was asking whether the United States was a principal obstacle to improvements in North-South relations. In addition, was it not desirable to shift US forces out of highly visible areas such as Seoul, reduce their numbers, and turn the command of forces over to the ROK? In addition, was the Team Spirit exercise necessary on an annual basis and at such a costly level?

Between September 1991 and January 1992 (on a few items, before then), actions were taken on all of these matters, as has been indicated. American forces were reduced and shifted in position, ROK command was strengthened, nuclear weapons were removed from the South, mutual inspection—North and South—was proffered, and the Team Spirit exercises were suspended for 1992. In addition, official talks were initiated in New York and at a higher level. It might be noted, incidentally, that these actions were all in line with the September 1991 proposals made by one private group, the Asia Society-sponsored Mission to Korea.[28]

Whether DPRK officials were prepared for the rapidity and scope of these changes is not clear, but there are some indications that certain actions took Pyongyang by surprise and required time for adjustment. Two basic messages appear to have been understood: A resolution of the nuclear issue was indispensable if North-South relations were to improve significantly, and progress in North-South relations was a critical factor in realizing improvements in relations with the United States and Japan. To put the US position succinctly—the United States shall not move ahead of ROK-DPRK relations, but neither shall it fall behind them.

As has been suggested, there remain many uncertainties about the extent—and the tempo—of progress in reducing tension on the Korean peninsula, the resolution of the issue of the DPRK nuclear program, the concrete steps possible in creating a network of ties between the two Koreas, and advances in cross-recognition or raising the level of dialogue between the two Koreas and the four major powers. The level of distrust—indeed, hatred—between the two Koreas has been extraordinarily high, a product not only of a tremendously destructive war but also of a series of subsequent incidents. Moreover, the two systems, both political and economic, are drastically different indeed, more so now that the ROK is experimenting with democracy.

It seems certain that the two governments will compete in seeking to capture and use the nationalist banners. Such terms as "independence," "national integrity," and "the historic oneness of the Korean people" will be coveted by both sides. The issue of unification has been highly politicized in both North and South. And it cannot be denied that despite the obstacles, an overwhelming majority of Koreans would like to see unification sooner rather than later—providing it takes the form they approve and does not bear undue costs.

There have been advances in the course of the past year that few could have envisaged. A fortuitous conjunction of events—both in the domestic circumstances of the two Koreas and in policy shifts on the part of the major powers—made this possible. Since these conditions seem likely to continue despite various twists and turns, cautious optimism is in order.

Notes

1. For two recent volumes presenting a comprehensive view of various facets of Korean developments in 1990, North and South, see Michael J. Mazarr, John Q. Blodgett, Cha Young-koo, and William J. Taylor, Jr., eds., *Korea 1991—The Road to Peace* (Boulder, CO: Westview, 1991); and Donald N. Clark, ed., *Korea Briefing, 1991* (Boulder, CO: Westview, 1991).

2. Kim's New Year's address is available in Press Release No. 1 of the DPRK Permanent Observer Mission to the United Nations (henceforth, PR, DPRK), January 1, 1991.

3. The commonwealth concept is discussed in Hongkoo Lee, "Call for Building National Community," carried in *Information Service on the Unification Question of the Korean Peninsula*, a publication of the National Unification Board, ROK, February 25, 1991, pp. 3-11.

4. On recent trends with respect to the DPRK economy, see Karoly Fender, "Economic Problems of the Democratic People's Republic of Korea in the 1980s," paper prepared for an international seminar in Taipei, June 24, 1990, and reproduced

in *ibid.*, pp. 31-42; Il-Dong Koh, "Complementarity of Industrial Structures Between North and South Korea," paper for the Institute of East Asian Studies, East-West Center, Korean Association for the Study of Socialist Societies (henceforth, IEAS-KASSS) Berkeley, California, conference, December 11-13, 1991; Hacheong Yeon, "Prospects for North-South Korean Economic Relations and the Evolving Role of Korea in Northeast Asian Economic Development," Korea Development Institute publication, Seoul, 1991.

5.   For further details, consult Rhee Sang-Woo, "North Korea in 1991—Struggle to Save *Chuch'e* Amid Signs of Change," *Asian Survey*, January 1992, pp. 56-63; and Toshio Watanabe, "North Korea's Worst Enemy Is Still Itself," *Asian Wall Street Journal Weekly*, January 14, 1991, p. 1.

6.   For an insightful analysis, see B. C. Koh, "Foreign Policy Implications of Domestic Political Developments in the Two Koreas," paper presented at the IEAS-KASSS conference, December 11, 1991.

7.   Details of the agreement are given in "S-N Agree to Form Joint Sports Teams," *Korea Update*, Seoul, March 4, 1991, pp. 1-2.

8.   See "South Korean Army 'General' Cannot Be Recognized as Senior Member of 'U.N.' Forces' Side to MAC," PR, DPRK, No. 10, March 28, 1991.

9.   See *Rodong Sinmun* commentary of April 27, 1991, as summarized in PR, DPRK, No. 15, April 27, 1991.

10.   The full text of the statement is reproduced in PR, DPRK, No. 19, May 28, 1991, 3 pp.

11.   The demand of the DPRK for a nonaggression declaration to be signed by both governments and a draft of a proposed declaration are contained in PR, DPRK, No. 22, June 25, 1991, 8 pp.

12.   A succinct analysis of theories and trends with respect to security issues is contained in Norman D. Levin, *Security Trends and U.S.-ROK Military Planning in the 1990s* (Santa Monica, CA: Rand, 1991).

13.   "South-North Economic Ties Continue to Expand," *Korea Update*, Seoul, October 28, 1991. An earlier account is carried in the *Japan Times*, April 4, 1991, p. 1.

14.   Details of this and other regional developments are set forth in Sung-Hoon Kim, "Prospects for Regional Economic Cooperation in Northern Asia: The Republic of Korea's Perspective," paper for the IEAS-KASSS conference, December 11-13, 1991. In addition, see Hajime Izumi, "Prospects for North Korean Participation in the Regional Economy," paper presented at this same conference.

15.   The details are presented in *Korea Update*, October 28, 1991, pp. 1-2.

16.   Two fine background articles contained in Chong-Sik Lee, ed., *In Search of a New Order in East Asia* (Berkeley, CA: IEAS, 1991) are Han Sungjoo, "Prospects for Peace and Unification on the Korean Peninsula," pp. 177-189; and Chong-Sik Lee, "North and South Korea at a Crossroad," pp. 190-206.

17.   For details, see "South Korea Offers North Mutual Inspection of Nuclear Facilities," *Korea News-Views*, Korean Information Office, Embassy of Korea, Washington, DC, December 11, 1991, 2 pp.

18.   The full text of the agreement was published by both Southern and Northern sources. See "Agreement on Reconciliation, Nonaggression, and Cooperation and

Exchange Between the North and the South," *Korea News-Views*, December 12, 1991, and PR, DPRK, No. 31, December 14, 1991.

19.   For the official statement by Roh, see "A Special Announcement on a Nuclear-free Korean Peninsula," *Korea News-Views*, December 18, 1991, 6 pp.

20.   For the full text, see "New Year Address of President Kim Il Sung," PR, DPRK, No. 1, January 1, 1992, 8 pp.

21.   See "DPRK Foreign Ministry Spokesman Issues Statement on Nuclear Inspection Problem," PR, DPRK, No. 2, January 7, 1992.

22.   "Team Spirit to be Canceled for this Year," *Korea Background Information*, Embassy of the Republic of Korea, Washington, DC, January 7, 1992.

23.   Don Oberdorfer, "North Korean Leader Promotes Son," *Washington Post*, January 24, 1992, p. A-19.

24.   For background and diverse perspectives on Soviet policies in Asia, see Robert A. Scalapino and Gennady I. Chufrin, eds., *Asia in the 1990s: American and Soviet Perspectives* (Berkeley, CA: IEAS, 1990).

25.   Chae-Jin Lee, "U.S. and Japanese Policies Toward Korea: Continuity and Change," paper for the IEAS-KASSS conference, December 11-13, 1991.

26.   For essays on China's recent foreign policies, see Allen Whiting, ed., *Chinese Foreign Policy*, special issue of *Annals of the American Academy of Political and Social Science*, January 1992.

27.   For a recent overview of US policies in Asia, including policies toward the two Koreas, see Robert A. Scalapino "The United States and Asia: Future Prospects," *Foreign Affairs*, Winter 1991/1992, pp. 19-40.

28.   For an updated report on the mission's work, see "Divided Korea—Report of the Asia Society Study Mission" (New York: Asia Society, 1992).

10

America and the
Cambodian Peace Agreement

Robert G. Sutter

ON OCTOBER 23, 1991, an agreement was signed in Paris establishing terms for peace in Cambodia that promised to end the protracted civil war in that country. For over a decade the Cambodian conflict was a focal point of US-Soviet, Sino-Soviet, and regional differences. Both regional and global powers moderated longtime policies to take more accommodating stances that facilitated progress toward a Cambodian peace accord. Most important were the shift in Soviet policy begun under the leadership of Mikhail Gorbachev and Vietnam's withdrawal of most if not all of its forces from Cambodia in 1989 and its 1991 decision to reverse a policy of truculent hostility to China.

Détente among global and regional powers with an interest in Cambodia added impetus to the efforts of some of the leaders of Cambodian factions to seek peace. The process was slow and difficult. A major peace conference in Paris in 1989 had failed to achieve results. An internationally agreed framework for peace, established in August 1990 by the five permanent members of the UN Security Council (the Perm Five), had remained stalled for over a year, in part because the competing Cambodian factions would not agree on the specifics for power sharing, disarmament, and other sensitive issues in the postwar transition to a new internationally sanctioned civil government.

The views of this article are those of the author and not necessarily those of the Congressional Research Service, Library of Congress.

The peace plan signed in Paris on October 23, 1991, gave a strong role to a United Nations peacekeeping force, the UN Transitional Authority in Cambodia (UNTAC). It will monitor the end of outside military assistance, disarm combatants, and control key government administrative functions until a new Cambodian government is established. The UN will also play a key role in repatriating over 300,000 displaced Cambodians along the Thai border and other Cambodian refugees and in organizing nationwide elections for a new government in Cambodia. The UN contingent is expected to number around 20,000 personnel, and cost estimates for the entire UN effort—including refugee repatriation—top $3 billion. Elections are not expected to be held for some time, perhaps in 1993.

For the United States, the fluid political situation since the late 1980s promising a negotiated end to the Cambodian civil war prompted a series of unprecedented initiatives from those in Congress critical of the Bush administration's policy. Through letters to the administration, congressional resolutions, and legislation dealing with foreign assistance and other matters, Congress pushed the administration to adjust policy to perceived changing circumstances in the decade-long Cambodian conflict.

Most in Congress supported Bush administration-led efforts to reach a comprehensive peace settlement in Cambodia under the auspices of the five permanent members of the UN Security Council. But progress toward a peace settlement was slow, and there was widespread concern that the so-called Perm Five plan would enhance the legitimacy of the Khmer Rouge or fail to check what some perceived as the rising power and influence of that feared group of communist insurgents. Congressional critics saw the US policy of providing modest amounts of overt and covert nonlethal support to two noncommunist insurgent groups loosely aligned with the Khmer Rouge as playing into the hands of the communist insurgents. They took steps to cut off US aid to the noncommunist insurgents and to open greater contacts, including giving some humanitarian aid, to people under the rule of the Vietnamese-backed government in Phnom Penh. Some members of Congress pressed on procedural grounds for an end to US covert aid to the noncommunist Cambodian insurgents. In particular, they were uneasy over the protracted use of US covert operations, which were subject to limited congressional oversight. They wanted the program in Cambodia to be cut back or subjected to more open congressional oversight.

Seeking a broad consensus in Congress, administration officials and their many supporters in Congress made adjustments in policy while continuing to emphasize support for the Perm Five plan, assistance to the noncommunist resistance, and restricted US interaction with Phnom Penh and Hanoi. Arrangements finally reached reflected new US attempts to restrict the power and influence of the Khmer Rouge, to provide US aid to people under Phnom Penh's rule as well as to the noncommunist insurgents, to phase out US covert aid to the insurgents, and to open official contacts with both Phnom Penh and Hanoi over a Cambodian settlement.

The internal US policy debate did not stop with the signing of the October 1991 peace agreement. A December 3, 1991, letter to President Bush signed by half the Congress warned that US support for the UN peace plan was in jeopardy if the plan was seen as playing into the hands of the Khmer Rouge. Congressional support for the financial backing needed to carry out the expensive UN plan was also in question in early 1992 because of federal budget constraints and election-year politics.

Earlier Efforts to Achieve Peace

The October 1991 Paris peace accord is to bring an end to a thirteen-year-old conflict in Cambodia. That conflict was brought about by Vietnam's December 1978 invasion of Cambodia and the establishment of a pro-Vietnamese client government in Phnom Penh, the Cambodian capital. Vietnam's actions were politically and financially supported by the Soviet Union. The client government, known in recent years as the State of Cambodia (SOC), was opposed by armed forces of the communist Khmer Rouge and two smaller noncommunist resistance forces led respectively by Prince Norodom Sihanouk, former head of state, and Son Sann, former prime minister (see Table 10.1). All three resistance forces were backed by China, but China concentrated its resources on the Khmer Rouge, a longtime ally.

China had supported the Khmer Rouge rise to power in Cambodia in 1975 partly to counter Vietnam's growing power, and the relationship continued even though the Khmer Rouge carried out brutally radical policies resulting in the deaths of over one million Cambodians. At bottom, the Chinese and Khmer Rouge had strong common interests in keeping Cambodia independent in the face of a newly unified Vietnam's desire to create a postwar Indochinese order that would put Phnom Penh under Hanoi's influence. The Vietnamese appeared especially intimidating after their victory over the United States. They commanded a battle-hardened

Table 10.1 Military-Political Groups Active in Cambodia Before October 1991 Peace Accord

Leader(s)/ Name of Organization	Political Status	Foreign Policy	Estimated Force Strength[a]
Heng Samrin/ Hun Sen/ State of Cambodia (SOC) (communist)	In power (supported by Vietnamese[b])	Pro-Vietnamese; pro-Soviet	40,000-48,000 main force; 50,000 organized militia, 50,000 unorganized militia
Khieu Samphan Ieng Sary Pol Pot/ Democratic Kampuchea (DK) (communist; also known as Khmer Rouge)	Participated in Coalition Government of Democratic Kampuchea (CGDK). Maintained the foreign affairs portfolio in the CGDK.	Anti-Vietnamese; close ties with China	35,000-40,000 well trained, well equipped
Son Sann/ Khmer People's National Liberation Front (KPNLF) (noncommunist)	Participated in the CGDK. Son Sann was prime minister.	Anti-Vietnamese; prononaligned and noncommunist nations	12,000-15,000
Norodom Sihanouk/ Sihanouk National Army (ANS) (noncommunist)	Participated in the CGDK. Sihanouk sometimes served as president.	Anti-Vietnamese; prononaligned (leader often resides in China and North Korea)	18,000-20,000

[a]Precise US government estimates of forces in Cambodia are classified. These general estimates were confirmed during a telephone conversation with officials in the Department of State.
[b]Vietnam says all of its troops left Cambodia by September 1989. China, Sihanouk, and others claimed that after September 1989, thousands of Vietnamese troops remained "disguised" as SOC troops.

Sources: Far Eastern Economic Review, annual Asia yearbooks, and *Asian Survey*, January issues from the mid-1980s to the present.

army that was the fifth largest in the world and that continued to receive strong material and political support from the USSR.

The two noncommunist resistance forces led by Prince Sihanouk and former Prime Minister Son Sann received modest material support and political backing from the United States and the Association of Southeast

Asian Nations (ASEAN members are Thailand, Malaysia, Singapore, Indonesia, the Philippines, and Brunei). Thailand allowed supplies to reach the insurgents through its territory and provided safe haven to over 300,000 displaced Cambodians who represented the core population base for the Cambodian insurgents. Meanwhile, international support for the Cambodian resistance was registered annually at the United Nations in votes on which side—the Vietnamese-backed government or the resistance forces—should represent Cambodia in the UN. The United States took the lead in maintaining an international economic embargo against Vietnam until it withdrew its forces and assisted in reaching a Cambodian peace accord.[1]

For over a decade, the SOC and its Vietnamese and Soviet backers were at an impasse with the Cambodian resistance and its international backers in China, ASEAN, and the United States. In the late 1980s, the new Soviet leadership of Mikhail Gorbachev showed more interest than past Soviet governments in capping the estimated annual expenditure of $3 billion to aid its Indochinese clients. Gorbachev also wanted to break out of Moscow's isolation in the region caused by Soviet association with Vietnam's military occupation. Meanwhile, the battlefield situation in Cambodia remained at a stalemate, and Vietnam's internal economic situation continued to deteriorate. A major transition in Vietnam's leadership in 1986 and 1987 brought to power younger leaders who seemed at least somewhat more open to possible compromise in Cambodia.

In 1988, Vietnam announced it would withdraw its troops from Cambodia—a process it said was complete by September 1989, although later reports showed thousands of Vietnamese still remained, at least temporarily. Concurrently, peace talks among the Cambodian factions and interested international parties became more active, leading to the first Paris conference on Cambodia held in August and September 1989. The 1989 conference broke down in disagreement over differing views on several issues held by the SOC and Vietnam on one side and the resistance forces and China on the other.

The 1989 Paris conference participants had particular difficulty resolving the question of what role the Khmer Rouge would play in a future reconciliation government in Cambodia.[2] Resistance leader Prince Sihanouk demanded that the Khmer Rouge be included in an interim, four-party coalition government that would rule prior to elections. Sihanouk said this would be the best way to monitor the activities of the radical group.[3] SOC Premier Hun Sen said the Khmer Rouge could participate in a national council that would prepare for elections, but he ruled out any role for the group in a provisional government. He said he would be willing to have Sihanouk return to Cambodia as head of state, but diplomats participating in the conference said Hun Sen refused to discuss specific terms for sharing power.

Other unresolved issues included the role of the UN in monitoring the Vietnamese troop withdrawal, the question of whether the word "genocide" should be used to describe the earlier Khmer Rouge rule, and what to do about the thousands of Vietnamese residents living in Cambodia. The Khmer Rouge demanded that all of these people return to Vietnam.

The Cambodian parties appeared to harden their positions during the month-long conference. Diplomats did not expect the conference to reconvene until after the Cambodian factions had a chance to test their strength on the battlefield.

As Sihanouk insisted on a prominent role for the Khmer Rouge in a proposed transition government, Hun Sen stepped up his criticism of the prince and suggested that it might no longer be possible for the two men to reach an agreement to share power. This was in contrast to a meeting earlier in the year in Jakarta when the two leaders, who had met a half dozen times since December 1987, seemed much closer to an agreement. In May 1989, Sihanouk had said he would be willing to return to Phnom Penh and join forces with Hun Sen if Vietnam withdrew its remaining troops; Phnom Penh agreed to drop references in its constitution to the "leading role" of the communist party and to introduce a multiparty political system in which all factions, including the Khmer Rouge, were allowed to participate. The prince had also said he expected that the Khmer Rouge would reject any power-sharing arrangement with Hun Sen, allowing him to pursue a separate agreement with Phnom Penh.

By the end of July 1989, the conciliatory relations between Sihanouk and Hun Sen had turned hostile, and the prince had adopted the firm position on including the Khmer Rouge that led to the impasse at the Paris conference in August. After the August meeting, both leaders seemed intent on testing the military strength of the other before returning to the negotiating table. China, ASEAN, and most Western countries were expected to continue supporting the resistance coalition and isolating the Phnom Penh government in an attempt to force the Vietnamese-backed government to agree to a political role for the Khmer Rouge in a settlement.

The months leading up to the 1989 Paris meetings also saw a flurry of diplomatic activity, including a round of talks among all four Cambodian factions, ASEAN, and Vietnam in Jakarta in February; several visits by Hun Sen to Thailand, which had long supported the resistance; and discussions between China, which armed the coalition, and the Soviet Union, which backed Phnom Penh. China and Vietnam also held their first talks in nearly a decade, and the United States debated whether it should send arms to the noncommunist resistance.

Even though the 1989 talks failed, international interest in reaching a settlement continued. The Soviet Union, which took no strong action to avoid the collapse of communism in Eastern Europe and faced major problems at home, seemed more anxious than ever to cut its losses through a diplomatic solution to problems in Indochina. China was now willing to deal pragmatically with Gorbachev about Indochina and other problems, having welcomed the Soviet leader in May 1989 to the first Sino-Soviet summit meeting in thirty years. That meeting was marked by the mass pro-democracy demonstrations in Beijing and other cities that were finally put down by bloody force in June. Although much of the West turned away from China in horror, Gorbachev and Asian leaders tended to keep open contacts in an effort to find solutions to common problems, including Cambodia. For their part, Beijing leaders showed greater flexibility and accommodation in dealing with former adversaries, possibly in an effort to appear less isolated after the massacre at Tiananmen Square. Facing a continuing dilemma in Cambodia and diminishing Soviet support, Vietnam's leaders took the initiative to conduct secret high-level meetings with China in an effort to smooth the path toward peace in Cambodia and to deal pragmatically with other problems.

For their part, ASEAN members were also anxious to see peace restored on mutually agreeable terms. They worried about the future balance of power in the region now that the Soviet Union was withdrawing, the United States and China seemed preoccupied with other issues, and Japan was playing an increasingly important economic and political role in the region. It seemed clear that ASEAN members needed to find ways to keep open channels of communication to all powers having an interest in the region and work hard to resolve sources of tension like Cambodia that threatened regional stability. Indonesia and Singapore moved to open formal diplomatic ties with China, and the ASEAN states worked diligently to foster an internationally sanctioned peace agreement on Cambodia that would be acceptable to the competing factions and their respective backers. ASEAN members were concerned that the problem of the Khmer Rouge had to be handled in a way that would reduce the insurgents' threat to regional peace and enhance prospects that a Cambodian peace settlement would allow for the economic integration of Indochina into the vibrantly growing region.[4]

By 1990, the Perm Five were able to reach common ground on a broad outline and specific aspects of a plan for a Cambodian settlement. The continued thaw in US-Soviet and Soviet-Chinese relations boosted the process of reconciliation among the big powers. But Vietnam and the SOC in Phnom Penh on one side, and the three resistance forces backed by China and others on the other, remained at an impasse over the establishment of an interim regime in Cambodia, disarmament of combatants, election procedures, and other questions. The logjam was not broken until Vietnam markedly shifted its policy toward China in 1991. Faced with quickly evaporating support from the former Soviet bloc and unable to make rapid headway in its efforts to reach out to the United States, Japan, and others in the West, Vietnam decided to reverse its previous hostility to China. China was ready to reciprocate. Domestic and diplomatic uncertainties in China had been compounded by the collapse of communism in the Soviet bloc and in much of the Third World. Beijing also presumably saw the Vietnamese accommodation as meeting China's long-standing goal that any settlement in Cambodia must preclude Vietnamese domination of Indochina.

China and Vietnam conducted a series of high-level meetings in 1991 that coincided with rapid progress in peace talks among the heretofore seemingly irreconcilable Cambodian parties. In June, a series of meetings among the Cambodian parties began to produce significant progress toward a peace agreement. A Cambodian Supreme National Council (SNC), set up under the UN Perm Five plan, began to function. The SNC consisted of twelve members, six from the SOC and two each from the three resistance forces. Hun Sen's SOC had compromised in acquiescing to the Khmer Rouge's return to Phnom Penh as part of the SNC, but Sihanouk softened the impact by moving closer to a power-sharing arrangement with Hun Sen. The Khmer Rouge occasionally balked at conditions that acted to curb their influence but China, now reconciled with Vietnam, applied pressure along with the other Perm Five members and ASEAN to keep the Khmer Rouge in line. By late August, the Cambodian parties agreed to a cease-fire, ending outside military support, demobilizing combatants, and providing for future elections. The stage was set for the terms of the October 23, 1991, agreement.

The US Role and Policy Debate

The American policy debate during the period leading up to the Cambodian peace accord was based on long-standing interests that often conflicted. US policymakers disagreed on steps necessary to strike a balance between ensuring that Vietnam withdraw from Cambodia and preventing a power vacuum that might be filled by the reviled Khmer Rouge.[5]

The United States—along with China, Thailand, and other members of ASEAN—wanted to push back the Soviet-supported Vietnamese expansion in Cambodia. For many years, US policy followed the lead of US treaty ally Thailand and other members of ASEAN and of China in giving political support and modest amounts of nonlethal military support to the armed resistance against the Vietnamese occupiers and their Cambodian client government. The United States avoided all contacts with the Khmer Rouge, the strongest of the loosely connected resistance groups, which received support mainly from China. The United States supported the other two groups, both noncommunist, led by Prince Sihanouk and former Prime Minister Son Sann.

The United States also strongly opposed a return to power of the Khmer Rouge. Though driven from power by the Vietnamese, the Khmer Rouge regrouped along the Thai-Cambodian border and grew in size and strength as an insurgency opposing the Vietnamese and their client regime, the SOC. Pol Pot and other senior leaders responsible for the atrocities of the 1970s have remained central to Khmer Rouge policies and practices up to the present.

As the Vietnamese withdrew and peace negotiations became more active in the late 1980s, the Bush administration became more deeply involved in brokering a settlement. US policy emphasized the importance of peace negotiations led by the five permanent members of the UN Security Council.

US efforts to strengthen the two noncommunist resistance groups included both covert and overt assistance and other means. The United States provided more than $3 million in nonlethal equipment and supplies annually to the noncommunist resistance from 1985 to 1988; the amount was increased for FY 1989 to $5 million and to $7 million for FY 1990. A reportedly larger amount of covert assistance, also for nonlethal equipment, was provided. Such US support was intended to continue to apply pressure on Vietnam and its Phnom Penh client to compromise on a

Cambodian peace settlement. The assistance helped sustain the two resistance groups as a viable noncommunist force in a postsettlement Cambodia, especially vis-à-vis the more powerful forces of the communist SOC
and the communist Khmer Rouge.

Many in Congress, including members of both parties, believed the
Bush administration struck the right balance in supporting the Perm Five
plan, continuing to assist the noncommunist resistance, and maintaining
US economic and political restrictions against the SOC and Vietnam. During 1989 and 1990, however, there emerged in Congress a bipartisan group
of vocal and powerful critics who pushed for changes in US policy on Cambodia.[6] They judged that the terms and slow progress of the Perm Five
peace plan enhanced the legitimacy of the Khmer Rouge and failed to
check its rising power and influence in Cambodia. US aid to the noncommunist resistance, critics argued, played into the hands of the Khmer
Rouge and weakened the SOC, the Cambodian faction best equipped to
offset Khmer Rouge power. The critics included the Majority Leader and
chairman of the Appropriations Committee in the Senate, the chairman of
the Foreign Operations Appropriations Subcommittee in the House, and
scores of others. They pressed for a cutoff of US aid to the noncommunist
insurgents and the opening of aid, trade, and other contacts with people
under the administration of the SOC.

The administration and its supporters in Congress recognized the need
for at least tactical adjustments in the face of this pressure. Otherwise,
there was a real risk that US funding for Cambodian operations would be
abruptly ended, which would severely compromise the US ability to play a
continuing role in the peace process. As a result, administration officials
and their supporters in Congress worked together to modify policy while
continuing to emphasize support for the Perm Five plan. During the year,
new US attempts were made in the peace negotiations and elsewhere to
establish frameworks to restrict the power and influence of the Khmer
Rouge, to provide US aid to people under Phnom Penh's rule as well as to
the noncommunist insurgents, to phase out covert aid to the insurgents,
and to open official contacts with both Phnom Penh and Hanoi in pursuit
of a Cambodian settlement.

Events in late 1990 and 1991 sharpened the debate between Bush administration supporters and critics. Disagreements lay quiescent during
much of this period as US policymakers focused on the Persian Gulf crisis.
But the defeat of Iraq and the requirements of the authorization and

appropriations process brought criticism of US Cambodian policy to the fore again by spring 1991. The issues included the following:

■ There was widespread concern that the Perm Five peace plan had reached an impasse. Backed by Vietnam, the SOC remained reluctant to give up military power and political authority, asserting that it felt threatened by rising Khmer Rouge power.

■ Concurrently, the Khmer Rouge reportedly was expanding its political influence in the Cambodian countryside and had developed economic enterprises that would help sustain it if outside support were cut off.

■ A series of State Department and US General Accounting Office reports required by law or requested by the Senate Foreign Relations Committee detailed the extent of cooperation between forces of the noncommunist opposition and the Khmer Rouge. They also revealed the amount of US aid flowing to the noncommunist resistance through the auspices of the so-called (Bill) McCollum Amendment and found that 200 tons of surplus Defense Department commodities provided under that program from 1987 to 1989 were not counted as part of the US overt aid to the noncommunist resistance at that time. The reports also disclosed that the $100 million US contribution to the UN Border Relief Operations from 1983 to 1989 represented about 30 percent of the total cost of the program that helped to feed, shelter, and provide basic medical care for the 300,000 displaced Cambodians located in camps along the Thai border, including the 70,000 Cambodians located in camps controlled by the Khmer Rouge.[7]

■ By early 1991, there was considerable congressional discontent over the fact that the administration was slow to conduct a US Agency for International Development "needs" assessment involving the people under control of the SOC. Critics disapproved of the allocation of US assistance between the noncommunist resistance and needy Cambodians under SOC control. US assistance went to the former and neglected the latter.

The strong debate between administration supporters and congressional critics provided the backdrop for a third, less clearly articulated viewpoint on the Cambodian crisis.[8] There were many in and out of government who shared the moral concerns voiced by administration backers and detractors regarding the desirability of restoring peace and territorial integrity to Cambodia and restricting the power of the Khmer Rouge. But they tended to believe that the United States should be more realistic in acknowledging American ignorance of the forces at work inside Cambodia. They pointed to the limited influence of the United States among the local and regional actors with a basic stake in the situation in Cambodia and the checkered record of US policy in recent years—policy that entailed American attention being pushed toward one "solution" after another, only to find each solution to be less than satisfactory. These critics argued that in American domestic politics, the legacy of the US experience in the Vietnam War still impeded US policy toward Indochina.[9] In the end, however, those who tended to prefer a less active and involved US approach to Cambodian-related questions were overtaken by the more impassioned participants in the debate.

The Paris Peace Accord

The signing of the October 1991 Paris peace agreement brought the process of restoring peace in Cambodia to a new stage. The signatories were the four Cambodian factions, the regional powers with an interest in the conflict (including Vietnam, China, and Thailand), the United States, the Soviet Union, Japan, France, the United Kingdom, India, Australia, and nine others. The terms of the agreement represented an ambitious UN effort to organize Cambodia's administration, its military affairs, and elections and to oversee refugee resettlement and the human rights situation. Implementation of the plan faced serious difficulties from the outset, not the least of which was continued US debate over how closely and in what ways the United States should support the changing order in Cambodia.

- Agreement on the administration issue was for the SOC and the three resistance groups to continue to administer the territory and population they control until a new government is formed. Five key areas of government authority (defense, interior, foreign affairs, finance, and information) will be under the control of the UN Transitional Authority in Cambodia (UNTAC), the UN peacekeeping presence in Cambodia. The Supreme National Council (SNC), made up of representatives of the four Cambodian parties, is a representative of Cambodian sovereignty that will have the right to offer advice to UNTAC, which will comply with the advice if there is a consensus in the SNC or if the advice is consistent with the Paris agreement. If there is no consensus in the SNC, Prince Sihanouk as head of the SNC will be the ultimate decisionmaker. If he is unable to make a decision, a special representative of the UN secretary-general will have that responsibility.

■ On the military issue, UNTAC is responsible for monitoring the withdrawal of all foreign forces and advisers and the cessation of outside military assistance. It must locate and confiscate caches of weapons and military supplies and supervise the regrouping and relocating of all forces to specially designated cantonment areas. UNTAC must also disarm and demobilize 70 percent of all forces. The remaining 30 percent of the SOC and resistance forces are either to be incorporated into a new national army after the creation of a new Cambodian government, or they will be demobilized at that time.

■ As for elections, the UN is to educate voters and organize all aspects of free elections for a 120-member constituent assembly based on proportional representation in each province. The assembly will draft and approve a constitution, by a two-thirds vote, and then transform itself into a legislature, which will create a new Cambodian government.

■ All parties pledged to promote respect for human rights to prevent "practices of the past," a reference to the deaths of a million Cambodians caused by the Khmer Rouge. UNTAC is to develop a human rights program and investigate abuses. The UN will monitor the human rights situation even after elections.

The meetings among the four Cambodian factions and interested international parties in the months leading up to the Paris conference in October 1991 assured that the peace agreement would be signed without too much controversy. The SOC had reluctantly acquiesced to the return of the Khmer Rouge to Phnom Penh as part of the SNC. China was pressing the Khmer Rouge to behave constructively in the transition period. Sihanouk presumably saw an opportunity to break with the Khmer Rouge and work more closely with Hun Sen and the international community in securing a leading role for himself as the leader of a nonaligned, noncommunist Cambodia. In addition, the United States and other outside powers—perhaps even including China—were determined to do what they could to assure that the peace agreement would provide the framework for restoration of peace in Cambodia and restrict the possible return to power of the Khmer Rouge.

Press reports after the Paris conference emphasized the difficulty of implementing the accord. Many said the transition period—from the signing of the peace accord in October 1991 until a new government is formed—would likely be eighteen months or more. Elections were not expected until after all refugees and displaced persons—numbering over 350,000—had been resettled, which could take more than a year. A particular problem was the widespread use of mines, which made transportation and resettlement very difficult.

During the weeks after the signing of the peace agreement, Prince Sihanouk and other resistance leaders returned to Phnom Penh along with US, Chinese, and other diplomats. In November 1991, there were growing signs that Sihanouk's faction was aligning more closely with Hun Sen's SOC. At the same time, a mob of demonstrators attacked the site of Khmer Rouge offices in Phnom Penh and beat and threatened to kill its senior representative, Khieu Samphan. A meeting of the SNC in Thailand on December 3 ended with an agreement that the Khmer Rouge representatives would return to Phnom Penh amid improved security arrangements.

Another round of violent demonstrations—this time directed against reported corruption in the SOC—took place on December 21. Khieu Samphan returned briefly to Phnom Penh on December 30. The SNC at a meeting that day urged prompt deployment of UN peacekeeping forces to Cambodia. US Representative Stephen Solarz visited Phnom Penh on January 1, 1992, and also urged quick UN deployments.

Major determinants of how thoroughly the plan can be implemented are the size, scope, and support given to UNTAC and other aspects of the UN effort. Estimates of the potential size of the UNTAC presence ranged up to 20,000 personnel. UNTAC was not expected to be fully functional for several months. In October 1991, the UN Security Council approved the UN Advance Mission in Cambodia (UNAMIC). UNAMIC, which consisted of 268 military and civilian personnel and was the initial component of UNTAC, dealt with problems of disarming mines and establishing communications and other technical support for UNTAC. The UNAMIC office opened in Phnom Penh in December 1991.

The head of UNTAC, Yasushi Akashi, visited Cambodia in late January 1992 amid repeated military clashes and other breaches of the peace accords. Prominent critics in Cambodia were gunned down in Phnom Penh, violence that prompted the imposition of a 10 PM-to-dawn curfew. In February 1992, 700 Thai soldiers began mine-clearing efforts in areas along the Cambodian-Thai border. Also in February, the UN secretary-general approved a plan calling for about 20,000 UN personnel to partici-pate in a $1.2 billion program for Cambodia. A military contingent of 15,000 was to supervise the cease-fire, verify the withdrawal of foreign forces, and disarm and demobilize combatants; 3,600 UNTAC police would oversee police work in Cambodia, and 1,800 personnel would super-vise voter registration.

Several developed countries and China said they were ready to con-tribute at least modest amounts of financial support for UN efforts to re-turn displaced persons and assist in reconstruction and recovery. Press re-ports highlighted the potential major role to be played by Japan. In late 1991, Tokyo was considering a change in legislation that would have al-lowed the dispatch of up to 2,000 peacekeeping forces, including members of the Japanese Self-Defense Forces, to Cambodia. However, strong polit-ical opposition blocked the move. The Japanese government sent a mis-sion to study Cambodia's economy at the end of 1991, and it planned to host an international donor conference on Cambodia in 1992. After the UN secretary-general approved the February 1992 plan calling for about 20,000 UN personnel to be involved in Cambodia, it was reported that the total cost of the UN effort—including refugee resettlement—would be close to $3 billion and that Japan was expected to pay about one-third of that amount.

Issues for US Policy

Secretary of State James Baker and other US officials disclosed at the Paris conference in October 1991 that the United States would establish a liaison office in Phnom Penh headed by a senior US Indochina expert, would lift the US-backed embargo, and would establish economic relations with Cambodia as soon as UNAMIC arrived and began to implement the settlement. Secretary Baker also took the opportunity to offer a harsh US condemnation of the Khmer Rouge. The US liaison office in Phnom Penh opened in November 1991; President Bush announced the lifting of the US embargo against Cambodia on January 4, 1992.

Few members of Congress and leading commentators went on record strongly endorsing the Cambodian peace plan. More commonly seen in press commentary were warnings about the difficult road ahead, the danger posed by the return of the Khmer Rouge to Phnom Penh, and the expensive and possibly unwieldy UN role in Cambodia. A "Dear Colleague" letter criticizing the accord began to circulate in Congress soon after the October 1991 signing. On December 3, 1991, a letter to President Bush signed by more than half of the Congress called for stronger US efforts to curb the Khmer Rouge and warned that US support for the peace plan was in jeopardy if the plan was seen as playing into the hands of the Khmer Rouge.[10]

In general, the basic question for US policy related to how closely the United States should associate with the current peace plan. On one side was the Bush administration and some members of Congress who argued that the plan represented the best that could be reached under admittedly difficult circumstances and contained safeguards sufficient to contain the Khmer Rouge and restore peace and stability to Cambodia. On the other side were those who had long opposed the administration's approach as fundamentally flawed; they would have preferred a strategy of working more closely with the SOC and Vietnam, if necessary, to prevent a resurgent Khmer Rouge. Between these opposing poles were US leaders who were reluctant to associate too closely with the Cambodian accord either because of its inclusion of the Khmer Rouge or its cost. There were also those mentioned earlier who thought the United States could not substantially influence developments in such a faraway country subject to historical animosities and heavily influenced by regional powers, notably Vietnam and China.

The importance of US support for the Cambodian peace plan was underlined by the trips to Washington, DC, in early 1992 of UNTAC Director Yasushi Akashi and SOC Prime Minister Hun Sen. Both officials appealed to administration leaders, members of Congress, and the press for signs of strong US support for the UN peacekeeping effort in Cambodia. Without a strong showing of US backing, they warned, other nations would fail to follow through with needed support, the UN presence would be scaled backed sharply or suspended, and Cambodia could revert to a state of civil war or internal anarchy that could presumably ease a return to power by the Khmer Rouge. The need for strong US support was seen as all the more pressing in view of Japan's inability to send peacekeeping forces to Cambodia and the Soviet Union's likely inability to pay its share of peacekeeping.

The calls for greater US support were poorly timed. US politicians were facing voters acutely concerned with domestic economic problems and critical of President Bush and some in Congress for devoting excessive attention and resources overseas. The Democrat-controlled Congress and the Republican administration were already repeatedly locking horns over rival tax, budget, and other financial proposals; the result was a standoff that boded ill for any significant increase in US spending abroad. In particular, a Bush administration proposal in early 1992 calling for $350 million for UN peacekeeping, with an emphasis on Cambodia over the next year, evoked strong criticism in Congress. The issue was not clear-cut for several reasons. First, it was unclear if the aid would come as a result of an appropriations bill, a continuing resolution, or some other mechanism. Second, the administration submitted the proposal as a "budget amendment" rather than a supplemental appropriations that would complicate adherence to rules of the Budget Enforcement Act. A third difficulty was the large size of the request, involving UN operations not only in Cambodia but in other contested areas as well. As it turned out, Congress in early April 1992 did approve a continuing resolution that provided about $200 million for UN efforts in Cambodia. Further US financial support would have to await congressional action for spending measures covering fiscal year 1993.

It seemed evident in mid-1992 that the administration would have to continue to work closely with Congress in order for its approach to Cambodia to succeed. The UN plan for Cambodia will probably falter without US funding—and that funding is impossible without congressional support. Congressional critics of administration policy were unhappy that the Paris agreement allowed the Khmer Rouge to return to Phnom Penh as a legitimate political force, and they were worried that the UN presence and other measures might not be enough to block its return to power. But enough critics in Congress were persuaded by the argument that the Paris accord provided the only viable means to prevent renewed Khmer Rouge ascendancy. They now are particularly concerned that the United States open quickly economic, political, and other ties with the SOC and its leader, Hun Sen. The critics are certain to watch closely how the administration and other governments implement the accord.

Notes

1.   For useful background on the Cambodian conflict and the search for peace, see Elizabeth Becker, *When The War Was Over: The Voices Of Cambodia's Revolution and Its People* (New York: Simon & Schuster, 1986), 502 pp.; Frederick Z. Brown, *Second*

Chance: The United States and Indochina in the 1990s (New York: Council on Foreign Relations, 1989), 163 pp.; Nayan Chanda, *Brother Enemy: The War After the War* (San Diego, CA: Harcourt Brace Jovanovich, 1986), 479 pp.; Nayan Chanda, "Civil War in Cambodia?" *Foreign Policy*, No. 76 (Fall 1989), pp. 26-43; David P. Chandler, *A History of Cambodia* (Boulder: Westview, 1992); David P. Chandler, *The Tragedy of Cambodian History: Politics, War, and Revolution Since 1945* (New Haven: Yale University Press, 1991), 396 pp.; Dick Clark, *The Challenge of Indochina: An Examination of the US Role* (Aspen, CO: Institute for Humanistic Studies, 1991), 40 pp.; Evelyn Colbert, "Stand Pat," *Foreign Policy*, No. 54 (Spring 1984), pp. 139-155; Bernard K. Gordon, "The Third Indochina Conflict," *Foreign Affairs*, Vol. 65 (Fall 1986), pp. 66-85; John McAuliff and Mary Byrne McDonnell, "Ending the Cambodian Stalemate," *World Policy Journal*, Vol. 7 (Winter 1989-90), pp. 71-105; Stephen J. Morris, "Vietnam's Vietnam," *Atlantic Monthly*, Vol. 255 (January 1985), pp. 70, 75, 78; Stephen J. Solarz, "Cambodia and the International Community," *Foreign Affairs*, Vol. 69 (Spring 1990), pp. 99-115; Nathaniel Thayer, "Cambodia: Misperceptions and Peace," *Washington Quarterly*, Spring 1991, pp. 179-191.

2.   See assessment in Far Eastern Economics Review, *Asia 1990 Yearbook*, pp. 102-103.

3.   The prince's stance at this time was said to demonstrate his strong dependence on China for continued support. In any event, the mercurial prince remained strongly wedded to this position until the months leading up to the signing of the October 1991 Paris accord. Then he seemed to begin to tilt closer to the SOC and its prime minister, Hun Sen. Speculation about the prince's shift pointed to several possible motives: a response to greater SOC flexibility; the shift in China's position after its reconciliation with Vietnam in 1991; and an assessment that the 1991 peace framework would give the prince enough international support to break with the reviled Khmer Rouge.

4.   See assessments in Far Eastern Economic Review, *Asia 1991 Yearbook*, pp. 93-94; Justis M. van der Kroef, "Cambodia in 1990," *Asian Survey*, January 1991, pp. 94-102; and Frederick Z. Brown, "Cambodia in 1991," *Asian Survey*, January 1992, pp. 88-96.

5.   See, among others, Clark, *The Challenge of Indochina*, pp. 9-16.

6.   For a review of the US policy debate, see US Congress, House Committee on Foreign Affairs, *Congress and Foreign Policy 1990* (Washington, DC: US Government Printing Office, 1991), pp. 97-106.

7.   *Ibid.*

8.   See discussion in congressional staff seminar reviewed in Clark, *The Challenge of Indochina*, p. 11.

9.   Reviewed in *ibid.*, pp. 9-12.

10.   For further information, see the *Indochina Digest*, Indochina Project, Washington, DC, December 6 and 13, 1991.

11

The United States, El Salvador, and the Central American Peace Process

Thomas Dodd

HISTORICALLY, US INTEREST IN Central America has focused on the need to secure free and unimpeded transit across that region. Direct intervention, often diplomatic but sometimes military, has been necessary to pursue global US economic and strategic goals.

States in the region have had to grapple with economic and political problems made worse by extraregional states motivated by geopolitical interests. From a confederation of countries in the nineteenth century to a single judicial system and a common market in the twentieth, these nations have turned when possible to multilateral diplomacy to further their own interests.

As so often in the past, Central America in the 1980s was a focal point of US-Soviet rivalry. Each superpower had surrogates in the region and backed rebel forces undermining the authority of neighboring countries. Despite its Cold War backdrop, however, US policy in Central America was a contentious issue in US domestic politics. Debates raged in Congress and across the nation over US involvement in the civil war in El Salvador and support for the Nicaraguan resistance.

Despite turmoil in the wider world around them, Central America's leaders crafted a plan for a settlement of regional civil wars, ending insurgencies, and beginning democratization. Three elements—domestic, regional, and global—shaped a new approach to Central America's crisis, of which the Salvadoran civil war was but one segment. How did these factors combine to provide the real impetus for peace in El Salvador? How

Map 11.1 Central America

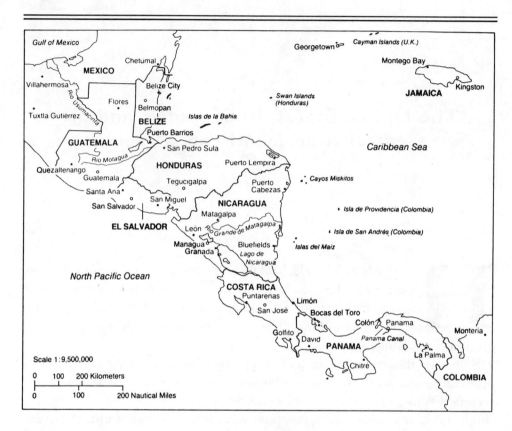

Reprinted, by permission, from Richard Fagen, *Forging Peace: The Challenge of Central America* (Basil Blackwell, Inc., 1987; copyright © PACCA 1987), p. xii.

did regional efforts weigh in? The story of how one of Central America's longest and most bitter internal conflicts finally ended has to sweep broadly to include events occurring not only in Central America but in domestic US politics and in superpower relations as well.

Ending Conflict in El Salvador

The Salvadoran civil war, in which more than 75,000 people lost their lives over a period of twelve grim years, finally ended in the tall United Nations (UN) headquarters building in New York City. It was virtually at the stroke of the New Year 1992, in the last few minutes of his tenure as

UN secretary-general, that Javier Pérez de Cuéllar arranged the peace accord between the Salvadoran government and rebel forces.

Later, Bernard Aronson, US assistant secretary of state for Latin American affairs, unexpectedly encountered several Salvadoran rebel military commanders in a New York restaurant, among them Joaquin Villalobos, Salvador Sanchez Ceren, and Schafik Handal. The chance meeting marked the first time since 1980 that, after the United States had spent $4 billion propping up Salvadoran governments fighting guerrilla forces, a Washington official of Aronson's rank had met with insurgent leaders. Aronson spoke to the guerrilla commanders, remarking that the encounter was a kind of catharsis for everyone in that it was an important occasion to let the rebels know the war was over for the United States as well. Fidel Recinos, another of the guerrilla leaders present, replied that everyone in El Salvador, government and insurgent forces, had changed too.[1]

The negotiations between the government and the Farabundo Marti National Liberation Front (FMLN) lasted eighteen months and resulted in an agreement that, within a broad framework of conditions and guarantees, transformed the guerrilla forces into civilians and provided for their future security. A formal signing ceremony took place on January 16, 1992, in Mexico City. By October 31, 1992, 6,000 guerrilla troops are to be disarmed under UN auspices. El Salvador's President Alfredo Cristiani made a commitment to reform society by promoting respect for human rights, strengthening civilian institutions, and establishing a smaller regular armed force. Although the accord marked a significant breakthrough for all parties in war-torn El Salvador, external factors such as the collapse of the Soviet Union and the end of Cuba's role as a regional force placed unique pressure on the FMLN and ended its hopes of overthrowing the government.

El Salvador, at the end of 1991, was no longer the center of Cold War tensions that Alexander Haig had pointed to during his confirmation hearings as secretary of state in 1980. When Mikhail Gorbachev later promised to withdraw troops from Afghanistan in 1988, he urged the end of Cold War confrontations in other parts of the world, among them Central America.[2] The scope and depth of the dramatic changes that had occurred in US-Soviet relations were demonstrated once again when both nations, in a joint statement issued in December 1991, urged government and rebel forces to reach an agreement on an internationally supervised cease-fire and to implement measures aimed at national reconciliation.[3]

The Salvadoran peace accord also reflected a triumph for collective diplomatic action in Central America. It came after years of painstaking

efforts by the region's national leaders to bring an end to civil conflict
through several regional peace agreements between states and reconciliation within countries.

Divergence of US and Central American Interests in the 1980s

When the leftist Sandinista National Liberation Front (FSLN) in
Nicaragua ousted longtime dictator and Washington ally, Anastasio Somoza in July 1979, the event riveted US attention on Central America.
The Sandinistas were now dominating Nicaraguan politics, were assisting
leftist guerrillas in El Salvador, and had already developed close relations
with the Soviet bloc, particularly Cuba.[4] US policy, particularly during the
Reagan administration, focused almost exclusively on isolating Nicaragua,
seeking to overthrow the government by supporting counterrevolutionar-
ies (the Contras), and protecting Nicaragua's neighbors against the conta-
gion of leftist revolutions. Washington's Central American allies—Costa
Rica, Honduras, Guatemala, and El Salvador—initially shared US concerns
about Nicaragua.

Washington also pushed for reform in the rest of Central America, urging moderate military officers to turn power over to civilian regimes in El
Salvador, Honduras, and Guatemala. El Salvador created a civilian military
junta in late 1979 and held presidential elections in 1984; the Honduran
military turned power over to civilians in 1981. The same transition took
place in Guatemala in 1985. In 1980, during the Carter administration,
Washington began allocating large sums of money to the El Salvadoran
government fighting the FMLN, Nicaragua's ally.

As time passed, however, many Central Americans began to see US policy toward Nicaragua as a failure. The Contras, backed by Washington,
were unable to topple the Marxist regime. Political polarization and economic disruption mounted in the region, causing floods of refugees. As
early as 1983, several Latin American countries—Venezuela, Colombia,
Panama, and Mexico, known as the Contadora group—tried to mediate
conflicts in the area. This diplomatic front had emerged in 1976 supporting the ratification of a Panama Canal treaty. Essentially, these states were
engaging in a time-honored diplomatic strategy of creating juridical means
through arbitration and mediation to preclude intervention in the internal
affairs of Latin American states. Meeting again in January 1983, they
focused on Central America's crisis and proposed a plan to end internal

political strife in each state and to terminate military assistance from out-side powers, namely the United States and the Soviet Union.

The effort failed for several reasons. Among them were Mexico's mounting debt and reliance on the United States for help and Venezuela's growing lack of enthusiasm for the militant Sandinista regime. Washington rejected outright the Contadora plan largely because it lacked enforce-ment mechanisms and thus left US security interests unattended. While the Contadora group was trying but failing, leaders in Central America began to criticize Washington's single-minded focus on a military solution to the Nicaraguan problem. Washington's abrupt rejection of the Latin American diplomatic initiative also caused resentment.

In 1987, the presidents of five Central American states—José Napoleon Duarte Fuentes (El Salvador), Marco Antonio Vinicio Cerezo Arevalo (Guatemala), José Azcona Hoyo (Honduras), Daniel Ortega Saavedra (Nicaragua), and Oscar Arias Sanchez (Costa Rica)—drew up a regional peace plan, named after Arias, its architect. This was a collective diplomatic initiative, designed by the area's top political leaders to reach an accommo-dation with Nicaragua and recognize the legitimacy of the Sandinista regime. However, the proposal also had a broader objective: It sought peaceful relations among all governments and the resolution of civil war within states, particularly in Nicaragua, El Salvador, and Guatemala.

The plan was one agreement, but it had five agendas representing the interests of each Central American nation. The Sandinistas in Nicaragua looked favorably on a regional peace, their legitimacy having been debili-tated by war and a growing economic crisis. They had become heavily de-pendent on the Soviet bloc for military assistance. Moreover, many San-dinista leaders were willing to accept some changes in the Nicaraguan po-litical system if Washington would cut off aid to the Contra guerrillas. Costa Rica, with no army, faced a growing Nicaraguan armed force; Costa Rican leaders feared that unless the Sandinistas were restrained by a treaty, the country could fall under Nicaraguan influence. El Salvador's government was anxious to end its civil war with the FMLN, which in turn was being aided by the Sandinistas. Honduras supported a Central American peace plan principally because it wanted its border with Nicaragua pacified and assurances that Washington would help resettle the thousands of Contras and other refugees in the area. Last, Guatemala, like El Salvador, wanted to negotiate a peace agreement with its rebels—who had been fighting for more than twenty-five years—and bring them into the political process.

The Arias Peace Plan

The Arias peace plan had three elements. First, all countries, including the United States, had to end their support for guerrilla forces. US aid to the Contras and Nicaraguan, Cuban, and Soviet support of the Salvadoran FMLN would have to stop. Second, all Central American states had to agree to democratize their political processes. Last, each state had to begin national reconciliation by allowing all opposition groups to enter the political system.[5]

The US response to the Arias plan disappointed its proponents. Still wedded to its policy of isolating Nicaragua and ousting the leftist Sandinista government, Washington presented the Reagan-Wright plan, devised by the White House and James C. Wright, Jr., at that time Speaker of the House.[6] This proposal, presented to the region's presidents in August 1987 at their summit, called for a negotiated cease-fire in Nicaragua, only after which Washington would suspend military assistance to the Contras. The Central American presidents rejected the US plan and proceeded to implement their own regional peace process.

The Arias peace plan did not produce immediate changes in Central America's political landscape, and Central Americans were fully aware that a final resolution to the region's political crises could not be attained without US support.[7] Yet the leaders involved felt notable results would eventually emerge from the peace process. They felt prospects for economic aid from Europe might in time reduce their dependence on the United States and similarly bring pressure on Nicaragua to democratize. Moreover, their efforts to strengthen democracy through the Arias plan would assist new civilian regimes emerging in the mid-1980s. Making Nicaragua their first priority, the Arias peace-plan participants continued their work.

At Tesoro Beach in El Salvador, on February 14, 1989, they proposed a plan for voluntary demobilization, repatriation, or relocation of Nicaraguan Contras and their families either in that country or in third states.[8] Nicaragua, signing the agreement, promised in turn to hold presidential and legislative elections on February 25, 1990.[9] Clearly, Central American leaders had taken a notable step: resolving, without any assistance from the United States, one of the most contentious issues between Washington and the region. The Tesoro Beach accord offered the first indication that elements of the Arias plan could be implemented.

Washington: Building Bipartisanship

President Bush, in office only a few weeks, took note of the positive steps entailed in the Arias plan and the pledge from the Sandinistas to hold elections. The Tesoro Beach accord opened wide the possibility of closer cooperation with Washington because it did not fix a date for the Contras to abandon their cause, thereby satisfying its supporters as well as opponents in the US Congress.

With none of the ideological zeal of President Reagan, President Bush and Secretary of State James Baker displayed a more pragmatic approach toward Central America. Abandoning military force as key to its regional policy, the administration shifted to diplomatic pressure on Nicaragua as provided in the Tesoro accord, working with the region's leaders. Undoubtedly, the change in US policy reflected political reality—Congress would no longer support military assistance to the Contras. The president and his secretary of state concluded that without a consensus at home, bipartisanship on Central American issues would be almost impossible to achieve. Cooperation with Congress appeared to be as important to the new administration as the substance of policy itself.[10]

After several weeks of negotiations with leaders of the House and Senate, a bipartisan agreement was concluded for a new US approach to Central America. The accord, signed at the White House on March 24, 1989, focused on Nicaragua, clearly one of the most contentious issues dividing the executive and legislative branches for almost a decade. Specifically, it was agreed that the United States would pursue three objectives: promoting democracy in Nicaragua, convincing Nicaragua to stop subverting and destabilizing its neighbors, and ending Soviet-bloc ties that threatened US and regional security.[11]

In an effort to ensure that the Tesoro Beach accord would have some effect, the administration pursued a carrot-and-stick approach. Carrots would be the lifting of the trade embargo on Nicaragua, restoring US aid, and improving diplomatic relations. But if Nicaragua failed to adhere to the proposals, including the holding of free elections, Washington would, in turn, wield the stick and tighten its embargo as well as renew military support for the Contras. The executive-legislative agreement also provided for extending humanitarian assistance to the Contras through February 28, 1990, after the planned Nicaraguan elections. The pact created a bipartisan approach to US policy in Central America and, equally significant, recognized for the first time the Arias peace plan as the key mechanism for bringing about a cease-fire, democratization, and national reconciliation in all Central American states.

The change in US policy—from pursuit of a military solution in Nicaragua to cooperation with the regional peace process—reflected the administration's desire to move beyond Nicaragua to pursue what it saw as larger issues. Improved relations with all of Latin America, unencumbered by an unpopular US stance in Central America, was clearly in the US interest. The United States wanted to work closely with its southern neighbors in pursuit of free-market economies and economic growth as well as deal with narcotics and environmental issues.[12] Just as important, President Bush needed congressional help on other administration initiatives, including a free-trade agreement with Mexico and the Enterprise for the Americas Initiative, announced in June 1990, providing for relief of official debts.

Washington Follows a Central American Agenda

The 1989 executive-congressional agreement fit well in the context of the ongoing Central American peace process. Remaining elements of the Arias plan, namely elections in Nicaragua and an end to civil war in El Salvador and Guatemala, were essentially adopted as part of Washington's policy objectives.

The Tesoro Beach accord had established a detailed plan for democratization in Nicaragua by opening the political process to all groups. The promised elections would include the presidency, the legislature, and, for the first time, municipal offices. A Supreme Electoral Council was to be named with representatives from all opposition parties. The summit also had called for the presence of international observers during the election period, who would come principally from the United Nations and the Organization of American States (OAS). Last, the Tesoro Beach agreement provided for the demobilization of the Contra force under a plan set up by specialized organizations of the United Nations.

Later, a meeting of the region's presidents at Tela, Honduras, on August 7, 1989, concentrated on the mechanisms for the relocation, repatriation and breakup of the Nicaraguan Contra forces. Specifically, an accord reached set up an International Commission of Support and Verification (CIAV, its Spanish acronym) to be administered by the secretaries-general of the OAS and the UN.[13] The CIAV was assigned specific tasks, among them disarming the Contras, establishing reception centers for returning forces, hearing complaints about their treatment, and distributing food and medical supplies.

The Tela accord also named observers from the UN and OAS to ensure that insurgent forces operating in several states, including Nicaragua and El Salvador, no longer received aid from countries outside the region. Peacekeeping forces included observers from Canada, West Germany, and Spain. Along with the verification teams, "surveillance missions" from these states, the UN, and the OAS would patrol Honduran, Nicaraguan, and El Salvadoran borders.[14]

Elections in Nicaragua

Unlike Panama, where a US invasion in 1989 cost lives and treasure, transition in Nicaragua was peaceful. The democratic elections pursued and orchestrated in a multilateral diplomatic effort brought an end to the unpopular regime in the country. They also made possible reintegration of the Contras into Nicaraguan society. Violeta Chamorro's defeat of Sandinista leader Daniel Ortega in February 1990 marked a watershed in Nicaraguan history and a turning point in US-Central American relations. It was the first time a free political contest had taken place in Nicaragua since 1932. For Washington, the installation of the new president removed the last major regional force openly antagonistic to it.

But Chamorro's election was primarily a Nicaraguan triumph. It was a stunning mandate to create a new government. The elections swept an overconfident Sandinista president from power, but also gave Daniel Ortega's party, the FSLN, a significant bloc of seats in the National Assembly and control of the country's defense units.

Bringing her campaign slogan and the Arias peace-plan goal of "national reconciliation" into effect, the president named Humberto Ortega, brother of former president Daniel, as commander of the army. In return, Chamorro was assured that the military would support her objective of bringing the Contra forces into the country's political process. In addition, the army was cut back from over 80,000 to less than 28,000. For the first time, the chief executive became both minister of defense and commander in chief of the nation's armed forces.[15]

Four months later, in June 1990, the Protocol of Managua was signed by Humberto Ortega and Galeano Franklin, director of the political arm of the Contras. It stipulated that some 30,000 hectares of land would be given to Contra troops. They were also allowed to keep a security force and be represented in local municipal councils. Shortly after the agreement was signed, 18,000 Contras turned in automatic rifles and sixty-two US-made Red Eye surface-to-air missiles.

Several confrontations have occurred between the Contras and government forces since 1990 over such matters as the restoration of confiscated lands. An adjudication commission composed of representatives of cooperatives, Contra forces, and former landowners has so far been moderately successful in resolving conflicts.[16]

President Chamorro's accomplishments included restructuring and reducing the size of the military and security forces, reintegrating to a significant degree Contras into the country, and drafting a recovery plan for the nation's destroyed economy. Each of these tasks has been pursued through a *concertación* (a dialogue between political antagonists)—a process unknown in Nicaragua's past. These brief, tenuous steps toward internal reconciliation, carried out as outlined in the Arias peace plan, indicate that moderates in the country's major parties, once on the periphery of politics, have returned home and accepted the profound changes that have occurred since the ouster of Anastasio Somoza in July 1979. And for the United States, another ally and a democratic regime emerged in the region. The restoration of democracy in Panama and Violeta Chamorro's election victory removed any semblance of a regional threat to US interests. Equally important, these two developments ended Washington's rationale for a military victory over rebel forces in El Salvador.

The Effect on El Salvador

Central American summits from 1989 through 1991 held to agendas that focused on ending conflicts within countries. Washington's new determination to work for these objectives through support for the regional process was conducted in a low-keyed manner. It allowed Central American leaders to determine the pace and procedures for government and rebel forces in El Salvador to negotiate an end to the civil war.

The Tela (Honduras) meeting in August 1989 and the San Isidro de Coronado (Costa Rica) summit the following December called on the UN to implement a peace plan that included the creation of a peacekeeping force to halt cross-border incursions throughout Central America. The UN force was to monitor Contra bases in Honduras and patrol El Salvador's borders as well. At the San Isidro de Coronado meeting, with elections already scheduled in Nicaragua, the Central American leaders were able to focus their attention on the festering internal conflict in El Salvador. They asked the UN to do three things: first, help resume a dialogue between the FMLN and the government; second, whenever possible, increase verification of any agreements made; and third, begin work on the demobilization of rebel forces.[17]

Later, in the fall of 1990, the United States urged the Soviet Union to cooperate in a Salvadoran peace settlement and help end the conflict. Specifically, Washington asked Moscow to establish diplomatic relations with San Salvador, hoping to create a major setback for the leftist rebels. The Soviet Union had already halted arms shipments to the Sandinista regime in early 1989 and had helped persuade the Nicaraguan government to call elections. The United States was instrumental in arranging several meetings between Soviet Foreign Minister Yuri Pavlov and Manuel Pacas, his Salvadoran counterpart in Washington. Pavlov's deputy, Jan Burliay, visited El Salvador's President Alfredo Cristiani and suggested diplomatic relations be established. At the same time, he offered to intercede with Cuba to encourage the rebels to negotiate.

Ending bipolar confrontation in Central America and El Salvador in particular gave new strength to the region's peacemaking process. Yet when Congress turned its attention to El Salvador after appropriating funds for economic recovery in Panama and Nicaragua, complications arose. Unlike in the Panama and Nicaraguan cases, Washington had given its unqualified support to an incumbent government in a civil war. US pledges of support were still being counted on. To complicate the situation, rebel guerrilla forces had launched a nationwide offensive in November and December 1989 and had shown significant strength. At the same time, six Jesuit priests were assassinated by elements of the US-supported Salvadoran army. When prosecution of the case lagged and human rights continued to be violated, Congress withheld half of El Salvador's $85 million in military aid to pressure President Cristiani's government to reform the military and punish human rights offenders. At the same time, Congress warned guerrillas that beginning a military offensive would be challenged and pressed both sides to accept any UN proposals for a cease-fire.[18]

In April 1990, the UN persuaded government and guerrilla representatives to undertake monthly talks under its auspices as recommended at the December 1989 San Isidro summit. With Central American leaders pressing for negotiations, Congress using its leverage on funding, and the UN setting a plan for ending the conflict, El Salvador's government and FMLN negotiators made some progress. From April to November 1990, six meetings deadlocked over the issues of armed forces reduction and human rights abuses, but two positive elements emerged: First, the UN was given authority by the parties to monitor human rights. Second, El Salvador's newly created Inter-Party Commission's proposals for teams of international observers to monitor the March 1991 legislative and mayoral elections were agreed upon. Just as significant, government and rebel negotiators allowed a UN mediator, Peruvian diplomat Alvaro de Soto, to continue his peacemaking efforts.

The March 1991 congressional elections in El Salvador marked a significant breakthrough toward political reconciliation. The right-wing ARENA (National Republican Alliance) took 50 percent of the vote, electing thirty-nine people to the legislature, and Christian Democrats received 20 percent. Three parties of the left associated with the FMLN and calling themselves Democratic Convergence received about 16 percent of the vote and obtained eight seats in Congress.[19] Ruben Zamora, a member of the left and once a militant guerrilla, was installed as vice president of the National Assembly. The near impossible took place as Roberto D'Aubuisson, a founder of ARENA and allegedly linked to death squads that eliminated thousands of people in the 1980s, voted for the leftist. With the installation of former rebels in the Congress, it was becoming clear that the FMLN was no longer seeking a military victory but social and economic changes by constitutional means.[20]

With the political arm of the FMLN (Democratic Convergence) in the political process and conceding along with government officials that a military standoff existed, the FMLN military commanders agreed to negotiate a cease-fire before all other political issues were resolved. This was an issue on which the UN-mediated talks had foundered.[21] Consequently, negotiations proceeded at an accelerated pace. Hard-line rebel military leaders like Fidel Recinos now joined negotiations in April 1991, indicating a willingness to discuss concrete provisions for a military truce.[22]

The Salvadoran Congress, meanwhile, approved for the first time in history several constitutional changes that were agreed to by government and rebel negotiators as part of a cease-fire. These included the creation of a civilian police force to take over internal security from the army, the election of supreme court judges, and a tribunal to supervise political contests.

But several issues still remained difficult to settle, among them how insurgent forces could be incorporated into the army. UN Secretary-General Pérez de Cuéllar proposed, and both sides agreed, that rebel groups be assured of representation in the new police force.[23] At this point, on September 24, in New York, both sides created a framework of conditions and guarantees that assured rebel soldiers a new role in Salvadoran society. A compromise reached in September stipulated that rebels drop their demand that the armed forces be dissolved or integrated with insurgent forces. In exchange, the government promised to purge the military of brutal and corrupt officers and reduce its size. A ten-member National Commission for the Consolidation of Peace was established to work out the details of the accord. The guerrillas and the government named two members each, and the other six were selected by political parties in the National Congress. The UN and the Roman Catholic Church were named observers on the commission.[24]

Several weeks later, on November 14, the FMLN announced it was unilaterally suspending all offensive operations, dropping its demand that the army remain outside the insurgent zones until a cease-fire was negotiated. President Cristiani promptly responded that the military would undertake similar action.[25] A major roadblock to a temporary cease-fire had fallen. Yet to be resolved was the command of a new civilian police force located in rebel-held territory and the amount of land the government would provide rebels in those regions.[26]

Though general provisions had been made in September for a cease-fire, neither side felt assured that these would be implemented and enforced. To move the two sides beyond their mistrust, four countries calling themselves Friends of the Salvadoran Peace Process—Mexico, Venezuela, Colombia, and Spain—offered to support a UN plan for overseeing any agreement to be carried out. Moreover, as an incentive to sign an accord, the "Four Friends" promised to undertake efforts to obtain funds for the reconstruction of the country. This was an endeavor rebels and government negotiators agreed needed to be undertaken. The UN, the Four Friends, and the United States persuaded negotiators to sign a cease-fire agreement just before midnight on December 31 to go into effect by February 1, 1992. In an unprecedented move to guarantee that a cease-fire would take place as promised, rebel and government representatives agreed that if they failed to settle remaining differences by January 10, the UN would have the power to decide them.[27]

On January 16, in Mexico City, the US-backed Salvadoran government and the rebels signed a detailed peace treaty. It ended twelve years of civil war that killed 1 percent of the Salvadoran population of 5.2 million and displaced one-fifth of the nation's people. Following are the key elements of the peace treaty:

- The UN-monitored cease-fire effective date was set for February 1, 1992.
- The FMLN begins the process of dismantling its rebel forces, the deadline for which was set for October 31, with all weapons handed over to the UN.
- Political prisoners will be freed.
- The FMLN becomes a legal political party in El Salvador.
- The national police changes from military to civilian control and former rebel fighters are allowed to serve in it. Its new director will be named by President Cristiani from three candidates nominated by the National Commission for the Consolidation of Peace, including representatives from the government, FMLN, and political parties. Within a period of twenty-one months, approximately 6,000 members are expected to have been graduated from a new police academy. The paramilitary National Guard and Treasury Police are to be disbanded.
- The armed forces are to be reduced by 50 percent. The government is to submit a plan and timetable to the UN. The cuts will include 12,000 to 13,000 combat troops and approximately 19,000 operational support units. A land redistribution program will give land to fighters and peasants on both sides.
- Government military intelligence is to be dismantled along with US-trained elite infantry battalions.
- Weapon permits issued to civilians by the military will be canceled, and weapons collected.
- The National Commission for the Consolidation of Peace will review members of armed forces with the aim of purging the worst human rights violators.
- A socioeconomic forum will be established made up equally of representatives of business, labor, and government. (A similar institution was created in Nicaragua in spring 1990). The forum will draw up a national reconstruction plan with proposals from the FMLN. Its specific task will deal with economic and social stabilization, labor legislation, and a consumer-protection code. A reconstruction fund set up

by the government will receive ongoing assistance from the UN Development Fund.[28]

Just as the Contadora process in 1982 and the Arias peace plan of 1987 demonstrated a collective approach to the Nicaraguan crisis, the same process brought about a cease-fire agreement in El Salvador. The Tela and San Isidro Central American summits in August and December 1989 provided the framework for mediation in El Salvador.

Summary

Looking at Central America in the 1980s, one could describe it as an arena for superpower rivalry, brutal wars, displaced people, and worsening poverty. But now that El Salvador's civil conflict is ending and opportunities are opening up for wider participation in government, a total of six freely elected civilian leaders in the region preside over democracies, however fragile they may be. These states, with the exception of Panama, have experienced peaceful transitions of power. Regional diplomacy set the agenda for an end to civil wars, though it is still working on ending the insurgency in Guatemala. It is also creating a climate to support ever-stronger democratic governments. What remains to be resolved are the age-old problems of inegalitarian societies and poor distribution of wealth. A regional parliament of elected representatives met for the first time in October 1991 in Guatemala. It set long-term goals for itself involving political-economic cooperation to lead toward a common market and continued efforts for democratization.

Both internal events and outside pressures, regional and extraregional, made a peace accord in El Salvador possible. The origins of the conflict, as in other Central American states, reached back to the 1960s and 1970s, an era of rapid economic growth. Social changes emerging from uneven development gave rise to new groups demanding participation in the political process. But El Salvador's governmental institutions refused to make room for these groups. Efforts to accommodate more participation were thwarted, thereby radicalizing political forces. The country was polarized by ideological extremes. Leftist guerrillas fought to overthrow the entire structure of the state. The militant right vowed to destroy even the most moderate of political reformers. The origins of the civil war were essentially internal, but the Cold War fostered and sustained them. Washington bolstered incumbent Salvadoran regimes with counterinsurgency training and money. The Soviet Union, through Cuba, supported the revolutionaries.

US policy of providing military assistance to the Salvadoran government, opposing a rebel victory, and prodding the government to hold elections encouraged elements on the right to moderate their position on total destruction of the FMLN forces. Continued pressure in the 1980s from the US Congress on human rights violations and the withholding of funds for military equipment added pressure for a peace process to begin and continue. The fall of the Berlin Wall (1989), the Sandinista electoral defeat (1990), and the collapse of the Soviet Union (1991) made guerrilla leaders realize that the destruction of the Salvadoran state was no longer possible. The FMLN had not been persuasive that its campaigns of sabotage and assassination would improve the lot of the vast majority of the Salvadoran people.

Political moderates on the left, like their counterparts on the right, sought a political center in a peace process begun by Central American presidents in 1987. Equally important, Washington abandoned its unilateral objectives of toppling a Sandinista regime in Nicaragua and supporting a Salvadoran government military victory and worked to strengthen the regional peace process. The Salvadoran agreement addressed the long-term causes of its twelve-year civil war. It provided wider participation for the left as long as it abandoned armed conflict and, at the same time, ended government-sponsored military praetorianism.[29]

Simón Bolívar, a leader of the independence movement in Latin America, once said Central America would become the "Emporium of the Universe," a crossroad for the world. It did—but exclusively for the interests of extraregional powers competing for control of the area. The Central American architects of the peace process took charge of their history the way Bolívar intended in the early nineteenth century. If not becoming the center of the world then, today these nations have become managers of their own destiny through regional collective action, taking preemptive steps to avoid intervention.

Will Washington shift its focus on Central America from close attention to indifference now that a peace agreement has been established in El Salvador? The simple fact is that Central America will no longer be as important a security consideration to the United States as it was during the Cold War. Yet, like its neighbors in the rest of the Western Hemisphere, Central America will be more significant for different reasons.[30]

Approximately 23 million people of Latin American ancestry live in the United States. A substantial percentage come from Central America and the Caribbean. Immigration and migration are expected to continue and will profoundly affect such domestic policy issues as education, public health, business, politics, and employment. Abraham Lowenthal has observed that "Latin America's problems and opportunities may become understandable as virtually 'domestic' concerns in the United States."[31]

For decades, Washington looked to Latin America for military stations and raw materials; today it seeks markets for its products and hopes for cooperation on such issues as drugs, the environment, and human rights. A clear-cut US policy for the region may not emerge, but a new set of issues will compel Washington to continue paying attention to Central America.

Central America has begun its search for a place in a changing world where the interests of one state may be more effectively pursued through regional association and multilateral diplomacy. In turn, Washington ultimately accepted the need to replace unilateral action with multilateral approaches.[32] It must be remembered that the Contadora efforts and the Arias peace plan were not always welcomed in Washington. The United States may have learned that restraint in the post-Cold War era, especially in a regional conflict, can create a successful outcome.[33]

Notes

1. Tim Golden, "The Salvadorans Make Peace via Negotiated Revolution," *New York Times*, January 5, 1992, p. A-9.
2. Stephan Rosenfeld, "Straight Talk About Hot Spots," *Washington Post*, June 3, 1988, p. A-19.
3. "US Soviet Statement in El Salvador: Peace Negotiations," *US Department of State Dispatch*, December 9, 1991, p. 2.
4. Nina Serafino, "Overview: Central American Dilemmas and US Policy," *CRS Review* (Library of Congress), February 1989, p. 1.
5. "Central America and Panama, Major Issues for Congress," *CRS Issue Brief*, November 16, 1990, p. 4.
6. John Felton, "Baker Woos Hill with Call for Bipartisanship," *Congressional Quarterly*, November 16, 1990, p. 4.
7. *Ibid.*
8. Tesoro Beach, El Salvador, February 14, 1989. "Text of Accord by Central American Presidents," *New York Times*, February 16, 1989, p. A-14.
9. "Plan to Disarm the Contras Revives Policy Debate," *Congressional Quarterly*, February 18, 1989, p. 345.
10. Robert Pear, "Behind the Transformation of Central American Policy," *New York Times*, April 16, 1989, p. E-2.
11. "Bipartisan Agreement Reached on Central American Policy," *Congressional Quarterly*, March 25, 1989, p. 669.

12. N. Serafino, L. Storrs, and M. Taft, "Latin America: An Overview of US Policy and Challenges in 1991," *CRS Report for Congress*, February 19, 1991.

13. Nina Serafino, "Central America Peace Prospects: US Interests and Response," *CRS Issue Brief* (Library of Congress), August 30, 1990, p. 7.

14. *Ibid.*

15. Serafino, "Central American Peace Prospects," p. 10.

16. *Diario Las Americas*, June 3, 1990, p. 6.

17. FBIS (Foreign Broadcast Information Service) LAT. 89, 237, December 12, 1989, p. 5.

18. Serafino, Storrs, and Taft, "Latin America: An Overview of US Policy Challenges in 1991," p. 3.

19. *Latin American Weekly Report*, March 21, 1991, p. 1. The Democratic Convergence, which formed the political wing of the FMLN, consisted of three parties: (1) the Popular Social Christian Movement, led by Ruben Zamora, first to return to legal political activity, (2) the National Revolutionary Movement, established by the late Guillermo Ungo, and (3) the Social Democratic party.

20. Lee Hockstader, "Salvadorans Moving to End Civil War," *Washington Post*, May 5, 1991, p. A-29.

21. Mark Uhlig, "Salvadorans and Rebels Open Talks to End Their Civil War," *New York Times*, April 5, 1991, p. A-6.

22. *Ibid.*

23. Shirley Christian, "Salvador Chief Says Bars to Peace Are Overcome, But Others Demur," *New York Times*, September 24, 1991, p. A-16.

24. *Latin American Report*, October 10, 1991, p. 2.

25. Shirley Christian, "Salvadoran Rebels to Halt Attacks: Government Sees an End to War," *New York Times*, November 15, 1991, p. A-1.

26. *Ibid.*, p. 16.

27. Edward Cody, "Salvadorans Sign Accord Ending 12-Year War," *Washington Post*, January 17, 1992, p. A-27.

28. Lee Hockstader, "As Conflicts Wane, Central America Strives for Long-Term Stability," *Washington Post*, January 19, 1992, p. A-20. See also "National Agenda for Peace in El Salvador," *Washington Update* (Washington, DC), Vol. 3, No. 7 (January 1992), pp. 1-2.

29. Charles Lane, "War and Remembrance: Peace at Last in El Salvador," *New Republic*, February 24, 1992, p. 10.

30. Abraham Lowenthal, "The United States and Latin America in the 1990s: Changing US Interests and Policies in a New World," Inter-American Dialogue, Washington, DC, 1991, p. 17.

31. *Ibid.*, p. 1.

32. *The Americas in a New World—The 1990 Report of the Inter-American Dialogue* (Aspen, CO: Aspen Institute, 1990) pp. 4, 6.

33. Terry Lynn Karl, "El Salvador's Negotiated Revolution," *Foreign Affairs*, Vol. 71 (Spring 1992), p. 163.

12

Choosing the World's Top Diplomat

Donald F. McHenry

IN 1991, THE UNITED NATIONS (UN) faced the task of electing a new secretary-general. Javier Pérez de Cuéllar, a Peruvian diplomat, had been a dark-horse candidate when he was elected to the post in 1981. At the time, he had announced his intention to serve only a single five-year term, but had been prevailed upon to serve a second term. Now, Pérez de Cuéllar gave every indication that he would retire.

The election of a secretary-general in 1991 was, arguably, more significant than any since the election of the first, Trygve Lie, in 1945—more significant even than the election of Dag Hammarskjöld, who for all of his subsequent outstanding performance and deserved acclaim, was not elected with great expectations. For the first time, a secretary-general could be chosen free of the shadow of the Cold War. Rather than look for the individual least likely to rock the boat so delicately balanced between East and West, there was an opportunity to select the most outstanding individual available, an individual who might lead the UN toward the full realization of the potential its founders envisioned.

Indeed, throughout 1991, particularly in light of the UN's role in expelling Iraq from Kuwait, there was genuine excitement about the UN's potential. It had played a significant role in settling conflicts in Namibia, Angola, Afghanistan, and Nicaragua; and it was engaged in negotiations in El Salvador, Cambodia, Yugoslavia, and the Sahara.

The election of a new secretary-general in 1991 was also especially significant within the UN itself. After forty-five years, the Secretariat was in considerable need of overhaul. A new secretary-general was expected not only to carry the heavy additional duties of a reinvigorated organization, but also to reorganize the Secretariat, recruit new staff, and introduce new efficiencies and greater fiscal responsibility.

Despite the importance of the decision, or maybe because of it, the process of electing Boutros Boutros-Ghali of Egypt as the sixth secretary-general of the UN was long and difficult. The UN could not escape its past. Indeed, the past complicated and limited the selection process, no matter how much the member countries protested otherwise.

The UN Charter says very little about the qualifications of the secretary-general or about the manner in which the individual is selected. The selection, more technically the "appointment," is by a majority of the General Assembly on the nomination of the Security Council. Since substantive actions of the Security Council are subject to veto by any one of the five permanent members, the support or acquiescence (abstention or nonparticipation in the vote) of the five permanent members and enough of the remaining vote of the council to constitute a majority is essential. In the history of the UN, there has never been any question whether the General Assembly would appoint the individual nominated by the Security Council. In contrast, the nomination process in the Security Council has been subject to prolonged disagreement, usually behind the scenes.

Two factors in 1991 focused early attention on the election. The first was the sad memory of the revelations following the completion of the term of Pérez de Cuéllar's predecessor, Kurt Waldheim of Austria. It was revealed that during World War II, Secretary-General Waldheim served in an elite Nazi unit that was accused of committing atrocities. He denied participating in acts of atrocity, but whatever the truth regarding the nature of his service, he repeatedly lied about his wartime service. In his memoirs and in response to numerous inquiries, he had repeatedly stated he had been wounded early in the conflict and had spent the remainder of the war in school.[1]

The Waldheim record focused attention on the manner in which the secretary-general is elected. A former Austrian foreign minister and representative to the UN, Waldheim emerged victorious in the election of 1971 as a compromise candidate after the Soviet Union had vetoed the candidate favored by the West, Ambassador Max Jacobsen of Finland. There had been apparently little, if any, effort to research Waldheim's record. Even a cursory search in the archives of the UN would have revealed the true nature of his wartime service. Nor, in truth, had there been any systematic effort to examine closely the records of any of the other holders of the office of secretary-general.

Waldheim's record as secretary-general had been lackluster at best, but in their embarrassment at the revelations about his war record, both East and West tended to ignore the fact that he had performed in exactly the uninspiring manner expected of a compromise candidate. He would have been reelected had not China persistently vetoed him in favor of a Third World candidate.

The second factor that focused early attention on the election was the belief that the world's renewed reliance on the UN required an individual capable of making the organization effective in new and difficult situations. Early on, numerous discussions were held and studies written on ways to improve the election process and define the qualifications needed in a new secretary-general. At the same time, there were similar studies on ways to reorganize the UN and the specialized agencies to make them more responsive and efficient.

Among the most authoritative of such studies were one by Brian Urquhart and Erskine Childers, *A World In Need of Leadership: Tomorrow's United Nations*,[2] and *A Successor Vision: The United Nations of Tomorrow*,[3] a report of an international panel assembled by the UN Association of the United States of America. Both studies occurred well in advance of the 1991 UN election, in the case of the UN Association almost three years in advance. The recommendations by Urquhart and Childers were particularly significant in light of Urquhart's forty-year UN service, the last twelve as under secretary-general in charge of peacekeeping.

A number of recommendations in the two studies are similar. Urquhart and Childers respond affirmatively to their own questions: "Would an alternative to the present haphazard, increasingly parochial, predominantly political process in fact produce better results? And would governments, not to mention candidates, be prepared to accept the kind of scrutiny, expert advice, and wider canvassing which are considered both normal and essential in great enterprises in the non-governmental and private sector?"[4] For Urquhart and Childers, the essential elements of an improved selection process are

- Serious consideration by governments of the necessary qualifications for the post, as indicated, among other things, by probable future demands on the UN.
- A single seven-year term.
- The cessation of the practice of individual campaigning.
- Agreed rules as to nominations and a timetable for the process.

■ A well-organized search, in good time, for the best qualified candidates worldwide.

■ Removal of the initiative from self-perceived or nationally sponsored candidates.

■ The inclusion of women candidates in the search in comparable numbers to men.

■ A mechanism for the proper assembly of biographical material and for the assessment and checking of the qualifications, personal suitability, and record of the candidates.

■ High-level consideration of candidates by governments, in consultation with parliamentary leaders and important nongovernmental bodies, before a final decision.

These and other recommendations had little effect on the process of selecting the secretary-general in 1991. The term of the post was not changed, no search committee was established (the idea reportedly having been opposed by France), and numerous candidates campaigned actively or subtly for the office. There was one woman candidate, Gro Brudtland, the prime minister of Norway. And although it is likely that the qualifications for the office and the records of candidates were considered at high levels of governments—presumably more thoroughly than in previous elections—without a systematic search committee or publicly agreed-upon qualifications, the process was not advanced much beyond what existed in previous elections.

In the final analysis, UN members found it difficult to break away from the baggage of past elections. Among the heaviest bags to carry was the argument that it was now the turn of an African to be secretary-general. The process, as in previous years, was mired in political maneuvering and national ambitions.

Africa's Turn

In the five previous elections, three secretaries-general had come from Europe (Lie from Norway, Hammarskjöld from Sweden, and Waldheim from Austria), one from Asia (U Thant of Burma), and one from South America (Pérez de Cuéllar). None was from Africa. Accordingly, there was a widespread belief among Africans that it was "Africa's turn." It was also a belief supported by those who wished to rotate the position among geographical groups. More important, other countries were reluctant to oppose Africa's turn openly for fear of being accused of discriminating against Africans. In these circumstances, most countries, not wishing to elevate geography as the prime qualification for office, rejected the idea that it was "Africa's turn" but, sensitive to the discrimination charge, expressed confidence that qualified African candidates were available. On the record, Africans were themselves reluctant to assert geography as the prime consideration for the appointment. But there was no doubt about their sentiments. The OAU formally endorsed a list of African candidates. In September 1991, the foreign ministers of the 102-member Non-Aligned Movement endorsed Africa's nominees at the movement's meeting in Accra, Ghana. Finally, as if to drive home their determination, a number of African representatives threatened to oppose a Security Council nomination in the UN General Assembly if the nominee were not an African.

Historically, the geographical origin of the secretary-general had not been nearly as important as the individual's and his country's political orientation. Neutrality between East and West had been a more important qualification for the first four secretaries-general. Only in the case of the departing Pérez de Cuéllar had geography been more significant. China had vetoed any non-Third World candidate, and Pérez de Cuéllar emerged from the deadlock between Waldheim, generally favored by the West, and Salim Salim of Tanzania, a Third World candidate repeatedly vetoed by the United States.

The Third World had an additional pressing concern about the origin of the new secretary-general. The end of the Cold War had significantly reduced the Third World's pivotal role as a balance between East and West. The appointment of a secretary-general from the Third World was seen as important in restoring Third World influence.

Campaigning for the Job

Although the chief administrative officer of many countries is elected after a vigorous campaign, there has been concern that a campaign is not the appropriate process to select the secretary-general. In fact, the UN Charter specifies that the secretary-general shall be "appointed," not "elected," by the General Assembly after nomination by the Security

Council.[5] In reality, this apparent effort to emphasize the secretary-general's position as that of chief administrative officer and to downgrade the person's role as chief political officer of the UN was always doomed to fail.

In 1991, any effort to minimize the importance of campaigning for the position of secretary-general failed miserably. Some campaigned openly and actively; others simply made their availability known. A number of names surfaced as possible dark-horse candidates or candidates whose names might be put forward only in the event of a deadlock. Clearly, the notion of "Africa's turn" discouraged a number of candidates from allowing their names to be considered.

The OAU put six names forward: Minister of Finance Bernard Chidzero of Zimbabwe; Kenneth Dadzie, a Ghanaian UN official who serves as executive director of the UN Conference on Trade and Development; Egyptian Deputy Prime Minister Boutros Boutros-Ghali, a former minister of foreign affairs; James Jonah, a UN official from Sierra Leone who had held a number of high-level UN positions; Olusegun Obasanjo, former head of the military government of Nigeria, who had presided over the return of civilian rule to the country; and Nguema François Owono, a former Gabonese minister of culture. Other possible candidates included Prime Minister Gro Brudtland of Norway; Prince Sadruddin Aga Khan, former UN High Commissioner for Refugees and frequent designee for high-level UN assignments; Foreign Minister Raul Manglapus of the Philippines; and Foreign Minister Hans van den Broek of the Netherlands. Frequently mentioned were Olara Otunnu, former foreign minister of Uganda and Ugandan representative to the UN and currently president of the International Peace Academy; Tommy Koh, former Singapore ambassador to the UN and to the United States and currently serving as the chairman of the 1992 UN Conference on the Environment; Martti Ahtisaari, former UN under secretary-general for administration and the secretary-general's special representative for Namibia; and Jan Eliassen, the Swedish ambassador to the UN.

Some forms of campaigning were more discreet than others. In the cases of Boutros-Ghali and Chidzero, the heads of state of Egypt and Zimbabwe actively supported their nationals. The candidates themselves took steps to advance their cause. Boutros-Ghali, thought to be vulnerable on the grounds of age and health, signed up for a physical examination at Walter Reed Army Medical Center. Otunnu, concerned that France would oppose anyone who did not speak French, took leave to study French. Otunnu, however, had a problem he could not overcome: Exiled from

Uganda, he was opposed by his government. In the circumstances, he was omitted from the list of those endorsed by the OAU. Thus, Otunnu's name was never formally advanced despite the view of many that he would have been among the strongest of the African candidates.

There seemed to be agreement, intellectually, on the importance of the position and the need to avoid the selection pitfalls of the past, but this concern did not lead the world's leaders to change significantly the process followed in earlier years. One measure of the extent to which there was widespread longing to raise the political level of candidates can be seen in the names floated as possible candidates but never seriously considered. The list included Margaret Thatcher, former prime minister of the United Kingdom; Mikhail Gorbachev, outgoing president of the Soviet Union; and Jimmy Carter, former president of the United States.

Still another hope at an early stage was that Pérez de Cuéllar would agree to serve a third term. This would postpone the tough successor decision. Pérez de Cuéllar, who had already reversed his announced intention to serve a single term, seemed for a while to be open to a new term, reportedly having told Bush that he would not leave the organization in the lurch. Finally, however, he issued a Shermanesque statement and indicated that he intended to clear out his desk at the end of the year.

The most popular guessing game was the identity of the individual supported by the United States, apparently in the belief that the views of the world's only remaining superpower would carry the day. Rumor had it that President Bush supported Sadruddin Kahn, perhaps because Bush played tennis with him, but the White House denied the report. One report that did have a ring of truth was that it was the United States that nominated Prime Minister of Canada Brian Mulroney on an early ballot.[6] As handled, it was an effort doomed to fail. Already in deep political trouble at home and a lame duck if his UN candidacy was successful, Mulroney was immediately put on the spot at home to confirm or renounce his candidacy. Only after some confusion did he issue a statement taking himself out of the race.[7] To have had any chance of success, Mulroney should have been named only in the event of a deadlock or with prior agreement on him as the nominee. Otherwise, it was too difficult for Mulroney to overcome the disadvantages of being a sitting prime minister and the inclination of member countries to honor "Africa's turn."

In the end, rather than a search committee or sustained and serious high-level consideration that might have improved the process, the election came down to those who campaigned for the position or who allowed their names to go forward. As a practical matter, the selection was limited to African candidates.

The Election Process

The secret ballot and the special role of the permanent members of the Security Council combine to surround the process of selecting a secretary-general with all the mystery of selecting a pope. The difference, of course, is that the UN representatives are not sequestered, and every representative is available—sometimes eager—to reveal how votes were cast. The Security Council first sought to get all nominations on the table and agreed on October 1 as the date for a final decision on the nomination of a new secretary-general. They took a series of straw votes with the aim of eliminating those who did not have sufficient support. African candidates dominated the voting. No non-African received more than five votes. Boutros-Ghali and Chidzero led the voting with Obasanjo a more distant third. However, the procedure made it impossible to tell whether the abstentions and negative votes each candidate received included the fatal negative vote of a permanent member.[8]

Next, the council sought to determine which candidates would fail because of the opposition of a permanent member. This step, which was accomplished by having the permanent members cast blue ballots, revealed that Sadruddin Khan was the only non-African candidate to avoid one or more negative votes from a permanent member. Even so, support for Khan was weak.[9]

Now having a list of names unlikely to attract a veto, the Security Council started a series of votes to determine who could get nine votes. The first ballot produced no winner. Boutros-Ghali and Chidzero had the most votes, but neither received the required number for election. Based on corridor discussions, it was widely believed that the next ballots would be equally inconclusive and that the resulting deadlock would allow a new name, presumably outside of the OAU list or even the Africa's-turn limitation. However, it was reported that at this point France intervened. Apparently catching the United States napping, the French persuaded the nonpermanent members of the Security Council, particularly the Third World members, that a further deadlock would leave the procedure open to a move by the United States to inject a dark-horse candidate. In the next round of voting, Boutros-Ghali emerged with the requisite number of votes, edging out Chidzero who narrowly led the previous ballot.[10]

Publicly, no one spoke negatively about the election of Boutros-Ghali. His nomination satisfied the Africa's-turn requirement, though no doubt most Africans thought of a black African when they spoke of Africa's turn. The French were satisfied, because they had demonstrated diplomatic finesse and because Boutros-Ghali was fluent in French. He also had a solid record. He is highly educated, thoughtful, and articulate in English, French, and Arabic. An experienced diplomat, having won high praise for his work on the Camp David accords and for the tireless and effective manner in which he lobbied the African states to maintain Egyptian membership in the OAU after the Arabs had expelled Egypt from the Arab League. But he has had no experience running a large bureaucracy. Through no fault of his own, he had been repeatedly passed over for the position of foreign minister, largely because he is a Christian in an overwhelmingly Muslim country.

Privately, there was widespread concern that the UN had missed an opportunity to improve its election process and perhaps incrementally improve the quality and even the structure of its leadership. Nonetheless, the United States and the United Kingdom reportedly overcame their initial lack of enthusiasm and rallied around Boutros-Ghali as the best of a limited choice.

Perhaps the concern will prove to be misplaced. Boutros-Ghali could not have become secretary-general at a more opportune time. An astute secretary-general may be able to turn the current esteem for the UN into a force for change—perhaps more change than the advocates of change find tolerable. Even Boutros-Ghali's age might work to his advantage. Like Pope John who attained office at an advanced age, Boutros-Ghali, at age sixty-nine, will probably stay only one term and aspires to no higher office. He can assert the power of independence. If a favorable political climate continues, Boutros-Ghali may be exactly the leader needed at the UN in this time of far-reaching changes.

Notes

1.   See, for example, Brian Urquhart, *A Life in Peace and War* (New York, Harper & Row, 1987), pp. 227-228.

2.   Brian Urquhart and Erskine Chiders, *A World in Need of Leadership: Tomorrow's United Nations* (Uppsala: Dag Hammarskjöld Foundation, 1990).

3.   *A Successor Vision: The United Nations of Tomorrow* (New York: United Nations Association of the United States of America, 1988).

4.   Urquhart and Childers, *A World in Need of Leadership*, pp. 29-30.

5.   UN Charter, Article 97.

6.   Paul Lewis, "Bid for UN Post Is Led by Zimbabwe and Egypt," *New York Times*, October 26, 1991, p. A-3.

7.   "Mulroney Withdraws from UN Contest," *New York Times*, October 29, 1991, p. A-13.

8.   The various votes are reported in the *New York Times* from October 26 to November 12, 1991.

9.   Paul Lewis, "Egyptian Leads Voting for UN Post," *New York Times*, November 12, 1991, p. A-3.

10.   Paul Lewis, "Security Council Selects Egyptian for Top UN Post," *New York Times*, November 22, 1991, p. A-1.

DEPARTMENTS

LOOKING AHEAD:
DIPLOMATIC CHALLENGES
OF 1993

Steven Philip Kramer

T HE END OF THE COLD WAR not only has created new diplomatic problems and opportunities but it has also changed the nature of international relations in basic ways. During the Cold War, the world was divided into three parts—the East, the West, and the nonaligned. Ideology played a major part in keeping these groups internally united while divided from one another. The United States and the Union of Soviet Socialist Republics (USSR) dominated and led the first two blocs because of military, especially nuclear, preeminence. There were no direct wars between the two blocs, but they fought proxy wars around the globe, vying for influence and allies and introducing superpower rivalry to many civil conflicts in Third World areas. The role of international organizations, notably the United Nations, was limited, because UN action could occur only under the unusual circumstance of East and West finding a common interest. Regional organizations that included members aligned with both East and West were stymied.

The situation is very different today. The division of the world into three blocs is over. With the collapse of the Soviet bloc, the cohesion of the Western bloc is declining, and the nonaligned bloc—never possessed of much more than a tenuous negative identity—has no further raison d'être. The split between haves and have-nots, most of the latter in the South, is a loose division with many exceptions and little internal coherence. Russia, despite its nuclear capacity, does not play a world leadership role. The United States, the self-proclaimed sole remaining superpower, has lost much of its influence over its allies as the importance of military power has declined in relation to economic power. The salience of ideology in the Cold War sense has disappeared. Former East-bloc nations

compete in abandoning all trappings of communism and demonstrating
their commitment, at least rhetorical, to the doctrines of democracy and
the free market, the sole entrée into today's polite international society. As
ideology has waned, history and geography have thrust into greater prominence nationalism and religion, which had been suppressed in East-bloc
nations. There also has been a trend toward deinternationalizing many
Third World conflicts. As the former USSR withdrew from involvement,
often followed by the United States, the local antagonists, no longer financed in the style to which they had grown accustomed, were more likely
to compromise. The end of the Cold War has made it possible for regional
organizations and the United Nations to serve as peacemakers in many of
these conflicts.

An old set of problems moves toward resolution even as new classes of
problems emerge. The year 1993 will be an important one for both types.
What then are the major diplomatic challenges facing the world in the upcoming year?

Attaining Political and Economic Stability
in the Former USSR

The euphoria felt in the West after the demise of communism in the
Soviet Union was soon replaced by recognition of the enormous problems
facing its successor states—and the rest of the world. These problems fall
into several categories:

- Reviving the problem of nuclear weapons on non-Russian territory
  (decided in principle by the protocol to the START treaty).
- Establishing mutually acceptable boundaries and peaceful relations
  between and within the successor states. Former intrastate boundaries, in some cases artificial, became interstate boundaries overnight.
  Ownership of the forces and facilities of the Soviet military was called
  into question. The most serious of these problems involves conflicting
  Russian and Ukrainian claims on the Crimea and on the Black Sea
  Fleet. So far, the conflicts between Russia and Ukraine have been
  only verbal, but there has been violent confrontation between Armenia and Azerbaijan and nationalities conflicts in Moldova and Georgia, to cite only a few examples. Any number of potential conflicts
  could spill over former Soviet borders to become international conflicts.

- Establishing stable, legitimate, and perhaps democratic regimes in the successor states, avoiding the creation of a revanchist, nationalist regime in Russia, and preventing the emergence of an arc of instability along the boundaries of the former Soviet Union.
- Preventing economic collapse and embarking on a successful program of economic reform that might lead eventually to the creation of modern free-market economies.
- Avoiding public health threats resulting from lack of medicine and clean water and ecological disaster stemming from unstable nuclear reactors and decades of unsafe disposal of industrial waste.

Whereas in the past, the West mobilized to counter the "Soviet threat," it now must find the means to help prevent social, political, and economic collapse and internecine conflict in the former Soviet Union.

Dealing with the Problems of Eastern Europe

The situation is both better and worse in the former East bloc. Some of these nations, far more advanced economically and politically than the nations of the former USSR, are engaged in the consolidation of political democracy and the creation of market economies. The process requires assistance from the West and from international organizations. These nations seek integration into the European Community (EC) and security guarantees, above all from the North Atlantic Treaty Organization (NATO).

Czechoslovakia, Hungary, and Poland stand out as the most advanced states. All have functioning, elected democratic governments—which is not to say that they are exempt from political problems. Other than the Czech-Slovak tension, however, they are largely exempt from nationalities problems. All three have signed association agreements with the EC. If they can be helped through a difficult transition process, they could become EC members by the end of the century.

The Balkans are more problematic. Bulgaria and Romania lag in both economic and political reform. Albania is extremely backward and suffers from self-imposed isolation. The Yugoslav federation, like the USSR, has decomposed but in a much more violent way, with Serbia bent on creating a Greater Serbia by forcibly appropriating large parts of other republics containing significant Serbian minorities.

The Yugoslav crisis constitutes a model for several of the new kinds of challenges of the post-Cold War era:

■ The problems created when internal boundaries of a federal state become the boundaries of independent states, which in turn relates to
the problems of overlapping nationalities in Eastern Europe and the
former Soviet Union.

■ The problem of preventing a Yugoslav civil war from becoming a regional war. Albanian interests are involved in Kosovo, Islamic and
Turkish interests in the treatment of Moslems in Bosnia, Hungarian
interests in Vojvodina, and Greeks and Bulgarians are concerned
about the Macedonian question.

■ The appropriate role of regional organizations and the UN in reacting
to violent behavior of small states against their neighbors or internal
minorities.

The Yugoslav situation, even in the most optimistic prognosis, will remain
a problem in 1993 and may turn out to be the tip of a new "Eastern question."

Arms Control and Nuclear Proliferation

The end of the Cold War has created enormous challenges and risks in
the area of arms control and nuclear proliferation. The most notable result
has been the end of nuclear confrontation between the United States and
the USSR. The year 1993 will be important for the implementation of
START and the movement toward removal of nuclear weapons from all
former Soviet republics other than Russia. Other challenges will be maintaining centralized command and control over Russian nuclear systems
and continuing cuts in Russian and US nuclear arsenals as the possibility
of conflict continues to diminish.

The threat of superpower nuclear holocaust has now been replaced by
the lesser but still real danger of nuclear proliferation. States still want to
catch up with nuclear neighbors—Pakistan with India and China, the
Arabs with Israel. There is also the greater possibility today of nonnuclear
states obtaining technology or weapons from the outside. One of the critical issues of 1993 will be whether North Korea will be willing to forgo
building an atomic bomb to escape international isolation.

The dangers of nuclear proliferation are matched by the dangers of proliferation of chemical, bacteriological, ballistic, and high-tech conventional
weapons, all of which need to be dealt with in 1993.

Fostering Regional and International Solutions to Third World Conflicts

During the Cold War, neither superpower was indifferent to the fate of any part of the Third World, even areas of minimal economic, strategic, or sentimental interest. Local conflicts attracted big-power attention, often intervention. These included conflicts in Nicaragua, El Salvador, Afghanistan, Angola, Namibia, and Cambodia and in the Horn of Africa. Great-power rivalry helped keep the pot boiling, especially in the Middle East.

The Soviets and then the Russians dramatically reduced aid to former clients and guerrilla movements, and the American need to block Soviet international efforts has disappeared. Local forces are now showing more willingness to turn to outside mediation—in many cases the UN. Supporting regional international mediation efforts, including financially, will be among the challenges of 1993.

Also important in 1993 may be the future of the "orphans" of the communist world, notably Cuba and North Korea and to a lesser extent Vietnam and Laos, whose regimes will attempt to find an equilibrium between maintaining political control and undertaking the economic reforms that will enable them to end their international isolation.

Supporting Democracy

It is not only in former communist states that a transition to democracy is being attempted. In Latin America, there are now freely elected governments in most countries. But free elections do not always translate into a fully functioning democracy and the rule of law. Latin American democracies are threatened by economic difficulties and debt, weakness or absence of civilian control over the military, pronounced social inequalities, lack of assimilation of Indian populations, and, in some cases guerrilla movements. Such events as the attempted military coup in Venezuela, the presidential coup in Peru in 1992, and the army's deposing of President Jean-Bertrand Aristide in Haiti indicate the fragility of democratic trends. Nevertheless, OAS efforts to press hard for restoration of democracy in Haiti and Peru are a new and positive phenomenon that would not have been possible without democracy's having been established as the norm in the hemisphere.

In Asia, one great challenge in 1993 will be achievement of a settlement in Cambodia under UN auspices acceptable to but not dominated by the Khmer Rouge. The year will also provide an opportunity for consolidation of democracy in the Philippines and South Korea. Whether China can pursue economic reform successfully without political reform and whether the aging Chinese leaders can keep a lid on the democratic movement there are two questions that may be answered in the coming year.

In Africa, there has also been a trend away from the rule of old "Big Men" and one-party states. Although some leverage has been exerted by the West through economic aid, the impetus has been internal. The risk in some cases is that the collapse of dictatorial regimes will result in tribal conflict. In addition, the same economic forces that destabilized dictatorships will, if unchecked, undermine democratic successors.

The year will also be critical for the success of the process of creating multi-racial democracy in South Africa through adoption of a new constitution. The results in the most economically advanced state of Africa will affect the dynamics of the rest of sub-Saharan Africa.

Limits to National Sovereignty?

The Cold War made it impossible to deal with the inherent contradiction between the seemingly absolute rights of states to oppose interference in their internal affairs and the equally absolute commitments to human rights contained in such documents as the UN Charter. US and Soviet willingness to meddle in the affairs of other nations in practice was matched by a theoretical exaltation of the concept of national sovereignty as an absolute, in part to prevent such intervention.

The end of the Cold War and the aftermath of the Persian Gulf War raise the question of the rights and obligations of outside states to react to flagrant violations of human rights within other states, not only by refusing aid but also by using economic, political, or even military means. If pursued, the concept of limits on sovereignty would mark the beginning of an attempt to reconcile the rights and obligations of sovereignty. The World Bank and International Monetary Fund (IMF) have imposed stringent requirements on the economies of nations seeking their assistance, thereby limiting in practice, if not in theory, the exercise of fiscal and monetary sovereignty.

Sovereignty questions appear in other contexts as well. The EC has moved beyond being a mere free market toward political unity, but is not yet a federal state. As the Community accepts new members, probably beginning with European Free Trade Association (EFTA) states such as Sweden, Austria, and Finland, the need to devise a new institutional framework with concomitant changes in the nature of sovereignty will occur.

The multinational states of the former Eastern bloc are going through the opposite process, analogous to the breakup of the Ottoman and Austro-Hungarian empires. But unlike the situation in 1918, the West and international organizations are encouraging efforts to avert economic nationalism and beggar-thy-neighbor policies, even if they cannot prevent the political disintegration they generally fear. Even Canada runs a serious risk of breaking apart unless the relationship between Quebec and the rest of Canada can be negotiated.

Role of Regional Organizations

Regional organizations have gained in importance as a result of the end of the Cold War. Geography has returned as a vital political factor.

The most important issue for Europe in 1993 may be the resolution of the problem of ratification of the EC's Maastricht treaty. The Maastricht accords, concluded in December 1991, provided for a deepening of economic cooperation leading to a common currency, for greater political cooperation with the goal of a common foreign policy, and for coordinated security policy leading eventually to a common defense. National parliaments and the general public were not, however, closely involved in the discussions leading up to Maastricht. When the Danish referendum of June 1992 rejected the treaty, it not only complicated ratification of a treaty that required unanimous consent by all twelve EC members, but it also reopened debate on the substance of European unity. The ratification problem will delay enlargement—the EC will be reluctant to admit new members until the ratification issue is resolved—as well as consideration of changes in the institutional mechanism and governance of the EC so that it can function with a larger membership.

European unification also affects plans for European security. Since the end of the Soviet threat, there has been a debate on this subject in which the United States and France have been at loggerheads. Although the French advocate a continued American role in Europe and the United States accepts the legitimacy of a specifically European security system, there is sharp division about the nature and implications of US-European security relations. In concrete terms, the United States has advocated widening NATO's mission and was instrumental in the creation of the North Atlantic Cooperation Council (NACC), which serves a liaison function with the countries of the East. The French have supported strengthening the Conference on Security and Cooperation in Europe (CSCE), which now includes Europe, the states of the former Soviet Union, the United States, and Canada. They also want to use the Western European Union (WEU) as an executor of EC policy and have concluded an agreement with Germany to create a joint Franco-German army corps, which is open to contingents from other EC members.

New Pan-European or multilateral organizations have been suggested or established. The French have come up with the idea of a European confederation, which so far has little support. The European Bank for Reconstruction and Development (EBRD) has been more successful. The Italians initiated the Hexagonale, a loose system of cooperation that included Italy, Austria, Hungary, Czechoslovakia, Poland, and Yugoslavia. The importance of the Council of Europe's role in supporting human rights and democracy and bringing together parliamentarians has increased, and membership has become a sort of imprimatur for democratic legitimacy.

The Organization of American States (OAS) has made serious efforts to resolve the dilemmas of the Haitian and Peruvian coups. Whether the OAS can successfully pursue collective security in the hemisphere, and whether unilateral action by the United States can be made a thing of the past, may well be tested in 1993. The intervention by the Economic Community of West African States (ECOWAS) in Liberia to end a bloody civil war constitutes a new kind of collective security in Africa. If ECOWAS can solve the Liberian impasse, collective security in Africa will have advanced a major step forward.

Not only are organizations like the OAS and ECOWAS showing greater vigor in security, but there also has been an increase in regional economic cooperation, some of it inspired by the example of the EC, some of it by fears that the EC marks the beginning of the formation of regional trading blocs. Efforts to ratify the North American Free Trade Association (NAFTA) including the United States, Mexico, and Canada will continue in 1993. Efforts at broadening this to other nations of the Western Hemisphere may occur as well. Development of the Asian Pacific Economic Cooperation (APEC) is also proceeding. It will include Asian and non-Asian nations of the Pacific Rim.

The United Nations

A key question for 1993 will be whether the UN can fulfill renewed hopes for its effectiveness. Issues UN members must address are

- Resolving the UN's financial problems. The cost of peacekeeping operations has skyrocketed. The United States, among others, has not met its obligations.
- Making the Security Council responsive to the new balance of forces in the world. Japan, Germany, and India claim the right to permanent seats. If such seats were accorded, would it be at the expense of present permanent members? How should the European union emerging from Maastricht be represented? Finally, how would increasing the number of permanent members (and thus of vetoes) or changing the composition of the Security Council affect its newfound efficacy?
- Considering the creation of a permanent UN military force. Harvard professor Joseph Nye, for example, advocates "a UN rapid deployment force of 60,000 troops formed from earmarked brigades from a dozen countries."[1]

The Middle East

The problems of the Middle East, multifaceted and intimately related as they are, defy optimism. Following are some of the key challenges of 1993:

- Eliminating the threat that Iraq and Libya pose to their neighbors and the international community.
- Striving for continued peace in Lebanon and consolidating a political settlement.

- Encouraging Iran to develop normal relations with neighboring states and to become a useful member of the international community.
- Pursuing progress in US-sponsored Middle East peace talks between Israel and its neighbors and Israel and the Palestinians.
- Working for a modus vivendi between Islam and the modern concept of a secular, pluralistic state.

This does not exhaust the list of diplomatic challenges for 1993. One can anticipate continued negotiations aiming at a successful completion of the Uruguay Round of the GATT talks, follow-ups to the 1992 Rio summit on the environment, and further efforts at international narcotics control—as well as at least some surprises.

Notes

1. Joseph Nye, "What New World Order?" *Foreign Affairs*, Vol. 71 (Spring 1992), p. 93.

DIPLOMATIC CHRONOLOGY

(Arranged Topically)

DIPLOMATIC RELATIONS

1991

August 25: Denmark, Norway, and Finland became the first nations to recognize the independence of the Baltic republics.

August 27: The European Community (EC) recognized Estonia, Latvia, and Lithuania as independent nations.

September 2: The United States recognized Estonia, Latvia, and Lithuania as independent nations.

September 5: After three American congressmen unfurled a banner commemorating the Tiananmen Square massacre on the square, the People's Republic of China (PRC) lodged a formal protest to the United States.

October 23: Meeting with Vietnamese Foreign Minister Nguyen Manh Cam, US Secretary of State Baker announced that the United States would move to normalize relations if Vietnam would provide information on missing US servicemen.

October 24: Israel reopened its embassy in Moscow after twenty-five years of closure.

November 5: The Vietnamese prime minister and communist party leader arrived in Beijing to initiate exploratory talks on reestablishing political and economic relations severed since 1979.

November 9: Syria announced it would permit the Palestine Liberation Organization (PLO) to reopen its representative offices in Damascus. The offices had been closed for eight years.

November 23: Vietnamese Deputy Foreign Minister Le Mai indicated that progress on negotiations with the United States to reestablish relations had progressed to the point where a breakthrough was imminent.

December 12: North and South Korea signed a treaty of reconciliation and nonaggression that provided for a modicum of communication and social exchange.

December 13: The five Asian, former Soviet, republics (Kirghizia, Tadzhikistan, Turkmenia, Uzbekistan, and Kazakhstan) agreed to join the Commonwealth of Independent States (CIS).

December 15: India and the PRC agreed to reopen consulates in Bombay and Shanghai and reopen their borders to trade.

December 17: The EC voted to recognize Slovenia and Croatia by January 15, 1992.

December 23: Germany recognized Slovenia and Croatia and upgraded its consulates in their capitals to embassies.

December 25: The United States, Canada, Israel, and the EC moved to recognize the independence of former Soviet republics Russia, Armenia, Ukraine, Kazakhstan, Byelorussia, and Kirghizia.

December 26: Kurdish demonstrators, protesting the killings of Kurds by the Turkish army, seized the Turkish consulate in Paris.

December 27: The PRC officially recognized Russia and the independence of the other Soviet republics. The announcement was accompanied by disparaging assessments of the likely future for the new states and global relations.

December 29: Iran curtailed freedom of movement for Swiss diplomats in the country in protest of the arrest of an Iranian in Switzerland on December 23. The Swiss embassy also represented US interests.

1992

January 4: In an apparent shakeup of the former Soviet embassy in Washington DC, Ambassador Viktor Komplektov was recalled to Moscow and was not expected to return.

January 7: Algeria announced it would sign the Nuclear Non-Proliferation Treaty in the near future.

January 14: Lebanon indicated it would allow the PLO to reopen its representative office in Beirut.

January 15: The EC recognized the independence of Slovenia and Croatia.

January 25: The presidents of Moldova and Romania met in Kishinev, Moldova, to strengthen relations and develop economic ties between the two nations. Neither leader called for a restoration of the political union that existed before World War II.

February 1: Russian President Boris Yeltsin and US President George Bush, meeting in the United States, declared a formal end to the Cold War and reaffirmed that relations between the two countries would continue on a cooperative basis.

February 4: The United States announced that embassy restrictions in Moscow were being relaxed and that Russians would now be eligible for employment in nonsensitive positions.

February 5: US Secretary of State James Baker indicated that the United States would move quickly on recognition of the Central Asian former Soviet republics in an attempt to counter growing Iranian influence.

February 11: On a tour of the Caucasus and Central Asia, Secretary Baker pledged US recognition of Moldova in the near future.

February 21: Saudi Arabia established relations with Uzbekistan, reportedly in a move to counter growing Iranian influence in the region.

February 27: German Chancellor Helmut Kohl indicated that Prague would have German support in its bid for EC membership.

February 29: Germany agreed to serve as mediator in the territorial dispute between Japan and Russia over the Kurile Islands.

March 16: Algeria ceased its representation of Iranian diplomatic interests in Washington, DC; Pakistan agreed to take over the Iranian interests section.

March 17: A car bomb destroyed the Israeli embassy in Buenos Aires, Argentina.

_____ The PLO reported that it was conducting discussions with Jordan to form a federation as a means of pressuring Israel to withdraw from the West Bank. Israel has long stated it would not negotiate with the PLO or an independent Palestinian state.

March 20: An open-skies treaty was agreed to in Vienna during meetings of the Conference on Security and Cooperation in Europe (CSCE). The treaty allows reconnaissance flights over the former Soviet Union, Europe, and North America as a confidence-building measure.

April 6: The EC recognized the independence of Bosnia and Herzegovina.

April 7: The United States recognized the independence of Slovenia, Croatia, and Bosnia and Herzegovina.

April 10: South African President F. W. de Klerk returned from negotiations in Nigeria without having obtained any pledge to renew diplomatic relations.

April 11: Belgium expelled four Russian diplomats following a security operation that uncovered a large spy network that had continued to function over the past two years. Belgium Foreign Minister Willy Claes filed a formal protest in Moscow and commented that such activity would endanger Western aid.

April 20: Bush administration officials acknowledged that the United States was considering a break in relations with the Serbian-controlled Yugoslav state in response to Serbian attacks on the former Yugoslav republics.

April 28: Serbia and Montenegro proclaimed the establishment of a smaller Yugoslav nation and a de facto acceptance of the independence of the four other republics.

May 7: North and South Korea issued a communiqué outlining further steps toward reconciliation, including the reunification of families and the establishment of liaison offices and a joint military commission at Panmunjom.

May 11: EC nations recalled their ambassadors from Yugoslavia and indicated they would push for isolation of Belgrade in multilateral institutions.

May 13: North Korea returned the bodies of fifteen missing US servicemen from the Korean War.

May 22: The United States closed its diplomatic representation in Yugoslavia and expelled Yugoslav diplomats as part of a sanctions package to protest Serbian actions in Bosnia.

June 14: A US delegation arrived in Kabul, Afghanistan, for discussions on resuming diplomatic relations.

ENVIRONMENTAL DIPLOMACY

1991

July 9: The International Atomic Energy Agency (IAEA) urged Bulgaria to close its nuclear reactors for repairs. An IAEA report identified four of six Bulgarian nuclear reactors as operating under hazardous conditions.

August 27: The Bush administration declared its opposition to any exceptions in the United Nations (UN) ban on drift nets used in fishing.

September 8: The United States borrowed a European weather satellite to fill a gap in its weather-detection system.

September 20: An international meeting in Nairobi, Kenya, to discuss environmental proposals for the Conference on Environment and Development ended with little progress on the issue of carbon dioxide emissions.

September 23: Brazilian President Fernando Collor de Mello asserted at the opening session of the forty-sixth UN General Assembly that there was "an inescapable obligation" for nations to adopt environmental protection measures. He chided the United States for its resistance to carbon monoxide standards.

September 25: The European Commission forwarded a directive to the European Council proposing an energy tax to reduce emissions of carbon dioxide. The Commission indicated it would encourage other industrialized nations to adopt similar strategies.

_____ Prince Norodom Sihanouk of Cambodia called at the UN for a ban on the use of land mines, reflecting on the thousands of Cambodians maimed and killed by mines left over from the wars of the 1960s and 1970s.

October 4: Members of the Antarctic Treaty agreed to a ban on oil and mineral exploration in the region for a fifty-year period.

November 26: Japan agreed to comply with a UN moratorium on the use of huge nets for fishing in the northern Pacific Ocean.

December 17: Forty-five nations of the CSCE endorsed the European Energy Charter, calling for increased Western imports and help in developing the energy sectors of Eastern Europe.

December 21: The UN General Assembly passed a resolution calling for a global moratorium on drift-net fishing to be implemented within one year.

December 27: Iceland announced it would withdraw in 1992 from the International Whaling Commission, which imposed a moratorium on commercial whaling in 1986.

1992

March 2: At the opening of a UN meeting on the environment, the EC announced it would support a call for more money to be devoted to helping developing countries comply with environmental legislation.

March 10: At the Convention on International Trade in Endangered Species in Kyoto, Japan, five African nations agreed to retain stringent international standards on trade in elephant hides and meat. The United States, Japan, Morocco, and Canada refused to agree to a total ban on the fishing of blue fin tuna, though they acquiesced to a voluntary reduction of tuna catches by 50 percent.

March 23: At a five-week conference on the environment at the UN, the United States received strong criticism from both industrialized and developing countries for its refusal to commit additional environmental aid or to set specific limits on the emissions of gases that contribute to global warming.

_____ The EC announced a restriction on the permissible sulfur content of heating oil and diesel fuel.

March 25: Finland reported that it had detected an increase in radioactivity believed to have come from a nuclear power reactor near St. Petersburg (formerly Leningrad). Russia confirmed a small amount of gas had been released, but contended that radioactivity levels were back to normal.

April 4: At a meeting of the 160-nation UN Conference on Environment and Development in New York, a draft document entitled Rio Declaration on Environment and Development was passed committing the industrialized nations to help the poorer nations to achieve growth without environmental degradation. The draft resolution was to be considered at the Rio conference in June.

April 8: France announced a moratorium on nuclear testing in the South Pacific and pledged to renew the moratorium next year if other nuclear powers followed suit.

April 28: US officials acknowledged that the United States had informally offered to curb the increase in gas emissions of US factories as a concession for the upcoming Rio talks but still refused to stabilize emissions at 1990 levels by the year 2000.

April 29: The US Energy Department announced it would no longer manufacture weapons-grade uranium.

May 1: Jean Ripert, chair of a UN negotiating committee on the environment, offered a compromise package for the Rio environmental talks by which industrialized nations would set a goal of limiting gas emissions to 1990 levels by the year 2000 but would not be required to meet that target level.

May 3: Russian officials acknowledged that the former Soviet Navy and icebreaking fleet dumped their radioactive waste in the Arctic Ocean for the past three decades.

May 9: President Bush announced he would attend the Earth Summit in Brazil in June.

May 13: The EC proposed a high energy tax on all types of fuel as a measure to limit the emission of gases that contribute to global warming.

May 21: The PRC detonated an underground nuclear device thought to be as large as one megaton.

May 22: Ninety-eight nations adopted a draft treaty to protect plant and animal species. The treaty was to be presented at the Rio summit in June.

May 29: US officials announced that President Bush would not sign the draft treaty on the protection of plant and animal species when it was presented at the Rio summit.

June 1: Responding to criticism of his environmental policy, President Bush announced an increase in foreign aid for forest conservation programs and challenged other nations to increase spending.

June 3: The Rio "Earth Summit" opened with UN Secretary-General Boutros Boutros-Ghali calling for an environmental collective security effort. Germany and Canada announced they would support a treaty outlining steps to protect biodiversity.

June 4: Brazil, Antigua and Barbuda, Australia, Belgium, Finland, Iceland, Israel, Liechtenstein, the Netherlands, New Zealand, Norway, and Uruguay signed a climate treaty that outlined steps to reduce gas emissions. Switzerland, Austria, and the Netherlands called for a more stringent set of standards to be developed, but the United States expressed its strong opposition to further steps.

June 5: Japan and Great Britain announced they would support the biodiversity treaty at the Rio summit, leaving the United States as the only industrialized country refusing to sign the pact.

June 6: Diplomats at the Rio summit announced they had achieved broad consensus to create a watchdog group to be called the Sustainable Development Commission. The commission would rely on public opinion and intergovernmental lobbying to encourage conformity with environmental treaties.

June 8: Japan announced it would substantially increase economic aid designated for environmental protection.

June 12: President Bush signed the climate treaty at the Rio summit and challenged other signatories to implement it more rapidly than mandated by the treaty's provisions.

June 13: Less-developed countries dropped their demand for specific goals for industrialized nations' funding of environmental projects in poorer nations.

June 14: The Rio summit concluded with 153 nations signing a global-warming treaty and a treaty to protect plant and animal species. The United States refused to sign the biodiversity treaty but signed the global-warming treaty after language setting exact targets was withdrawn.

INTERNATIONAL ORGANIZATIONS

1991

July 3: UN officials charged Iraq with blockading as many as 100,000 Shiite Muslims in the marshlands of southern Iraq in an effort to eliminate them.

July 4: Members of the UN inspection team reported that they were denied access to Iraqi nuclear equipment.

July 5: Iraq pledged to allow UN inspectors access to nuclear sites and indicated it would provide the UN Security Council with a complete listing of those sites in the near future.

July 8: Iraq divulged to the UN Security Council information regarding an extensive nuclear program that purportedly violated its adherence to the Nuclear Non-Proliferation Treaty and IAEA standards.

July 10: The United States made the first of five $36 million annual payments to the UN in an effort to pay off its long-standing debt.

July 11: Iraqi troops withdrew from southern marshlands under UN pressure to allow Shiite Muslim refugees access to food and medicine.

July 12: UN envoy Prince Sadruddin Aga Khan, head of the UN mission assessing Iraq's humanitarian needs, called for a relaxation of the UN embargo preventing Iraq from purchasing needed food and medical supplies.

July 13: UN inspectors asked Iraq for a list of nuclear-enrichment sites. The list would be forwarded to the Security Council and the sites subsequently inspected.

July 14: The United States and France indicated to the Security Council that they would support the renewed use of force against Iraq if the country did not comply with UN demands.

_____ Iraq supplied a list of nuclear facilities to UN inspectors but would not indicate whether the list was complete.

July 17: UN inspectors in Iraq announced their belief that Western bombing had destroyed Iraq's ability to produce enriched nuclear-weapons fuels before they could be produced.

_____ The Cambodian factions negotiating in Beijing elected Prince Norodom Sihanouk as president of the Cambodian Supreme National Council, which will govern the country in the process of transformation under the peace plan. The factions agreed to share a seat at the UN.

July 25: The UN Security Council began to discuss the possibility of removing selected sanctions on Iraq in order to allow it to pay for needed imports.

July 30: UN inspectors in Iraq announced that they had uncovered more than four times the amount of chemical weapons that Iraq had previously acknowledged were in existence.

August 1: The IAEA submitted a plan to the UN Security Council whereby the agency would hold complete control over the future of Iraqi nuclear technology.

August 2: A UN report asserted that Iraq was facing widespread famine due to a poor harvest and UN sanctions on the sale of oil.

August 5: Iraq admitted to having small amounts of weapons-grade plutonium that was created from spent fuel at a nuclear installation functioning under the safeguard regulations of the IAEA.

_____ South Korea applied for membership in the UN. North Korea had applied for separate membership on May 9, 1991.

August 7: The five permanent members of the Security Council agreed to continue sanctions but allow Iraq to sell up to $1.6 billion in crude oil to buy food and other humanitarian supplies. Iraqi Ambassador to the UN Abdul Amir A. al-Anbari denounced the offer as an infringement on Iraq's sovereignty and said Iraq would not comply.

August 8: Iraq divulged the location of 17.6 pounds of enriched uranium that it had kept hidden from previous UN inspection teams.

August 10: The PRC announced it was ready in principle to sign the Nuclear Non-Proliferation Treaty.

August 13: The United States reversed its initial position on open inspections under a proposed UN chemical weapons ban treaty and instead called for more restrictive inspections that would not jeopardize military secrets.

August 25: UN Secretary-General Javier Pérez de Cuéllar arrived in Geneva for three days of talks concerning Western hostages in Lebanon as well as speeches on the environment and humanitarian issues in Iraq.

August 27: Iranian UN representative Kamal Kharazzi conferred with Secretary-General Pérez de Cuéllar concerning the hostage situation in Lebanon. The UN head accepted an invitation to fly to Tehran September 10 for further discussions.

August 29: Secretary-General Pérez de Cuéllar expressed his alarm over the reported Iraqi attack of Bubiyan Island and pledged an investigation into the matter.

September 9: The UN reported renewed fighting between Kurdish rebels and Iraqi forces in northern Iraq.

September 10: UN inspectors in Iraq claimed that Iraqi forces required them to use Iraqi helicopters rather than their own equipment, a violation of the formal cease-fire agreement.

_____ Secretary-General Pérez de Cuéllar arrived in Tehran, Iran, to press for Iranian help in freeing the remaining Western hostages in Lebanon.

September 11: UN officials contended that Iraq was delaying the destruction of chemical, biological, and nuclear arsenals, part of the cease-fire agreement.

September 12: The UN team inspecting Iraqi missile systems was denied use of UN helicopters and announced it would leave Iraq without completing its mission.

September 16: A group of twenty-two industrial and developing countries, including the United States and other Security Council nations, announced a program of reform for the Secretariat to be presented when the forty-sixth session opened on September 17.

September 17: Saudi representative to the UN General Assembly, Samir Shihabi, was elected president of the General Assembly. Other first-day business of the organization included votes accepting North and South Korea, Estonia, Latvia, Lithuania, the Marshall Islands, and Micronesia as UN members, raising total membership to 166.

_____ The UN Security Council discussed troop escorts for the UN inspection team in Iraq, but Iraq indicated it was more willing to comply with the original terms of the cease-fire.

September 18: President Bush authorized US fighter escorts for UN helicopters inspecting Iraqi nuclear facilities.

September 19: The UN Security Council voted to allow Iraq to sell $1.6 billion worth of oil to pay for basic living necessities, but Iraq considered the "allowance" an affront to its sovereignty and said it may not sell the oil.

September 22: UN diplomats acknowledged that Iraq, in its latest letter to the Security Council, had failed to give assurances that UN inspectors would have unrestricted access to all areas while investigating the country's nuclear, biological, and chemical arsenals.

September 23: President Bush, speaking before the UN General Assembly, called for a repeal of

Resolution 3379 (passed in 1975) which states that Zionism is racism.

_____ Iraq detained a UN inspection team after they found and tried to remove secret Iraqi plans for the construction of nuclear weapons. Members of the Security Council, exasperated by continued Iraqi attempts to thwart the stipulations of the cease-fire agreement, began considering stronger measures that could be taken to enforce compliance.

September 24: The UN Security Council reported that Iraq agreed to UN use of non-Iraqi helicopters for its inspection missions in Iraq.

_____ President Bush ordered surface-to-air missiles deployed in Saudi Arabia in preparation for the deployment of combat aircraft to escort UN inspection teams in Iraq.

September 25: In a note to the Security Council, Iraq indicated that the UN inspection team would be freed once they and Iraqi officials had jointly documented and copied all the information in question.

September 26: After Iraq's compromise position and agreement to allow UN inspectors to take documents if they provided an inventory, President Bush halted the deployment of missiles and aircraft to Saudi Arabia. The UN accepted the Iraqi proposal but warned that inspectors would continue their mission to seek out and destroy Iraq's powerful arsenal of weapons of mass destruction.

September 28: Iraq freed the UN inspection team detained in a nuclear facility. The team indicated that it had retained possession of all documents it wanted to inspect. The documents named foreign suppliers of Iraq's nuclear program.

October 3: UN inspectors began helicopter overflights of Iraq in search of Scud missile sites.

October 7: UN inspectors reported the discovery of a building complex in Iraq that may have served as the headquarters of Iraq's nuclear-weapons program.

October 10: Director General Hans Blix of the IAEA asked member governments to provide intelligence about any countries that may be violating the Nuclear Non-Proliferation Treaty, in order to prevent the development of nuclear programs similar to Iraq's.

October 17: At a meeting of NATO defense ministers in Sicily, it was announced that NATO would destroy over 700 nuclear bombs for use by aircraft and stockpiled in arsenals throughout Western Europe.

_____ The PRC vetoed a Security Council resolution criticizing the Khmer Rouge party of Cam-

bodia for attempting to force refugees into areas of the country it controls.

October 21: Iraq confirmed to UN inspectors that the country had sponsored research on the construction of nuclear weapons.

October 23: The UN Security Council approved a plan for destroying all of Iraq's nuclear-related plants and equipment.

October 27: The EC declared Serbian Yugoslavia in violation of the latest cease-fire accord for its attacks on Croatia.

October 30: France issued warrants for the arrest of four Libyan government officials for complicity in the bombing of a French airliner over Africa in 1989.

November 5: The Soviet Union agreed to permit aerial inspections of its territory, paving the way for an open-skies treaty to be signed at the March 1992 CSCE meeting in Helsinki.

November 11: Members of the UN inspection team returned from Iraq and indicated they had found numerous chemical warheads on Iraqi weapons.

November 14: The United States and Scotland indicted two Libyan intelligence agents for the 1988 bombing of a Pan Am flight passing over Scotland. The two were believed to be in Libya.

November 21: Former Egyptian Deputy Prime Minister Boutros-Ghali won approval from the Security Council and General Assembly for the post of UN secretary-general.

November 24: The UN asked member nations to establish a $1 billion peacekeeping fund.

November 26: A UN report alleged that Iraq had concealed a substantial store of enriched uranium garnered from an unknown foreign source.

November 27: The UN Security Council pledged to send as many as 10,000 peacekeeping troops to Yugoslavia to enforce a cease-fire if sufficient resolve to keep that peace can be shown by the warring factions.

December 2: The UN Economic Commission on Europe released a report that forecast further declines in production in East European economies of 15 percent and nearly 6 percent in the Soviet Union.

December 5: The Israeli representative at the UN indicated that enough votes had been garnered to repeal the "Zionism is racism" provision of UN Resolution 3379.

December 6: IAEA Director Blix proposed measures to increase the agency's ability to safeguard nuclear material. The measures included special inspections of sites where the agency suspected violations and the creation of a special agency within the IAEA that would have access to other countries' intelligence agencies to pool information that might indicate violations.

December 8: Libya indicated that two suspects involved in the bombing of a Pan Am flight in 1988 were under house arrest pending further investigation. A Libyan judge said the two men might be tried in Libya but would not be extradited.

December 10: The UN General Assembly voted to establish a register of international arms sales that would allow nations to identify large buildups.

December 12: Japan announced it would support the movement within the UN to repeal the resolution equating Zionism with racism.

_____ UN Secretary-General Pérez de Cuéllar indicated he would soon recommend sending 10,000 troops in a peacekeeping force to Croatia to help bolster a cease-fire. France and Britain requested that the UN Security Council send military observers to support the EC contingent already in place.

_____ Brazil and Argentina announced they would soon accede to the IAEA safeguards and open their nuclear sites for inspection.

_____ Soviet Prime Minister Ivan Silayev signed, on behalf of the newly formed CIS, an agreement with the EC that would yield $520 million in technical aid.

December 16: The UN General Assembly voted to repeal the 1975 resolution equating Zionism with racism. The vote was 111-25.

December 17: The UN announced it was centralizing humanitarian relief efforts under a single coordinator who would have substantial authority to intervene in situations in which governments were obstructing the flow of aid.

December 18: Great Britain, France, and the United States agreed to put forward a resolution in the UN Security Council that would impose sanctions on Libya for its role in terrorist bombings of airplanes.

December 24: The Russian republic announced to the UN that it would formally assume the Soviet position within the organization, including the seat on the Security Council.

December 25: Israel's chief hostage negotiator, Uri Lubrani, criticized UN Secretary-General Pérez de Cuéllar's failure to determine the fate of a missing Israeli navigator, Captain Ron Arad.

December 27: Libyan leader Muammar Qaddafi invited Western observers to the trial of two agents accused of bombing Western airlines. Libya refused their extradition.

1992

January 1: Boutros-Ghali became the sixth secretary-general of the UN.

January 2: American, British, and French diplomats at the UN indicated that by accepting Russian assumption of the Soviet permanent seat, they had effectively postponed consideration of a restructuring and creation of new seats in the body.

January 5: Secretary-General Boutros-Ghali announced he would ask the Security Council to send fifty military observers to Yugoslavia to monitor the cease-fire.

January 14: Iraqi officials indicated to the UN inspection team that the country had purchased before the Gulf War substantial supplies of German components used in enriching uranium.

January 21: The UN Security Council passed Resolution 731 calling on Libya to extradite two suspects wanted in connection with the bombing of a Pan Am jet airliner in 1988.

January 25: UN Under Secretary-General Vasily Safronchuk visited Libya in an unsuccessful attempt to win extradition of the two suspects wanted in the West.

January 28: A UN inspection team in Baghdad was confronted and jostled by demonstrators while Iraqi police watched. The UN asserted that the incident was a breach of Iraqi pledges to cooperate with and protect the inspection teams.

January 30: At a CSCE meeting in Prague, ten of the former Soviet republics were admitted to the organization as independent states.

January 31: At a summit meeting of UN Security Council members, fifteen national leaders pledged to strengthen the UN's role in peacekeeping operations. At the summit, President Bush met Chinese Prime Minister Li Peng and criticized China's human rights record. President Bush also asked the Security Council to place sanctions on Libya.

February 3: Belgrade announced it would send Yugoslav troops to assist UN peacekeeping forces in Croatia if local Serbian leaders resisted the UN peace plan.

February 4: Iraq rejected a UN plan for monitoring its arms industry and again asserted it would not sell oil to pay for imports of needed medical aid and food.

February 5: The UN Security Council deplored Iraq's refusal to sell oil to pay for needed humanitarian goods and placed the blame for the situation totally on President Saddam Hussein.

February 7: UN officials announced that warring parties in the Somalian civil war had agreed to UN mediation in New York.

February 12: UN special envoy Cyrus Vance recommended the immediate deployment of a large UN peacekeeping force to Yugoslavia.

_____ Libya announced it would cooperate with French investigations of the two Libyan officials wanted for bombing a Pan Am commercial aircraft.

February 13: The five permanent members of the UN Security Council expressed their support for a UN peacekeeping mission in Yugoslavia.

February 16: Somali guerrillas agreed to allow the UN to bring food and medical aid into Mogadishu.

February 17: Secretary-General Boutros-Ghali called for the Security Council to support peacekeeping troops in Yugoslavia until a peaceful political settlement could be achieved, regardless of whether the countries involved supported such a mission.

February 19: The UN Security Council sent a special envoy to Iraq to demand the destruction of weapons.

February 21: The Security Council voted to send a 14,000-member peacekeeping contingent to Yugoslavia to monitor the cease-fire.

February 28: The UN Security Council issued a warning to Iraq to comply with the mandate of the special UN commission to oversee the destruction of Iraqi weapons.

_____ The UN Security Council voted to send 22,000 soldiers to support the peace plan in Cambodia. The cost of the peacekeeping mission was estimated at $2 billion.

February 29: Britain and France urged the UN Security Council to designate a special envoy for human rights and refugees to be sent to Iraq.

March 2: The United States rejected a Libyan proposal to extradite to a neutral site for trial the two suspects wanted in the West.

March 3: Members of the Security Council indicated that they were considering using frozen Iraqi assets in Western countries to pay for the destruction of Iraqi weapons and the importation into Iraq of humanitarian supplies.

March 5: The UN Human Rights Commission released a report citing twenty-two nations for human rights abuses.

March 10: At a meeting in Brussels of North Atlantic Treaty Organization (NATO) members and former members of the Warsaw Pact, a German proposal for international mediation of the Armenian-Azerbaijani conflict passed overwhelmingly. The conference also discussed a potential role for NATO involvement in the mediation process.

March 17: Secretary-General Boutros-Ghali expressed his willingness to organize economic and medical assistance following a devastating earthquake in Turkey.

_____ The Security Council voted to send representatives to Somalia to discuss the possibility of peacekeeping operations to enforce a cease-fire in the Somali civil war.

March 18: The UN announced it was sending an envoy to Bangladesh and Myanmar in hopes of stemming the flood of Muslim refugees from Myanmar.

March 23: Libya informed the UN secretary-general that the two Libyan officials wanted for felony charges in the United States and Britain would be extradited to the Arab League for trial.

March 25: The IAEA ordered Iraq to destroy the core of an industrial complex used in developing nuclear-missile technology.

_____ The United States, France, and Britain indicated they would press the Security Council to impose sanctions on Libya because it had failed to give a satisfactory reason why the accused had not been extradited.

March 26: Libya began an appeal before the International Court of Justice at The Hague to prevent Britain and the United States from taking action to force the extradition of two Libyan citizens to those countries to face felony charges.

March 27: The United States, Britain, and France warned China that a veto of UN sanctions on Libya would cost China trade preferences and other support from Security Council nations.

March 28: Libya accused the United States before the International Court of Justice of practicing terrorism and disregarding international law.

March 31: The Security Council voted to impose sanctions on Libya. The sanctions included a ban on flights in or out of the country and a prohibition of arms sales to the country.

April 2: Libya warned member states of the UN Security Council to withdraw all citizens residing in the country. The request followed a day of violence in which protesters attacked the embassies of those countries.

April 3: Member countries of the informal "Nuclear Suppliers Group" reached an accord in Warsaw that created detailed rules to limit the spread of machinery and material that could be used in constructing nuclear devices.

April 4: The Security Council passed a resolution condemning Israel for violence in the Gaza Strip.

_____ Libya rejected UN demands to extradite suspects allegedly involved in the 1988 bombing of a Pan Am airliner.

April 7: Iraq agreed to permit the destruction of the Al Atheer nuclear facility, considered the heart of the Iraqi nuclear program.

April 10: Iraq informed the UN special commission charged with destroying Iraq's nuclear weapons and facilities that surveillance overflights of Iraqi territory were a violation of its sovereignty and were not required by the commission's mandate. In the future, Iraq asserted, such flights risked being shot down.

April 11: The Security Council instructed Secretary-General Boutros-Ghali to press for resolution of the Cyprus conflict and to report back by July, after which the council would decide whether to continue funding for the peacekeeping force there.

April 12: The IAEA cautioned Japan that its plan to store large amounts of plutonium in the country for its civilian nuclear program could create fears of insecurity and environmental degradation among other Asian nations. The IAEA proposed that Japan place the plutonium under international custody.

_____ Libya agreed in principle to extradite the two officials suspected of participating in the bombing of a Pan Am flight.

_____ The Security Council voted to send 100 observers to Bosnia and Herzegovina.

April 13: The Arab League proposed to the Security Council that the two Libyan suspects wanted for trial in the West be sent to Malta as an alternative and that UN sanctions be postponed.

April 14: UN sanctions against Libya were implemented.

_____ The United Nations suspended its relief program in Sudan following a government offensive against rebel forces.

April 15: UN special envoy Vance appealed to Serbian leaders to halt the attack on Bosnia and Herzegovina. During a meeting with Serbian President Slobodan Milosevic and Yugoslavia's acting defense minister, Blagoje Adzic, Vance received assurances that Serbia would pursue a peaceful solution to the conflict.

April 24: The foreign ministers of Germany, France, and Poland called on the United Nations to send peacekeeping troops to Bosnia and Herzegovina. Secretary-General Boutros-Ghali asserted that such action under current conditions was not feasible.

May 4: North Korea submitted a list of nuclear-

related sites open for inspection to the IAEA.

May 10: Western diplomats in Sarajevo indicated that the UN High Commissioner for Refugees was considering asking the Security Council for troop escorts to bring economic and food assistance into embattled areas of Bosnia and Herzegovina.

May 13: Secretary-General Boutros-Ghali indicated that the UN would not send a peacekeeping force to Bosnia and Herzegovina and was considering the withdrawal of forces from Croatia as fighting renewed in the republic. Responding to diplomatic pressure, Serbian leaders announced a five-day cease-fire in Bosnia and Herzegovina.

May 14: A dramatic increase in the fighting in and around Sarajevo trapped 350 UN military and civilian personnel in their headquarters building.

May 15: UN officials negotiated another cease-fire in Sarajevo following a day of intense fighting in which many UN vehicles were destroyed and the headquarters was shelled.

_____ The UN Security Council urged Secretary-General Boutros-Ghali to continue the peacemaking efforts in Bosnia and Herzegovina.

May 16: After an inspection, IAEA Director Blix reported that a North Korean laboratory at Yongbyon had the capability to function as a plutonium-reprocessing center if additional equipment were added to the site. Blix indicated that an IAEA team would provide more details after another inspection in several weeks.

_____ UN peacekeeping forces and staff evacuated Bosnia and Herzegovina. Secretary-General Boutros-Ghali indicated that the evacuation was a transfer of headquarters and not an end to the mission.

May 19: UN inspectors from the IAEA reported that Iraq had been at least three years away from developing a nuclear weapon before the Gulf War.

May 22: Croatia, Slovenia, and Bosnia and Herzegovina were given membership in the UN.

May 28: The United States won the support of Britain, France, and Belgium in the Security Council for a total economic embargo of Yugoslavia.

May 29: Serbian forces in Bosnia and Herzegovina renewed artillery attacks on Sarajevo. Russia indicated it would support a total economic embargo against Yugoslavia. China and Zimbabwe indicated they would abstain when the measure was put to a Security Council vote.

May 30: The Security Council voted 13-0 to impose a complete package of trade sanctions against Yugoslavia.

June 8: The Security Council voted to expand the UN peacekeeping force in Bosnia so that the Sarajevo airport could be reopened and aid shipments could be resumed.

June 11: The United States indicated it would supply troops for the UN peacekeeping effort in Bosnia only on a relief basis. Additional UN forces arrived in Sarajevo in an attempt to reopen the airport for relief supplies.

June 13: The International Court of Arbitration in New York ruled in favor of Canada in a dispute over fishing areas off the coast of Newfoundland. France had claimed an area the size of Nova Scotia south of Miquelon Island as a French fishing zone.

June 14: UN officials warned the Khmer Rouge that its refusal to abide by the terms of the Paris accords and send its troops to UN camps for disarmament could destroy the peace process.

June 15: The Japanese parliament voted to allow Japanese troops to participate in UN peacekeeping missions.

INTERNATIONAL TRADE AND ECONOMICS

1991

July 5: Bank regulators in Britain, Luxembourg, and the Cayman Islands seized control of over $20 billion in assets from the Bank of Credit and Commerce International (BCCI) following revelations of fraud.

July 11: Japan paid the United States $500 million in support of military actions in the Gulf War.

July 16: At a summit of the Group of Seven (G-7) members in London, leaders of the major industrialized countries expressed support for Soviet reform efforts and special status within the International Monetary Fund (IMF).

July 23: The Soviet Union applied for full membership in the World Bank and IMF.

July 31: General Agreement on Tariffs and Trade (GATT) negotiators in Geneva voted to extend trade restrictions on textiles until the end of 1992.

August 19: Cuba requested a General Assembly debate on the legality of the thirty-year-old American trade embargo.

August 22: Japanese leaders said that the coup attempt in the Soviet Union made them less disposed toward aid and loans to the region.

August 28: UN Secretary-General Pérez de Cuéllar proposed that developed nations cancel or help pay most of Africa's $270 billion debt, just as the United States forgave much of Egypt's debt following the Gulf War.

September 19: The PRC denied reports that cheap exports were being manufactured at prison labor camps.

September 15: The IMF approved an $845 million restructuring plan for Peru following its announcement of a tough austerity program.

September 25: The Organization of Petroleum Exporting Countries (OPEC) agreed to a Saudi proposal to increase production by more than a million barrels a day to stabilize rising oil prices and allow the global economy to recover from its recession.

_____ Japan began to retaliate for a 63 percent tariff on computer screens that the United States imposed to protect its nascent industry.

_____ The United States forgave $259.5 million in Nicaraguan debt in recognition of improved ties.

October 7: The EC called on Japan and the United States to match the $2.4 billion it planned to give the Soviet Union in aid for the winter.

October 8: Saudi Arabia announced it would send $1 billion in aid to the Soviet Union this winter.

October 10: Kuwait announced it would seek $5 billion in reconstruction loans from commercial lenders.

October 13: The Group of Seven (G-7) industrialized nations offered to help the Soviet Union create an economic reform program.

October 22: The EC and the European Free Trade Association (EFTA) agreed to form a new economic common market, to be called the European Economic Area (EEA).

November 19: Eight of the twelve former Soviet republics agreed to accept a portion of the Soviet external debt in a meeting with G-7 ministers. Ukraine, Uzbekistan, Azerbaijan, and Georgia demurred from immediately signing such an agreement.

November 21: Representatives of the G-7 allowed the Soviet Union to defer repayment of $6 billion in loans for one year.

November 23: Argentina and Britain passed legislation allowing oil exploration of the continental shelf surrounding the Falkland Islands.

December 5: A US court of appeals ruled that under existing trade treaties between the United States and Japan, business was legally permitted to discriminate against top-level employees based on their country of citizenship. The suit was brought by American senior officials of the Japanese-owned company Quasar who felt they were discriminated against in reaching the highest company positions.

December 13: The European Court of Justice issued an opinion that the recently concluded trade agreement between the EC and the EFTA violated the EC's founding charter. The action would force the European Commission to consider the court's opinion and devise a solution.

_____ The World Bank announced it would arrange $700 million in loans for reconstruction of Lebanon.

December 14: President Bush told Mexican President Carlos Salinas de Gortari on his visit to Washington that the United States desired a free-trade pact with Mexico at the earliest possible date.

December 17: GATT participants were ordered to present their final offers for the Uruguay Round. Officials asserted that the trade talks were in danger of collapsing.

December 19: The German Bundesbank announced it would raise interest rates, even though other EC members had lobbied hard for a relaxed monetary policy.

December 20: GATT Director Arthur Dunkel announced a take-it-or-leave-it plan for ending the Uruguay Round. The comprehensive plan called for cuts in agricultural subsidies, a strengthening of intellectual property rights, an end to restrictions on textile imports, and the creation of liberal rules for trade in services.

December 26: Yugoslav officials warned that if the EC recognized the independence of Croatia and Slovenia, it would consider defaulting on its foreign debt.

December 28: The IMF delayed $63 million in loans to Kenya as a result of dissatisfaction with Kenyan economic reforms.

December 29: US Secretary of Commerce Robert Mosbacher blamed Japanese protectionism for the depth and persistence of the US recession.

_____ France and Iran signed a settlement of the $12 billion dispute over investments in France by the former shah of Iran.

1992

January 25: Germany resisted pressure from the G-7 finance ministers to lower interest rates.

February 2: The United States announced it was relaxing its economic embargo on Cuba by allowing AT&T to expand telephone service to the country.

February 19: Germany forgave $5.5 billion in debt owed by Poland.

February 21: The United States lifted sanctions on the PRC that prevented the sale or transfer of

high technology. In return, China pledged to abide by restrictions on the sale of missiles and missile technology.

February 22: Canada became the first Western country to approve credits to Ukraine.

March 1: Poland called for the IMF to consider, when designing stabilization programs, the special circumstances East European countries face in their transition to market economies.

March 2: The US Department of Commerce announced that Honda cars assembled in Canada did not contain enough North American input to qualify for duty-free entrance into the United States. Canada said it would file a challenge to the ruling.

March 12: GATT officials criticized the United States for increased reliance on antidumping measures as a means of restricting imports.

March 13: Ukraine announced it would share responsibility with Russia and the other CIS nations for the foreign debt of the former Soviet Union.

March 18: The Polish government passed an austerity budget that met IMF approval. The IMF had suspended a $2.5 billion credit package pending reductions in the budget deficit.

March 22: Trade talks between Chancellor Kohl and President Bush stalemated over the issue of farm subsidies. The United States had been pressing Germany to take a more forceful role in convincing the EC to compromise.

March 31: The IMF endorsed Russia's economic reform program, enabling the country to apply for membership and receive credits.

April 1: European and US negotiators reached a tentative agreement limiting government subsidies for the commercial aircraft industry.

April 3: Japanese officials declared that President Bush's announcement of a $24 billion aid package for Russia was premature, as details of the package had not been agreed to by the industrialized nations.

April 6: The EC lifted its remaining economic sanctions on South Africa in recognition of progress made in repealing apartheid.

April 15: An IMF report asserted that the former Soviet republics would require $44 billion in economic aid this year.

April 25: Canada agreed to ease restrictions on the import of US beer following intense negotiations in Washington and Ottawa.

April 27: The IMF and the World Bank offered membership to Russia and most other former Soviet republics.

April 29: The United States relaxed its economic embargo against Vietnam, allowing commercial sales of goods for basic human needs.

May 1: In negotiations with Citibank officials, Brazil agreed to reserve a portion of its central bank reserves to use as collateral for new terms on the repayment of over $41 billion in debt.

May 2: The United States threatened to implement sanctions against both countries if Russia sells to India missile technology that can be used in the development of long-range weapons.

May 3: The Kuwaiti central bank acknowledged that the government had incurred expenses of up to $65 billion in the past year, almost two-thirds of total global Kuwaiti assets.

_____ The United States threatened to introduce tariffs on over $1 billion worth of European imports following the EC's refusal to reduce oilseed subsidies.

May 5: France renounced a forty-six-year-old commercial aviation treaty with the United States that allowed American air carriers to increase the number of flights they offer in France without a commensurate increase in French access to the United States. The treaty would lapse one year after notice of termination.

_____ Chancellor Kohl called on Japan to increase financial assistance to the countries of Eastern Europe and the CIS. Kohl indicated that German assistance had reached its limit and that potential for great instability existed if more help was not forthcoming.

_____ Russia announced it would make the ruble fully convertible by August 1 at a fixed rate to the dollar (approximately at R80/US$). The exchange rate would be supported by a $6 billion fund established by Western governments.

May 6: The United States accused China of conspiracy to evade textile import duties.

May 11: The United States imposed trade bans on two arms and space research agencies in Russia and India after the Russian agency signed an agreement with its Indian counterpart to transfer Russian rocket technology.

May 15: Japan announced a $400 million aid package for the nations of Eastern and Central Europe but rejected aid to the former Soviet republics until territorial disputes are settled.

_____ In a national referendum, Swiss voters supported an application for the country to join the IMF and World Bank.

May 18: President Nursultan Nazarbayev of Kazakhstan signed an agreement with Chevron Corporation to develop the Tengiz oilfield, which will produce 700,000 barrels of oil per day.

_____ Switzerland announced plans to join the EC as well as the IMF and World Bank.

May 19: At a ministerial meeting in Paris, ministers from twenty-four Organization for Economic Cooperation and Development (OECD) nations called for a rapid conclusion to the Uruguay Round of the GATT talks.

May 21: The EC reached agreement on agricultural subsidy concessions that included sharp cuts in the level of subsidies as well as cuts in production ceilings.

May 29: The US Department of Commerce accused several former Soviet republics of dumping uranium on the US market.

June 2: The Bush administration announced it would seek to extend preferential trade ties to the PRC for the next year despite congressional criticism that China had been unresponsive to US human rights concerns.

June 6: Saudi Arabia warned foreign oil companies exploring in disputed territories on the Saudi-Yemeni border that they must withdraw from the area or face possible military retaliation.

_____ Zaire seized assets of all foreign oil companies in an attempt to end fuel shortages.

June 7: A report by a Japanese government advisory council accused the United States of unfair trade practices and supported greater use of GATT enforcement mechanisms as an alternative to bilateral negotiations.

REGIONAL DIPLOMACY

AFRICA

1991

July 3: A conference of Ethiopian political factions adopted a charter for establishing a transitional government and endorsing the right of self-determination.

July 5: Nelson Mandela was elected to be African National Congress (ANC) President at the first ANC conference in South Africa.

July 9: The International Olympic Committee, meeting in Lausanne, Switzerland, lifted its ban on South African participation.

July 10: The United States removed most of its economic and cultural sanctions against South Africa.

July 14: Israel repealed its package of economic and cultural sanctions against South Africa, though it continued to impose an embargo on military exports.

August 1: The ANC called for a conference of all South African political parties as soon as possible to force the government toward a framework for interim rule.

August 26: The South African government drafted the outlines of a new constitution that would provide for a governing executive council of representatives of leading political parties and provide for free elections.

September 4: South African President de Klerk outlined a plan for a two-chamber legislature that would be elected by universal suffrage.

September 9: Leaders of the ANC and Inkatha Freedom party stressed their commitment to peace and negotiations with the government despite the recent renewal of factional violence. ANC leaders met with President de Klerk and released a statement contending that progress had been made in areas of mutual interest.

September 11: Nearly 100 South Africans died in the previous four days from factional violence between ANC and Inkatha Freedom party supporters.

September 17: The leaders of Côte d'Ivoire, Gambia, Burkina Faso, Guinea-Bissau, Mali, Senegal, Liberia, and the Liberian rebel forces reached an agreement on the demilitarization of Liberian rebel forces and a provisional end to the civil war.

September 24: France and Belgium sent troops to Zaire to protect Westerners during looting by troops challenging President Mobutu Sese Seko's rule.

September 29: Angolan rebel leader Jonas Savimbi returned to Luanda to begin a political campaign for the presidency in elections expected in 1992.

October 26: The ANC and Pan-African Congress announced they had reached agreement on the representation and agenda of a conference for all parties in South Africa to debate a new constitution.

November 5: The ANC called for a conclusion to a two-day strike that effectively brought South Africa's economy to a standstill.

November 12: About 2,500 black South African miners were sent home from the major gold mines following an intense outbreak of ethnic violence in which sixty-nine workers were killed.

November 13: ANC leader Mandela indicated that the all-party conference to discuss constitutional approaches to the repeal of apartheid was likely to begin by the end of the month.

November 16: A West African peacekeeping force began deployment in Liberia, putting an end to the twenty-month civil war.

November 29: France mobilized troops to assist General Gnassingbe Eyadema of Togo in reinstating his power following an attempted coup.

November 30: Twenty political organizations in South Africa concluded a set of meetings that laid the groundwork for a general convention in late December.

December 5: While visiting the United States, ANC leader Mandela sought to tie the repeal of economic sanctions against South Africa to the establishment of a multiparty interim government.

December 8: Concluding its first legal congress in forty years, the South African Communist party pledged to support Cuba in its struggle "against US imperialism" following the reduction of Soviet support in the last year.

December 10: South African President de Klerk canceled a planned trip to the Soviet Union pending stabilization of the situation in Moscow.

December 11: A group of 120 South African exiles returned to the country under a UN-negotiated amnesty.

December 12: The Congo began expelling as many as 30,000 Zairians who were living illegally in the country.

December 13: The UN General Assembly called on nations to begin restoring ties to South Africa in recognition of its steps to repeal apartheid.

_____ Zairian Prime Minister Nguza Karl-i-Bond left the United States after a visit claiming that American officials had indicated their desire to see democracy come to the country.

_____ The United States nearly doubled its emergency assistance to Somalia after UN officials refused to organize further assistance for casualties of the civil war.

December 19: The South African government and the African National Congress reached a compromise in preliminary negotiations for the Convention for a Democratic South Africa (CODESA) conference. All parties to the conference would commit themselves politically and morally to implementing any decisions reached, though decisions would have no legal standing.

December 20: The CODESA conference opened in Johannesburg with nineteen political parties represented. President de Klerk indicated that the government was prepared to negotiate changes in the constitution to allow an interim government until a new constitution could be drafted. De Klerk attacked the ANC for refusing to disband its military wing, a criticism that prompted sharp rebukes from ANC leader Mandela.

_____ Belgium began air transport of relief supplies to the Somalian capital, Mogadishu.

December 21: The CODESA conference in South Africa concluded with the appointment of five working groups to prepare issues, including a referendum on an interim government, and to report back to the conference early next spring.

December 31: The Security Council gave tacit support to guidelines drawn up by Secretary-General Pérez de Cuéllar for a referendum in the Western Sahara.

1992

January 3: France sent 450 more paratroopers to Chad to protect French property and citizens during the civil war.

_____ UN Under Secretary-General James O.C. Jonah flew to Somalia for talks on the potential for the UN to act as a mediator in the civil war.

January 4: After meeting with leaders of both sides, Under Secretary-General Jonah professed skepticism about a UN role in the Somalian negotiations.

January 5: Eritrean officials offered mediation services in resolving the civil war in Somalia.

January 7: Algeria announced it would sign the Nuclear Non-Proliferation Treaty in the near future.

January 20: Nineteen of South Africa's political parties met to begin working out details that would lead to a constitutional convention.

January 22: The US accused Libya of continuing the manufacture and stockpiling of chemical weapons.

February 8: The World Bank agreed to lend Ethiopia $672 million to help in the reconstruction of the country following more than two decades of civil war.

February 14: A cease-fire agreement was reached by the two Somali factions that had fought a bitter civil war for the past three months.

February 16: The UN agreed to provide food relief to Somali civilians if the truce continued to hold.

February 20: After a defeat in a local South African election, President de Klerk announced he would hold a national referendum on his policies of repealing apartheid.

March 7: Former South African President P. W. Botha announced he would not support the referendum March 17 calling for a continuation of measures to repeal apartheid.

March 17: A referendum in South Africa giving President de Klerk a mandate to proceed with constitutional revision and dismantle the apartheid system passed by a two-to-one margin.

March 23: The South African government announced a series of measures designed to create a series of advisory councils in place of an interim government, reserving for itself greater power in the transition process. The ANC denounced the proposal as a step back from progress made over past weeks.

March 30: The South African government proposed to create a two-chamber legislature to replace Parliament and agreed with the ANC to set up an interim government within three months.

_____ The United States officially asked former Angolan guerrilla leader Jonas Savimbi for explanations of alleged human rights violations.

April 1: Violence raged in Alexandra, South Africa, as supporters of the Inkatha Freedom party battled ANC supporters.

April 23: President de Klerk proposed to bring black leaders into an interim government with an executive council composed of elected officials replacing the presidency.

April 25: ANC President Mandela rejected President de Klerk's power-sharing plan as an attempt to refurbish the existing government rather than a true democratic redistribution of power.

April 30: President Joseph Momoh of Sierra Leone was overthrown in a coup d'état and fled to neighboring Guinea.

May 15: Negotiations in the CODESA working groups deadlocked over the size of the legislative margin of approval for constitutional provisions covering regional issues.

May 16: Negotiators recessed the CODESA working-group talks until June without any resolution of the deadlock.

June 17: At least forty people were killed in the South African township of Boipatong when Zulu-speaking men, allegedly assisted by South African police, went on a brutal rampage.

June 20: President de Klerk visited Boipatong but was driven from the scene of the June 17 massacre by an angry mob.

June 23: The ANC announced it was withdrawing from talks on the political future of South Africa due to alleged government support of township violence.

ASIA AND THE PACIFIC

1991

July 4: Britain and the PRC reached an agreement by which Hong Kong would be able to build a new airport under Chinese loan guarantees and the PRC would be given more influence in Hong Kong affairs as the 1997 reversion from British rule approaches.

July 17: The United States and the Philippines agreed to a new ten-year lease of the Subic Bay naval complex while US forces withdraw from Clark Air base.

August 1: South Korea proposed to hold arms talks on nuclear and military issues with North Korea.

August 20: Seven Sri Lankan Tamils committed suicide when surrounded by Indian police who were seeking the assassins of former Prime Minister Rajiv Gandhi.

August 22: Four members of an American human rights group were detained overnight in the PRC before being expelled from the country.

August 27: The Cambodian government and opposition groups reached agreement to cut military forces by up to 70 percent and allow UN supervision of the remaining forces.

_____ The United States and the Philippines signed an agreement providing for ten more years of American naval presence at Subic Bay.

August 29: The four groups negotiating Cambodian peace concluded talks in Thailand without a formal agreement but were optimistic that an agreement could be reached by the end of the year.

September 2: British Prime Minister John Major arrived in the PRC for discussions about the future of Hong Kong and to sign an agreement to build a new airport there.

September 5: Prime Minister Major sought to reassure Hong Kong that China would abide by the joint 1984 agreement between China and Great Britain.

September 9: A preliminary vote in the Philippine Senate showed a majority against renewing the Subic Bay Naval Base lease with the United States.

September 10: Grigory A. Yavlinsky, a vice-chairman of the Soviet transitional economic committee, acknowledged Japanese rights to the southern Kurile Islands, though Russian President Yeltsin had recently reiterated Russian claims to the island chain.

September 12: Vietnam and the PRC announced that Vietnamese leaders would travel to Beijing for meetings aimed at normalizing relations.

September 15: Philippine President Corazon Aquino declared that she would seek a national referendum if the Senate voted down a bill extending the American lease of Subic Bay Naval Base.

September 16: The Philippine Senate voted to reject the agreement allowing the United States to continue using the Subic Bay Naval Base.

September 17: President Aquino revoked an eviction notice for US forces at Subic Bay, extending their presence at least one year.

_____ The United States and Japan agreed to study (1) US sales of autos to Japan and (2) US sales of auto parts to Japan and to Japanese companies in the United States.

September 19: The Japanese Parliament began debate on legislation to allow troops to participate in UN peacekeeping actions.

_____ President Aquino declared she would seek to overrule the Philippine Senate's vote if the people demanded a referendum. The announcement was seen as a retreat from her previous assertion that she would take the vote to the people.

September 24: South Korean President Roh Tae Woo addressed the UN General Assembly, the first time any leader of either Korea had addressed the assembly as a member. He proposed a three-phased plan for reunification based on a commitment by North Korea to repudiate its nuclear program and allow international inspections.

October 2: Vietnam agreed to the forced return of refugees who fled the country for economic reasons.

October 4: After losing the support of party elders, Japanese Prime Minister Toshiki Kaifu announced he would not seek reelection.

October 22: North and South Korea resumed ministerial talks in Pyongyang. North Korea again refused to allow international inspection of its nuclear facilities.

October 23: The government of Cambodia signed a UN-brokered peace agreement by which former Cambodian leader Prince Norodom Sihanouk would become president of an interim Supreme National Council. The peace agreement also called for the demobilization of each faction's armies and the repatriation of all Cambodian refugees.

October 24: North Korea dropped its demand that South Korea sever its alliance with the United States as a precondition for normalization of relations.

November 4: Imelda Marcos returned to the Philippines to face charges and to mount a campaign for the presidency.

November 5: President Bush's trip to Asia was canceled.

November 8: Hong Kong began the deportation of a large group of refugees back to Vietnam.

_____ President Roh announced that South Korea would not seek to produce nuclear weapons after the United States withdrew its arsenal from the nation.

November 11: US Secretary of State Baker called on Japan to transcend "checkbook diplomacy" and take a more active role in promoting democracy and free trade.

November 13: Secretary Baker expressed American concern while in Seoul over the suspected North

Korean plan to develop nuclear weapons.

_____ Japan's new prime minister, Kiichi Miyazawa, declared that normalization with North Korea could begin only if the latter repudiated its nuclear program.

November 14: Prince Sihanouk returned to Cambodia after nearly twenty years of exile as leader of the coalition Supreme National Council that would lead the country back to normalcy.

November 15: While in Beijing, Secretary Baker pressed Chinese leaders about the release of prisoners and arms sales.

_____ The Cambodian peace process came under strain as the government refused to build memorials to the victims of the Khmer Rouge leadership in the late 1970s.

November 16: Prince Sihanouk declared his support for genocide trials against Khmer Rouge leaders for mass slayings during their administration. The declaration was made as Khmer Rouge officials were preparing to return to Cambodia to participate in an interim government.

November 17: Secretary Baker concluded a three-day trip to China with no progress made on the issue of human rights and vague Chinese reassurances to reconsider their sales of missiles to the developing world.

_____ The Afghanistan government called for wide-ranging talks to end the twelve-year-old civil war.

November 20: US and South Korean officials involved in talks with North Korea demanded the cancellation of North Korean nuclear programs in advance of an agreement.

_____ Prince Sihanouk was declared president of Cambodia by the Vietnamese-installed Cambodian government.

November 21: US Secretary of Defense Dick Cheney halted the US reduction of forces in Korea pending greater certainty of the extent of North Korean nuclear capabilities.

November 26: North Korea offered international inspection of its nuclear facilities in return for commensurate inspections of US facilities in South Korea to confirm that the United States was withdrawing all nuclear weapons from the Korean peninsula.

November 27: Senior Khmer Rouge leader Khieu Samphan was attacked and injured by demonstrators after he arrived in Phnom Penh to take up his position as called for by the UN peace treaty.

November 29: The UN General Assembly passed a resolution rebuking the government of Myanmar for its refusal to surrender power to the National League for Democracy, which won 80 percent of the vote in the 1990 elections, and for continued human rights abuses.

December 5: After President Bush's refusal to apologize for the American use of atomic weapons in World War II, Japanese officials indicated that it was unlikely Japan would apologize for the Pearl Harbor attack on the occasion of the fiftieth anniversary December 7.

December 6: Prince Sihanouk called for restraint from Cambodians in allowing the Khmer Rouge to return to Cambodia. Though emphasizing he was not calling for forgiveness of genocide, Sihanouk announced he would not seek to create a coalition government absent the Khmer Rouge.

_____ President Bush invited chief executive officers (including the heads of the Big Three auto companies) to accompany him on his trip to Japan.

December 7: Fiftieth anniversary of Pearl Harbor.

December 10: North Korean Prime Minister Yon Hyong Muk met with his South Korean counterpart in Seoul for a fifth round of talks aimed at reducing tensions.

December 11: South Korea and the United States announced their willingness to allow North Korean inspection of civilian and military sites in return for reciprocal rights.

December 13: North and South Korea adopt, after two days of talks, an Agreement on Reconciliation, Nonaggression, and Exchanges and Cooperation between the South and the North.

December 15: Former Cambodian Prime Minister Son Sann, leader of the US-backed Khmer People's National Liberation Front, returned to Cambodia calling for unity and peace.

December 18: South Korea announced that all nuclear weapons in the country had been removed.

_____ The United States lifted an embargo on organized travel to Vietnam.

December 19: North Korean leader Kim Il Sung denied Western reports that his country was pursuing development of nuclear weapons and introduced a proposal for international inspection of North Korean nuclear-research centers.

December 21: As numerous demonstrations swept through Cambodia, Khmer Rouge officials were told that returning to the capital at the moment would be ill-advised.

December 26: North Korea pledged to join an IAEA safeguards agreement that would allow international inspection of secret nuclear-research centers.

December 27: The Philippines declared that the United States must withdraw from the Subic Bay Naval Base by the end of 1992, ending an American military presence there since the Spanish-American War of 1898.

_____ President Bush called for a two-year extension of the voluntary restraint agreements on machine tools with Japan and Taiwan.

December 28: North and South Korea resumed talks concerning nuclear weapons and inspections.

December 30: The Supreme National Council of Cambodia, the joint governing council set up as part of the UN framework for peace, met for the first time in Cambodia when Khmer Rouge officials returned to the country.

_____ Japan announced a series of steps intended to invigorate economic growth and increase the value of the yen relative to the dollar. The move was seen as a demonstration of Japan's willingness to increase imports and pacify American trade critics in anticipation of President Bush's arrival in Japan January 7.

December 31: North and South Korea initialed an agreement banning nuclear weapons on the Korean peninsula, but the methods and procedures for ensuring compliance had yet to be determined.

1992

January 1: Upon the arrival of President Bush in Sydney, Australia, Australian Prime Minister Paul Keating lashed out at US trade restrictions and subsidies on agriculture.

_____ The United States and the CIS announced an agreement to cease all military aid to their allies in Afghanistan. Pakistan declared it would not be bound by the agreement.

January 2: While visiting Australia, President Bush tried to enlist Asian help in pressuring Europe to reduce agricultural subsidies.

January 3: President Bush arrived in Singapore for a one-day stopover before traveling to Korea and Japan. He praised Singapore's policy of free trade, which has yielded sustained economic growth.

January 4: Cambodian officials pledged to speed the release of prisoners as part of the UN-sponsored peace.

January 5: President Bush warned South Koreans against too-rapid progress in normalizing relations with North Korea before adequate provisions for monitoring North Korean nuclear-weapons programs were developed.

January 6: The US Senate committee reviewing the issue of missing servicemen in Vietnam announced it was sending a mission to Laos, Cambodia, and Vietnam to talk with officials.

January 9: President Bush and Prime Minister Miyazawa agreed to a US-Japan Global Partnership Plan of Action. Japan pledged to increase imports of US autos, auto parts, computers, and other goods.

January 17: Japan formally apologized to Korea for forcing Korean women to serve as prostitutes for Japanese soldiers during World War II.

January 19: Japanese Speaker of the House Sakurauchi claimed that American workers are lazy and illiterate and that America had become "Japan's subcontractor."

January 22: Los Angeles canceled a $122 million railcar contract with Sumitomo.

_____ House Majority Leader Richard Gephardt introduced a bill that would require Japan to reduce its trade surplus by 20 percent per year for five years.

January 30: North Korea signed a nuclear-safeguards agreement permitting international inspection of its nuclear facilities.

_____ The United States asserted that China was continuing to sell missile technology to Syria and Pakistan despite statements that it would refrain from such activity.

_____ China indicated it would consider participating in nuclear arms reduction talks once Russia and the US had scaled their arsenals down to a size roughly equivalent to China's arsenal.

February 3: Riots in Vietnamese refugee camps in Hong Kong left twenty-one dead and over one hundred injured.

_____ Prime Minister Miyazawa stated that Americans' determination "to produce goods and create value has loosened sharply."

February 7: Pakistan confirmed that it had a nuclear-weapons capability but asserted that the country had not built a bomb and would not transfer its technology to other countries.

_____ Three Afghan rebel factions endorsed a UN peace plan calling for a cease-fire and the creation of an interim government composed of an assembly of all parties.

February 21: Attorney General William Barr announced that the US government would soon change its antitrust policies to allow Justice Department lawsuits against the American operations of foreign cartels.

March 2: The US Customs Department ruled that Honda Motor Company owed $18.6 million in tariffs on the grounds that Honda Civics imported from Canada had less than 50 percent North American content.

March 7: Hong Kong officials announced that no Vietnamese sought refuge on its territory in the past month.

March 10: India offered to begin discussions with the United States aimed at curbing the spread of nuclear weapons in Asia.

March 11: Japan was asked by UN officials to contribute $1 billion and deploy civilian personnel in support of UN peacekeeping efforts in Cambodia.

March 12: Japan's Liberal Democratic party approved a bill to raise the maximum fine for antitrust violations from 5 million to 100 million yen. The Japan Fair Trade Commission had originally requested an increase to 300 million yen.

March 14: India agreed to join naval operations with the United States and to intensify negotiations aimed at curbing nuclear proliferation in South Asia. The agreements were seen as part of an improvement in relations between the two countries.

_____ North and South Korea reached agreement on inspection of each other's nuclear facilities by mid-June.

March 15: Yasushi Akashi, a senior UN diplomat, arrived in Cambodia to initiate officially the UN peacekeeping effort in the country. Even as he arrived, fighting broke out north of Phnom Penh.

March 18: Bangladesh Prime Minister Khaleda Zia arrived in the United States for talks concerning economic aid and the plight of Myanmar Muslims taking refuge in her country. The UN indicated it would send an envoy to the area to mediate the refugee problem.

_____ Afghanistan President Muhammad Najibullah indicated he would resign in favor of a UN-sponsored peace plan that would set up an interim government.

March 25: Refugee workers in Cambodia asserted that Khmer Rouge guerrillas were attempting forcibly to direct returning refugees into areas of the country in which they were in control.

March 30: The UN peacekeeping force in Cambodia began overseeing the repatriation of an estimated 370,000 Cambodian refugees from Thai border camps.

April 10: The North Korean parliament ratified an agreement to allow inspection of the country's nuclear facilities.

April 11: The government of Afghanistan agreed to a UN plan to establish a neutral council to govern the country until an interim government could be established. Several guerrilla leaders rejected the proposal, but most groups supported it.

April 15: North Korea released a videotape showing footage of nuclear facilities that the United States had alleged were part of a huge nuclear-weapons development complex.

April 16: Afghanistan President Najibullah was deposed and arrested as he sought to flee Kabul. Rebel troops were surging toward the capital unchecked.

April 17: Afghanistan mujahidin rebel groups surrounded Kabul and demanded the surrender of the army.

April 20: Cambodia's four factional groups signed UN Charter covenants that form the International Bill of Human Rights.

April 21: Speaking on a trip to India, UN Secretary-General Boutros-Ghali asserted he would make national reconciliation in Afghanistan a priority issue in the months ahead.

April 24: Islamic guerrillas from six major rebel groups began occupying Kabul as the government maintained control over only the city center. Leaders of the six groups reached agreement on the composition of a fifty-member interim council to assume power when the final vestiges of the government had collapsed.

April 25: Islamic rebel groups captured the city of Kabul, ending fourteen years of civil war between the communist regime and Islamic opposition in Afghanistan.

April 28: Sibgatullah Majadedi, elected leader of the ruling council of Islamic guerrillas in Afghanistan, arrived in Kabul to assume power from the former government. Majadedi declared a general amnesty.

April 29: Afghanistan guerrillas secured control of the capital and announced an unconditional cease-fire.

April 30: Ahmad Shah Masood, leader of the strongest Afghan guerrilla organization, entered Kabul and took charge of security. He denounced Gulbuddin Hekmatyar, whose own hard-line Islamic group fired rockets on the city from its southern base.

May 2: Islamic party leader Hekmatyar asserted that his guerrilla force would attack Kabul within three days if other militia forces did not withdraw from the capital.

May 5: Intense fighting broke out between forces loyal to Hekmatyar and interim President Majadedi. Residents described the fighting as far more intense than had previously been experienced against the former communist regime.

May 6: A cease-fire was declared in Kabul while various rebel groups attempted to bring the Islamic party into a coalition government.

_____ North Korea gave the IAEA names of previously unknown facilities involved in its nuclear program.

May 7: Four different mujahidin rebel groups claimed to have governmental authority in Kabul and all of Afghanistan.

May 12: Vietnam, Hong Kong, and Great Britain reached an agreement that allowed Hong Kong to continue the forced repatriation of Vietnamese refugees living in detention camps in Hong Kong.

May 22: North Korean soldiers skirmished with South Korean army troops south of the demilitarized zone for the first time since 1986.

May 30: India successfully tested a two-stage medium-range missile capable of a range of 1,500 miles.

June 3: Chinese police prevented a demonstration marking the third anniversary of the Tiananmen Square incident and arrested seven foreign journalists attempting to cover the demonstration.

June 13: Soldiers of three of Cambodia's four rival groups began reporting to UN missions in preparation for disarmament and demobilization. The Khmer Rouge refused to send its soldiers to the camps, in contravention of the UN-brokered peace treaty.

EUROPE

1991

July 1: The Soviet Union and five East European nations meeting in Prague formally dissolved the Warsaw Pact.

_____ Chancellor Kohl threatened to cancel economic aid to Yugoslavia if the army was deployed against Slovenia or Croatia.

July 2: The Yugoslav army attacked Slovenia, vowing to crush the drive for independence.

July 3: Northern Ireland peace talks collapsed.

July 4: Yugoslavia demanded that Slovenia accept an immediate cease-fire and relinquish control over border posts. Slovenia rejected the ultimatum.

July 5: The EC suspended economic aid to Yugoslavia and imposed a ban on arms sales to the belligerents in the civil war.

_____ The Russian parliament voted to support in principle the Union Treaty proposed by Soviet President Mikhail Gorbachev.

July 7: The Serbian-dominated government of Yugoslavia agreed to allow Slovenia limited control over its border posts as a concession to avert a war of independence. The agreement was combined with an immediate cease-fire in EC-brokered negotiations.

_____ Fighting broke out between Serbs and Croat national guardsmen in Croatia.

July 8: The United States announced its support of the EC arms embargo on Yugoslavia.

July 10: The Slovenian parliament voted to accept the EC-brokered compromise cease-fire agreement with Yugoslavia.

_____ Boris Yeltsin was inaugurated as the first directly elected president of Russia.

July 14: US Secretary of State Baker and Soviet Foreign Minister Aleksandr Bessmertnykh concluded three days of negotiations on the remaining obstacles to a strategic arms treaty, announcing that all but one highly technical issue had been resolved.

July 15: Fifty EC observers were deployed in Yugoslavia.

July 17: The Soviet Union and the United States reached agreement on a Strategic Arms Limitation Treaty that effectively cut the strategic arsenals of the two superpowers by 25 to 35 percent. President Bush and President Gorbachev announced the treaty would be signed on July 31 at a summit in Moscow.

July 18: Yugoslavia ordered its army to withdraw from Slovenia, effectively conceding independence to the republic.

July 22: Fighting between the Serbian minority and Croatian national guard again erupted as leaders of the six Yugoslav republics met in Belgrade to discuss proposals for reconstituting the federation.

July 24: Nine of the fifteen Soviet republics agreed to a decentralized system of power sharing in supporting President Gorbachev's draft Union Treaty.

July 29: The EC announced it would add fifty more personnel to its Yugoslav observer force, effectively doubling the size of the contingent.

July 31: President Bush and President Gorbachev signed the Strategic Arms Reduction Treaty (START), which reduced the number of long-range nuclear weapons on each side. Concurrently, the two leaders pledged to sponsor a Middle East peace conference in October.

_____ The Yugoslav republic of Croatia offered its Serbian minority a peace plan containing significant concessions in terms of home rule that were designed to meet the minimum demands of the Serb minority.

August 3: Croatia accepted an EC cease-fire plan, but Serbian leader Slobodan Milosevic rejected the proposed deployment of an armed peace-keeping force in the region.

August 6: The EC called for greater international pressure on the parties to the Yugoslav civil war to solve their differences peacefully.

August 7: Italy announced it was considering the forced repatriation of thousands of Albanian refugees who fled their country in the past weeks.

_____ Chancellor Kohl threatened Serbia with economic sanctions if violations of cease-fire agreements continued.

August 8: At an emergency meeting of the CSCE member nations in Prague, Yugoslavia agreed to an expansion of the EC observer force in Croatia.

_____ Turkish army regulars attacked Kurdish rebels inside the Iraqi border.

August 14: Italy announced it would allow 1,000 Albanians to remain pending a review by an immigration committee. Over 17,000 Albanians had been shipped home in the previous few days.

August 18: An emergency committee composed of Kremlin hard-liners took control of the Soviet Union, alleging that Soviet President Gorbachev had taken ill while vacationing in Yalta.

_____ Troops and armor of the Yugoslav national army crossed into Croatia.

August 19: As Soviet conservatives sought to reimpose Communist party control over the country, Russian President Yeltsin rallied resistance to the coup from his headquarters at the Russian parliament building.

_____ Increased fighting in Croatia threatened the shaky truce; forty-two people died during the weekend.

_____ President Bush rejected the legitimacy of the emergency committee governing the Soviet Union and called for the restoration of Gorbachev to his office as president. The US State Department issued a warning against travel to the USSR.

_____ Chancellor Kohl warned the new Soviet government that a change in economic policies or human rights would endanger the flow of economic aid from Europe.

_____ The United States, Great Britain, and Canada froze economic assistance to the Soviet Union; NATO and the EC planned for meetings of foreign ministers later in the week.

August 20: In Moscow, various military units and personnel sought to protect the Russian parliament and Russian President Yeltsin from an expected attack by the Soviet army. Rumors spread concerning disarray within the new leadership. The presidents of the Ukraine and Kazakhstan republics denounced the leaders of the coup.

_____ The Estonian parliament declared full and immediate independence from the USSR.

_____ President Bush said the United States would refuse normal relations with the coup leadership.

_____ Canada demanded an independent medical inspection of President Gorbachev to confirm his alleged illness.

_____ The EC during an emergency meeting at The Hague halted all economic aid to the Soviet Union.

August 21: Lithuanian security forces exchanged fire with Soviet troops in an apparent coup attempt near the parliament building in Vilnius.

August 22: President Gorbachev returned to Moscow after the failed coup attempt, meeting with Russian President Yeltsin and replacing key heads of government ministries.

_____ Latvia voted to outlaw the Communist party and called for the arrest of its leader for his alleged role in the Soviet coup attempt.

_____ Croatia gave the Serbian-dominated federal government until August 31 to withdraw its troops from Croatian territory or it would be treated as a foreign occupying force and Croatia would order a total mobilization.

August 24: Ukraine declared its independence from the Soviet Union.

August 25: Byelorussia followed the Ukraine by declaring its independence from the USSR. Moldavia announced it would hold a referendum the next day.

August 26: Russia asserted it would not allow other republics to secede from the union if they were to take areas with large Russian populations with them. Leaders of Kazakhstan warned, in turn, that significant border disputes leading to war were possible.

August 27: Yugoslavia and Croatia agreed to a ceasefire. But Croatia also announced it was ready to announce a general mobilization of troops to supplement the forces that had been fighting against the Serbian-dominated Yugoslav army.

_____ Russia and Kazakhstan joined Kirghizia and President Gorbachev in calls for retention of some form of union among the breakaway Soviet republics.

_____ Moldavia became the seventh Soviet republic to vote for independence from the Soviet Union.

August 28: Delegates of the Russian republic and Soviet parliament flew to Ukraine to convince leaders there to remain in the union.

_____ The latest Yugoslav cease-fire was broken by fierce fighting between Yugoslav and Croatian forces.

_____ Russian President Yeltsin announced that he and Soviet President Gorbachev would convene a conference to discuss the future security of Soviet nuclear weapons.

August 29: The Soviet parliament voted to suspend the activities of the Communist party until investigation of its role in the attempted coup could be completed.

_____ EC envoy Henry Wijnaendts reported after visiting Yugoslavia that the federal army was definitely supporting Serbian positions in the conflict with Croatia.

September 1: The Congress of People's Deputies of the USSR approved the formation of an interim confederation of sovereign states. Only seven of the fifteen republics participated in the interim structure.

September 2: Yugoslavia agreed to additional EC observers to monitor a cease-fire.

September 5: A large demonstration erupted in Tbilisi, Georgia, protesting President Zviad Gamsakhurdia's alleged dictatorial rule.

September 7: An EC-sponsored peace conference on Yugoslavia began work at The Hague. It failed to make any progress.

September 9: Macedonia became the third Yugoslav republic to vote for secession.

September 11: President Gorbachev announced he would begin discussions with Cuban leader Fidel Castro to remove Soviet troops from the island.

_____ Croatia shut down the oil pipeline that supplied Serbia.

_____ Meeting in Paris, Greek and Turkish officials failed to resolve their differences over Cyprus.

September 12: President Gorbachev asked the EC and G-7 nations for urgent food relief worth up to $7 billion.

_____ Serbian forces severed access of the Croatian capital to the Dalmatian coast.

September 15: The Yugoslav army intensified fighting in Croatia following Croatia's blockade of Yugoslav army garrisons.

September 16: The Yugoslav air force attacked the Croatian capital of Zagreb for the first time since fighting had broken out two months earlier.

_____ The EC, under Dutch leadership, proposed sending a peacekeeping force to Yugoslavia under the auspices of the Western European Union (WEU).

_____ President Bush and Chancellor Kohl declared that the West should provide humanitarian aid to the Soviet Union for the winter, though no specifics were announced.

_____ Former head of East German intelligence Markus Wolf requested asylum in Austria.

September 17: Hours after the fourth cease-fire was declared, the Yugoslav air force and artillery units attacked Zagreb with an intense battery of shells.

_____ The Canadian National Defense Department announced it was cutting its forces in the European region by 80 percent as a result of the reduced military threat to Western Europe.

September 19: The Soviet Union doubled its request for food aid to $14.7 billion from the EC after figures showed that oil exports had fallen by 50 percent.

_____ After a long and divisive debate, the EC rejected a proposal to send a peacekeeping force to Yugoslavia and instead called on the WEU to strengthen the 200-member EC observer force in the country.

September 22: The Armenian republic agreed to negotiations with neighboring Azerbaijan concerning territorial disputes related to the territory Nagorno-Karabakh. President Yeltsin agreed to act as mediator.

_____ Croatian and Yugoslav forces agreed to another cease-fire after three days of a federal army offensive.

_____ Georgian opposition forces occupied radio stations in Tbilisi protesting President Zviad Gamsakhurdia's alleged dictatorial rule.

September 23: An agreement between Armenia and Azerbaijan was signed that would submit the dispute over Nagorno-Karabakh to negotiations. The agreement mandated an immediate cease-fire.

September 24: President Gamsakhurdia of Georgia called for supporters to rally in Tbilisi and throw out rebel forces.

September 25: The UN Security Council voted to embargo the sale of weapons and military equipment to Yugoslavia.

_____ A secret meeting of belligerent factions in Yugoslavia was held in which agreement was reached to "maintain and fortify" the three-day-old cease-fire.

_____ German Foreign Minister Hans-Dietrich Genscher called for the inclusion of East-bloc nations in the EC.

September 27: The United States announced a sweeping unilateral cut in strategic and tactical nuclear weapons deployed abroad. The US strategic command was taken off alert status. President Gorbachev welcomed the move as a major step toward disarmament but indicated he would need further time to study the proposals before he could consider commensurate reductions.

October 2: Croatian President Franjo Tudjman appealed to the Yugoslav army for a cease-fire and pledged to end the Croatian blockade of army barracks.

October 4: Croatia and Yugoslavia agreed to a sixth cease-fire during a meeting at The Hague.

October 7: The Yugoslav air force bombed the presidential palace in Zagreb, nearly killing two top Croatian officials and the Croatian head of the federal government.

October 8: Poland and the Soviet Union reached agreement by which the Soviet Union would withdraw the rest of its troops from Poland by the end of 1992. The agreement also allowed Poland to join other security alliances.

October 10: At a meeting of the leaders of Serbia and Croatia at The Hague, Croatian President Tudjman rejected an agenda that included discussion of a continued Yugoslav federation because Croatia had already declared its independence.

October 15: The United States offered to negotiate limits on antimissile systems with the Soviet Union.

_____ Serbia and Croatia announced a cease-fire after meetings with Soviet President Gorbachev in Moscow.

October 17: The Yugoslav army began a new offensive against Croatia as negotiators prepared to meet at The Hague for discussions on Yugoslavia's future shape.

_____ Ukraine rejected a proposed free-market association for the Soviet republics on the grounds that it would infringe on Ukraine's sovereignty.

October 21: President Gorbachev opened a new session of the Soviet parliament, although five of the twelve republics did not send a delegation.

October 22: The Ukrainian parliament approved measures to create an independent army of 400,000 soldiers.

October 23: Serbian leaders meeting in Belgrade approved a plan to reconstruct a Yugoslav state based on Serbian-controlled territory.

October 28: The EC warned Serbian leaders to accept an EC peace plan or face sanctions.

October 31: Twenty-seven West and East European governments issued a communiqué from Berlin that called for more stringent enforcement of border controls to prevent the surge in illegal migration.

November 5: Lord Carrington, chairman of the European conference attempting to mediate peace in Yugoslavia, warned Serbia that continued refusal to compromise would cause the EC to suspend the peace process.

November 6: Ukraine and Moldavia signed the economic free-trade zone agreement passed by the former Soviet republics on October 17.

November 7: At a NATO summit meeting in Rome, alliance leaders agreed to extend formal links to members of the former Warsaw Pact, but would not offer security guarantees.

November 8: The EC voted to place sanctions on Yugoslavia for its persistence in using force and urged the UN Security Council to embargo oil exports to the country.

_____ NATO ended a two-day meeting in Rome with a warning to the Soviet Union and its fragmenting republics to keep nuclear weapons under centralized control.

November 9: The United States indicated it would join the EC in imposing economic sanctions on Yugoslavia.

November 11: The Russian parliament rejected President Yeltsin's bid to impose emergency rule in the Muslim autonomous republic of Checheno-Ingush that had voted to break away from Russia.

_____ A meeting in Bonn between German Chancellor Kohl and British Prime Minister Major ended inconclusively as the two leaders failed to resolve differences over European unity.

November 13: Great Britain, France, and Belgium announced they were drafting a resolution to send a UN peacekeeping force to Yugoslavia if the warring factions agreed to a cease-fire.

_____ Prime Minister Major indicated that Britain would back a plan for a single European currency by the end of the century if the goal of a closer federal union were abandoned.

November 14: President Gorbachev received assurances from seven republics (but not the Ukraine) that they would participate in negotiations aiming at a "Union of Sovereign States."

November 15: French and German leaders agreed to press the United Kingdom for greater concessions on European unity prior to the Maastricht summit of EC leaders in December.

November 17: President Yeltsin issued a number of decrees to assert Russian autonomy over its natural resources, abolish export and import controls, and float the ruble after the new year.

November 18: WEU member nations offered to provide warships so that a "humanitarian corridor" from Yugoslavia to Italy could be built that would allow refugees to flee the civil war.

November 20: President Gorbachev sought emergency funds from the Soviet parliament, but the Russian republic rejected the appropriation.

November 23: Croatia and Serbia signed a cease-fire agreement in Geneva that could lead to the deployment of a UN peacekeeping force.

November 25: Representatives of the former Soviet republics met in Moscow and refused to sign a treaty forming a new political union under the leadership of President Gorbachev. The representatives indicated that all legislation considered would have to be referred back to the national parliaments.

November 27: President Bush announced that his administration now hoped to recognize expeditiously an independent Ukraine and other former Soviet republics as soon as it was feasible.

November 29: President Bush told a group of American-Ukrainians that he would expedite recognition of the Ukraine if the independence referendum passed. In contrast, Yeltsin announced his opposition to independence for the Ukraine. The EC announced it would take a more cautious approach to Ukrainian recognition.

_____ President Yeltsin refused the Soviet government's request for an extension of funds, effectively shutting down the Soviet government indefinitely.

_____ The Yugoslav army began withdrawing from Croatian army barracks in occupied Croatia. Despite flare-ups throughout the Croatian republic, the fourteenth cease-fire generally seemed to be holding.

_____ If the Ukraine voted for independence in its upcoming referendum, Romania announced it would demand negotiations over disputed territories taken after World War II.

November 30: President Yeltsin agreed to finance the Soviet government payroll temporarily and guarantee enough credits to meet the minimal needs of the Kremlin apparatus.

December 1: Ukrainian voters overwhelmingly passed a referendum calling for independence. President Gorbachev congratulated the republic but expressed hope that the Ukraine would join a union of independent republics.

_____ Leonid M. Kravchuk, a former Communist party ideologue in the Ukraine, won the republic's first presidential election. Kravchuk called for "collective management" to control and eventually destroy nuclear weapons held among the four former Soviet republics. President Yeltsin extended recognition to the newly independent Ukraine.

_____ EC foreign ministers, meeting in Brussels, lifted sanctions on all Yugoslav republics except Serbia and Montenegro after EC military observers released a report blaming the Serbian-controlled Yugoslav army for the recent escalation in the civil war.

_____ Portugal, Spain, Greece, and Ireland called for more EC aid to be directed toward the poorer areas of the EC.

December 5: Stipe Mesic, Croatian representative to the rotating Yugoslav presidency, resigned after a resumption of Yugoslav army attacks on Croatian cities. Mesic had not attended many of the presidency committee sessions, which were dominated by Serbia and its allies.

_____ President Gorbachev warned of a growing supply crisis in Moscow and called for international aid to the city.

December 6: UN special envoy Cyrus Vance warned that the latest breakdown in the Yugoslav truce threatened the introduction of UN peacekeeping forces as mediators in resolving the civil war.

_____ The United States repealed preferential trade status and canceled a textile agreement that allowed the Yugoslav federal government to distribute export quotas.

December 7: President Yeltsin called for the formation of a commonwealth of sovereign states as an alternative to President Gorbachev's version of a confederation of independent republics.

December 8: Members of the EC met in Maastricht, the Netherlands, to determine the future of political and monetary union.

_____ Leaders of the Ukraine, Byelorussia, and Russia declared that the USSR had ceased to exist and established a Commonwealth of Independent States (CIS) while meeting in the Byelorussian city of Brest. Though all three founder states are Slavic nations, the commonwealth was declared open to all former republics of the Soviet Union. The republics also called for the creation of new "coordinating bodies" headquartered in Minsk to handle defense, foreign affairs, and the economy.

_____ Yugoslavia's warring republics reached accord on a tentative plan to end Croatia's blockade of Yugoslav army barracks, a precondition for the Yugoslav army to enter another cease-fire agreement.

December 9: President Gorbachev rejected the formation of a commonwealth and the decentralization of the Soviet Union. The Bush administration said it would continue to recognize the Soviet Union.

_____ Meeting at Maastricht, the Netherlands, EC members agreed to establish a single currency and central bank by 1999. Britain supported the agreement but retained an option not to participate in monetary integration.

December 10: The Ukraine and Byelorussia ratified the commonwealth agreement. President Gorbachev met with defense officials in an attempt to win support of the army in the struggle for control of the nation.

_____ EC members agreed to work toward a common defense policy and closer political union as well as economic and monetary union. Britain was again allowed the flexibility to adopt only those EC resolutions that it deemed suitable.

December 11: Soviet President Gorbachev met with Russian President Yeltsin to discuss differences over the proposed CIS. No announcement was made following the meeting. The Kazakhstan republic indicated it was reconsidering its initial opposition to the group and would consider membership, thereby bringing the four nuclear powers under a single group.

_____ Members of the Ukrainian parliament called for the prosecution of President Gorbachev for his alleged role in covering up disasters related to the Chernobyl nuclear accident.

_____ Russian authorities gave former East German leader Erich Honecker two days to leave the country.

December 12: Secretary Baker outlined a plan for integrating the former Soviet republics into the international community. The plan called for a global conference in Washington in January 1992 to organize a cohesive response to the changes under way.

December 13: The five Asian and formerly Soviet republics of Kirghizia, Tadzhikistan, Turkmenia, Uzbekistan, and Kazakhstan agreed to join the CIS.

_____ Chancellor Kohl said that the agreements reached at Maastricht would lead to eventual political union.

December 14: North Korea offered former East German leader Honecker temporary refuge for medical treatment.

December 15: The Russian republic formally asked the United States for recognition while Secretary Baker was in Moscow.

_____ The Security Council decided not to press the issue of German recognition of Slovenia and Croatia and thus would not pass a resolution forbidding recognition of the republics.

_____ The Chilean embassy in Moscow refused to evict former East German leader Honecker for humanitarian reasons.

December 17: President Gorbachev announced that by the new year, the USSR would cease to exist.

_____ President Nursultan Nazarbayev of Kazakhstan told visiting Secretary Baker that he would oppose a Russian monopoly on nuclear weapons and its assumption of the UN Security Council seat.

_____ Chancellor Kohl indicated that Germany would move to recognize Slovenia and Croatia soon but would not exchange diplomatic personnel until January. The decision was seen as a compromise to other EC countries that wanted to delay recognition until after the civil war.

December 18: The leaders of Russia, Ukraine, Byelorussia, and Kazakhstan agreed to make the necessary cuts in their nuclear arsenals to meet the treaty obligations signed by President Gorbachev with the United States.

December 19: President Yeltsin took control of the remaining bureaucracies of the Soviet state, including the Foreign Ministry, the KGB, and the Soviet parliament.

December 20: The Yugoslav republic of Bosnia and Herzegovina applied for EC recognition as an independent state.

_____ Russia began to remove nuclear weapons from Ukraine. It was estimated that the process would take up to six months.

_____ The former Soviet republics began a series of meetings in Alma-Ata, Kazakhstan, to determine the future framework of political and military relations.

_____ At a meeting of NATO and former Warsaw Pact countries in Brussels, Russian Ambassador to Belgium Nikolai Afanasyevsky presented a letter from President Yeltsin advising the conference to strike all references to the "Soviet Union."

December 21: A CIS, composed of Azerbaijan, Armenia, Byelorussia, Kazakhstan, Kirghizia, Moldavia, Russia, Tadzhikistan, Turkmenia, Uzbekistan, and the Ukraine, was signed into existence in Alma-Ata, Kazakhstan. However, important details concerning the military and nuclear weapons were set aside due to lack of agreement. The ministers present accepted in advance the resignation of President Gorbachev.

_____ Secretary Baker reiterated his call for a conference of Western nations in Washington to coordinate aid to the Soviet Union.

December 23: Russian President Yeltsin, during a telephone call with President Bush, asked for American recognition of Russia. Bush responded that American recognition would promptly follow Soviet President Gorbachev's resignation.

_____ Germany recognized Slovenia and Croatia and upgraded its consulates in their capitals to embassies.

_____ Bosnia and Herzegovina appealed to the UN to deploy peacekeeping forces at the earliest possible moment.

December 25: President Gorbachev resigned. Within hours, the United States recognized Russia, Armenia, Ukraine, Byelorussia, Kazakhstan, and Kirghizia, as well as the new commonwealth.

_____ After independence, several of the former Soviet republics made changes in their names:

Byelorussia – Belarus
Kirghizia – Kyrgyzstan
Moldavia – Moldova
Tadzhikistan – Tajikistan
Turkmenia – Turkmenistan

December 26: Defense ministers of the former Soviet republics met in Moscow to discuss the Soviet army and nuclear arsenal. Ukraine and Belarus had announced their intention to transfer all ICBMs to Russia, but Kazakhstan expressed its concern that Russia would have a monopoly on nuclear weapons.

_____ Yugoslavia announced it was drafting plans for a smaller federation that could include captured Croatian territory.

December 28: President Yeltsin signed an executive order to begin land reform this winter as an important step toward economic reform.

December 29: A Georgian cease-fire was ignored by both sides as government troops expelled opposition forces from the parliament building housing President Gamsakhurdia's government.

_____ The Yugoslav air force attacked cities in central Croatia, but the army denied it had used surface-to-surface rockets in attacks south of Zagreb.

December 30: Meeting in Minsk, Belarus, the former Soviet republics agreed to institute a joint command for the management of nuclear weapons, but lacking agreement for a unified military, the republics conceded that separate armies would have to be permitted.

December 31: Serbian and Yugoslav officials formally agreed to the deployment of a UN peacekeeping force. UN special envoy Vance negotiated throughout the day to win Croatia's backing for the peace plan.

1992

January 1: Croatia formally accepted a UN proposal for the deployment of a peacekeeping force in the warring regions of Yugoslavia.

January 2: Georgian opposition leaders announced the formation of a military council to take power from President Gamsakhurdia.

_____ Croatian and Yugoslav forces agreed to a fifteenth cease-fire.

January 3: The United States called for full IMF and World Bank membership for Russia, Ukraine, Kazakhstan, Belarus, Kyrgyzstan, and Armenia in recognition of the republics' commitments to implementing far-reaching economic reforms.

_____ During a progovernment demonstration in Tbilisi, Georgia, opposition gunmen fired automatic weapons into the crowd, killing two demonstrators.

January 4: Ukrainian officials ordered all military personnel based on its soil, including the Black Sea fleet, to take an oath of allegiance to the country. The move significantly raised tensions with Russia, which considered itself in command of the former Soviet forces.

_____ UN special envoy Vance returned to New York to report on the latest Yugoslav cease-fire.

January 5: Georgian President Gamsakhurdia proposed a national referendum under UN monitoring to decide the issue of who should rule the newly independent country.

January 6: President Gamsakhurdia fled the country as opposition forces took over the Georgian parliament building where he had been headquartered.

_____ The chief of the Soviet forces remaining in the Baltic states, Colonel Vladimir Kandalovsky, asserted it would be three years until Soviet forces had left the area, due to complications with "sorting things out."

January 7: A Yugoslav army MiG fighter shot down an EC observer-force helicopter, killing the five WEU military observers on board. The Yugoslav leadership expressed its dismay and promised an investigation.

January 8: Yugoslav Defense Minister Veljko Kadijevic resigned following the downing of the EC observer-force helicopter. Kadijevic's replacement, General Blagoje Adzic, formerly chief of staff, was considered more pro-Serbian and therefore less likely to support the UN-sponsored peace. UN officials declared no further monitoring would occur until Yugoslav officials guaranteed the observers' safety and a thorough investigation of the shooting of the helicopter had occurred.

January 10: President Yeltsin asserted Russian sovereignty over the Black Sea fleet, which Ukraine also claimed.

_____ Serbs in Bosnia and Herzegovina proclaimed their autonomy.

January 11: Acting Minister of Defense General Blagoje Adzic pledged the support of the Yugoslav army for the UN peace plan.

_____ Russia and Ukraine agreed to establish a working group of experts to negotiate a settlement for the Black Sea fleet dispute.

January 16: The EC recognized the independence of Slovenia and Croatia.

January 23: A forty-seven nation two-day conference in Washington ended with little progress achieved in designing an aid package to benefit the former Soviet Union. Various conferees announced bilateral emergency aid programs, but little coordination or strategy emerged from the talks.

January 27: Azerbaijani forces attacked the town of Stepanakert in Nagorno-Karabakh, killing at least sixty people.

January 28: President Yeltsin reasserted Russia's claims to the Black Sea fleet while visiting the fleet in its home port of Novorossisk.

January 29: President Yeltsin and President Bush proposed further cuts in their respective nuclear arsenals by as much as 60 percent.

January 30: Croatian President Tudjman demanded that Croatia should have the right to appoint local officials under a UN peace plan in areas currently occupied by Serbian forces.

February 6: President Tudjman reversed his earlier position and accepted the UN peace plan unconditionally.

_____ Leaders of the four former Soviet "nuclear" republics agreed to abide by the terms of the START treaty while transferring the arsenals to Russia for destruction.

February 7: The US announced a plan to employ Russian scientists to prevent them from selling their expertise to other countries.

February 14: At a meeting of the CIS nations in Minsk, a deadlock occurred as Ukraine rejected a proposal to create a single military apparatus.

_____ Citizens of the Greek state of Macedonia protested against potential EC recognition of the former Yugoslav republic of Macedonia under that name.

February 17: Meeting in Moscow, President Yeltsin and Secretary Baker agreed to US assistance in helping Russia dismantle its nuclear-weapons stockpile and retraining Soviet nuclear engineers for civilian work.

February 21: The UN Security Council voted to support a UN peacekeeping force to be deployed in contested areas of Yugoslavia if the Yugoslav army and the Croatian national guard withdrew from occupied positions.

February 23: Croatia's ethnic Serbian leader Milan Babic accepted a UN plan to deploy peacekeeping troops in Croatia to enforce a cease-fire.

February 24: Belarus laid claim to territory incorporated within Lithuania but indicated that it wanted to resolve the dispute peacefully.

February 25: Canada announced it would withdraw all combat troops from Europe by the end of 1994.

February 27: Yugoslav President Milosevic indicated his support of the impending UN peacekeeping deployment, calling it the beginning of a peaceful solution to the crisis.

March 1: Voters in Bosnia and Herzegovina supported a referendum calling for independence and separation from Yugoslavia.

March 2: The last brigade of former Soviet troops serving as a buffer between Armenia and Azerbaijan began pulling out of the region. Azerbaijan claimed that Armenian militants had massacred as many as 1,000 civilians in the town of Khojaly in the past week. Armenia denied the claims, but reporters entering the village found dozens of bodies scattered about the city.

March 3: Canadian Prime Minister Brian Mulroney responded to US criticism of Canada's decision to withdraw troops from Western Europe and participate more fully in UN peacekeeping operations by noting that global strategic needs were fundamentally different, money needed to be spent in different ways, and the United States should not criticize because it was years behind in its UN contributions.

March 8: UN peacekeeping forces arrived in Yugoslavia in an effort to prevent resumption of the civil war.

_____ Former President Gorbachev began his first visit abroad since tendering his resignation. Gorbachev toured Germany, where he called for greater Western assistance for the former Soviet republics.

March 9: Diplomatic representatives of Britain, Turkey, and a coalition of Islamic nations began attempts to mediate a cease-fire in the conflict between Azerbaijan and Armenia in the Nagorno-Karabakh.

March 11: President Bush indicated that his administration was considering contributing to a multi-billion-dollar international fund to stabilize the ruble, but did not have a "blank check" to increase other forms of aid to Russia.

_____ Turkish Prime Minister Suleyman Demirel warned Western nations that the conflict over Nagorno-Karabakh could turn into a holy war of Muslims against Christians if overt and biased support was given to the Armenians. He pledged to resist pressures on Turkey to intervene on the side of Azerbaijan.

March 12: Ukraine announced it was suspending the transfer of tactical nuclear weapons to Russia because it had not received a guarantee that the weapons were being destroyed.

March 13: Secretary-General Boutros-Ghali asked former US Secretary of State Cyrus Vance to serve again as a UN special envoy—this time in a mediating role in the Azerbaijani-Armenian conflict.

March 14: UN peacekeeping forces began setting up positions in Yugoslavia to enforce a cease-fire.

March 15: At a meeting in Iran, Armenian and Azerbaijani negotiators reportedly agreed to a cease-fire in the conflict over Nagorno-Karabakh. The agreement also included an exchange of prisoners and the repeal of mutual economic sanctions.

March 16: President Yeltsin ordered the creation of a separate Russian Ministry of Defense as a first step toward a separate Russian army. His move followed failed attempts to create a unified defense structure within the CIS.

March 18: An EC-sponsored plan to divide Bosnia and Herzegovina into three distinct regions while keeping it a united and independent country received approval by the various ethnic groups involved. The approval reportedly would allow EC members to recognize immediately the republic's independence.

_____ President Yeltsin announced he had received assurances from Ukraine that battlefield nuclear-weapons stockpiles would be transferred to Russia for storage and destruction. There was no confirmation from Ukraine.

March 20: During a summit of the CIS in Kiev, Ukrainian President Kravchuk strongly criticized the Russian republic and the commonwealth for accomplishing so little. He also denied reports that he had reversed his decision to cancel the transfer of nuclear weapons to Russia.

_____ Minutes after the departure of Iranian mediators from Nagorno-Karabakh following a visit by UN special envoy Vance, the cease-fire broke down.

_____ The United States and Russia announced the formation of a joint committee to review cases of missing servicemen dating back to World War II.

March 22: Citizens of the Tatar region in Russia voted to explore independence.

March 24: The head of the UN peacekeeping force in Yugoslavia issued an appeal to halt cease-fire violations and threatened that the UN may halt the deployment of its peacekeeping force.

March 25: The Ukrainian parliament voted to replace the ruble with its own coupon currency April 1.

March 26: The CIS navy asserted that it had intercepted a US submarine in Russia's northern waters and chased it into international waters.

_____ Germany announced it was halting the sale and delivery of military equipment to Turkey until it received assurances that the equipment was not being used in attacks on Kurdish separatists.

March 27: The level of violence between Kurdish separatists and Turkish military forces dramatically increased following Turkish attacks on Kurdish strongholds. The *New York Times* termed the

situation a "near full-scale revolt."

_____ Israel criticized Chancellor Kohl for welcoming Austrian President Kurt Waldheim to Germany. President Waldheim's visit was the first official trip to a foreign country since his 1986 election.

_____ The leaders of Bosnia and Herzegovina called on the UN to deploy peacekeeping forces in the country.

March 30: Turkish President Turgut Ozal in a newspaper interview accused Germany of meddling in other countries' affairs, making a comparison to Hitler's Germany. Chancellor Kohl denounced the comments.

April 1: President Bush and Chancellor Kohl announced a $24 billion aid package for Russia, including bilateral aid, debt reduction, and ruble stabilization. Seven industrial democracies were reported to be contributing to the fund.

_____ During a NATO meeting in Brussels, Russian defense officials indicated to Secretary Cheney that a separate Russian army of 1.3 million troops would be deployed in defensive positions in western Russia. Included in the NATO meeting for the first time were delegates from the states of the former Warsaw Pact. The delegates received assurances that NATO would cooperate in matters of reorganization, military reform, and environmental cleanups.

_____ President Yeltsin issued a decree assuming leadership of the Moldovan army in an attempt to quell civil disturbances raging through the republic.

April 2: Polish President Lech Walesa ended a five-day visit to Germany, the first by a Polish leader since independence in 1918. He announced that "a new era in relations between Germany and Poland is beginning." Walesa recounted the political strengthening of relations but received no new promises of economic aid from Germany.

April 3: Serb forces attacked Muslim and Croatian forces in Bosnia and Herzegovina in an attempt to block the EC's recognition of the republics.

April 4: Bosnia and Herzegovina mobilized the national guard and reserve forces to repel the Serbian invasion.

April 7: President Yeltsin issued a decree placing the Black Sea fleet under Russian command as a rebuke to Ukrainian pretensions.

April 9: Russian President Yeltsin and Ukrainian President Kravchuk agreed to establish a commission to work out a plan for redistribution of the Black Sea fleet.

April 11: The Russian parliament voted to reduce

some of the powers of the presidency and called on President Yeltsin to resign from his post as prime minister.

_____ Ukraine announced it would begin to construct its own navy while awaiting a decision on the future status of the Black Sea fleet.

April 13: The cabinet of President Yeltsin threatened to resign following parliamentary attempts to weaken the country's economic program.

April 14: Breaking the EC-brokered cease-fire, Serbian Yugoslav army troops invaded Bosnia and Herzegovina.

April 15: The United States warned the Serbian leadership of Yugoslavia that it would seek a suspension of Yugoslavia's membership in the CSCE if the Yugoslav army did not withdraw from Bosnia and Herzegovina within fourteen days.

April 16: UN special envoy Vance pressed Serbia to end the attack on Bosnia and Herzegovina and abide by a cease-fire.

April 17: The Serbian-controlled Yugoslav army surrounded Sarajevo, the capital of Bosnia and Herzegovina, and reportedly hijacked six UN relief trucks loaded with food supplies.

April 23: Leaders of Bosnia and Herzegovina's three main ethnic factions reached an agreement to introduce a cease-fire and resume the negotiations brokered by the EC in Portugal.

May 2: The Yugoslav army captured and detained President Alija Izetbegovic of Bosnia and Herzegovina at Sarajevo airport as he returned from the EC-sponsored talks in Lisbon. The Yugoslav army dramatically increased the intensity of fighting in Sarajevo as it sought to consolidate gains made over the past week.

May 3: President Izetbegovic was released as the Yugoslav army came under intense international criticism for detaining him.

May 6: Speaking in Fulton, Missouri (site of Winston Churchill's Iron Curtain speech), former President Gorbachev criticized the West for initiating the nuclear-arms race and described the end of the Cold War as not a victory by one side but "a shattering of the vicious circle into which we had driven ourselves."

May 7: President Yeltsin issued a decree creating a new and separate Russian army.

_____ President Rakhman Nabiyev of Tajikistan fled the capital (Dushanbe) as Islamic and pro-democracy forces took control of the country. A revolutionary council was formed, its aim being to create an Islamic state.

May 9: Yugoslavia announced a major shake-up of its top military leadership, including the resignation of Defense Minister Adzic and the chief of military forces in Bosnia and Herzegovina.

_____ Armenian forces overran the last remaining Azerbaijani stronghold in the disputed territory of Nagorno-Karabakh, giving them effective control of the enclave.

May 12: EC observers quit Bosnia and Herzegovina because of the continued violence in the region. Serbian officials asserted that the EC and US decisions to withdraw ambassadors from Belgrade showed Western bias against Serbia.

May 16: UN staff and peacekeeping troops evacuated Bosnia, moving to Belgrade.

May 19: Kazakh President Nursultan Nazarbayev and President Bush signed an agreement by which Kazakhstan would sign the Nuclear Non-Proliferation Treaty and pledged to become a nonnuclear state within the decade.

_____ Bosnian Foreign Minister Haris Silajdzic criticized Western inaction in stopping the invasion of his country, drawing a parallel to the failure of the West to respond to Nazi Germany's advance pre-World War II.

May 20: Serbian leaders indicated they would not release as many as 5,000 Bosnians being held in Sarajevo until the government of Bosnia ended the blockade of Yugoslav army barracks.

May 21: Russia declared the 1954 grant of the Crimea to Ukraine null and void. Crimea declared its desire for independence.

_____ Serbian soldiers allowed 5,000 refugees to leave Sarajevo after the Bosnian government pledged to supply food to soldiers of the Yugoslav army surrounded in their barracks.

May 22: The United States announced a package of sanctions against Yugoslavia that included the closing of representative offices.

_____ France and Germany announced the creation of a 35,000-member joint army corps that could serve as the base for a future European army.

May 23: The four former Soviet nuclear states and the United States signed an agreement to abide by the terms of the 1991 START treaty. Ukraine, Belarus, and Kazakhstan also pledged to transfer their nuclear arsenals to Russia for destruction.

May 24: Secretary Baker called for UN sanctions against Yugoslavia while at a meeting in Lisbon to discuss Soviet aid.

_____ Citizens of Kosovo, Yugoslavia, voted in a referendum to establish a separate presidency and regional assembly.

May 25: Moldova accused Russia of militarily supporting the separatist Dniester region. The

Moldovan parliament indicated it would consider declaring a state of war against Russia at its next session.

May 26: Yugoslavia pledged to assist the UN peace-keeping operations in Bosnia and to assist in the movement of relief supplies into Sarajevo.

_____ Turkey and Russia agreed to work toward a peaceful resolution of the Armenian-Azerbaijani conflict.

June 2: Danish voters rejected in a referendum the EC treaty on political and monetary union negotiated at Maastricht in December 1991. The negative vote technically voided the treaty, which required ratification by all twelve signatory countries to be implemented.

June 3: France and Germany issued a statement of regret concerning the Danish referendum on EC unity but asserted their commitment to continuing the quest for unity and called on other member states to ratify the treaty by the end of the year.

June 4: NATO ministers agreed in principle to support the CSCE with military forces for peace-keeping activities when called upon.

June 5: President Slobodan Milosevic reiterated his contention that all Yugoslav regular army troops had been withdrawn from Bosnia and Herzegovina and that the irregular troops continuing the fighting in the republic were not under his government's control.

_____ Signatories of the 1990 treaty concerning conventional forces in Europe reaffirmed their commitment to adhere to its provisions at a meeting of the North Atlantic Cooperation Council (NACC) in Oslo, Norway.

June 8: Bosnian President Izetbegovic appealed to the United States for military assistance in stopping the bombardment of Sarajevo.

June 9: Secretary Baker concluded talks with Russian Foreign Minister Andrei Kozyrev in Washington, DC, but failed to reach a consensus on further cuts in strategic arms.

June 10: President Yeltsin accused the United States of seeking a strategic advantage in current arms talks.

_____ EC finance ministers from Germany, Britain, and France rejected an EC Executive Committee proposal to increase funding to the Community's four poorest members.

June 12: Protestant and Catholic parties in Northern Ireland agreed in principle to establish a joint committee to discuss the future of the British province.

_____ Secretary Baker and Foreign Minister Kozy-rev reported progress during further negotiations in London.

June 15: During a visit to the United States, Albanian President Sali Berisha expressed fear of Serbian threats to the Albanian minority living in the Kosovo region of Serbia.

_____ Britain announced it was removing tactical nuclear weapons from ships and aircraft.

_____ In an interview while en route to Washington, DC, President Yeltsin said that some American prisoners of war apparently had been transferred to Soviet labor camps during the Vietnam era. He concluded that "some of them may still be alive."

June 16: President Bush and President Yeltsin announced agreement on massive arms reductions. The agreement called for the elimination of all land-based, multiple-warhead missiles and drastic cuts in the number of warheads to a total of 3,000 to 3,500 on each side.

June 17: In an address to a joint session of the US Congress, President Yeltsin called for swift action on aid to the former Soviet republics.

_____ The United States granted most-favored-nation status to Russia and liberalized regulations on investment in Russia.

June 19: By a large majority, Irish voters approved the Maastricht treaty on political and economic union.

June 21: Russian army troops were reported to be fighting on the side of Slavic separatists in Moldova.

June 23: President Yeltsin and President Kravchuk signed an accord that settled in principle a number of disputes between Russia and Ukraine. The two nations agreed to split the Black Sea fleet and share and jointly finance the fleet's home bases.

MIDDLE EAST

1991

July 1: Palestinian Liberation Organization (PLO) guerrillas and Lebanese army soldiers clashed after negotiations aimed at getting the PLO to withdraw from southern Lebanon collapsed.

July 4: The PLO agreed to turn over heavy weapons to the Lebanese army in a move that enhanced Lebanese control over the south.

July 7: The Gulf Cooperation Council (Egypt, Syria, Saudi Arabia, Kuwait, Bahrain, Qatar, Oman, and the United Arab Emirates) postponed negotiations on the creation of a unified military force to supplement and replace US forces in the region.

_____ Israel asserted that the withdrawal of PLO forces from southern Lebanon did not reduce the security threat faced by the country from its northern neighbors, and therefore Israel declared it would not withdraw from its security zone.

July 9: The five permanent members of the UN Security Council meeting in Paris committed themselves to the elimination of weapons of mass destruction in the Middle East and to restrain the supply of conventional weapons.

July 14: Syrian President Hafiz al-Assad accepted in principle the US proposal for a Middle East peace conference in which Israel would negotiate with the Palestinians separately from the Arab nations.

July 18: Syria formally accepted a joint US-Soviet invitation to attend peace talks with Israel.

_____ Iraq contended that it had divulged the location of all nuclear plants and technology.

July 19: Egyptian President Hosni Mubarak called for an end to the forty-three-year-old Arab boycott of Israel in return for an Israeli pledge to cease the construction of new settlements in the occupied territories.

July 20: Saudi Arabia announced it would support the Egyptian proposal to suspend the Arab boycott of Israel. Saudi Arabia and Lebanon announced they would attend the Middle East peace talks.

_____ After the completion of American withdrawal from an enclave in northern Iraq, Kurdish forces took control of many cities after skirmishing with Iraqi forces.

July 21: Jordan announced it would send a delegation to the Middle East peace talks.

July 22: Israel indicated that given Syria's pledge to attend a Middle East peace conference and negotiate with Israel, it would reconsider its opposition.

July 24: Israel reiterated its demand that no Palestinians from outside the occupied territories and East Jerusalem be allowed to attend a Middle East peace conference as part of a Palestinian delegation.

July 25: France indicated its support for East Jerusalem's Palestinians being allowed representation at a Middle East peace conference.

July 31: President Bush announced in Moscow that he was sending Secretary Baker to Israel to receive official reaction to the announcement that the United States and the Soviet Union would be sponsoring a Middle East peace conference in October.

August 1: Israel gave conditional approval to a Mid-

dle East peace conference, reasserting its demand that the Palestinian delegation not include Palestinians from outside the occupied territories.

August 3: Secretary Baker asked Moroccan King Hassan II to attend the proposed peace talks and help persuade the Palestinians to send a delegation.

August 4: A PLO spokesman announced that the organization was prepared to send a delegation to the proposed Middle East peace conference. PLO leader Yasir Arafat denied the announcement.

August 6: Yasir Arafat demanded that the United States ask him to choose the members of a Palestinian delegation to the peace conference.

August 8: British hostage John McCarthy was released after five years of captivity in Lebanon.

_____ Israel announced it would exchange 375 Lebanese prisoners for seven Israeli soldiers missing in Lebanon.

August 11: American hostage Edward Tracy and French hostage Jerome Leyraud were released in Beirut.

August 18: Iranian Foreign Minister Ali Akbar Velayati reported a positive trend in his talks with pro-Iran fundamentalist groups holding Western hostages.

_____ Iraq returned over $700 million in gold taken during its invasion of Kuwait.

August 21: Egyptian President Mubarak called for the lifting of economic sanctions against Iraq so that the government could purchase food and medicine.

_____ Israeli Prime Minister Yitzhak Shamir declared his qualified willingness to attend a Middle East peace conference.

August 25: King Hussein met with Yasir Arafat to discuss the peace process and a joint Jordanian-Palestinian delegation, though no agreement was reached.

August 28: Kuwait announced it had repelled an armed Iraqi group attempting to infiltrate the island of Bubiyan.

August 29: The chief of the Lebanese Christian Army who fought against the government for two years, General Michel Aoun, left Beirut for France. The Lebanese government vowed to begin the process of reconstruction following years of civil war.

September 1: Lebanon and Syria signed a comprehensive security pact providing for an exchange of information and coordination of military action.

September 5: Iran indicated that the fate of Western

hostages in Lebanon was linked to Israel's willingness to free Arab prisoners. Israel had repeatedly declared it would not free Arab prisoners until seven Israeli servicemen missing in Lebanon were accounted for.

September 8: Prime Minister Shamir declared that despite US opposition, his administration would continue building settlements in the occupied territories.

September 11: Israel released fifty-one Arab prisoners and the bodies of nine guerrillas in exchange for information about the death of one of its servicemen missing in Lebanon.

September 12: The Bush administration announced it was opposed to further aid for Israel until the details of the Middle East peace conference were resolved.

_____ Israel received the body of one of seven servicemen missing in Lebanon.

September 15: Iran rejected Lebanon's request for compliance with the Lebanese peace agreement calling for withdrawal of military forces from the country. Iranian Foreign Minister Ali Akbar Velayati indicated that the Revolutionary Guard forces would not leave until southern Lebanon was liberated from Israeli forces.

September 17: After ending a two-day visit to Israel, Secretary Baker announced that the United States would not provide loan guarantees if Israel did not guarantee that no new settlements would be constructed in occupied areas.

September 18: A high-placed Iranian official, Mohammed Javad Larijani, indicated that the ten Western hostages in Lebanon were likely to be released by the end of the year.

September 19: Prime Minister Shamir publicly questioned the impartiality of the United States acting as a mediator in the Middle East peace process.

_____ Kuwait and the United States signed a ten-year security agreement to "enhance postwar security and stability in the Gulf." The agreement did not provide for a US military presence in the country.

September 22: Iran registered its criticism of the US-Kuwait military pact and any prolonged American presence in the region.

September 23: Yasir Arafat endorsed US efforts to sponsor a Middle East peace conference but offered no suggestions on how to resolve the issue of Palestinian representation.

September 24: British hostage Jack Mann was released from captivity in Lebanon.

September 25: Secretary Baker and Israeli Foreign Minister David Levy agreed to put the divisive question of loan guarantees for housing of Russian émigrés aside to discuss other problems, including the proposed Middle East peace conference.

_____ The United States released military aid to Jordan in hopes of spurring the Middle East peace conference.

September 26: Syria announced it would not participate in the regional phase of the Middle East peace talks because of the inclusion of other Arab nations in the multilateral talks.

September 29: After a five-day session of the "Palestinian Parliament," Yasir Arafat won a mandate to support a Middle East peace conference without direct PLO involvement.

October 16: Syria announced it would negotiate directly with Israel at the Middle East peace talks but would not attend a regional-issues session unless Israel agreed to withdraw from occupied territories.

October 17: Visiting Jerusalem, Secretary Baker failed to gain pledges from Israel that it would participate in the Middle East peace talks. Israel demanded assurances that the PLO would not represent Palestinians living in occupied territories.

October 20: The Israeli cabinet voted to send a delegation to the Middle East peace talks, though one party of the ruling coalition announced it would withdraw from the government as a consequence.

October 21: Western hostage Jesse Turner was released by his captors in Lebanon after Israel released fifteen Arab prisoners.

October 23: Members of the Arab delegations heading for the Madrid Middle East peace talks met in Damascus to outline unified positions on potential substantive issues. The various countries agreed not to reach a separate agreement with Israel.

October 26: Yasir Arafat indicated he would abide by whatever agreements were signed by the Palestinian delegation to the Middle East peace talks in Madrid.

October 30: President Bush and President Gorbachev opened the Middle East peace talks in Madrid.

October 31: The delegations to the Middle East peace talks in Madrid exchanged heated opening statements but proceeded without any party quitting the talks.

_____ Iran asserted that the nuclear technology it had acquired from China was to be used for peaceful purposes.

November 1: The opening session of the peace talks

in Madrid closed with no progress except an air-
ing of respective positions. Syria declined to
meet with Israel directly in one-on-one follow-up
negotiations, but Jordan and the Palestinian delegation agreed to meet with the Israeli delegation
on November 3.

November 3: Israel and the Palestinian delegation to
the peace talks agreed to discuss the issue of self-
rule in the occupied territories.

November 5: Secretary Baker criticized Israel for
opening new settlements for Soviet immigrants
in the occupied territories and jeopardizing the
peace process.

November 7: Israeli helicopter gunships attacked
Lebanese guerrilla positions near the city of
Tyre, Lebanon.

November 8: Saudi Arabia announced it would buy
fourteen Patriot missile batteries from the United
States to defend against the threat of further Iraqi
missile attacks.

November 11: Palestinians in the occupied territories announced they had created "political committees" to advise the Palestinian negotiating
team at the Middle East peace talks.

November 13: The Israeli parliament voted to in-
struct its negotiating team that continued occupation and settlement of the Golan Heights was not
negotiable.

November 14: The Iraqi government and Kurdish
rebels reached an accord entailing a withdrawal
of Kurdish forces from major cities in northern
Iraq in exchange for an end to the partial blockade of Kurdistan territory.

November 16: Iraq ordered residents of two Kurdish
villages in the northern part of the country to
evacuate their homes.

November 17: Iran criticized the United States for its
attempts to prevent the sale of nuclear technology to Iran.

November 18: Hostages Terry Waite and Thomas
Sutherland were released from captivity in
Lebanon.

November 22: The United States extended formal
invitations to Israel, the Palestinians, and Arab
nations to attend a second round of peace talks
beginning December 4 in Washington.

November 23: After Britain unfroze Iraqi funds, Iraq
freed a British businessman who had been imprisoned over five years. Iraq also agreed to allow
the United Nations to operate humanitarian missions for another six months but again declined to
sell oil to pay for needed supplies.

_____ Syria said it would delay assenting to a new
round of peace talks until Israel agreed to discuss
the surrender of territory.

November 25: The United States offered concrete
proposals to the negotiation parties of the Middle
East peace talks, including Israeli withdrawal
from Golan, as a means to push the talks toward
substantive issues.

November 27: The United States and Iran signed an
agreement on a compensation package covering
various military equipment paid for but not delivered to Iran just before the 1979 revolution.

_____ Israel rejected the US call for a second round
of peace talks in Washington, asserting that further talks should occur in the Middle East.

November 28: Syrian Foreign Minister Farouk al-
Sharaa asserted that Israel was attempting to sabotage the Middle East peace talks by delaying
their start and making unacceptable demands.

December 2: Israel announced it would boycott the
first day of the second round of Middle East
peace talks, slated to begin in Washington on
December 4, to protest the short notice given by
Secretary Baker. State Department officials predicted that the talks would begin on December 8
with all participants.

_____ American hostage Joseph Cicippio was released by his Lebanese captors after more than
five years in captivity.

December 4: American hostages Alann Steen and
Terry Anderson were released by Lebanese captors after more than five years in captivity.

_____ Israeli negotiators failed to attend the first
scheduled day of peace talks in Washington.

December 5: The three Arab delegations that arrived
in Washington for the peace talks called on
Washington to set a firm date and ensure that Israel would attend.

December 6: Meeting with representatives of Israeli
and Arab delegations, US negotiators attempted
to reach a consensus on when to begin the next
round of peace talks. Israel indicated it would be
ready to begin talks on December 8, but Arab
representatives declined because the date was
the fourth anniversary of the uprising in the occupied territories.

_____ Kurdish leaders claimed they had uncovered
evidence of mass extermination in villages that
were razed during the Iraqi offensive on Kurdish
insurgents. A human rights watch group, Middle
East Watch, announced it would send a team to
investigate the charges.

December 8: Israeli negotiators arrived in Washington for talks with Arab delegations and agreed to
start the talks the next day. But they insisted that
the Palestinian-Jordanian delegation meet with
them in one room, in contrast to the demands for
two rooms by the Arab delegations.

December 10: The second round of Middle East peace talks began with significant exchanges between Israel and Syria and Israel and Lebanon. Talks among the Palestinians, Jordan, and Israel continued to be stalemated over the composition of the delegations.

December 12: The Middle East peace talks in Washington were extended one week as the negotiating parties cited progress on the issue of Palestinian representation and movement toward substantive discussions.

December 15: Israeli authorities imposed restrictions on the movement of Palestinians at night after two night attacks on Israeli citizens.

December 18: The Middle East peace talks in Washington adjourned after ten days of discussions about procedures and agendas.

December 20: Israel announced it had arrested three suspected terrorists in southern Lebanon and was questioning them.

December 21: Israel released the three Arab suspects to the International Red Cross after questioning.

December 22: Former hostage and Church of England envoy Terry Waite denied reports, stemming from his reported meetings with US Marine Colonel Oliver North, that he had known about the American arms-for-hostages deal.

_____ A body left along a Beirut street was reported to be the remains of American Lieutenant Colonel William Higgins, commander of a UN observer group monitoring the Lebanese-Israeli border in 1988.

_____ Israel agreed to new Middle East peace talks to begin in Washington on January 7, but expressed a desire to hold subsequent talks nearer to the troubled region.

December 24: UN negotiator Giandomencio Picco left Syria after failing to make progress in his efforts to free two German hostages being held in Lebanon.

December 25: General Avihu Bin-Nun, commander of the Israeli Air Force, alleged that the United States had a contingency plan in the Gulf War that would have allowed Israeli retaliation for Scud missile attacks.

_____ Iraqi opposition groups were invited to Syria to discuss tactics to oust Iraqi leader Saddam Hussein. The invitations were extended by Ayatollah Mohammed Baqer al-Hakim, an Iraqi cleric, after meetings with Syrian President al-Assad.

December 27: France asked Switzerland to extradite an Iranian accused in the assassination of a former Iranian prime minister in Paris in summer 1990.

1992

January 1: Israel announced it was planning to devote two-thirds of its 1992 budget for public housing toward the development of new settlements on the West Bank and the Gaza Strip.

January 2: Iraq released two Americans and a Filipino who had been arrested after entering Iraq through the demilitarized border with Kuwait.

_____ Israel announced it would expel twelve Arabs who were accused of terrorist activities in occupied territories.

January 3: Palestinian representatives to the Middle East peace talks in Washington announced that they would not attend the next session to protest the Israeli decision to expel twelve Palestinians from the occupied territories.

_____ The United States accused Iraq of blocking international aid to nearly 18 million people.

January 4: Syria, Lebanon, and Jordan joined the Palestinians in delaying participation in the next round of peace talks.

January 5: The Israeli delegation to the peace talks left for Washington, claiming that the Arab delegations would attend the talks though they had announced a boycott.

January 6: The UN Security Council condemned the Israeli decision to expel twelve Palestinians accused of participating in terrorist activities. The United States voted in favor of the resolution.

_____ Arab delegations boycotted the Middle East peace talks that were to have continued today in Washington.

January 7: After the UN Security Council voted to condemn Israel for the expulsion of twelve Palestinians, Arab delegations announced their willingness to return to the negotiating table for peace talks in Washington. Israel expressed surprise and bitterness at US support for the resolution.

January 13: The Middle East peace talks moved into substantive discussions in Washington after a compromise formula allowed Israel to negotiate with Palestinians with a few Jordanians present.

January 14: The peace talks in Washington quickly became stalemated as all sides attempted to control the agenda. The coalition partners of Prime Minister Shamir threatened to bring down the government if Shamir instructed his negotiators to offer a plan for limited Palestinian self-rule in the occupied territories.

January 20: The United States asserted that Iran had paid the captors of Western hostages in Lebanon up to $1 million per hostage for their release.

January 24: Secretary Baker told Israeli Ambassador

Zalman Shoval that US aid must not be used for new settlements in occupied territories.

January 28: Middle East regional-issue peace talks began in Moscow absent a Palestinian delegation, which was forbidden to attend by the United States and Russia because of the presence of Palestinians from outside the West Bank and Gaza Strip.

January 30: The Middle East peace talks in Moscow concluded with the formation of five working groups to discuss specific regional issues. Though the issue of Palestinian representation was not resolved, delegations from twenty-four nations attended the conference.

February 16: Israeli forces attacked a motorcade in Lebanon, killing the leader of the pro-Iranian Party of God.

February 20: Israeli troops broke through UN barricades in southern Lebanon to attack a Shiite Muslim base from which several rocket attacks on Israel had been launched.

February 24: Secretary Baker again linked continued US loan guarantees to an Israeli decision to halt new settlements in occupied territories.

February 26: Israel proposed a scheme of limited self-rule for the Palestinians living in occupied territories.

February 27: Iraq indicated it would not comply with UN Security Council demands unless trade restrictions were relaxed.

March 3: The Palestinian delegation to the Middle East peace talks submitted a plan to the Israeli delegation that detailed a framework for self-government in the occupied territories. Israel rejected the plan after equating it with the establishment of an independent Palestinian state.

March 4: The third round of the Arab peace talks concluded in Washington.

March 7: A senior Israeli embassy security officer was killed by a car bomb in Ankara, Turkey. Two militant Islamic groups claimed responsibility.

March 9: A North Korean ship suspected by US military officials of carrying Scud missiles evaded a US naval task force and docked in an Iranian port.

March 10: Members of the Third World caucus of the UN Security Council told Deputy Prime Minister Tariq Aziz that Iraq must pledge total compliance with terms of the UN-brokered cease-fire before any discussion of removing economic sanctions could occur.

March 11: Deputy Prime Minister Aziz, speaking before the UN Security Council, asserted that Iraq had destroyed all weapons of mass destruction in compliance with Security Council directives. He stated that Iraq did not plan to destroy equipment used in the manufacture of such weapons, as directives calling for such action were an infringement of Iraq's sovereignty.

March 12: The UN Security Council reprimanded Iraq for its noncompliance with the terms of the cease-fire, instructing Deputy Prime Minister Aziz that it wanted to see "deeds, not words."

_____ King Hussein met with President Bush in Washington, DC, and pledged to help secure full Iraqi compliance with Security Council demands.

_____ President al-Assad of Syria asserted that the United States was attempting to strip the Arab world of its military power, which would force Arab countries to accept Israeli terms in the peace talks.

March 13: Israel denied unofficial US accusations that it shared Patriot missile technology with China.

_____ A US aircraft carrier task force entered the Persian Gulf, replacing a force that had been previously operating in the area and reinforcing Security Council demands on Iraq.

_____ A second North Korean ship suspected of carrying Scud missiles docked in Iran after US defense officials decided not to board the ship.

March 16: During a summit between Secretary Cheney and Israeli Defense Minister Moshe Arens, Arens again denied reports that Israel had shared military technology with China. He offered to allow inspections by American observers.

March 17: The UN Security Council informed Iraq that it must destroy its ballistic missile equipment within one week or face potential military intervention.

March 19: The UN Security Council implored Iraq to consider seriously a new oil pact that would allow it to export oil to purchase needed humanitarian supplies, fund UN activities in the country, and compensate victims of the war. Iraq had rejected such a pact in the past as an infringement of its sovereignty.

March 20: In a letter to the Security Council, Iraq agreed to UN demands that it destroy all ballistic missile equipment. Iraq also admitted to having hidden ballistic missiles and chemical warheads from UN inspectors.

March 21: A UN inspection team arrived in Baghdad to begin the process of destroying Scud missile equipment that Iraq recently had divulged.

March 23: Prime Minister Shamir accused the United States of attempting to rearrange Israel's borders by restricting new settlements even before the peace talks had reached any conclusions.

March 25: A Lebanese newspaper, *An Nahar*, reported that Syria and Iraq discussed the potential for Iraq to pump oil through a pipeline to Syria's Mediterranean coast.

March 30: Iraqi military forces attacked Kurdish villages and towns in an apparent violation of the cease-fire agreement.

April 1: Israeli troops clashed with Palestinians in the Gaza Strip, killing four and wounding dozens.

April 2: The State Department announced that an investigation of the allegation that Israel sold Patriot missile technology to China had inconclusive results.

_____ A human rights report released by an Israeli group alleged that torture of Palestinian prisoners by Israeli security forces had become commonplace.

_____ The United States announced that Israel and Arab negotiators had agreed to a fifth round of peace talks in Washington on April 27.

April 5: The Iranian air force bombed an alleged Iranian rebel base just inside the Iraq border. Iranian embassies in ten countries were attacked by demonstrators in response.

April 15: Iran expelled Arab residents from Abu Musa, an island in the Persian Gulf that it administers jointly with the United Arab Emirates.

April 17: Prime Minister Shamir accused the United States of reaching a secret agreement with the Arab nations in which the United States would withdraw $10 billion in US loan guarantees to Israel in exchange for Arab participation in the Middle East peace talks.

April 27: Syria announced it would temporarily lift a travel ban for its resident Jewish population and said that it expected nearly all 4,500 citizens to leave the country immediately.

April 28: Israel indicated that it would not attend regional peace talks on economic development and refugees if Palestinians from outside the West Bank and Gaza Strip attended as part of an Arab panel.

April 29: Israel offered Palestinians the right to operate their own hospitals and to hold pilot municipal elections.

April 30: The fifth round of Arab-Israeli peace talks concluded in Washington with no apparent progress.

May 6: Israel announced it would boycott the economic development and refugee regional talks because Palestinians from outside the occupied territories would be attending.

May 8: The United States announced it had informa-

tion linking Iran to the bombing of the Israeli embassy in Buenos Aires on March 17.

May 9: Iran denied the US allegation that it had played a role in the Buenos Aires bombing.

May 12: Arab delegations to the Middle East peace conference in Ottawa dealing with the Palestinian refugee question asserted the right of Palestinians to return to their homes evacuated when Israel was created in 1948. The United States indicated it supported those rights in principle.

May 16: The US military announced it was assisting in the removal of thirty tons of documents from Iraq that purportedly indicated a campaign of torture and persecution of Kurds by Iraqi leaders.

May 18: In a move to pacify Israel, the United States asserted that the 1948 Palestinian "right of return" issue was not part of the current Middle East peace talks.

June 3: Egyptian President Hosni Mubarak met with Syrian President Hafiz al-Assad in Damascus to discuss the fighting between Israeli forces and Muslim guerrillas in southern Lebanon and how those actions could affect the Middle East peace conference.

_____ The United States canceled scheduled military exercises with Jordan, citing Jordan's inability or unwillingness to stop the flow of goods reaching Iraq in contravention of the UN embargo.

June 23: Israel's opposition Labor party won a decisive victory over the ruling Likud party in national parliamentary elections.

WESTERN HEMISPHERE

1991

July 31: The Bush administration announced its support for US economic aid to Peru to combat narcotic production despite the human rights record of the country.

August 17: Secretary-General Pérez de Cuéllar sent a letter to American and Soviet foreign ministers pleading for help in prodding El Salvador toward reinvigorating the peace talks under way for fifteen months between the government and the Farabundo Marti National Liberation Front.

August 25: President Alfredo Cristiani of El Salvador stated that the main issue preventing a peace accord was a demand by rebel forces that some units be integrated into the country's military.

August 27: Former Nicaraguan President Daniel Ortega criticized Russian President Yeltsin for measures taken against the Soviet Union and Soviet Communist party.

September 5: Argentina, Brazil, and Chile signed an agreement to ban the manufacture and use of chemical weapons.

September 12: The Soviet Union announced it was withdrawing all troops from Cuba.

September 19: The El Salvadoran government and rebel forces tentatively agreed to undisclosed proposals by the UN secretary-general. Negotiations continued.

September 22: Secretary-General Pérez de Cuéllar proposed to the El Salvadoran government that rebel military forces be integrated into a civilian police corps, a counterproposal to the rebel leaders' demand that they be incorporated into the army.

September 25: While meeting at the UN under the mediation of Secretary-General Pérez de Cuéllar, El Salvadoran government representatives and five guerrilla commanders reached agreement on a framework for peace and scheduled cease-fire talks to begin October 12.

September 30: Haitian soldiers seized President Jean-Bertrand Aristide. The United States suspended aid and indicated it would not recognize the new military government.

October 2: The Organization of American States (OAS) condemned the military coup in Haiti.

October 3: Deposed President Aristide appealed to the UN for assistance in restoring democracy to his country.

October 4: A delegation from the OAS arrived in Haiti for negotiations aimed at returning President Aristide to office.

October 7: The Haitian legislature invoked an article of the constitution that declared the presidency vacant until the return of exiled President Aristide could be negotiated between the military and the OAS. Members of the Haitian army terminated the negotiations and made OAS negotiators leave the country.

October 8: The OAS proposed tougher sanctions on Haiti following the failed negotiations.

October 29: The United States announced a trade ban on Haiti.

November 7: The United States held on Coast Guard ships over 200 Haitian refugees picked up while fleeing their country.

November 14: El Salvadoran rebel forces announced a suspension of offensive actions.

November 15: The OAS announced it had reached an agreement with the Haitian parliament to allow exiled President Aristide to return and set

up a constitutional government.

November 16: A US congressional investigation into the killings of six Jesuit priests in El Salvador in 1989 concluded that high-level army officers were responsible.

November 20: The United States began transferring Haitian refugees to a troop ship anchored at the Guantanamo Bay Naval Base in Cuba.

December 2: The US Navy announced it was expanding its refugee center at Guantanamo Bay Naval Base to accommodate as many as 10,000 Haitians expected to arrive in the next week, though the United States had refused to grant the refugees political asylum. Over 4,000 Haitians fled the country in the preceding week.

December 11: A UN report indicated that seventy-three Haitians who were voluntarily repatriated were quickly arrested upon their return.

December 14: Secretary-General Pérez de Cuéllar invited the El Salvadoran government and rebel opposition to the UN for the next round of talks aimed at resolving the civil war.

December 19: The United States forcibly repatriated twenty-two Haitians who had been camped at Guantanamo Bay Naval Base.

December 27: President Cristiani agreed to fly to New York to invigorate the UN-sponsored peace talks.

1992

January 1: The El Salvadoran government and opposition guerrilla forces announced a cease-fire brokered by Secretary-General Pérez de Cuéllar in the closing minutes of his administration. The final peace agreements were to be signed in Mexico City on January 16 and the formal cease-fire to take effect February 1.

January 3: A Cuban helicopter pilot and thirty-three others defected to the United States.

January 8: OAS representatives announced that exiled President Aristide had accepted a compromise in which he would endorse the nomination of a leading political rival for the office of prime minister if his opponents would allow him to return to Haiti.

January 16: The El Salvadoran government and guerrilla forces signed an armistice ending the twelve-year-old civil war.

February 1: The United States began to deport Haitian refugees back to their country after the Supreme Court lifted an injunction preventing the forced return of the refugees.

February 15: Officials from the office of the UN

High Commissioner for Refugees reported that significant numbers of Haitian refugees currently at Guantanamo Naval Base had already been repatriated and fled Haiti more than once.

February 20: Leaders of Caribbean nations met in Kingston, Jamaica, for summit talks to develop a response to the crisis in Haiti. After the meeting, the leaders called for stronger measures against Haiti, including an economic blockade and joint military intervention.

February 25: President Aristide signed an agreement with acting Prime Minister Rene Theodore to return to Haiti from exile and form a national unity government.

March 7: The outbreak of cholera on a flight from Argentina through Peru that landed in the United States led to recriminations among government officials as to who was responsible for failure to control transmission of the disease.

March 19: The Haitian parliament failed to approve an internationally brokered agreement that would have allowed deposed President Aristide to return.

March 20: The OAS began discussing sanctions against Haiti after it rejected a peace settlement.

April 2: At a ceremony commemorating the tenth anniversary of the Falklands war, Argentine President Carlos Saul Menem asserted that Argentina would regain control of the islands by the end of the century but would accomplish the task through diplomatic means.

_____ The United States seized a Belize-registered tanker that delivered diesel fuel to Haiti in contravention of a US embargo. The OAS indicated that the tanker had filed a false manifesto of cargo upon departing New York.

April 6: Leaders of South American nations and the Bush administration condemned the suspension of democracy by Peruvian President Alberto Fujimori. President Fujimori dissolved parliament and arrested opposition leaders in response, he claimed, to imminent revolt, terrorism, and corruption.

April 9: A US court found former Panamanian leader General Manuel Noriega guilty on eight of ten charges, including cocaine trafficking, racketeering, and money laundering.

April 11: Peruvian Foreign Minister Augustino Blacker criticized the Bush administration for using intense diplomatic pressure to isolate President Fujimori.

April 25: A Peruvian fighter plane attacked and shot down a US air transport plane over the Pacific Ocean. Governments of both countries sought to minimize the repercussions.

April 21: Secretary Baker indicated in a speech to the Council on Foreign Relations that the United States should seek to implement a policy of "collective engagement" in which the country would seek to be a leader of coalitions rather than a lone superpower.

May 15: US officials reported that the tide of Haitian refugees being picked up in the Caribbean Sea had dramatically increased as living conditions in Haiti worsened following sanctions.

May 17: The OAS supported stronger sanctions against Haiti, including a denial of port rights to ships that deliver goods to the island and a request to the EC to halt trade with the country.

May 21: US officials announced that the Coast Guard would no longer pick up Haitian boat refugees unless their craft was in immediate danger of sinking.

May 24: US officials announced that the Coast Guard would forcibly return all Haitian refugees found on boats fleeing their homeland.

May 29: US officials announced that the refugee camp at Guantanamo Naval Base would shortly be closed as a further step in pressuring Haitian leaders to return President Aristide to his elected office.

June 1: The Bush administration announced it was expanding antidrug smuggling efforts in Jamaica and the Dominican Republic.

June 2: The Haitian military named Marc Bazin, a former World Bank official and businessman, to serve as premier of a new consensus government backed by the military and parliament.

June 11: President Bush had to leave a rally in Panama, his first stop on the way to the Rio environmental summit, when demonstrators were sprayed with tear gas that drifted over the president's podium.

SOURCES

Christian Science World Monitor
The Economist
Europe
Facts on File
Foreign Broadcast Information Service news summaries
Keesing's Record of World Events
New York Times
Washington Post
Wall Street Journal

ACRONYMS
AND ABBREVIATIONS

ALCM	air-launched cruise missile
ANC	African National Congress
ANS	Sihanouk National Army
APAC	Auto Parts Advisory Committee
APEC	Asian Pacific Economic Cooperation
ARENA	National Republic Alliance (El Salvador)
ASEAN	Association of Southeast Asian Nations
BCCI	Bank of Credit and Commerce International
CGDK	Coalition Government of Democratic Kampuchea
CIAV	International Commission of Support and Verification
CIS	Commonwealth of Independent States
CODESA	Convention for a Democratic South Africa
CSCE	Conference on Security and Cooperation in Europe
DK	Democratic Kampuchea
DLP	Democratic Liberal Party (South Korea)
DPRK	Democratic People's Republic of Korea (North Korea)
EC	European Community
EBRD	European Bank for Reconstruction and Development
ECB	European Central Bank
ECOWAS	Economic Community of West African States
EEA	European Economic Area
ECU	European currency unit
EFTA	European Free Trade Association
EMU	economic and monetary union
FMLN	Farabundo Marti National Liberation Front
FSLN	Sandinista National Liberation Front
G-7	Group of Seven
GATT	General Agreement on Tariffs and Trade
GDP	gross domestic product
GDR	German Democratic Republic
GNP	gross national product
IAEA	International Atomic Energy Agency
ICBM	intercontinental ballistic missile
IGC	intergovernmental conference
IMF	International Monetary Fund
INF	intermediate-range nuclear forces
KPNLF	Khmer People's National Liberation Front

MAI   Multilateral Assistance Initiative
MBA   Military Bases Agreement (US-Philippines)
MBFR   mutual and balance force reduction
MIRV   multiple independently targeted reentry vehicle
MITI   Ministry of International Trade and Industry (Japan)
NACC   North Atlantic Cooperation Council
NAFTA   North American Free Trade Association
NATO   North Atlantic Treaty Organization
NPT   Non-Proliferation Treaty
OAS   Organization of American States
OAU   Organization of African Unity
OECD   Organization of Economic Cooperation and Development
OPEC   Organization of Petroleum Exporting Countries
PACT   Philippine-American Cooperation Talks
PLO   Palestine Liberation Organization
PRC   People's Republic of China
PRI   Institutional Revolutionary Party (Mexico)
PRK   People's Republic of Kampuchea
R&D   research and development
ROK   Republic of Korea (South Korea)
SII   Structural Impediments Initiative (US-Japan)
SLBM   submarine launched ballistic missile
SLCM   sea-launched cruise missile
SNC   Supreme National Council (Cambodia)
SNF   short range nuclear forces
SOC   State of Cambodia
SOFA   Status of Forces Agreement (US-Philippines)
SPD   Social Democratic Party (Germany)
SRAM-T   short range attack missile-tactical
SSD   safety, security, and disarmament (of nuclear weapons)
START   Strategic Arms Reduction Treaty
UNAMIC   UN Advance Mission in Cambodia
UNTAC   UN Transitional Authority in Cambodia
USCFTA   United States-Canada Free Trade Agreement
USSR   Union of Soviet Socialist Republics
WEU   Western European Union

BIBLIOGRAPHY

Abel, Christopher, and Colin M. Lewis, eds., *Latin America: Economic Imperialism and the State: The Political Economy of External Connection from Independence to the Present.* Atlantic Highlands, NJ: Humanities, 1992.

Armstrong, David, and Erik Goldstein, eds., *The End of the Cold War.* Portland, OR: International Specialized Book Source, 1991.

Bailey, Kathleen C., *Doomsday Weapons in the Hands of Many: The Arms Control Challenge of the '90s.* Champaign: University of Illinois Press, 1991.

Balzer, Harley D., *Five Years That Shook the World: Gorbachev's Unfinished Revolution.* Boulder, CO: Westview, 1991.

Bard, Michael Geoffrey, *The Water's Edge and Beyond: Defining Limits to Domestic Influence on United States Middle East Policy.* New Brunswick, NJ: Transaction, 1991.

Benedick, Richard E., *Ozone Diplomacy: New Directions in Safeguarding the Planet.* Cambridge, MA: Harvard University Press, 1991.

Bergner, Jeffrey T., *The New Superpowers: Germany, Japan, the U.S., and the New World Order.* New York: St. Martin's, 1991.

Beschloss, Michael, *The Crisis Years: Kennedy and Khrushchev, 1960-1963.* New York: Harper Collins, 1991.

Bevin, Alexander, *The Strange Connection: U.S. Intervention in China 1944-72.* Westport, CT: Greenwood, 1992.

Bhagwati, Jagdish, *The World Trading System at Risk.* Princeton, NJ: Princeton University Press, 1991.

Bhagwati, Jagdish, and Hugh T. Patrick, eds., *Aggressive Unilateralism: America's 301 Trade Policy and the World Trading System.* Ann Arbor: University of Michigan Press, 1990.

Black, Ian, and Benny Morris, *Israel's Secret Wars: The Untold History of Israeli Intelligence.* New York: Grove Weidenfeld, 1991.

Bos, J.M.M. van den, *Dutch EC Policy Making.* Utrecht: ISOR, 1991.

Bosner, Charles F., ed., *Toward a North American Common Market.* Boulder, CO: Westview, 1991.

Brands, H. W., *Inside the Cold War: Loy Henderson and the Rise of the American Empire, 1918-1961.* New York: Oxford University Press, 1991.

————, *Bound to Empire: The U.S. and the Philippines*. New York: Oxford University Press, 1992.

Brinkley, Douglas, and Clifford Hackett, eds., *Jean Monnet: The Path to European Unity*. New York: St. Martin's, 1991.

Brown, J. F., *Surge to Freedom: The End of Communist Rule in Eastern Europe*. Durham, NC: Duke University Press, 1991.

Brown, Sheryl J., and Kimber M. Schraub, eds., *Resolving Third World Conflict: Challenges for a New Era*. Washington, DC: US Institute of Peace, 1992.

Buckley, Kevin, *Panama: The Whole Story*. New York: Simon & Schuster, 1991.

Buckley, Roger, *U.S.-Japan Alliance Diplomacy 1945-1990*. New York: Cambridge University Press, 1992.

Calabrese, John, *China's Changing Relations with the Middle East*. London and New York: Pinter, 1991.

Caldwell, Dan, *The Dynamics of Domestic Politics and Arms Control: The SALT II Ratification Debate*. Columbia: University of South Carolina Press, 1991.

Chi, Wang, *History of U.S.-China Relations: A Bibliographical Resource Guide*. McLean, VA: Academic Press of America, 1992.

Cimbala, Stephen J., *Conflict Termination in Europe: Games Against War*. Westport, CT: Greenwood, 1990.

————, *Force and Diplomacy in the Future*. Westport, CT: Greenwood, 1992.

Clifford, Clark, with Richard Holbrooke, *Counsel to the President: A Memoir*. New York: Random House, 1991.

Cohen, Raymond, *Negotiating Across Cultures: Communication Obstacles in International Diplomacy*. Washington, DC: US Institute of Peace, 1991.

Collins, Michael J., *Western European Integration: Implications for U.S. Policy and Strategy*. Westport, CT: Greenwood, 1992.

Conniff, Michael L., *Panama and the United States: The Forced Alliance*. Athens: University of Georgia Press, 1992.

Cooley, John K., *Payback: America's Long War in the Middle East*. Washington, DC: Brassey's, 1991.

Cordesman, Anthony H., *Weapons of Mass Destruction in the Middle East*. Oxford: Pergamon, 1991.

Cviic, Christopher, *Remaking the Balkans*. New York: Council on Foreign Relations, 1991.

Dacor Bacon House Foundation Staff, *American Diplomacy in the Information Age*. Lanham, MD: University Press of America, 1992.

Darwish, Adel, and Gregory Alexander, *Unholy Babylon: The Secret History of Saddam's War*. New York: St. Martin's, 1991.

Delgado Gomez-Escalonilla, Lorenzo, *Acción cultural y política exterior: La configuración de la diplomacia cultural durante el régimen franquista 1936-1945*. Madrid: Universidad Complutense, 1991.

DiLeo, David L., *George Ball, Vietnam, and the Rethinking of Containment*. Chapel Hill: University of North Carolina Press, 1991.

Dobson, Wendy, *Economic Policy Coordination: Requiem or Prologue?* Washington, DC: Institute for International Economics, 1991.

Doern, Bruce, and Brian W. Tomlin, *Faith and Fear: The Free Trade Story*. Toronto: Stoddart, 1991.

Doran, Charles F., and Stephen W. Buck, eds., *The Gulf, Energy, and Global Security*. Boulder, CO: Lynne Rienner, 1991.

Edwards, Geoffrey, ed., *Europe's Global Links: The European Community and Inter-Regional Cooperation*. New York: St. Martin's, 1991.

Franklin, Michael, with Marc Wilke, *Britain in the European Community*. New York: Council on Foreign Relations (for the Royal Institute of International Affairs), 1991.

Freedman, Lawrence, and Virginia Gamba-Stonehouse, *Signals of War: The Falklands Conlict of 1982*. London: Faber & Faber, 1990.

Freedman, Robert O., *Moscow and the Middle East*. New York: Cambridge University Press, 1991.

————, ed., *The Intifada: Its Impact on Israel, the Arab World, and the Superpowers*. Miami: University of Florida Press, 1991.

Freney, Michael A., and Rebecca S. Hartley, *United Germany and the United States*. Washington, DC: National Planning Association, 1991.

Fu, Jen-kun, *Taiwan and the Geopolitics of the Asian-American Dilemma*. Westport, CT: Greenwood, 1992.

Gaddis, John Lewis, *The United States and the End of the Cold War: Implications, Reconsiderations, Provocations*. New York: Oxford University Press, 1992.

Garfinkle, Adam, *Israel and Jordan in the Shadow of War: Functional Ties and Futile Diplomacy in a Small Place*. New York: St. Martin's, 1992.

George, Alexander L., *Forceful Persuasion: Coercive Diplomacy as an Alternative to War*. Washington, DC: US Institute of Peace, 1992.

Gerson, Allan, *The Kirkpatrick Mission: Diplomacy Without Apology, America at the United Nations, 1981-1985*. New York: Free Press, 1991.

Glass, Charles, *Tribes with Flags: A Dangerous Passage Through the Chaos of the Middle East.* New York: Atlantic Monthly, 1991.

Glennon, Michael J., *Constitutional Diplomacy.* Princeton, NJ: Princeton University Press, 1991.

Golan, Galia, *Soviet Policies in the Middle East: From World War II to Gorbachev.* New York: Cambridge University Press, 1991.

Gorbachev, Mikhail, *The August Coup: The Truth and the Lessons.* New York: Harper Collins, 1991.

Gotlieb, Allan, *I'll Be With You in a Minute, Mr. Ambassador: The Education of a Canadian Diplomat in Washington.* Toronto: University of Toronto Press, 1991.

Gould, Harold A., and Sumit Ganguly, eds., *The Hope and the Reality: U.S.-India Relations from Roosevelt to Reagan.* Boulder, CO: Westview, 1992.

Granatstein, J. L., and David J. Bercuson, *War and Peacekeeping: From the Boer War to the Gulf War.* Toronto: Key Porter, 1991.

Graubard, Stephen R., *Mr. Bush's War.* New York: Hill & Wang, 1992.

Grin, John, *Military-Technological Choices and Political Implications: Command and Control in Establishing NATO Posture and a Non-Provocative Defence.* New York: St. Martin's, 1991.

ter Haar, Barend, *The Future of Biological Weapons.* Center for Strategic and International Studies Washington Paper #151. New York: Praeger, 1991.

Haglund, David G., *Alliance Within the Alliance: Franco-German Military Cooperation and the European Pillar of Defense.* Boulder, CO: Westview, 1991.

Hampson, F. O. and C. J. Maule, *Canada Among Nations 1990-91: After the Cold War.* Ottawa: Carleton University Press, 1991.

Harding, Harry, *A Fragile Relationship: The United States and China Since 1972.* Washington, DC: Brookings, 1992.

Harle, Vilho, and Jyrki Iivonen, eds., *Gorbachev and Europe.* New York: St. Martin's, 1991.

Harries, Owen, ed., *America's Purpose: Visions of U.S. Foreign Policy.* San Francisco: Institute for Contemporary Studies, 1991.

Harrington, Joseph F., and Bruce J. Courtney, *Tweaking the Nose of the Russians: Fifty Years of American-Romanian Relations, 1940-1990.* Boulder, CO: Columbia University Press, 1991.

Henkin, Louis, et al., *Right vs. Might: International Law and the Use of Force.* New York: Council on Foreign Relations, 1991.

Howard, Michael, *The Lessons of History.* New Haven, CT: Yale University Press, 1991.

Hurtig, Mel, *The Betrayal of Canada*. Toronto: Stoddart, 1991.

Inoguchi, Takashi, *Japan's International Relations*. Boulder, CO: Westview, 1992.

Irie, Akira, *Japanese Diplomacy*. Tokyo: Chuo Koron-sha, 1991.

Islam, Shafiqul, ed., *Yen for Development: Japanese Foreign Aid and the Politics of Burden-Sharing*. New York: Council on Foreign Relations, 1991.

Jackson, Robert H., *Quasi-States: Sovereignty, International Relations, and the Third World*. New York: Cambridge University Press, 1991.

Jensen, Kenneth M., ed., *Origins of the Cold War: The Novikov, Kennan, and Roberts 'Long Telegrams' of 1946*. Washington, DC: US Institute of Peace, 1991.

Jervos, Robert, and Seweryn Bialer, eds., *Soviet-American Relations After the Cold War*. Durham, NC: Duke University Press, 1991.

Johnson, Haynes, *Sleepwalking Through History: America in the Reagan Years*. New York: Norton, 1991.

Jones, Howard, intro. by, *Major Issues in American Diplomacy: Essays and Documents from the 1890's to the Present*. Chicago: Lyceum IL, 1991.

Kaminski, Bartlomiej, *The Collapse of State Socialism*. Princeton, NJ: Princeton University Press, 1991.

Kampelman, Max M., *Entering New Worlds: The Memoirs of a Private Man in Public Life*. New York: Harper Collins, 1991.

Kanet, Roger E., and Edward A. Kolodziej, eds., *The Cold War as Cooperation: Superpower Cooperation in Regional Conflict Management*. Baltimore, MD: Johns Hopkins University Press, 1991.

Kaplan, M.J.G.P., and A.H.G. Rinnooy Kan, *Onderhandelen*. Schoonhoven, The Netherlands: Academic Service, 1991.

Kapteyn, P., *Onderhandelen in beschaving*. In *Het Europees labyrint*. Meppel and Amsterdam: Boom and SISWO, 1991.

Kemp, Geoffrey, *The Control of the Middle East Arms Race*. Washington, DC: Carnegie Endowment for International Peace, 1991.

Keohane, Robert O., and Stanley Hoffmann, *The New European Community*. Boulder, CO: Westview, 1991.

Khan, Riaz M., *Untying the Afghan Knot: Negotiating Soviet Withdrawal*. Durham, NC: Duke University Press, 1991.

Kim, Young C., and Gaston J. Sigur, eds., *Asia and the Decline of Communism*. New Brunswick, NJ: Transaction, 1991.

Korn, David A., *The Making of United Nations Security Council Resolution 242*. Washington, DC: Institute for the Study of Diplomacy, 1992.

Kovrig, Bennett, *Of Walls and Bridges: The United States and Eastern Europe*. New York: New York University Press, 1991.

Kremenyuk, Victor A., ed., *International Negotiation: Analysis, Approaches, Issues*. San Francisco, CA: Jossey-Bass, 1991.

Laird, Robbin, *The Europeanization of the Alliance*. Boulder, CO: Westview, 1991.

Langley, Lester D., *Mexico and the United States: The Fragile Relationship*. Boston: G. K. Hall, 1991.

Leffler, Melvyn P., *A Preponderance of Power: National Security, the Truman Administration, and the Cold War*. Stanford, CA: Stanford University Press, 1992.

Leonard, Thomas M., *Central America and the United States: The Search for Stability*. Athens: University of Georgia Press, 1991.

Long, David E., and Bernard Reich, *International Relations of the Middle East: Contemporary Issues*. Boulder, CO: Westview, 1992.

Lowenthal, Abraham F., ed., *Exporting Democracy: The United States and Latin America*. Baltimore, MD: Johns Hopkins University Press, 1991.

Macchiarola, Frank J., and Robert B. Oxnam, eds., *The China Challenge: American Politics in Asia*. New York: Academy of Political Science, 1991.

Mangold, Tom, *Cold Warrior*. New York: Simon & Schuster, 1991.

Marks, John, and Igor Beliaev, eds., *Common Ground on Terrorism: Soviet-American Cooperation Against the Politics of Terror*. New York: Norton, 1991.

Mayall, James, and Anthony Payne, eds., *The Fallacies of Hope: the Post-Colonial Record of the Commonwealth Third World*. Manchester: Manchester University Press, 1991.

Menges, Constantine, *The Future of Germany and the Atlantic Alliance*. Washington, DC: The American Enterprise Institute, 1991.

Michta, Andrew, *East Central Europe After the Warsaw Pact: Security Dilemmas in the 1990s*. Westport, CT: Greenwood, 1992.

Migliazza, A., and E. Decleva, *Diplomazia e storia delle relazioni internazionali: Studi in onore di Enrico Serra*. Milan: Giuffré, 1991.

Miller, Robert Hopkins, *Inside an Embassy: The Political Role of Diplomats Abroad*. Washington, DC: Congressional Quarterly Books, 1992.

Morgan, William D., and Charles S. Kennedy, *The U.S. Consul at Work*. Westport, CT: Greenwood, 1991.

Muravchik, Joshua, *Exporting Democracy: Fulfilling America's Destiny*. Washington, DC: The American Enterprise Institute, 1991.

National Academy of Sciences, *Finding Common Ground: U.S. Export Controls in a Changing Global Environment*. Washington, DC: National Academy Press, 1991.

Nelson, Daniel N., *Balkan Imbroglio: Politics and Security in Southeastern Europe*. Boulder, CO: Westview, 1991.

North, Oliver L., and William Novak, *Under Fire: An American Story*. New York: Harper Collins, 1991.

Oberdorfer, Don, *The Turn: From the Cold War to the New Era*. New York: Poseidon, 1991.

Odom, William E., *On Internal War: American and Soviet Approaches to Third World Clients and Insurgents*. Durham, NC: Duke University Press, 1992.

Parker, William N., *Europe, America, and the Wider World, Vol. 2: America and the Wider World*. New York: Cambridge University Press, 1991.

Payne, Richard J., *The West European Allies, the Third World, and U.S. Foreign Policy*. Westport, CT: Greenwood, 1991.

Pinder, John, *The European Community and Eastern Europe*. New York: Council on Foreign Relations (for the Royal Institute of International Affairs), 1991.

Prins, Gwyn, ed., *Spring in Winter: The 1989 Revolutions*. Manchester and New York: Manchester University Press, 1991.

Reston, James, *Deadline: A Memoir*. New York: Random House, 1991.

Robinson, Linda, *Intervention or Neglect: The United States and Central America Beyond the 1980s*. New York: Council on Foreign Relations, 1991.

Rosenthal, Joel H., *Righteous Realists: Political Realism, Responsible Power, and American Culture in the Nuclear Age*. Baton Rouge: Louisiana State University Press, 1991.

Salinger, Pierre, and Eric Laurent, *Secret Dossier: The Hidden Agenda Behind the Gulf War*. New York: Penguin, 1991.

Sater, William F., *Chile and the United States: Empires in Conflict*. Athens: University of Georgia Press, 1991.

Schwartz, Thomas Alan, *America's Germany*. Cambridge, MA: Harvard University Press, 1991.

Schwok, René, *U.S.-E.C. Relations in the Post-Cold War Era*. Boulder, CO: Westview, 1991.

Serra, Enrico, *Professione: Diplomatico*. Milan: Angeli, 1991.

Shin, Hee Suk, *Japanese Foreign Policy*. Seoul: Eul Lyu Moon Hwa Sa, 1991.

Shoemaker, Christopher C., *The NSC Staff: Counseling the Council*. Boulder, CO: Westview, 1991.

Shulman, Holly Cowan, *The Voice of America: Propaganda and Democracy, 1941-1945*. Madison: University of Wisconsin Press, 1991.

Smith, Geoffrey, *Reagan and Thatcher*. New York: Norton, 1991.

Smith, James A., *The Idea Brokers: Think Tanks and the Rise of the New Policy Elite.* New York: Free Press, 1991.

Smith, Jean Edward, *George Bush's War.* New York: Henry Holt, 1992.

Smolansky, Oles M., *The USSR and Iraq: The Soviet Quest for Influence.* Durham, NC: Duke University Press, 1991.

Sodaro, Michael J., *Moscow, Germany, and the West from Khrushchev to Gorbachev.* Ithaca, NY: Cornell University Press, 1991.

Stares, Paul B., *Command Performance: The Neglected Dimension of European Security.* Washington, DC: Brookings, 1991.

Stein, Arthur A., *Why Nations Cooperate: Circumstance and Choice in International Relations.* Ithaca, NY: Cornell University Press, 1991.

Stephan, Paul B. III, and Boris M. Klimenko, eds., *International Law and International Security: Military and Political Dimensions.* Armonk, NY: M. E. Sharpe, 1992.

Tamnes, Rolf, *The United States and the Cold War in the High North.* Brookfield, VT: Gower, 1991.

Trapans, Jan Avreds, ed., *Toward Independence: The Baltic Popular Movements.* Boulder, CO: Westview, 1991.

Trebilcock, Michael J., Marsha A. Chandler, and Robert Howse, *Trade and Transitions.* New York: Routledge, 1991.

Ullman, Richard H., *Securing Europe.* Princeton, NJ: Princeton University Press, 1991.

United Nations, *Modern Law of Diplomacy: External Missions of States and International Organizations.* New York: United Nations, 1992.

United States Institute of Peace, *A Directory of U.S. Resources on the Rule of Law for the Independent States of the Former Soviet Union.* Washington, DC: US Institute of Peace, 1992.

Vernon, Raymond, Debora L. Spar, and Glenn Tobin, *Iron Triangles and Revolving Doors: Cases in U.S. Foreign Economic Policymaking.* New York: Praeger, 1991.

Vogel, Ezra F., *The Four Little Dragons: The Spread of Industrialization in East Asia.* Cambridge, MA: Harvard University Press, 1991.

Wallace, Helen, ed., *The Wider Western Europe: Reshaping the EC/EFTA Relationship.* London and New York: Pinter (for the Royal Institute for International Affairs), 1991.

Wallace, William, ed., *The Dynamics of European Integration.* London and New York: Pinter (for the Royal Institute for International Affairs), 1991.

Wallerstein, Immanuel, *Geopolitics and Geoculture: Essays on the Changing World System.* New York: Cambridge University Press, 1991.

Webber, Philip, *New Defence Strategies for the 1990s: From Confrontation to Coexistence.* New York: St. Martin's, 1991.

Wettig, Gerhard, *Changes in Soviet Policy Toward the West.* Boulder, CO: Westview, 1991.

Wyatt, Marilyn, ed., *CSCE and the New Blueprint for Europe.* Washington, DC: Institute for the Study of Diplomacy and the Center for German and European Studies, 1991.

Yohannes, Okbazghi, *Eritrea: A Pawn in World Politics.* Gainesville: University of Florida Press, 1991.

INDEX